A Special Issue of
Cognitive Neuropsychology

The Cognitive Neuroscience of Face Processing

Edited by

Nancy Kanwisher
Massachusetts Institute of Technology, Cambridge, USA

and

Morris Moscovitch
*University of Toronto at Mississauga, and Rotman Research
Institute, Baycrest Centre for Geriatric Care, Toronto, Canada*

Psychology Press
a member of the Taylor & Francis group

To my wife Jill, and my children, Elana and David
(M.M.)

Psychology Press Ltd, Publishers
27 Church Road
Hove
East Sussex
BN3 2FA
UK

http://www.psypress.co.uk

British Library Cataloguing-in-Publication Data

A catalogue record for this book is available from the British Library

ISBN: 0-86377-614-0

Typeset by Quorum Technical Services Ltd, Cheltenham
Printed and bound in the United Kingdom by Henry Ling Ltd, Dorchester

Contents*

The Cognitive Neuroscience of Face Processing: An Introduction
Nancy Kanwisher and Morris Moscovitch   1

Effect of Image Orientation and Size on Object Recognition: Responses
   of Single Units in the Macaque Monkey Temporal Cortex
E. Ashbridge, D.I. Perrett, M.W. Oram, and T. Jellema   13

Structural Encoding and Identification in Face Processing:
   ERP Evidence for Separate Mechanisms
Shlomo Bentin and Leon Y. Deouell   35

Models of Face Recognition and Delusional Misidentification:
   A Critical Review
Nora Breen, Diana Caine, and Max Coltheart   55

Facial Expression Recognition by People with Möbius Syndrome
Andrew J. Calder, Jill Keane, Jonathan Cole, Ruth Campbell,
   and Andrew W. Young   73

Structural Encoding Precludes Recognition of Face Parts in
   Prosopagnosia
Beatrice de Gelder and Romke Rouw   89

Attentional Modulations of Event-related Brain Potentials
   Sensitive to Faces
Martin Eimer   103

Early Commitment of Neural Substrates for Face Recognition
Martha J. Farah, Carol Rabinowitz, Graham E. Quinn,
   and Grant T. Liu   117

Is Face Recognition Not So Unique After All?
Isabel Gauthier and Nikos K. Logothetis   125

---

* This book is also a special issue of the journal *Cognitive Neuropsychology* which forms
Issues 1, 2 and 3 of Volume 17 (2000).

Does Visual Subordinate-level Categorisation Engage the
  Functionally Defined Fusiform Face Area?
Isabel Gauthier, Michael J. Tarr, Jill Moylan, Adam W. Anderson,
  Pawel Skudlarski, and John C. Gore   143

Age-related Changes in the Neural Correlates of Degraded
  and Nondegraded Face Processing
Cheryl L. Grady, A. Randy McIntosh, Barry Horwitz,
  and Stanley I. Rapoport   165

Localised Face Processing by the Human Prefrontal Cortex:
  Face-selective Intracerebral Potentials and Post-lesion Deficits
K. Marinkovic, P. Trebon, P. Chauvel, and E. Halgren   187

Super Face-inversion Effects for Isolated Internal or External
  Features, and for Fractured Faces
Morris Moscovitch and David A. Moscovitch   201

ERPs Evoked by Viewing Facial Movements
Aina Puce, Angela Smith, and Truett Allison   221

Prosopamnesia: A Selective Impairment in Face Learning
Lynette J. Tippett, Laurie A. Miller, and Martha J. Farah   241

Response Properties of the Human Fusiform Face Area
Frank Tong, Ken Nakayama, Morris Moscovitch, Oren Weinrib,
  and Nancy Kanwisher   257

Localised Face Processing by the Human Prefrontal Cortex:
  Stimulation-evoked Hallucinations of Faces
J.P. Vignal, P. Chauvel, and E. Halgren   281

Subject Index   293

COGNITIVE NEUROPSYCHOLOGY, 2000, 17 (1/2/3), 1–11

THE COGNITIVE NEUROSCIENCE OF FACE PROCESSING: AN INTRODUCTION

Nancy Kanwisher

Massachusetts Institute of Technology, Cambridge, USA

Morris Moscovitch

University of Toronto at Mississauga, and Rotman Research Institute, Baycrest Centre for Geriatric Care, Toronto, Canada

Faces are extraordinarily rich sources of information. From one glance, you can determine the person's age and sex. You know where he or she is looking. You can read mood. If the person is familiar, you know who it is. For most of us, faces are a unique class of visual stimulus: What else do we look at more often or care about more deeply? The very fact that faces have been so special to us and to our primate ancestors makes them a fascinating test case for many of the central questions in cognitive neuroscience. To what extent does visual cognition rely on domain-specific processing mechanisms? How do these specialised cognitive mechanisms arise? How autonomous are they, and how do they interact with other cognitive systems?

The centrality of faces in our lives, however, poses a thorny problem for researchers. What visual stimuli can serve as adequate controls, matched for interest, biological relevance, and visual expertise? Few investigators would disagree that faces are visually special, but it's not easy to discover exactly how and why they are unique.

Not easy, but worth the effort. Exploiting the gamut of techniques from cognitive neuroscience, research on face processing is now making substantial progress. The articles in the present issue use single-unit recording, event-related potentials (ERPS), fMRI, cortical microstimulation, and behavioural testing of patients with brain damage.

These studies, together with recent related studies published elsewhere, have helped us gain traction on the long-standing questions of how faces are perceived, how their processing differs from that of nonface stimuli, and how the interaction of evolutionary and experiential forces has produced a neural mechanism that still outperforms the best computer vision algorithms. Here we synopsise the main advances that have been made by the research reported in this volume.

RECENT PROGRESS IN UNDERSTANDING FACE PROCESSING

The Multiple Components of Face Processing

Given the diversity of information that can be extracted from a face, we might expect face perception to be accomplished by a system with multiple components (Bruce & Young, 1986). Indeed, evidence from neuropsychology suggests that dissociable neural systems exist for the recognition of individual faces, the discrimination of emotional expressions, and the discrimination of the direction of overt attention (i.e. gaze). The articles in the present issue advance this story further in several respects.

Requests for reprints should be addressed to Morris Moscovitch, Department of Psychology, University of Toronto at Mississauga, Mississauga, Ontario, Canada L5L 1C6 (Email: momos@credit.erin.utoronto.ca).

MM was supported by NSERC grant A8437 and NK was supported my NIMH grant 56037 and a Human Frontiers grant.

Two papers investigate an ERP marker of face-specific processing called the N170, described earlier by Bentin, Allison, Puce, Perez, and McCarthy (1996; see also Jeffreys, 1996). Bentin, Deouell, and Soroker (1999) demonstrate that the N170 is unaffected by the familiarity of the face presented (see also Rossion et al., 1999), although later ERPs occurring 250msec to 500msec after stimulus presentation are sensitive to face familiarity. These results are taken as evidence that the N170 reflects a fairly early stage of the visual analysis of faces rather than the recognition process itself. Puce et al. (this issue) investigated the ERP responses to moving eyes and moving mouths, and found that the N170 was greater over the left hemisphere for open mouth stimuli (relative to closed mouths), whereas the N170 was greater over the right hemisphere for averted gaze than directed gaze. These findings may reflect the recruitment of left-hemisphere lip-reading mechanisms by moving mouths and the recruitment of specialised gaze mechanisms of the right hemisphere. Related results reported recently by Puce, Allison, Bentin, Gore, and McCarthy (1998) using fMRI suggest that the neural mechanisms in both cases may lie in the region of the superior temporal sulcus (STS), a region that has been implicated in several prior studies in the analysis of biological motion (Bonda, Petrides, Ostry, & Evans, 1996).

Two papers in this volume use behavioural evidence from patients with neurological disorders to provide new information about the functional organisation of the face processing system. Tippet et al. (this issue) provide evidence for a dissociation between the learning of new faces, and the recognition of old faces. They studied patient CT who exhibits an impairment of face learning, or "prosopamnesia," while retaining near normal performance on tasks requiring recognition of previously-learned faces and tasks requiring learning of other visual forms. Although many theorists might assume that mechanisms involved in learning new faces would largely overlap with those involved in recognising and remembering known faces (Dubois et al., 1999; Gorno Tempini et al., 1998), the evidence from this patient suggests otherwise. As such it provides an interesting parallel to

neuropsychological patients who lose the ability to learn the appearance of new places despite retaining the ability to recognise old places and the ability to learn new faces (Habib & Sirigu, 1987; Landis, Cummings, Benson, & Palmer, 1986). Collectively, these cases demonstrate a surprising degree of domain specificity in the mechanisms involved in visual learning. One possibility is that these category-specific learning deficits arise from disconnections between visual recognition systems and the hippocampal formation.

Calder et al. (this issue) investigated three patients with Möbius syndrome, a congenital disorder producing facial paralysis. After finding that these patients showed little or no impairment in the recognition of facial expressions, these authors conclude that the ability to produce facial expressions is not a necessary prerequisite for their recognition.

Two paired papers report the results from several different techniques applied to an intriguing single case of an epilepsy patient who had depth electrodes implanted for presurgical mapping. Marinkovic et al. (this issue) report large face-specific potentials from several different electrode sites in the patient's right ventrolateral prefrontal cortex. These results are consistent with the face-specific responses reported recently in the frontal cortex of macaques (Ó Scalaidhe, Wilson, & Goldman-Rakic, 1997). Interestingly, these sites appear to be very focal, as similar responses were not found in electrode loci only 1.5mm medial or lateral to the active site. As Marinkovic et al. (this issue) note, this pattern of multiple, very small, face-selective regions would probably not be resolvable with current PET and fMRI techniques. Vignal et al. (this issue) further report the stunning result that when the frontal electrode sites showing face-specific responses were subsequently stimulated, the subject reported seeing a series of faces! Further, after surgical excision of the cortex surrounding the same right prefrontal sites, the patient was found to have a deficit in the recognition of emotional expressions, particularly fear. This deficit, however, had largely disappeared when the patient was retested 3 years later. Although these tantalising results do not resolve the precise role of the right ventrolateral prefrontal cortex in face processing, they do demonstrate that very small foci within this region are selectively involved in some aspects of face processing. Grady et al. (this issue) also report evidence for frontal involvement in face recognition tasks; see following.

Finally, the paper by Breen et al. (this issue) considers several accounts that have been proposed for covert face recognition in prosopagnosia and delusional misidentification syndromes such as Capgras syndrome (a condition in which the patient has a delusional belief that someone they know has been replaced by an impostor). Breen et al. (this issue) argue that both syndromes can be accounted for in terms of a model of face processing in which both covert and overt recognition are mediated by the ventral stream, after which the system bifurcates into one stream that processes semantic and biographical information about the seen face, and another stream responsible for generating the affective response to faces.

Thus the papers in this section provide evidence for a number of distinct components of the face processing system: (1) an early N170 response to faces whether familiar or unfamiliar, probably originating in ventral occipitotemporal cortex; (2) lateral cortical responses to face motion probably in the vicinity of the STS; (3) a functional dissociation of face recognition from face learning; (4) another dissociation between the production and the recognition of emotional expressions; (5) multiple discrete focal regions in right prefrontal cortex involved in working memory for faces and/or in extracting or responding to emotional expressions in faces; and (6) a dissociation between two different ventral pathways involved in face processing, one for extracting semantic and biological information about faces, and the other for producing appropriate affective responses to faces.

Face-specific Processing vs. Individuation of Within-class Exemplars

The impression gained from the papers discussed above is that cognitive neuroscientists have been generally successful at identifying the neural substrates involved in extracting the different types of information conveyed by faces. One conclusion that may be drawn from these studies is that each of these neural substrates are face-specific processing components that together form a system which is itself face-specific. This conclusion is endorsed by many investigators but it is by no means universally accepted. Other investigators take the view that the function of the system, and by implication its components, is to discriminate between similar exemplars of the same category. According to these investigators, faces are the prototypical stimuli on which this system operates, but not the exclusive ones.

Although in principle the debate applies equally to all the subcomponents of the system, its focus has been on the early components of face recognition centred on the mid-fusiform gyrus, designated the fusiform face area (FFA) by Kanwisher, McDermott, and Chun (1997; see also McCarthy, Puce, Gore, & Allison, 1997). Tong et al. (this issue) show that this area is activated by a wide variety of face stimuli (including cartoon faces and cat faces) compared to other nonface objects. They argue that this region is selectively involved in some aspect of the perceptual analysis of faces such as the detection of a face in an image or the structural encoding of the information necessary for face recognition.

By contrast, Gauthier et al. (this issue) argue that the FFA is more active when subjects make subordinate-level classifications than basic-level classifications (e.g. classifying a particular canine as a beagle rather than a dog). It is not immediately apparent how to reconcile these data with prior studies showing a response in the FFA that was at least twice as great during discriminations between faces as during within-class discriminations between hands (Kanwisher et al., 1997), houses, and backs of human heads (Tong et al., this issue). One possibility is that the large region activated by subordinate-level categorisation in Gauthier et al.'s (this issue) study reflects in part the greater difficulty of the subordinate-level task. Another possibility is that the discrepancy arises because Gauthier et al. used a different technique to identify the FFA from that originally proposed by Kanwisher et al. (1997). For example, they assumed that the FFA occupies a square-shaped region of cortex. It is therefore possible that the region/s identified in their study are partially or completely nonoverlapping with the FFA as originally defined by Kanwisher et al. (1997) and as identified in subsequent studies by Kanwisher and colleagues (Kanwisher, Tong, & Nakayama, 1998; Kanwisher, Stanley, & Harris, 1999; Tong, Nakayama, Vaughan, & Kanwisher, 1998; Tong et al., this issue).

Development of Recognition Systems

Two of the papers concerned with the development of face and object recognition systems are also concerned with the problem of specificity. Farah and her colleagues (this issue) present a single-case study of Adam, a 16-year-old boy who became prosopagnosic following bilateral infarction in the occipital lobes at one day of age. Formal testing revealed that Adam could recognise objects much better than faces, leading Farah et al. to conclude that this case provides evidence for an innate face-specific mechanism whose function cannot be assumed by other structures despite ample opportunity and time to do so (but see Ballantyne & Trauner, 1999). Farah et al.'s argument would have carried more weight had they tested Adam on within category discriminations, especially in light of the observation that his recognition of living things is impaired. In support of Farah et al.'s conclusion, however, Bentin et al. (1999) report a case of a developmental prosopagnosic whose N170 response to faces is severely reduced but who has no difficulty making within-class discriminations on various nonface categories (see also Eimer & McCarthy, 1999).

Taking their lead from the seminal studies by Diamond and Carey (1986) on development of expertise in recognising dogs, Gauthier and Logothetis (this issue) argue that through extensive training, specialised mechanisms can be acquired whose characteristics will resemble, and may even overlap or be identical with, those used to recognise faces. As evidence, they cite Gauthier and Tarr's work on recognising "greebles" (artificially created creatures whose members bear a family resem-

blance to one another), and Logothetis' work on training monkeys to recognise paperclip figures. In both cases, Gauthier and Logothetis show that regions in inferotemporal cortex "learn" to respond to items on which the individual has recently been trained. However, it is not clear whether the regions responsive to "greebles" in humans are the same as those claimed to be selectively involved in the perception of faces (Kanwisher et al., 1997; McCarthy et al., 1997) because of the differences in the techniques used to localise face-selective regions (as discussed earlier). In monkeys, the region responsive to newly learned objects is well anterior to the regions typically found to be responsive to faces. Further, no cells have yet been found that are strongly responsive to both paperclips (after training) and faces. The existence of such cells is predicted by the hypothesis that common mechanisms are involved in all expert subordinate-level categorisation. Future work using fMRI in monkeys should provide an excellent way to survey a large cortical territory at a variety of stages during the acquisition of extensive expertise with novel objects. This work, in combination with studies of the deficits that result from brain damage, will be crucial in resolving the debate about the specificity of visual recognition systems. They may also help answer the even more fundamental question: why is the inferotemporal cortex such a fertile ground for cultivating modules that are specialised for processing complex visual stimuli ranging from words to faces?

Configural and Part-based Processes in Face and Object Recognition

As difficult as it is to resolve the debate concerning the existence of face-specific neural mechanisms, it is even more difficult to determine what processes might distinguish recognition of faces from that of objects. A popular hypothesis is that object recognition is analytic and part-based whereas face recognition is holistic and configural. Yin's (1969) finding that inversion impairs recognition of faces more than that of other objects supported this hypothesis because inversion impairs the perception of the spatial configuration among features on which face recognition depends more than identification of the features themselves, which would suffice for much of object recognition. This finding also established inversion as a marker of face-specific processes and a tool for investigating what makes face-recognition special. Building on this tradition, de Gelder and Rouw (this issue) replicated Farah's observation of an "inverted inversion effect" in prosopagnosic patients, that is, better performance on inverted than upright faces. Like Farah, Wilson, Drain, and Tanaka (1995), de Gelder and Rouw account for this effect in terms of the mandatory operation of a damaged holistic processing system, which is engaged by upright but not inverted faces. However, de Gelder and Rouw further show a similar benefit in prosopagnosics for inverted compared to upright stimuli even for animal faces and objects. They account for this result by arguing that the holistic system is also engaged by upright objects and when it is damaged in prosopagnosia it interferes with the operation of the part-based system necessary for object recognition.

Moscovitch and Moscovitch (this issue) discovered that requiring subjects to identify people from photos of inverted internal or external features and from those of inverted fractured faces lead to a "super inversion effect", in which performance dropped to about 20% correct compared to about 70% for intact inverted faces. The super inversion effect in controls resembles the inversion effect for intact faces in CK, a person with object agnosia but otherwise normal recognition of intact upright faces. If the object system is needed for recognition of intact inverted faces, as CK's performance indicates, then the super inversion effects in normal people suggest that some type of configural, orientation-specific information is also needed for recognising intact inverted faces, and possibly also objects. Moscovitch and Moscovitch conclude that both the face and object system use configural and orientation-specific information, but of different types. The face system works on representations of orientation-specific global configurations formed primarily by internal facial features. The object system, on the other hand, integrates information about individual features which themselves may be orientation-specific, with information about local or categorical relations among those features.

One would expect that inversion effects for faces that are so apparent at the behavioural level would have a clear neural correlate. Moreover, if inverted faces are indeed processed as objects as many claim, then they should activate brain regions involved in object processing more than would upright faces. Ashbridge et al. (this issue), recording from single units in a STS, found orientation-selective cells (as well as size-selective cells), the majority of which responded to upright faces and bodies whose size was in the normal range. Ashbridge et al. concluded that the ease of recognising upright over inverted faces is a statistical phenomenon based on the number of neurons involved in processing faces in one or the other orientation. Although this interpretation may account for some of the inversion effect, it does not explain why recognition of inverted faces is related to the integrity of the object recognition system, rather than simply to damage to the face system.

In examining the effects of face inversion on the FFA, Tong et al. (this issue; as well as Kanwisher et al., 1998) found only a slight reduction in activation, with the response to inverted faces remaining much higher than that to objects (see also Aguirre, Singh, & D'Esposito, 1999; Haxby et al., 1999). If inverted faces are treated as objects, why should the two engage the FFA to such different degrees? A solution suggested by Moscovitch and Moscovitch is that the object system forms a representation of the face based on information congruent with its operating characteristics, which it then transfers to the FFA for further processing. The FFA, in turn, sends its output to more anterior regions for identification. Thus, even inverted faces should activate the FFA, though not as strongly, and at a delay, compared to upright faces. Consistent with this hypothesis, Haxby et al. (1999) found that inverted faces activated object processing regions more than upright faces did, and they activated the face system including the FFA at a longer delay than did upright faces.

System Wide Distributed Networks in Face Recognition

The study by Grady et al. (this issue) demonstrates that regions not traditionally considered part of the posterior neocortical face system contribute to face recognition, and that their activity levels, as well as the levels of the posterior recognition system, vary with the clarity of the stimulus and the age of the individual. For example, increasing degradation of face stimuli was associated with greater activity in prefrontal cortex in both age groups, presumably because the frontal lobes were recruited in order to allocate additional cognitive resources to stimulus analysis. The old and young, however, differed in a number of ways. In the undegraded condition, the older adults showed greater activity than the young in prefrontal cortex, suggesting that sensory loss in the elderly may have led to some loss in clarity even for the undegraded stimulus. By contrast, the young showed greater activity in parietal and prestriate cortex, reflecting their greater reliance on posterior perceptual mechanisms for stimulus analysis. When the stimuli were degraded, there were striking differences between the young and old adults in the correlations between brain activity and recognition, both in posterior neocortex and in the hippocampus and the thalamus.

Grady et al.'s results indicate that face recognition is not as automatic as a modular account would have one believe. This view is reinforced by Eimer's finding that attention affects even the early N1 components that are specifically sensitive to faces. As in Grady et al.'s study, attentional influences interacted with stimulus properties such that attention affected N1 amplitude in posterior sites for centrally presented faces, but not for peripheral ones. One possible account of the lack of attentional effects for peripherally presented faces is that foveal projections may have preferential access to the ventral visual system where the FFA is located. Another possibility is that peripherally-presented faces may act as exogenous cues such that all peripheral stimuli are maximally attended, swamping any effect of the task.

Both Grady et al.'s and Eimer's (this issue) findings support and extend previous findings by Wojciulik, Kanwisher, and Driver (1998) that the FFA is not a passive system but one whose activity is modulated by attention that is either internally generated or elicited by external factors such as stimulus quality and location. It is interesting to speculate whether the frontal system recruited in Grady et al.'s study acts on posterior face-specific sites directly, or indirectly through the face-specific regions in prefrontal cortex that were identified by Marinkovic et al. (this issue) and Vignal et al. (this issue, corresponding to the face-specific neurons in macaques discovered by Ó Scalaidhe et al., 1997).

FUTURE DIRECTIONS

The articles in this issue advance our understanding on many of the key questions in the cognitive neuroscience of face processing. Yet many of the core questions in this area are still largely unanswered. We conclude by suggesting several critical areas where future research on face processing may be able to make the most headway.

The Functional Organisation of Face Processing

The central task of the cognitive neuroscience of face processing is to characterise the functional organisation of the face processing system, including an enumeration of the components of that system, a precise description of what each component does and how it works, and an understanding of how the components interact in real-world face processing tasks.

The increased involvement of new cognitive neuroscience techniques has provided a wealth of new candidate components of the face processing system. The present issue illustrates this progress with articles that provide evidence for different roles for left and right hemisphere STS systems involved in processing face movements (Puce et al., this issue; Ashbridge et al., this issue), frontal areas involved in face processing (Marinkovic et al., this issue; Vignal et al., this issue; Grady et al., this issue), a posterior mechanism for the structural encoding of faces (Bentin & Deouell, this issue; see also George et al., 1999), different systems involved in the production and perception of emotional expressions (Calder et al., this issue), and others in the emotional responses to faces (Breen et al., this issue), as well as evidence that non-face-specific mechanisms may play an important role in processing inverted faces (Aguirre et al., 1999; Haxby et al., 1999; Moscovitch & Moscovitch, this issue). Although the research in each of these areas is making substantial progress, we are still far from having a definitive account of the precise processes that are involved in each. To take just one example, despite the extensive recent research on the fusiform face area, it is not yet clear whether this region is involved simply in the detection of faces (Tong et al., this issue), the structural encoding of faces (George et al., 1999), or the subordinate-level categorisation of nonface objects (Gauthier et al., this issue). Thus one obviously important direction for future research is to determine more precisely the role of each of the functional components of face processing.

The proliferation of new cognitive neuroscience techniques for studying face processing, however, raises a new challenge: How are we to relate the findings collected from different techniques? Is the generator of the N170 observed with ERPs the same as that for the face-selective N200 observed with subdural strip electrodes (McCarthy, Puce, Belger, & Allison, 1999)? (Bentin et al., 1996, argue that it is not.) Does prosopagnosia result from the loss of the FFA, or rather from some other part of the face-processing system? Answers to these questions will be crucial if any effort to bring coherence and unity to this field is to succeed. One way to approach this question is to run closely matched experiments on the same individuals using two or more of these techniques, enabling a qualitative comparison of the functional properties of each neural marker. It will also be important to conduct similar studies in people with neurological disorders to determine whether damage to these areas produce the types of deficits predicted from functional studies in normal subjects. As yet, there are only a few studies that have applied the new techniques to investigate individuals with brain damage (e.g. Eimer & McCarthy, 1999).

An even greater challenge arises in relating data across species. Is the STS region in monkeys homologous to the human FFA, STS, or neither? Do monkeys have a region of face-selectivity in ventral cortex homologous to the FFA? A major limitation in answering this question has been the difficulty of recording from many cortical regions simultaneously in monkeys. However, the advent in the last year of techniques for running fMRI experiments on monkeys (Logothetis, Guggenberger, Peled, & Pauls, 1999) greatly improves the prospect for progress in this area by providing a way to run closely matched studies in monkeys and humans, enabling a direct comparison of the data collected across species.

Thus a major direction for future research will be to attempt to bridge across techniques, different human populations, and species. This effort is bound to provide a much richer and more precise picture of the involvement and function of each of the functional components in face processing.

Lessons from Machine Vision

Although our special issue did not include papers on this topic, a wealth of recent research in computer vision has been directed toward the development of algorithms for machine face recognition (Hallinan, Gordon, Yuille, Giblin, & Mumford, 1999). This work is relevant to our efforts to understand human face recognition in two ways. First, machine vision has long informed the study of human vision by providing counterintuitive insights about just which aspects of a visual task pose the greatest computational challenge. To the extent that any aspect of face perception poses special computational demands, we might expect the brain to exhibit a greater degree of cortical specialisation in its solution to that problem. Second, computer vision algorithms can be thought of as candidate theories of human recognition, specified with unusual precision and therefore eminently testable by behavioural and other techniques. In the long run the goal of a cognitive theory of face recognition should be to transcend the vague terminology now in use (e.g. "holistic processing") by achieving a precise characterisation of each component of face processing in terms of the actual algo-rithms involved. Thus one important direction for the cognitive neuroscience of face processing in the future will be a greater integration of the field with computational approaches to face perception.

Face Processing: How Selective and How Special?

Many of the articles in this issue address the selec-tivity of different neural mechanisms for face pro-cessing. Demonstrating a greater response to one stimulus class than to another is not sufficient to make the case for selectivity; a large number of noninstances of the stimulus class must be shown to produce a much lower response. Single-unit physi-ologists have made the greatest progress toward this goal, as they have tested the response of individual "face cells" to a wide variety of stimuli (Gross, Roche-Miranda, & Bender, 1972; Perrett et al., 1991). ERP work (Bentin et al., 1996; Jeffreys et al., 1996) and fMRI studies (Kanwisher et al., 1999; McCarthy et al., 1999; Tong et al., this issue) are catching up, with substantial evidence for face-selectivity of both the N170 and the FFA. How-ever, note that claims of face selectivity amount to hypotheses that none of the infinite number of as-yet-untested stimulus categories will produce a response as great as that observed to faces. Any such claim may be refuted whenever a new stimulus cate-gory is tested and shown to produce a response as great as (or greater than!) faces. Given this situation it will be important for all neural markers of sup-posed face-specific processes to be tested on a wide range of nonface stimuli.

Nonetheless, even substantial evidence for face selectivity need not imply that faces are unique. After all, the brain could be populated by hundreds of discrete regions, each specialised to analyse a dif-ferent class of stimuli. Thus one important direc-tion for future research is to test a wider range of stimulus categories to see whether any other simi-larly selective responses to distinct categories can be found. Neuropsychological evidence for category-specific impairments suggests that faces may not be the only domain of specialisation; it will be impor-tant in the future to supplement this evidence with

fMRI and other neural measures in normal subjects (Downing & Kanwisher, 1999; Martin, Wiggs, Ungerleider, & Haxby, 1996).

A wider exploration of the range of stimulus selectivities found in the brain should provide a broader context in which to view the implications of face-selective mechanisms. Further, this enterprise may shed some light on the more fundamental question of the origins of cortical specialisation (Downing & Kanwisher, 1999). If the experience of the individual is important in shaping the organi-sation of visual cortex, then we might expect to find selective responses to stimulus classes with which modern individuals (but not their primate ances-tors) have frequent daily experience (e.g. cars and chairs). However, if the evolutionary experience of the species is the critical determinant, then we might expect to find cortical regions specialised for the visual analysis of stimulus classes (e.g. predators and flowers) critical to the survival of our primate ancestors but not to modern humans.

The type of representation that is used by a par-ticular specialised cortical system may also depend on whether evolution or experience plays the more prominent role in its origin. For stimuli such as faces, which are likely to be encountered by every member of the species, configural representations or templates may be most effective because the basic stimulus configuration is invariant across the envi-ronments in which individuals may live. Thus the predictability of species-specific stimuli may allow for the creation through evolution of complex pat-tern recognition systems. These systems are likely to be based on templates or configurational proper-ties that are tuned at birth to the relevant stimulus properties but that remain plastic through develop-ment (Johnson, 1999; Maurer, 1985; Valenza, Simion, Cassia, & Umilta, 1996).

A different type of recognition system would be needed for dealing with complex patterns whose presence in the environment is accidental and whose identification would depend on experience. Manufactured objects would be one such stimulus class. Further, animals, plants, and objects may be so different from one another that no single tem-plate or handful of templates could capture the stimulus characteristics of all of them. For these kinds of complex patterns, a part-based system would allow the necessary flexibility to represent heterogeneous classes of stimuli.

It may be significant that several category-specific representation systems are found in ventral extrastriate cortex in the lingual, fusiform, and parahippocampal gyri. Located between posterior regions that code for primary sensory features and anterior and lateral regions concerned with semantics and memory, the inferotemporal cortex is ideally situated to serve as a convergence zone for binding information across distributed sensory networks under the guidance of higher-order systems. Regions within this ventral pathway appear to be distinguished from each other by their location, by the type of information that is bound, and perhaps by the algorithms underlying the binding operations. Recent neuroimaging and single unit studies on repetition priming suggest that inferotemporal cortex is also rapidly modified by experience (Grill-Spector et al., in press; Wiggs and Martin, 1998), a feature that may be crucial for the creation of structural representation systems.

If different representational systems exist that are structurally separate and operate according to different principles, how do they share information with each other? Moscovitch and Moscovitch addressed this problem with regard to sharing of information between the face and object system. One possible solution is to use translation codes for communicating between two systems, and another is to form associations between coactivated systems so as to create new, inter-related units that embody information about both. Apart from some computational modelling, few studies have attacked this problem directly.

Origins of Cortical Specialisation

A final and crucial area for future research will be the effort to explore the origins of cortical specialisation. We have discussed several methods for tracking the effect of individual experience on cortical specialisation. An important complement to this work will be to investigate possible innate bases for specialised face recognition mechanisms. Advances in imaging technology may make it possible in the future to safely scan young children and infants, enabling the origins of cortical specialisations to be tracked directly throughout the development of the individual. fMRI studies of developing primates may also allow us to address closely related questions. In a similar vein, longitudinal imaging studies during recovery from brain damage should provide a better understanding of the mechanisms that cause cortex to become specialised.

REFERENCES

Aguirre, G.K., Singh, R., & D'Esposito, M. (1998). Timing and intensity of fusiform face area (FFA) responses to upright and inverted faces. *Society of Neuroscience Abstracts,* #355.8.

Aguirre, G.K., Singh, R., & D'Esposito, M. (1999). Stimulus inversion and the responses of face and object-sensitive cortical areas. *Neuroreport, 10,* 189-194.

Ashbridge, E., Perrett, D.I., Oram, M.W., & Jellema, T. (this issue). Effect of image orientation and size on object recognition: Responses of single units in the macaque monkey temporal cortex. *Cognitive Neuropsychology, 17,* 13–33.

Ballantyne, A.O., & Trauner, D.A. (1999). Facial recognition in children after perinatal stroke. *Neuropsychiatry, Neuropsychology and Behavioural Neurology, 12,* 82–87.

Bentin, S., Allison, T., Puce, A., Perez, E., & McCarthy, G. (1996). Electrophysiological studies of face perceptions in humans. *Journal of Cognitive Neuroscience, 8,* 551–565.

Bentin, S., & Deouell, L.Y. (this issue). Structural encoding and identification in face processing: ERP Evidence for separate mechanisms. *Cognitive Neuropsychology, 17,* 35–54.

Bentin, S., Deouell, L.Y., & Soroker, N. (1999). Selective visual streaming in face recognition: Evidence from developmental prosopagnosia. *Neuroreport, 10,* 823–827.

Bonda, E., Petrides, M., Ostry, D., & Evans, A., (1996). Specific involvement of human parietal systems and the amygdala in the perception of biological motion. *The Journal of Neuroscience, 16,* 3737–3744.

Breen, N., Caine, D., & Coltheart, M. (this issue). Models of face recognition and delusional misidentification: A critical review. *Cognitive Neuropsychology, 17,* 55–71.

Bruce, V., & Young, A. (1986). Understanding face recognition. *British Journal of Psychology, 77,* 305–327.

Calder, A.J., Keane, J., Cole, J., Campbell, R., & Young, A.W. (this issue). Facial expression recognition by people with Möbius syndrome. *Cognitive Neuropsychology, 17,* 73–87.

de Gelder, B., & Rouw, R. (this issue). Structural encoding precludes recognition of face parts in prosopagnosia. *Cognitive Neuropsychology, 17,* 89–102.

Diamond, R., & Carey, S. (1986). Why faces are and are not special: An effect of expertise. *Journal of Experimental Psychology: General, 115,* 107–117.

Downing, P., & Kanwisher, N. (1999). Where do critical modules come from? *Poster to be presented at the Annual Meeting of the Cognitive Neuroscience Society.*

Dubois, S., Rossion, B., Schiltz, C., Bodart , J.M., Michel, C., Bruyer, R., & Crommelinck, M. (1999). Effect of familiarity on the processing of human faces. *Neuroimage, 9,* 278–289.

Eimer, M. (this issue). Attentional modulations of event-related brain potentials sensitive to faces. *Cognitive Neuropsychology, 17,* 103–116.

Eimer, M., & McCarthy, R.A. (1999). Prosopagnosia and structural encoding of faces: Evidence from event- related potentials. *Neuroreport, 10,* 255–259.

Farah, M.J., Rabinowitz, C., Quinn, G.E., & Liu, G.T. (this issue). Early commitment of neural substrates for face recognition. *Cognitive Neuropsychology, 17,* 117–123.

Farah, M.J., Wilson, K.D., Drain, H.M., & Tanaka, J.R. (1995). The inverted face inversion effect in prosopagnosia: Evidence for mandatory, face-specific perceptual mechanisms. *Vision Research, 35,* 2089–2093.

Gauthier, I., & Logothetis, N.K. (this issue). Is face recognition not so unique after all? *Cognitive Neuropsychology, 17,* 125–142.

Gauthier, I., Tarr, M.J., Moylan, J., Anderson, A.W., Skudlarski, P., & Gore, J.C. (this issue). Does visual subordinate-level categorisation engage the functionally-defined fusiform face area? *Cognitive Neuropsychology, 17,* 143–163.

George, N., Dolan, R., Fink, G.R., Baylis, G.C., Russell, C., & Driver, J. (1999). Contrast polarity and face recognition in the human fusiform gyrus, *Nature Neuroscience, 2,* 574-580.

Gorno Tempini, M.L., Price, C.J., Josephs, O., Vandenberghe, R., Cappa, S.F., Kapur, N., &

Frackowiak, R.S.J. (1998). The neural systems sustaining face and proper-name association. *Brain, 121,* 2130–2118.

Grady, C.L., McIntosh, A.R., Horowitz, B., & Rapoport, S.I. (this issue). Age-related changes in the neural correlates of degraded and non-degraded face processing. *Cognitive Neuropsychology, 17,* 165–186.

Grill-Spector, K., Kushnir, T., Edelman, S., Avidan, G., Itzchak, Y., & Malach, R. (in press). Differential processing of objects under various viewing conditions in the human lateral occipital complex. *Neuron.*

Gross, C.G., Roche-Miranda, G.E., & Bender, D.B. (1972). Visual properties of neurons in the inferotemporal cortex of the macaque. *Journal of Neurophysiology, 35,* 96–111.

Habib, M., & Sirigu, A. (1987). Pure topographical disorientation: A definition and anatomical basis. *Cortex, 23,* 73–85.

Hallinan, P.L., Gordon, G.G., Yuille, A.L., Giblin, P.J., & Mumford, D.B. (1999). Two- and three-dimensional patterns of the face. Wellesley, MA: A.K. Peters.

Haxby, J.V., Ungerleider, L.G., Clark, V.P., Schouten, J.L., Hoffman, E.A., & Martin, A. (1999). The effect of face inversion on activity in human neural systems for face and object perception. *Neuron, 22,* 189–199.

Jeffreys, D.A. (1996). Evoked potential studies of face and object processing. *Visual Cognition, 3,* 1–38.

Johnson, M.H. (1999). Ontogenetic constraints on neural and behavioural plasticity: Evidence from imprinting and face processing. *Canadian Journal of Experimental Psychology, 53,* 77–90.

Kanwisher, N., McDermott, J., & Chun, M.M. (1997). The fusiform face area: A module in human extrastriate cortex specialized for face perception. *Journal of Neuroscience, 17,* 4302–4311.

Kanwisher, N., Stanley, D., & Harris, A. (1999). The fusiform face area is selective for faces not animals. *Neuroreport, 10,* 183–187.

Kanwisher, N., Tong, F., & Nakayama, K. (1998). The effect of face inversion on the human fusiform face area. *Cognition, 68,* B1–-B11.

Landis, T., Cummings, J.L., Benson, D.F., & Palmer, E.P. (1986). Loss of topographic familiarity: An environmental agnosia. *Archives of Neurology, 43,* 132–136.

Leung, T.K., Burl, M.C., & Perona, P. (1995). Finding faces in cluttered scenes using random graph matching. *International Conference on Computer Vision, Cambridge, MA.*

Logothesis, N.K., Guggenberger, H., Peled, S., & Pauls, J. (1999). Functional imaging of the monkey brain. *Nature Neuroscience, 2,* 555–562.

Marinkovic, K., Trebon, P., Chauvel, P., & Halgren, E. (this issue). Localized face-processing by the human prefrontal cortex: Face-selective intracerebral potentials and post-lesion deficits. *Cognitive Neuropsychology, 17,* 187–199.

Martin, A., Wiggs, C., Ungerleider, L., & Haxby, J. (1996). Neural Correlates of Category-Specific Knowledge. *Nature, 379,* 649–652.

Maurer, D. (1985). Infants' perception of facedness. In T.N. Field & N. Fox (Eds.) *Social perception in infants.* Norwood, NJ: Ablex.

McCarthy, G., Puce, A., Belger, A., & Allison, T. (1999). Electrophysiological studies of human face perception. *Cerebral Cortex, 9,* 431–444.

McCarthy, G., Puce, A., Gore, J.C., & Allison, T. (1997). Face-specific processing in the human fusiform gyrus. *Journal of Cognitive Neuroscience, 9,* 604–609.

Moscovitch, M., & Moscovitch, D.A. (this issue). Super face-inversion effects for isolated internal or external features, and fractured faces. *Cognitive Neuropsychology, 17,* 201–219.

Ó Scalaidhe, S.P., Wilson, F.A., & Goldman-Rakic, P.S. (1997). Areal segregation of face-processing neurons in prefrontal cortex. *Science, 278,* 1135–1138.

Perrett, D.I., Oram, M.W., Harries, M.H., Bevan, R., Hietanen, J.K., Benson, P.J., & Thomas, S. (1991). Viewer-centred and object-centred coding of heads in the macaque temporal cortex. *Experimental Brain Research, 86,* 159–173.

Puce, A., Allison, T., Bentin, S., Gore, J.C., & McCarthy, G. (1998). Temporal cortex activation in human subjects viewing eye and mouth movements. *Journal of Neuroscience, 18,* 2188–2199.

Puce, A., Smith, A., & Allison, T. (this issue). ERPs evoked by viewing facial movements. *Cognitive Neuropsychology, 17,* 221–239.

Rossion, B., Campanella, S., Gomez, C.M., Delinte, A., Debatisse, D., Liard, L., Dubois, S., Bruyer, R., Crommelinck, M., & Guerit, J.M. (1999). Task modulation of brain activity related to familiar and unfamiliar face processing: An ERP study. *Clinical Neurophysiology, 110,* 449–62.

Tippett, L.J., Miller, L.A., & Farah, M.J. (this issue). Prosopamnesia: A selective impairment in face learning. *Cognitive Neuropsychology, 17,* 241–255.

Tong, F., Nakayama, K., Moscovitch, M., Weinrib, O., & Kanwisher, N. (this issue). Response properties of the human fusiform face area. *Cognitive Neuropsychology, 17,* 257–279.

Tong, F., Nakayama, K., Vaughan, J. T., & Kanwisher, N. (1998). Binocular rivalry and visual awareness in human extrastriate cortex. *Neuron, 21,* 753–759.

Valenza, E., Simion, F., Cassia, V.M., & Umilta, C. (1996). Face preference at birth. *Journal of Experimental Psychology: Human Perception and Performance, 22,* 892–903.

Vignal, J.P., Chauvel, P., & Halgren, E. (this issue). Localized face-processing by the human prefrontal cortex: Stimulation-evoked hallucinations of faces. *Cognitive Neuropsychology, 17,* 281–291.

Wiggs, C.L., & Martin, A. (1998). Properties and mechanisms of perceptual priming. *Current Opinion in Neurobiology, 8,* 227–233.

Wojciulik, E., Kanwisher, N., & Driver, J. (1998). Modulation of activity in the fusiform face area by covert attention: An fMRI study. *Journal of Neurophysiology, 79,* 1574–1579.

Yin, R.K. (1969). Looking at upside-down faces. *Journal of Experimental Psychology, 81,* 141–145.

COGNITIVE NEUROPSYCHOLOGY, 2000, 17 (1/2/3), 13–34

EFFECT OF IMAGE ORIENTATION AND SIZE ON OBJECT RECOGNITION: RESPONSES OF SINGLE UNITS IN THE MACAQUE MONKEY TEMPORAL CORTEX

E. Ashbridge, D.I. Perrett, M.W. Oram, and T. Jellema

University of St Andrews, Scotland, UK

This study examined how cells in the temporal cortex code orientation and size of a complex object. The study focused on cells selectively responsive to the sight of the head and body but unresponsive to control stimuli. The majority of cells tested (19/26, 73%) were selectively responsive to a particular orientation in the picture plane of the static whole body stimulus, 7/26 cells showed generalisation responding to all orientations (three cells with orientation tuning superimposed on a generalised response). Of all cells sensitive to orientation, the majority (15/22, 68%) were tuned to the upright image. The majority of cells tested (81 %, 13/16) were selective for stimulus size. The remaining cells (3/16) showed generalisation across four-fold decrease in size from life-sized. All size-sensitive cells were tuned to life-sized stimuli with decreasing responses to stimuli reduced from life-size. These results do not support previous suggestions that cells responsive to the head and body are selective to view but generalise across orientation and size. Here, extensive selectivity for size and orientation is reported. It is suggested that object orientation and size-specific responses might be pooled to obtain cell responses that generalise across size and orientation. The results suggest that experience affects neuronal coding of objects in that cells become tuned to views, orientation, and image sizes that are commonly experienced. Models of object recognition are discussed.

INTRODUCTION

The visual system allows us to discriminate between objects of different orientation and size. The system also allows us to generalise across image transformations and identify an object as the same despite changes in view, orientation, and image size. How the visual system represents the appearance of objects to enable these recognition capacities is not resolved.

The study reported here investigates the effects of image transformation in orientation or size on object processing in the cortex of the anterior part of the superior temporal cortex (STSa) of the macaque monkey. This area was studied because it contains cells that are both selectively responsive to

Requests for reprints should be addressed to D.I. Perrett, School of Psychology, University of St Andrews, Scotland, KY16 9JU, UK.

E. Ashbridge is currently at the Division of Psychology, South Bank University, 103 Borough Road, London SE1 0AA, UK.

This research was funded by project grants from the UK MRC, BBSRC, the US ONR, and the HFSP. E. Ashbridge (née Wachsmuth) was supported by a UK SERC studentship. We acknowledge the contribution of N. J. Emery, L. K. Harrison, and J. K. Hietanen, who participated in some of the experiments. We are grateful for the support given by University technical and photographic staff and to Dr Walsh for comments.

the sight of one complex object—the face or head—and sensitive to viewing conditions (e.g. Bruce, Desimone, & Gross, 1981; Perrett, Rolls, & Caan, 1982; Perrett et al., 1985, 1991). The focus of studies on the face or head of previous studies (and the use of terms such as "face responsive" or even "face cells") is perhaps misleading as to the selectivity of the cells. A substantial proportion of cells that respond to the sight of the face are also sensitive to visual information arising from body regions other than the face (e.g. Wachsmuth, Oram, & Perrett, 1994). Cells may respond to the face when this is presented in isolation, but such cells often respond to the rest of the body when the head is occluded from sight. Not surprisingly, when both the head and body are visible the response is greater than that seen to the face alone. We therefore examined the effects of image transformations on whole body stimuli.

If an object's representation can be activated independent of the orientation or size of the object's image on the retina, then such a representation will here be referred to as "object-centred." On the other hand, if the object's representation is preferentially activated by a specific image orientation or size, then the representation will be referred to as viewer-centred" since activation depends on orientation and size relative to the viewer.

Scalp-recorded evoked potentials to the sight of faces show orientation and size specificity (Jeffreys, 1989, 1993; Jeffreys, Tukmachi, & Rockley, 1992), implying that faces are coded at a particular stage of the human visual system in a viewer-centred manner.

Neurophysiological studies of the ventral route of cortical processing have previously suggested that cells in early visual areas (V1, V2, V4) exhibit orientation-specific coding of elementary features of objects (Henry, Dreher, & Bishop, 1974; Kobatake & Tanaka, 1994). These cells project to inferotemporal (IT) cortex, where cells are selectively responsive to progressively more complex features but still exhibit orientation-specific responses (Kobatake & Tanaka, 1994; Tanaka, Saito, Fukada, & Moriya, 1991). IT cortex in turn projects to the cortex of the STSa (Seltzer & Pandya, 1978). This area contains cells selective for complex objects and which have previously been reported to respond irrespective of the stimulus orientation (Ashbridge, & Perrett, 1998; Perrett et al., 1982, 1985, 1988).

Studies of temporal cortex cell responses to faces have so far tested few orientations (often restricted to upright and inverted). The first aim of the present study is to determine the extent to which cells in the STSa show object-centred orientation invariance, or viewer-centred orientation specificity in their responses to whole bodies presented in multiple orientations. This allows us to address the question of how orientation in the picture plane is processed for one biologically important object and whether it is processed in a similar way to view (see Logothetis, Pauls, & Poggio, 1995; Perrett et al., 1991; Wachsmuth et al., 1994).

Furthermore, previous studies suggest mainly size-specific coding in V4 and IT and suggest a possible greater degree of size generalisation within STSa (Dobbin, Jeo, Fiser, & Allman, 1998; Ito, Tamura, Fujita, & Tanaka, 1995; Rolls & Baylis, 1986). The second aim of the study reported here is to measure the extent to which cells selective for complex objects in the cortex of the anterior STS generalise across different image sizes.

METHODS

Recordings of responses of single cells from five macaque monkeys (*Macaca mulatta*, two females wt. 4–8kg and three males wt. 5–8kg) were carried out. The techniques applied (including surgical and recording procedures) and results from previous cellular studies of these subjects have been previously described (Perrett et al., 1991; Wachsmuth et al., 1994).

Training and Fixation Task

Pre-surgical training: While in a primate chair, the subjects were trained to fixate on one of five LED lights presented on a white wall at eye level at a distance of 4 metres. For a block of 50 trials the position of the fixation LED light was constant. The monkey's task was to discriminate the colour of the LED that followed a short signal tone to obtain the monkey's attention. Licking resulted in fruit juice reward for the green LED. The monkey was to withhold licking in order to avoid delivery of a weak saline solution to the red LED. The LED stimuli were presented in pseudorandom order under computer control.

Visual Stimuli

Pictures of eight different views (at 45° intervals rotating from the front view, see Wachsmuth et al., 1994) of the whole body were taken. For each view, eight orientations in the picture plane were constructed (resulting in 64 different stimuli); 0° (upright), 45°, 90° (horizontal), 135°, 180° (inverted), 225°, 270° (horizontal), and 315°. The images were then projected onto a white wall at a viewing distance of 4m, resulting in an image size of 24.4° (1.73m) head to toe. For some cells testing was additionally performed with different views of the head without the body in view. Testing was normally performed with the fixation light at the centre of the test image, subsidiary testing to examine effects of receptive fields was performed with the centre of the image presented 10° above, below, or to the side of the LED fixation spot.

For size stimuli the same range of eight views were presented at four magnifications ranging from 100° (1.73m, head to toe height, subtending 24.4°), 75% (1.3m, 18.5°), 50% (0.87m, 12.3°) to 25% (0.43m, 6.2°) at the viewing distance of 4m. During daily life the monkey subjects saw humans at distances between 0.5 and 5m. The head to toe size of humans encountered by the subjects, at the projection distance of 4m, ranged between 1.5m and 1.8m.

Control stimuli included complex 2D and 3D objects of different sizes, shapes, textures and orientations (broom, lab coats, chairs, pictures of different animals, etc.), simple 2D geometrical shapes (bars, spots and gratings), and simple 3D forms (balls, cylinders, boxes, etc.).

Testing Methods

Every cell from which neuronal activity was recorded was first tested in an exploratory way by presenting a series of static and moving 3D objects (including bodies), and tactile and auditory stimuli. Where cells were found responsive to the face or body, they were tested for (a) selectivity between objects and (b) selectivity between views.

Selectivity Between Objects. This was studied by comparing responses to slide images of faces, bodies, and a minimum of five control objects of approximately equivalent shape, size, and complexity (e.g. a fire extinguisher, lab coat). Test comparisons were also made using videodisk images of heads, bodies, and a variety of laboratory objects. Sensitivity to species of primate was tested (less systematically) by comparing responses to photographs of monkeys and humans.

Selectivity Between Views. Each cell was tested with four views of the head and body (face, left and right profile, and back view) or with eight views (the same four views and four intermediate views). Cells found to be responsive to static views of the whole body but not to control objects were then further investigated for sensitivity to stimulus orientation and size. Size and orientation testing was performed with stimuli presented using the cell's preferred view (front, back, etc.) once this had been established. Stimuli were presented in blocks of trials, with five trials for each stimulus condition in a computer-controlled pseudorandom order.

Data Analysis

Since most cells in the anterior STS respond with a latency of 100msec (± 30msec), the magnitude of cell activity on individual trials was assessed over the 250msec time period occurring 100–350msec after stimulus onset. For some cells [with late response onset (> 200msec) or inhibitory responses (i.e. below S/A)] a 500msec time period (100–600msec post-stimulus) was used to assess cell activity.

Cell responses to the whole body presented in different orientations and sizes, control objects, and

S/A were compared on-line using a one-way ANOVA and post hoc tests [protected least significant difference (PLSD), Snedecor & Cochran, 1980] with a significance level of $P < .05$.

Orientation Tuning

A multiple linear regression analysis was performed to estimate the best relationship between response and second-order cardioid function of orientation of the stimulus (see Perrett et al., 1991). This regression analysis calculates the values of the coefficients b_{1-5} of the following equation for producing the highest correlation between cell responses and the angle of orientation.

$$R = b_1 + b_2 \cos (q) + b_3 \sin (q) + b_4 \cos (2q) + b_5 \sin (2q)$$

where R is the response, b_{1-5} are coefficients, and q is the angle of the body orientation. This equation was used to define the optimal angle of orientation (qmax), the maximum response at this orientation (Rmax), and the sharpness of tuning.

Population Response Analysis

All cells, independent of their response pattern, were included in a population analysis. For each cell, the neuronal responses to different test conditions (averaged from five trials) were normalised by applying the following formula: (R-S/A)/(Rmax-S/A) where R = response to test condition, Rmax = maximum response to any orientation or size (depending on the analysis), and S/A = spontaneous activity. The population response to each test condition was then computed from the average of the normalised single cell responses and was displayed after renormalising such that the maximum population response = 1, and population S/A = 0.

Histological Reconstruction

After each recording session, frontal and lateral X-radiographs were taken to localise the electrode. Micro-lesions (10 microamp DC for 30sec), made at the end of some electrode tracks and subsequently identified using standard histological techniques, allowed reconstruction of the electrode position within the brain. In addition, reference

markers were made by injection of RRP and the fluorescent dyes, true blue and diamadino yellow.

Once the last recording session had been completed, the monkey was given a sedating dose of ketamine followed by a lethal dose of barbiturate anaesthetic. After transcardial perfusion with phosphate buffered saline and 4% gluteraldehyde/paraformaldehyde fixative, the brain was removed and put into a series of sucrose solutions with increasing concentration (10, 20, and 30%), or alternatively 2% dimethylsulphoxide and 20% glycerol. Standard histological procedures followed.

RESULTS

From five subjects, 23% of anterior STS cells (1692 out of 7288 cells tested) were found to be visually responsive. These included cells selectively responsive to moving or static visual stimuli (see, e.g., Bruce et al., 1981; Oram, Perrett, & Hietanen, 1993). Of the visually responsive cells, a total of 26 cells were found to be selectively responsive to the whole body (i.e. with response to the whole human body significantly greater than that to control objects and S/A). These 26 cells were tested for selectivity to different whole body orientations in the picture plane. A total of 16 cells selectively responsive to the whole body were tested for size sensitivity. All of the cells included in this study were found unresponsive to the variety of control objects tested. Although sensitivity to identity was not tested systematically, no differences were noted in the response to the different experimenters. Moreover, the tested effects of image orientation and size were found to be comparable for images of humans and monkeys.

Generalisation Across Orientations

Seven cells (of 26 tested) responded to all orientations at a rate significantly above S/A and control stimuli. Four of these cells showed complete generalisation in that they responded without statistical difference to all orientations (see Fig. 1).

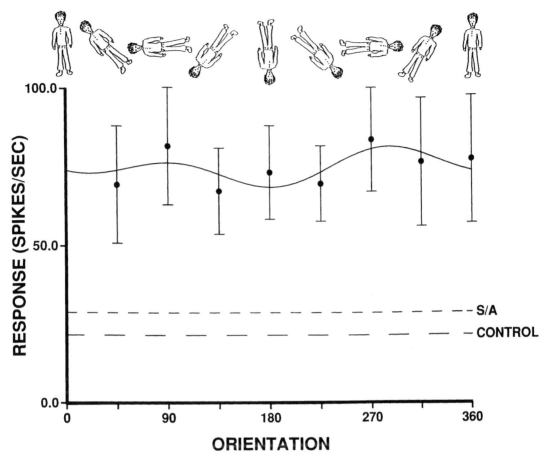

Fig. 1. *The responses of a cell displaying generalisation over body orientation. The mean responses (± 1SE) to the front view of the whole body presented in eight different orientations and spontaneous activity (S/A) are illustrated for one cell (E83_38.31). Orientation is defined as the angle of anti-clockwise rotation from upright (0° or 360°). The cell response showed no significant difference between different orientations tested (P > .5 PLSD each comparison), but the cell responded to all orientations at a rate greater than control stimuli (P < .05 each comparison) and S/A (P < .05 each comparison, except 45°, P < .06 and 135°, P < .067). Overall effect of conditions ANOVA: F(9,40) = 2.28, P < .05.*

Sensitivity to Orientation

The majority of cells (19/26) responded to only some rather than all orientations (e.g. Fig. 2). For the cell displayed in Fig. 2 the presence of the whole body presented in its gravitational upright orientation elicited the strongest response. The lower part of Fig. 2 displays responses of the same cell recorded on five individual trials with the whole body presented in its upright, two horizontal, and inverted orientations. Responses to the upright whole body occurred at approximately 180msec

after stimulus onset. Responses to horizontally presented bodies were reduced but remained at higher than pre-stimulus activity. When the whole body was presented inverted, however, there was no change in cell activity in comparison to the pre-stimulus period.

For the cell illustrated in Fig. 2, response latency changes with stimulus orientation. Most cells that exhibited orientation tuning did not exhibit changes in latency. Responses to suboptimal orientations were reduced in magnitude but began at the same latency as responses to preferred orientations.

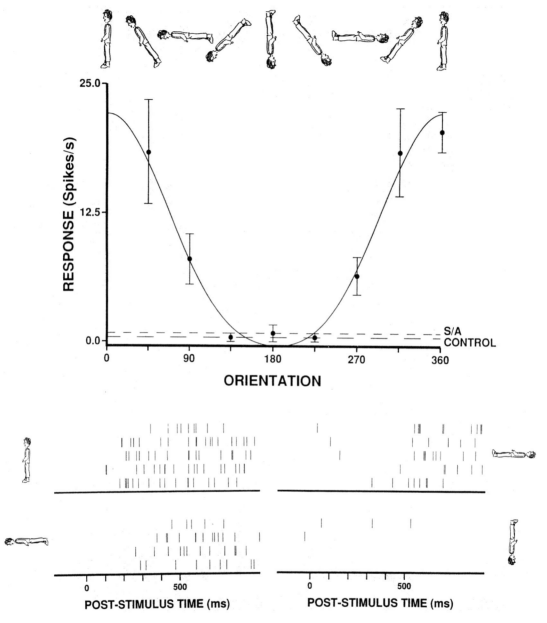

Fig. 2. *The responses of a cell displaying orientation tuning for upright bodies. Upper: The mean responses (± 1SE) to the side (90°) view of the whole body and spontaneous activity (S/A) are illustrated for one cell (E86_38.43). The curve is the best fit cardioid function, relating response to view. The cell exhibited tuning to the whole body stimuli in an upright orientation but responded to all orientations (except 135°, 180°, and 225°) at rates greater than to control stimuli and S/A. ANOVA: F(9,40) = 12.4, P < .0005. Lower: Rastergram displays of responses of the cell on five trials for four orientations. Each trial (originally in pseudorandom order) is represented by a single row of ticks, each tick indicates one action potential. Post-stimulus time is given at the figure base. The responses to the upright whole body (top left panel) were significantly different from responses to non-upright orientations (P < .005 each comparison).*

This behaviour is evident for the cell illustrated in Fig. 3, which responded to face images presented in a horizontal orientation at 200msec after stimulus presentation. The cell illustrated showed reduced responses to upright and inverted orientations but these responses also commenced approximately 200msec after stimulus onset.

Most cells (21/22) displayed an approximately monotonic tuning function. That is, the cells responded best to one orientation and showed a gradual decrease of response amplitude as the stimulus was rotated away from its optimal orientation (see following). One cell responded to two orientations of the front view of the body at a rate greater than intermediate orientations (see Fig. 4). This cell was unresponsive to the back view of the body; therefore responses to the front view were not simply attributable to orientation tuning for vertical stimuli.

Distribution of Orientation Tuning

The majority of cells (22/26, 82%) were selectively responsive for orientation in the picture plane. Although most of the tuned cells (16/22) were selective for orientations close to upright, cells were selective for non-upright orientations (e.g. Fig. 3) including three that were selective for inverted orientations. Figure 3 illustrates the responses of one cell to horizontal images of the face. The preference for this unusual orientation was found for both human and monkey faces. Figure 5 illustrates the responses of one cell tuned to orientations close to inverted. For the cell illustrated in Fig. 5 the sight of upright images of the body did not produce responses above spontaneous or controls.

Average Tuning Curve

The tightness of the tuning varied across the cells. Rotation of the stimulus away from optimal by 45° to 90° reduced most cell responses by half. To find the shape of orientation tuning in the picture plane a regression analysis for each cell was used to estimate the maximal response (Rmax) and the optimal

angle of orientation (qmax). Figure 6 (thin lines) illustrates the tuning curves for individual cells maximally sensitive to one orientation in the picture plane and where regression analysis provided a significant correlation between response and second-order cardioid function of orientation of the stimulus. Figure 6 combines different individual tuning curves, each being normalised by setting the mean S/A neuronal firing rate of each cell to 0 and the derived Rmax to 1.0. The peak normalised responses of each cell are expressed as a function of angle from optimal orientation (0°). If a normalised response curve falls below zero (i.e. response < average S/A), then the cell response is inhibited to that orientation of the stimulus.

Having established tuning curves for each cell tested with eight different orientations of the stimulus, an average tuning curve for these cells was produced. This is done by averaging the coefficients obtained from the individual regression analysis for each cell (Fig. 6, thick line).

Population Response to Different Orientations

The average response of 18 cells tested with eight angles was computed to provide an estimate of the total activity amongst the total population of cells responding to the sight of the body within the cortex of the anterior STS, and also to assess how such population activity was affected by stimulus orientation (Fig. 7). Note that this population response profile is different from that shown in Fig. 6, which estimates the average tuning of cells selective for orientation. Figure 7 indicates that, for the population, the response to the upright orientation of a whole body stimulus is higher than to other orientations in the picture plane. A gradual decline away from the upright orientation is observed. Nonetheless, the cell population responded to inverted stimuli at a rate significantly greater than that to controls [PLSD, $P = .005$, ANOVA: $F(8,136) = 11.7$, $P < .0005$]. This is because the population contains cells responsive to all orientations and cells tuned to inverted orientations.

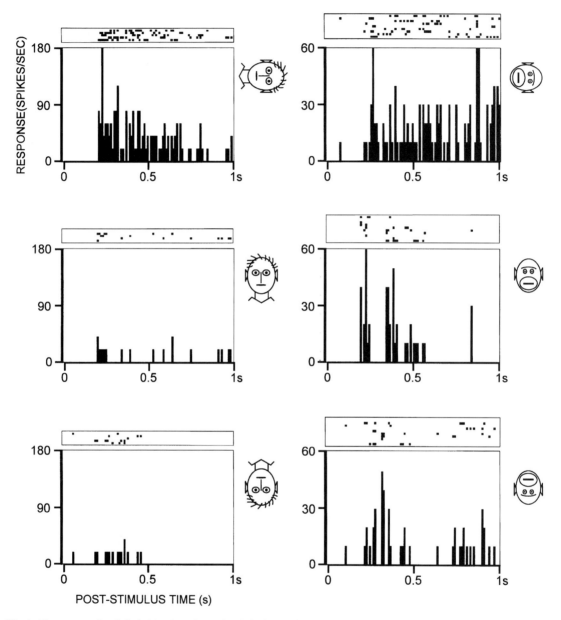

Fig. 3. *The responses of a cell displaying orientation tuning for horizontal faces. Rastergrams and peristimulus time histograms of the responses of one cell (S 128_2980) to different orientations of a human face (left) and a monkey face (right). Bin width is 10msec; spikes are indicated by black squares in rastergrams. The cell responded significantly more to a human face in the horizontal orientation than to upright or inverted orientations (P < .001, each comparison), ANOVA: F(2,12) = 53.9, P < .00001. Similarly for the monkey face, responses to the horizontal orientati n were greater than to the upright or inverted orientations (P < .001, each comparison), ANOVA: F(2,26) = 28.1, P < .002.*

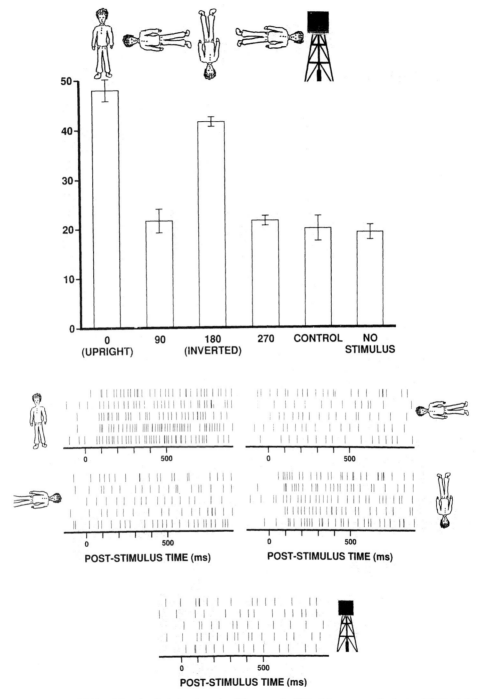

Fig. 4. *The responses of a cell with bimodal tuning for body orientation. Histogram (± 1SE) of the responses of a single cell (J69_29.04) to four orientations of the front view of the whole body. The cell responded more to inverted and upright orientations than to other orientations, control objects, or spontaneous activity (P < .0005 each comparison), ANOVA: F(5,24) = 45.8, P < .0005. Lower: Rastergram displays of cell activity (conventions as Fig. 2).*

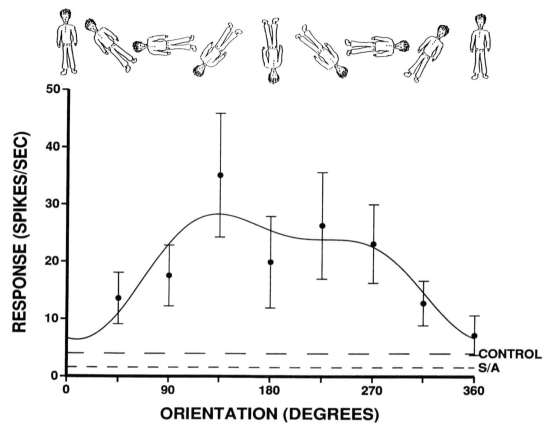

Fig. 5. *The responses of a cell tuned to non-upright body orientations. Histogram (± 1SE) of the responses of a single cell (E92_38.20) to eight orientations of the front view of the whole body. The cell responses to orientations close to inverted (135° and 225°) were greater than response to upright (0°), control objects, or spontaneous activity (P < .05 each comparison), ANOVA: F(9,40) = 2.7, P < .02.*

Generalisation Across Image Size

Of the 16 cells tested for size sensitivity, three cells showed size generalisation and responded to all image sizes (100% to 25%) at a rate greater than to S/A and control objects. Of these three cells, one showed no difference in response amplitude to different image sizes, whereas two cells displayed some size tuning superimposed on a generalised response (e.g. Fig. 8).

Sensitivity to Image Size

The remaining 13 cells (81%) were responsive to one (or more) but not all image sizes tested at a rate

greater than S/A and control objects, and hence showed size specificity (e.g. Fig. 9).

Thus, the majority of cells (15/16) showed sensitivity to size (including cells that displayed some size tuning superimposed on a generalised response, e.g. Fig. 8). Interestingly, all tuned cells were maximally responsive for the whole body at the largest (100%) or second largest (75%) projection size tested. These two sizes would correspond to images of real humans encountered at the projection distance. As for orientation, the response tuning to image size varied across cells. Some cells showed narrow tuning and responded to only one size of the body at a rate significantly different than to control objects and S/A, others showed broader tuning with the responses declining gradually as the

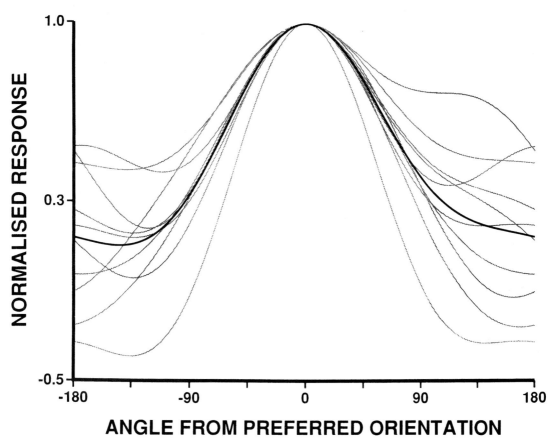

Fig. 6. *Tuning curves for cells sensitive to body orientation. Normalised tuning curves for cells exhibiting orientation sensitivity. The tuning curves are estimated from the best fit cardioid function relating response to an orientation. Spontaneous activity = 0 and maximal response = 1.0. Orientation is expressed as an angle of rotation from optimal orientation (θmax). Thick line: the average tuning curve from 10 orientation sensitive cells that gave a significant and good fitting regression curve.*

image size progressively decreased from the optimal size.

For comparison with other studies, reclassification was carried out with an effective response defined as greater than half the difference of the cell's maximal response and spontaneous activity. This showed that the majority of cells (75%, 12/16) that were selectively responsive to the body tolerated a size change of less than one octave. Of these, eight cells responded to only one particular size, either 75% or 100%, whereas four cells responded to both 75% and 100% size stimuli but not to the 25% size. The remaining 4/16 cells exhibited a more tolerant response pattern to stimulus size change. Two of the cells tolerated a size change of

one octave (from e.g. 50%–100%) and two cells tolerated a stimulus size change of at least two octaves (25%–100%).

Population Response to Different Image Sizes

All 16 cells were included in the population response analysis for Fig. 10. For each cell the response to different sizes was first normalised by setting the largest response (regardless of size) to 1.0 and S/A to 0. Two cells exhibited inhibitory responses and gave activity rates to the body stimuli that were lower than spontaneous activity or control stimuli. For these cells, response normalisation was

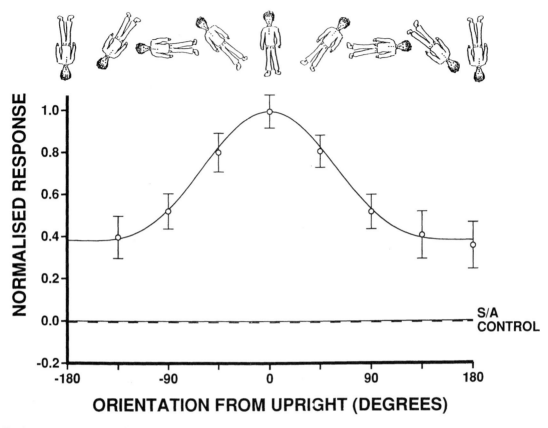

Fig. 7. *Population response to different body orientations. The mean response (± 1SE) for the population of cells responsive to the body at different orientations. The population response to each test condition was computed from the average of the normalised single cell responses (see Method) and was displayed after renormalising, such that the maximum population response = 1 and population spontaneous activity = 0.*

performed in an analogous manner except that the Rmax was defined as the response to the stimulus size that gave the greatest reduction from S/A. The graph displays a smooth degradation of response from maximum (100%) to minimum (25%). Even for the smallest image size of the body (25%), the population response was greater than the response to control, which was approximately zero (i.e. equal to S/A) [PLSD, $P = .021$, ANOVA: $F(4,60) = 24.8$, $P < .0005$].

Histological Reconstruction

The histological reconstruction showed that all cells reported in the present study were located in the upper and lower banks and the fundus of the anterior STS between 5 and 17mm anterior to the interaural plane (see Fig. 11). There was no observed clustering of cell types and no tendency for cells recorded at more anterior sites to show greater generalisation. For subject E, orientation-sensitive cells were found at anterior locations where the sulcus terminates in the temporal pole (see Fig. 11, lower left). Cells exhibiting size selectivity for the body were mainly located in the upper and to some extent in the lower bank of the anterior part of the anterior STS. For subject E, the size-sensitive cells were found in anterior regions of the STS (see Fig. 11, lower right).

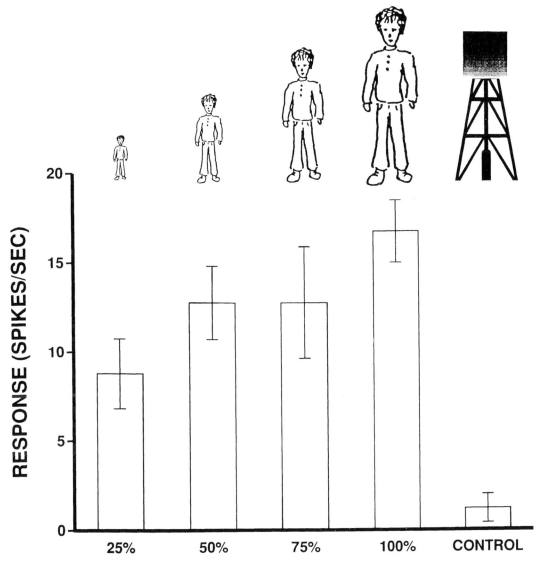

Fig. 8. *The responses of a cell displaying generalisation over body image size. The mean responses (± 1SE) to the whole body (front view) and to control objects are illustrated for one cell (E99_40.16). The cell showed generalisation in that all image sizes of bodies elicited a higher response than spontaneous activity (not shown) and control objects (P < .04 each comparison). The response also indicated size tuning since responses to largest three image sizes (100%–50%) were greater than that to the smallest image size (25%, P < .04 each comparison), ANOVA: F(5,24) = 9.6, P < .0005.*

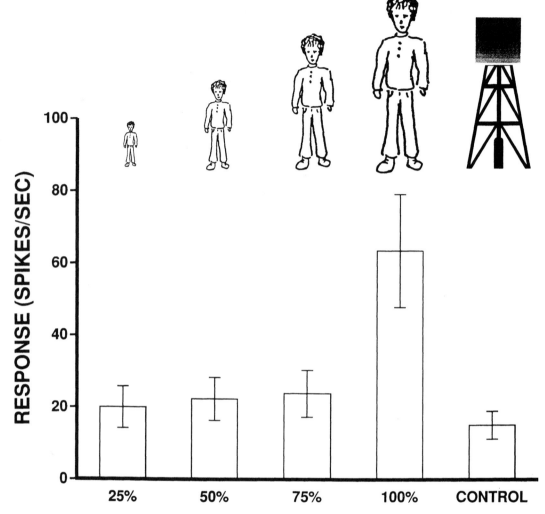

Fig. 9. *The responses of a cell displaying size tuning for large body image size. The mean responses (± 1SE) to the whole body (front view) and control objects are illustrated for one cell (E83_38.31). The cell's response to the largest body image (100%) was significantly greater than the response to smaller images of bodies (75%–25%) and controls (P < .003 each comparison). Responses to smaller body stimuli (75%–25%) were not significantly different from control stimuli (P > .4 each comparison), ANOVA: F(4,18) = 5.6, P = .004.*

DISCUSSION

Generalisation Along the Ventral Cortical Stream

It has been argued from previous observations that the further along the ventral stream one investigates the neuronal activity of cells, the greater the percentage of cells that generalise across viewing con-

ditions (such as orientation and size) in which an object is seen (Perrett et al., 1982, 1985, 1988). Studies of single cells in visual areas of the ventral stream leading up to the STSa support the contention that, while the selectivity between objects rises, the sensitivity to particular viewing conditions declines. As the ventral stream is progressed, cells become less sensitive to position (Desimone & Gross, 1979; Ito et al., 1995; Kobatake & Tanaka,

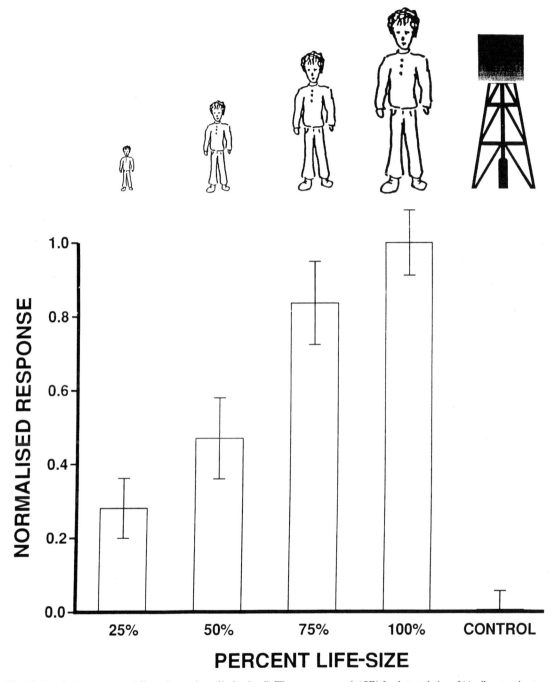

Fig. 10. *Population response to different image sizes of body stimuli. The mean response (±1SE) for the population of 16 cells responsive to the body at different sizes. The population response to each test condition was then computed from the average of the normalised single cell responses (see Method) and was displayed after renormalising such that the maximum population response = 1, and population spontaneous activity = 0.*

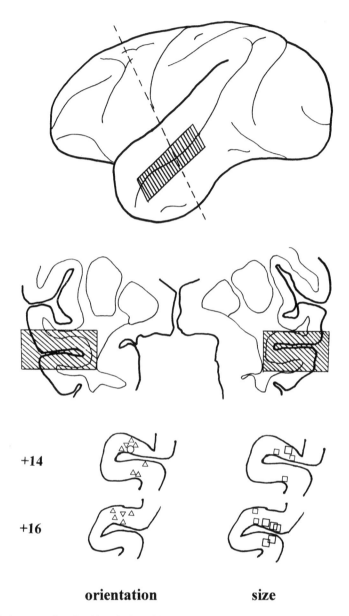

Fig. 11. *Histological reconstruction of position of cells sensitive and insensitive to body orientation and size. Upper: Side view of the brain. Study region (the anterior part of the superior temporal sulcus, STS) indicated by crosshatching, dashed line indicates plane of sections. Middle: A coronal section of the brain 12mm anterior to the interaural plane, anterior STS crosshatched. Lower: Frontal sections of the STSa in the right hemisphere of subject E, 14 and 16mm interior to the interaural plane. Left: The location of cells tuned to upright orientation of the body (triangles pointing up), cells tuned to non-upright orientations of the body (triangles pointing down), and cells generalising across all orientations of the body (circles). Right: The location of cells tuned to the largest (100%) image tested (large squares) and cells tuned to the 75% image size (small squares).*

1994; Tanaka et al., 1991) and show a greater tendency to generalise across object parts (Wachsmuth et al., 1994).

In contrast to the greater generalisation across position and components, the present investigation showed no marked tendency for cells to exhibit greater generalisation across orientation or size at more anterior recording sites. Indeed, cells selectively responsive to the sight of the body, yet showing orientation and size tuning, were found over a range of positions including very anterior sites within the STSa close to the temporal pole. Coding along the ventral pathway, therefore, does not appear to become independent of all viewing conditions.

Building View-general from View-sensitive Representations

Models of object recognition based on physiological evidence suggest the construction of view-independent representations by pooling the outputs across appropriate view-specific representations (e.g. Logothetis et al., 1995; Perrett & Oram, 1993). Such pooling operations can be based on simple learned association between different views of the same object seen in temporal succession as the object is rotated or as the viewer moves around the object (e.g. Perrett & Oram, 1993). Although these pooling operations were first conceived to account for generalisation across perspective view (Perrett et al., 1984, 1985), the same operations could account for generalisation in many domains (Földiák, 1991) including change in lighting conditions (Hietanen, Perrett, Oram, Benson, & Dittrich, 1992) or visibility of object part (Wachsmuth et al., 1994). In this same way responses of neurones selective for the head or body and capable of generalising across orientation (e.g. Fig. 1) could be formed by pooling outputs of orientation-sensitive cells (e.g. Fig. 2–5). Likewise, cells exhibiting size-tolerant responses to one object (e.g. Fig. 8) may owe their response characteristics to the pooled inputs of several cells with size-specific responses to the same object (e.g. Fig. 9). Experiencing the change in image size that happens when an object is approached may provide the basis

for the formation of cells with size-tolerant responses through the temporal association of inputs from cells selective for different image sizes.

Orientation-specific Neuronal Coding and Experience

The study reported here has shown that different STSa cell populations are selective for different object orientations of the same complex object (face/body). However, the majority (71%, 15/21) of cells that were sensitive to orientation of the face/body were found to be tuned to the upright orientation. This neuronal response pattern is similar to that found in IT for cells responsive to the face (Tanaka et al., 1991). It is therefore suggested that experience with one (upright) orientation of an object may enhance the neuronal representation for that object in the familiar viewing condition. Monkeys spend the majority of their time with their heads in an upright position and therefore their perceptual experience of heads and bodies will be biased (as in humans) to the gravitational upright. This biased experience may explain the predominance of cells tuned to the upright orientation.

It is interesting to note that the average *orientation* tuning curve for STSa cells responsive to body images is similar to the average *view* tuning curve obtained for STSa cells responsive to the head (Perrett et al., 1991), as well as the average *direction* tuning curve of motion-sensitive STSa cells (Oram et al., 1993).

Advantage of Orientation-specific Coding

What is the function of orientation-specific information in the ventral stream? First, computing such information is a useful and possibly essential stage in the processing leading to the identification of an object, even if later stages of the identification process discard orientation information through generalisation. Second, information about orientation is important in its own right. This is particularly evident for information about the face and body. The STSa appears to be a site that integrates information relevant to the interpretation of social signals, such as where other individuals are directing their attention and actions (Perrett et al., 1992; Walsh & Perrett, 1994). To recognise where an individual is attending requires orientation-specific and view-specific information about the head posture. The left profile view of the head in its upright orientation may indicate that an individual is attending to the viewer's left, but the same profile view rotated in the picture plane by 45° to 135° from upright (in an anti-clockwise direction) indicates that the individual's attention is directed towards the ground. More generally, to interpret the significance of an individual's posture and actions one needs to specify both the view and the orientation of the face, body, limbs, and hands.

Size-specific Neural Coding and Experience

The majority of cells studied here showed little tolerance to changes in size of body images. Only 4/16 cells tolerated a reduction of stimulus size by one octave (from 100% to 50%) and only two of these cells tolerated a change of two octaves (100% to 25%). Unfortunately, it was not possible to test a greater range of sizes in this study, since at the fixed projection distance of 4m, larger images of whole bodies would not fit onto the projection screen. If larger stimuli were tested, then only part of the body (e.g. a very large head or two extremely large eyes) would be visible on the screen. Previous findings (Perrett et al., 1991) indicate, however, that many cells selective for faces do respond to both very large faces (12.5° visual angle) and life-sized faces (4°) presented at 4m. Thus, the current study might have underestimated size tolerance because extra-large images were not tested. Nonetheless, the study has determined limits in the size tolerance of cells for stimuli decreasing from life-size at a constant viewing distance.

Previous studies have reported greater generalisation to image size in IT cortex. Ito et al. (1995) found 57% (16/28) of cells tolerated a size change of more than two octaves. The study of Ito et al., however, focused on cells responsive to simple geometrical forms. For such stimuli there is no defined life-size. The high degree of size-specific coding

reported here may be related to the response selectivity for complex biological stimuli. Life-size can be specified for images of biological objects at a given viewing distance. Studies of cells selectively responsive to faces and bodies show that the majority of size-specific cells are tuned to life-size images of these objects. Rolls and Baylis (1986) reported that 79% of size-specific face-responsive cells in IT and STSa were tuned to large faces (close to real life-size). In the present study, 16/17 cells selective for the head and body were maximally activated by the 75% or the 100% size images. At the projection distance these stimuli were life-sized. Figure 10 shows that the collective response of the cell population studied declines as image size is reduced from life size.

As with orientation tuning, the results for size tuning suggest a role of experience in shaping the response selectivity of cells in temporal cortex. Experience of an object over a particular range of distances and image sizes appears to result in a neuronal representation of that object at that range of image sizes experienced. This could explain the behavioural findings that images of familiar objects close to life-size (or to the image size experienced during training) are recognised faster than non-life-sized images (Besner, 1983; Jolicoeur & Besner, 1987). Indeed the greater the size change of stimuli between training and test, the greater the recognition impairment (Jolicoeur, 1987).

Size and Distance

The sensitivity to size exhibited by STSa cells appears to reflect tuning for "life-size" or absolute size. If this is true, then the cells' sensitivity to angular size (subtended at the retina) should change with distance. A cell selective for life-size bodies and optimally responsive to 18.5° stimuli at a test distance of 4m would be expected to show selectivity for 37° stimuli at a distance of 2m, and 9.75° stimuli at 8m to maintain the same selectivity for absolute size (Rolls & Baylis, 1986). The present study did not examine the possible interactions between sensitivity to angular size and distance but it would be an interesting focus for future work.

This is particularly the case because it is becoming increasingly apparent that information about object position is coded within the ventral stream of cortical processing. Dobbins et al. (1998) recently reported that cell responses within area V4 depend on the distance to visual stimuli. We have also found recently that many of the STSa cells responsive to faces, bodies and their movements are sensitive to distance and position of stimuli (Baker, Keysers, Jellema, & Perrett, in press; Baker, Keysers, Jellema, Wicker, & Perrett, 1999). Although one cannot present a real head at greater than life-size at any distance, with adjustments to viewing optics (e.g. in virtual reality environments) one could begin to isolate cues used by cells in the analysis of size of familiar objects.

Advantage of Size-specific Coding

To identify an object, which is argued to involve the ventral stream of visual processing, it is important to generalise across the different image sizes that occur when the object is seen from different distances. Recognising the specific size of an object, on the other hand, is important for interaction with objects. For example, the gap between the fingers must be adjusted appropriately to match the size of objects in order to pick them up. Cells in parietal cortex which are sensitive to information about object size and orientation (Taira et al., 1990; Sakata & Taira, 1994; Sakata et al., 1997) could be involved in guiding motor movements to enable such prehensile interactions with objects (Jeannerod, Arbib, Rizzolatti, & Sakata, 1995).

However, size can also carry information for social interactions between animals and therefore does play a role in object recognition. If, for instance, a monkey or human face is visible but very small, it does not constitute a threat. The face is either very small in absolute size, or it is a great distance from the viewer; neither constitute immediate danger. The size selectivity of the neuronal responses of cells located in the anterior part of the ventral stream may reflect this advantage of size-specific coding.

Behavioural Reaction Time and Neural Response Latency to Different Orientations or Sizes

The present study revealed that the population of STSa neurones activated by the sight of the head and body was less responsive the more the image orientation departed from upright (see Fig. 7) or was reduced from life-size (see Fig. 10). That is, more cells selectively responded to familiar orientations or sizes.

Such preferential representation of familiar orientations/sizes is reflected in the way activity accumulates in the entire cell population (Perrett, 1996; Perrett, Oram, & Ashbridge, 1998). Activity evoked by the face and body in familiar orientations and image sizes accumulates faster than that evoked by unusual orientations and sizes. Therefore at any given response threshold of the whole cell population, which might for example trigger behavioural reactions, responses to upright and life-size stimuli result in the shortest latencies. In other words the more cells there are responding to one orientation or size the less they have to "compete" with background noise and hence will reach the threshold faster. This argument is made considering the cells as a population. It is also true for the majority of cells considered individually: Weak responses to suboptimal image orientations or sizes commence at the same latency as strong responses to effective orientations and sizes (e.g. Fig. 3).

The decreased neural representation of unusual orientations or sizes may be sufficient to account for the decreased efficiency of recognition at unusual orientations (Jolicoeur, 1985: McMullen & Jolicoeur, 1992; Perrett et al., 1988; Phelps & Roberts, 1994; Tarr, 1995; Tarr & Pinker, 1989). Faces and bodies shown in unusual orientations would take longer to recognise because cell activity to these object orientations or sizes would be weaker and would take longer to exceed any threshold set for indicating the presence of a face/body. This account of recognition does not need to invoke "mental rotation" or "size normalisation" (Besner, 1983; Bundesen & Larsen, 1975; Larsen, 1985; Shepard & Metzler, 1971; Ullman, 1989) to explain increased time for processing unusual orientations (Perrett, 1996; Perrett et al., 1998).

Further, human scalp recordings of evoked potentials selective for face stimuli show an increase in latency and a decrease in amplitude of potentials as the face is rotated away from the upright orientation to the horizontal orientation (Jeffreys, 1989, 1993) and a small decrease in amplitude and latency for smaller faces (Jeffreys, 1989; Jeffreys et al., 1992). These evoked potentials presumably reflect large populations of neurones activated by the sight of faces and again indicate that neural activation is weaker to progressively more unusual orientations and sizes.

In conclusion, the physiological findings suggest a novel account for the recognition of familiar objects from unusual views. This account does not rely on "mental adjustment of size" (Besner, 1983; Bundesen & Larsen, 1975; Larsen, 1985; Shepard & Metzler, 1971) or "mental rotation" (Perrett, 1996; Perrett et al., 1998). Changes in the speed of recognition are taken to reflect the strength of size-, orientation-, and view-specific, neural representations of objects rather than the operation of transformational processes.

REFERENCES

Ashbridge, E., & Perrett, D.I. (1998). The physiology of shape generalisation (size and orientation). In: *Perceptual constancies: Why things look as they do* (pp. 192–209). Cambridge: Cambridge University Press.

Baker, C.I., Keysers, C., Jellema, T., & Perrett, D.I. (in press). Coding of spatial position in the superior temporal sulcus of the superior temporal sulcus of the macaque. *Current Psychology Letters.*

Baker, C.I., Keysers, C., Jellema, T., Wicker, B., & Perrett, D.I. (1999). *Temporal cortex and object permanence: Cells responsive to visual stimuli occluded from sight.* Manuscript submitted for publication.

Besner, D. (1983). Visual pattern recognition: Size pre-processing re-examined. *Quarterly Journal of Experimental Psychology, 35*, 209–216.

Bruce, C.J., Desimone, R., & Gross, C.G. (1981). Visual properties of neurons in a polysensory area in superior temporal sulcus of the macaque. *Journal of Neurophysiology, 46*, 369–384.

Bundesen, C., & Larsen, A. (1975). Visual transformation of size. *Journal of Experimental Psychology: Human Perception and Performance, 1*, 214–220.

Desimone, R., & Gross, C.G. (1979). Visual areas in the temporal cortex of the macaque. *Journal of Neuroscience, 4*, 2051–2062.

Dobbins, A.C., Jeo, R.M., Fiser, J., & Allman, L.M. (1998). Distance modulation of neural activity in the visual cortex. *Science, 281*, 552–555.

Földiák, P. (1991). Learning invariance from transformation sequences. *Neural Computing, 3*, 194–200.

Henry, G.H., Dreher, B., & Bishop, P.O. (1974). Orientation specificity of cells in cat striate cortex. *Journal of Neurophysiology, 37*, 1394–1409.

Hietanen, L.K., Perrett, D.l., Oram, M.W., Benson, P.J., & Dittrich, W.J. (1992). The effects of lighting conditions on responses of cells selective for face views in the macaque temporal cortex. *Experimental Brain Research, 89*, 157–171.

Ito, M., Tamura, H., Fujita, I., & Tanaka, K. (1995). Size and position invariance of neuronal responses in monkey inferotemporal cortex. *Journal of Neurophysiology, 73*, 218–226.

Jeannerod, M., Arbib, M.A., Rizzolatti, G., & Sakata, H. (1995). Grasping objects: The cortical mechanisms of visuomotor transformation. *Trends in Neuroscience, 18*, 314–320.

Jeffreys, D.A. (1989). A face-responsive potential recorded from the human scalp, *Experimental Brain Research, 78*, 193–202.

Jeffreys, D.A. (1993). The influence of stimulus orientation on the vertex-positive scalp potential evoked by faces. *Experimental Brain Research, 96*, 163–172.

Jeffreys, DA, Tukmachi, E.S.A. & Rockley, G.G. (1992). Evoked potential evidence for human brain mechanisms that respond to single, fixated faces. *Brain Research, 91*, 315–362.

Jolicoeur, P.E. (1985). The time to name disorientated natural objects. *Memory and Cognition, 13*, 289–303.

Jolicoeur, P. (1987). A size-congruency effect in memory for visual shape. *Memory and Cognition, 15*, 531–543.

Jolicoeur, P., & Besner, D. (1987). Additivity and interaction between size ratio and response category in the comparison of size-discrepant shapes. *Journal of Experimental Psychology: Human Perception and Performance, 13*, 478–487.

Kobatake, E., & Tanaka, K. (1994). Neural selectivities to complex object features in the ventral visual pathway of the macaque cerebral cortex. *Journal of Neurophysiology, 71*, 856–867.

Larsen, A. (1985). Pattern matching: Effects of size ratio, angular difference in orientation, and familiarity. *Perception and Psychophysics, 38,* 63–68.

Logothetis, N.K., Pauls, J., & Poggio, T. (1995). Shape representation in the inferior temporal cortex of monkeys. *Current Biology, 5,* 552–563.

McMullen, P.A., & Jolicoeur, P. (1992). The reference frame and effects of orientation on finding the top of rotated objects. *Journal of Experimental Psychology: Human Perception and Performance, 18,* 807–820.

Oram, M.W., Perrett, D.I., & Hietanen, J.K. (1993). Directional tuning of motion-sensitive cells in the anterior superior temporal polysensory area of the macaque. *Experimental Brain Research, 97,* 274–294.

Perrett, D.I. (1996). View-dependent coding in the ventral stream and its consequences for recognition. In: R. Caminiti, K.-P. Hoffmann, & A.J. Lacquaniti (Eds.), *Vision and movement mechanisms in the cerebral cortex* (pp. 142–151). Strasbourg: HFSP.

Perrett, D.I., Hietanen, J.K., Oram, M.W., & Benson, P.J. (1992). Organization and functions of cells responsive to faces in the temporal cortex. *Philosophical Transactions of the Royal Society of London, B, 335,* 23–30.

Perrett, D.I., Mistlin, A.J., Chitty, A.L, Smith, P.A.J., Potter, D.D., Broennimann, R., & Harries, M.H. (1988). Specialised face processing and hemispheric asymmetry in man and monkey: Evidence from single unit and reaction time studies. *Behavioural Brain Research, 29,* 245–258.

Perrett, D.I., & Oram, M. (1993). The neurophysiology of shape processing. *Image Visual Computing, 11,* 317–333.

Perrett, D.I., Oram, M.W., Harries, M.H., Bevan, R., Hietanen, J.K., Benson, R.J., & Thomas, S. (1991). Viewer-centred and object-centred coding of heads in the macaque temporal cortex. *Experimental Brain Research, 86,* 159–173.

Perrett, D.I., Oram, M.W., Hietanen, J.K., & Benson, P.J. (1994). Issues of representation in object vision. In M.J. Farah & G. Ratcliff (Eds.), *The neuropsychology of high-level vision* (pp.33–61). Lawrence Erlbaum Associates Inc.

Perrett, D.I., Oram, M.W., & Ashbridge, E (1998). Evidence accumulation in cell populations responsive to faces: An account of generalisation of recognition without mental transformations. *Cognition, 67,* 111–145.

Perrett, D.I., Rolls, E.T., & Caan, W. (1982). Visual neurons responsive to faces in the monkey temporal cortex. *Experimental Brain Research, 47,* 329–342.

Perrett, D.I., Smith, P.A.J., Potter, D.D., Mistlin, A.J., Head, A.S., Milner, A.D., & Jeeves, M.A. (1984). Neurons responsive to faces in the temporal cortex: Studies of functional organisation, sensitivity to identity, and relation to perception. *Human Neurobiology, 3,* 197–208.

Perrett, D.I., Smith, P.A.L., Potter, D.D., Mistlin, A.J., Head, A.S., Milner, A.D., & Jeeves, M.A. (1985). Visual cells in the temporal cortex sensitive to face view and gaze direction. *Proceedings of the Royal Society, London B, 223,* 293–317.

Phelps, M.T., & Roberts, W.A. (1994). Memory for pictures of upright and inverted primate faces in humans (*homo sapiens*), squirrel monkeys (*saimiri sciureus*), and pigeons (*columba livia*). *Journal of Comparative Psychology, 108,* 114–125.

Rolls, E.T., & Baylis, G.C. (1986). Size and contrast have only small effects on the responses to faces of neurons in the cortex of the superior temporal sulcus of the monkey. *Experimental Brain Research, 65,* 38–48.

Sakata, H., & Taira, M. (1994). Parietal control of hand action. *Current Opinion in Neurobiology, 4,* 847–856.

Sakata, H., Taira, M., Murata, A., Galese, V., Tanaka, Y., Shitake, E., & Kusunoki, M. (1997). Parietal visual neurons coding 3-D characteristics of objects and their relation to hand action. In O. Karnarth & P. Their (Eds.), *Parietal lobe contributions to orientation in 3D space.* New York: Springer.

Seltzer, B., & Pandya, D.N. (1978). Afferent cortical connections and architectonics of the superior temporal sulcus and surrounding cortex in the rhesus monkey. *Brain Research, 149,* 1–24.

Shepard, R.N., & Metzler, J. (1971). Mental rotation of three-dimensional objects. *Science, 171,* 701–703.

Snedecor, G.W., & Cochran, W.G. (1980). In *Statistical methods* (7th ed., pp. 215–237). Ames, IA: Iowa State University Press.

Taira, M., Mine, S., Georgopoulos, A.P., Murata, A., & Sakata, H. (1990). Parietal cortex neurons of the monkey related to the visual guidance of hand movements. *Experimental Brain Research, 83,* 29–36.

Tanaka, K., Saito, H., Fukada, Y., & Moriya, M. (1991). Coding visual images of objects in the inferotemporal cortex of the macaque monkey. *Journal of Neurophysiology, 66,* 170–189.

Tarr, M.J. (1995). Rotating objects to recognise them: A case study on the role of viewpoint dependency in the recognition of three-dimensional objects. *Psychonomic Bulletin Review, 2,* 55–82.

Tarr, M.J., & Pinker, S. (1989). Mental rotation and orientation dependence in shape recognition. *Cognitive Psychology, 5,* 233–282.

Ullman, S. (1989). Aligning pictorial descriptions: An approach to object recognition. *Cognition, 32,* 193–254.

Wachsmuth, E., Oram, M.W., & Perrett, D.A. (1994). Recognition of objects and their component parts: Responses of single units in the temporal cortex of the macaque. *Cerebral Cortex, 4,* 509–522.

Walsh, V., & Perrett, D.I. (1994). Visual attention in the occipitotemporal processing stream of the macaque. *Cognitive Neuropsychology, 11,* 243–263.

COGNITIVE NEUROPSYCHOLOGY, 2000, 17 (1/2/3), 35–54

STRUCTURAL ENCODING AND IDENTIFICATION IN FACE PROCESSING: ERP EVIDENCE FOR SEPARATE MECHANISMS

Shlomo Bentin and Leon Y. Deouell

Hebrew University of Jerusalem, Israel

The present study had two aims. The first aim was to explore the possible top-down effect of face-recognition and/or face-identification processes on the formation of structural representation of faces, as indexed by the N170 ERP component. The second aim was to examine possible ERP manifestations of face identification processes as an initial step for assessing their time course and functional neuroanatomy. Identical N170 potentials were elicited by famous and unfamiliar faces in Experiment 1, when both were irrelevant to the task, suggesting that face familiarity does not affect structural encoding processes. Small but significant differences were observed, however, during later-occurring epochs of the ERPs. In Experiment 2 the participants were instructed to count occasionally occurring portraits of famous politicians while rejecting faces of famous people who were not politicians and faces of unfamiliar people. Although an attempt to identify each face was required, no differences were found in the N170 elicited by faces of unfamiliar people and faces of familiar non-politicians. Famous faces, however, elicited a negative potential that was significantly larger than that elicited by unfamiliar faces between about 250 and 500msec from stimulus onset. This negative component was tentatively identified as an N400 analogue elicited by faces. Both the absence of an effect of familiarity on the N170 and the familiarity face-N400 effect were replicated in Experiment 3, in which the participants made speeded button-press responses in each trial, distinguishing among faces of politicians and faces of famous and unfamiliar non-politicians. In addition, ERP components later than the N400 were found to be associated with the speed of the response but not with face familiarity. We concluded that (1) although reflected by the N170, the structural encoding mechanism is not influenced by the face recognition and identification processes, and (2) the negative component modulated by face familiarity is associated with the semantic activity involved in the identification of familiar faces.

INTRODUCTION

Face recognition is an outstanding human visual ability. Despite the within-race overall physical similarity among faces, slight changes are sufficient to allow quick and unequivocal identification of a familiar face among tens and even hundreds of unfamiliar faces. Since this ability is not matched by the ability to identify other visual stimuli that are similarly complex and even more frequently encountered, it has been suggested that face recognition is achieved by a special-purpose mechanism that probably uses different processing strategies than those used for the visual identification of most other objects or animals (e.g. Tanaka & Farah, 1993; see also Farah, 1990). Empirical evidence

---

Requests for reprints should be addressed to Shlomo Bentin, Department of Psychology, Hebrew University of Jerusalem, Mount Scopus, 91905 Jerusalem, Israel (Email: msbentin@olive.mscc.huji.ac.il).

This study was supported by a grant from the US-Israel Binational Science Foundation. We thank Michael Fink and Gil Raviv for skilful assistance.

35

supporting this hypothesis was obtained in studies of monkeys and humans. In monkeys, single-unit recordings have revealed cells in the inferotemporal cortex that respond to monkey and human faces (Bruce, Desimone, & Gross, 1981; Desimone, 1991; Desimone, Albright, Gross, & Bruce, 1984; Perrett, Mistlin, & Chitty, 1987; Perrett et al., 1982; Young & Yamane, 1992) and face components (Perrett, Rolls, & Caan, 1982), but not to other complex stimuli such as snakes, spiders, or food (Baylis, Rolls, & Leonard, 1985; Desimone et al., 1984; Rolls & Baylis, 1986; Saito et al., 1986). In humans, the specificity of the face perception mechanism is suggested, for example, by the double dissociation between visual agnostic patients who cannot recognise objects while their ability to recognise faces is spared (e.g. Moscovitch, Behrmann, & Winocur, 1997) and prosopagnostic patients who cannot recognise familiar faces although they are able to identify other objects (Bentin, Deouell, & Soroker, 1999; for a recent review see De Renzi, 1997). In many cases, however, the impairment of the prosopagnostic patients was confined to the *identification* of faces (i.e. associating between a face and a person) whereas their ability to distinguish between faces and other visual stimuli and, in some cases, even to match between faces of the same individual seen from different angle, was significantly better or even intact (Benton & Van Allen, 1972; Malone, Morris, Kay, & Levin, 1982)[1]. This pattern led to a further dissociation between a specific visual mechanism responsible for the structural encoding of faces, and a "higher level" mechanism responsible for associating the structural representation of a face with semantic information about the person to whom

the face belongs (e.g. Benton, 1980). A model for face recognition in which such a distinction is explicit was suggested by Bruce and Young (1986). According to this model an abstract tridimensional structural representation of the face is initially constructed by a face-specific visual encoding process. This structural representation is compared with a set of face recognition units; if a positive match results, the person's identity nodes are activated in semantic memory. A recent study of brain event-related potentials (ERPs) provided tentative support for the specificity of a structural encoding mechanism for faces (Bentin, Allison, Perez, Puce, & McCarthy, 1996; cf. George, Evans, Fiori, Davidoff, & Renault, 1996; Jeffreys, 1993)[2].

Recording ERPs from the scalp of normal subjects, Bentin et al. (1996) found a negative potential peaking at about 170msec from stimulus onset (N170), which responded preferentially to human faces and isolated human eyes, but not to human hands, animal faces[3], items of furniture, cars, or nonsense stimuli preserving the illumination level of the faces. The N170 was distributed over a relatively circumscribed region at the posterior-inferior aspects of the temporal lobes, and was greater at right than at left hemisphere sites. Extensive investigations aimed at unveiling the stimulus-related characteristics of the N170 showed that it is not significantly affected by altering the spatial organisation of the inner components or by face inversion (Bentin et al., 1996; Bentin, & McCarthy, 1999), manipulations that are known to hamper the identification of faces. On the basis of these characteristics, Bentin et al. (1996) suggested that the N170 is probably associated with a face-specific structural encoding mechanism that might not be

---

[1] In fact, such considerations have led some authors to suggest that prosopagnosia is not a face-specific syndrome but a mild form of visual agnosia (Humphreys & Riddoch, 1987), or that the basic deficit of these patients involves the identification of an exemplar within a semantic category whose members are very similar (Damasio, Damasio, & Van Hoesen, 1982). The latter hypothesis was undermined, however, by studies of prosopagnostic patients who were very good distinguishing among cars (Sergent & Signoret, 1992), faces of sheep (McNeil & Warrington, 1993), as well as members of other categories (Farah, Klein, & Levinson, 1995).

[2] Neurophysiological evidence for a specific for face perception has been amply provided by PET studies (e.g. Haxby et al. 1993; Sergent, Ohta, & MacDonald, 1992), fMRI studies (e.g. Clark et al., 1996; Kanwisher, McDermott, & Chun, 1997; McCarthy, Puce, Gore, & Allison, 1997; Puce, Allison, Gore, & McCarthy, 1995), and intracranial ERP recordings (Allison et al., 1994a,b,c). These studies did not, however, address the dissociation between a structural encoding mechanism and a face identification mechanism.

[3] Apes were excluded.

directly involved in face identification. This hypothesis was tested in the present study by examining the effects of face familiarity on the N170 and other ERP components.

GENERAL METHOD

Participants

The participants were 60 undergraduate students with normal or corrected-to-normal vision. They participated in the experiment for class credit or payment.

Stimuli

The stimuli were 150 different portraits and 30 butterflies of different kinds. All stimuli were scanned high-quality photographs. They were presented in black and white using a high-resolution monitor and graphic-board. The exposure time of each stimulus was 350msec. Among the portraits, 60 were of unfamiliar people, 60 were of famous movie stars, TV personalities, sportsmen and sportswomen, and 30 were portraits of famous politicians. The familiarity of the photographed people was determined using the following procedure.

Photographs of 500 ostensibly known personalities from different professional fields were intermixed with 500 photographs of unknown people, and presented one-by-one on a computer screen to a random sample of 24 students from the same pool as the subjects in the present study. The participants in this pilot survey were instructed to judge the familiarity of each portrait by selecting one of four response categories: (1) Full recognition, including the name and the profession of the person; (2) Precise knowledge regarding who the person is, without remembering his or her name; (3) General feeling that the face is familiar without explicit knowledge of who the person is; and (4) Confident feeling that the face is unfamiliar. For the present study, we included in the "familiar faces" category only faces that were categorised in one of the first two categories by at least 85% of the subjects, and were not included in the fourth cate-

gory by any subject. "Unfamiliar faces" were those that were included in the fourth category by at least 90% of the subjects and were never included in the first two categories.

EEG Recording and Averaging

The EEG was recorded from 30 (Experiment 1) or 48 (Experiments 2 and 3) tin electrodes mounted on a custom-made cap (Fig. 1). The EOG was recorded with two electrodes, one located at the outer cantus of the right eye and the other at the infraorbital region of the same eye. The EEG and EOG were recorded with reference to the tip of the nose.

The EEG was continuously sampled at 250Hz, amplified × 20,000 with an analog band-pass filter of 0.1Hz to 33Hz, and stored for off-line analysis. For ERP averaging, the EEG was segmented into 1100msec epochs, starting 100msec before the stimulus. Epochs with EEG or EOG exceeding ± 100μV were excluded from the averaging. The baseline was adjusted by subtracting the mean amplitude of the pre-stimulus period of each ERP from all the data points in the epoch. Frequencies lower than 0.4Hz or higher than 19Hz (– 3dB points) were digitally filtered out from the ERPs after averaging.

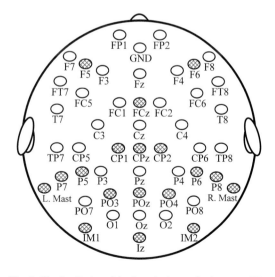

Fig. 1. *The distribution of the electrode sites on the electrocaps. The electrodes added for Experiments 2 and 3 are shaded.*

ERP Analysis

Averaged ERPs at each scalp site were used to calculate the overall scalp distribution of the electrophysiological activity presumably associated with face processing. On the basis of these topographies (and previous results), regions of interest were determined and the stimulus-type effects were statistically analysed only at these sites. ANOVAs were used to evaluate the statistical significance of the effects. Greenhouse-Geisser adjustment of degrees of freedom was applied whenever necessary.

EXPERIMENT 1

Previous results showed that the N170 is elicited by human faces regardless of whether or not the faces are relevant to the observer's task. In all the experiments reported by Bentin et al (1996), the participants' task was to silently count non-face targets while ignoring other stimulus types, including faces. The emergence of the N170 under these circumstances suggests that the face-processing mechanism with which the N170 is associated may be triggered automatically by the occurrence of a face in the visual field. However, automatic initiation does not imply that the process, once triggered, cannot be controlled, and that its activity cannot be shaped by top-down information. More specifically, as would be predicted by interactive-activation models of face recognition (e.g. Burton, Bruce, & Johnston, 1990; see also Burton, Bruce & Hancock, in press), it is possible that the construction of the structural representation of a face is facilitated by familiarity even if the face identity is not task-relevant. In addition, familiarity in general and face familiarity in particular may act as an exogenous, data-driven cue attracting attention to the face (for a comprehensive discussion of data-driven attention deployment, see Yantis, 1998). Experiment 1 was designed to explore this possibility by comparing the ERPs elicited by familiar faces with those elicited by unfamiliar faces while subjects were monitoring the screen for the occasional appearance of butterflies.

Method

Participants

The participants were 14 undergraduates (10 women), all right-handed according to self-report. One participant was excluded due to technical problems.

Stimuli

The stimuli were 60 unfamiliar faces, 60 faces of famous people (not including politicians), and 30 butterflies.

Task and Procedures

The participants were instructed to silently count the occasionally appearing butterflies and to ignore the faces. They were not told that some of the faces might be familiar to them. Following the application of the electrode-cap, the experiment was run within a single session lasting about 15 minutes. Two pauses were included, 1 every 50 trials. During the pause, the participants were asked how many butterflies they had seen up to that point, and were told to continue counting when the stimulus presentation resumed.

Results

Replicating previous results, faces elicited N170 potentials at the posterior temporal sites; at the same latency the butterflies elicited a much smaller negative-going deflection that did not cross the baseline (see Plate 1 of the colour section situated between pages 160 and 161).

The N170 potentials elicited by familiar and unfamiliar faces were similar in their scalp distribution and amplitude ($-6.1\mu V$ and $-6.0\mu V$, respectively; see Plate 1). For both type of faces the N170 recorded over right hemisphere sites were apparently larger ($-6.8\mu V$) than those recorded over the left hemisphere sites ($-5.3\mu V$). The statistical validity of these observations was tested by a three-way ANOVA. The factors were Familiarity (familiar, unfamiliar), Site (P7/8, PO7/8), and Hemisphere (left, right). The ANOVA showed that there was neither effect of familiarity [$F(1,12) < 1.00$] nor of site [$F(1,12) < 1.00$]. The hemisphere effect was conspicuous but failed to reach significance [$F(1,12)$ = 3. 1, P < 10].

In contrast to the absence of a familiarity effect on the N170, the ERPs elicited by familiar and unfamiliar faces seemed to diverge at most electrode sites during a later epoch of the waveform, starting at about 350msec. The two ERPs converged again at about 800msec from stimulus onset. The ERPs elicited by the familiar faces were more negative than these elicited by unfamiliar faces between 350 and 550msec, and more positive between 550 and 800msec, resulting in bi-phasic difference waveforms (Fig. 2)[4]. The latency of the negative peak in the difference waveform was at about 450msec, roughly corresponding with the peak of the N400 potential observed for faces (Bentin & McCarthy, 1994). The scalp-distribution of the difference, however, extended more posteriorly than the distribution of the "classical" N400 (Kutas & Hillyard, 1980). The positive

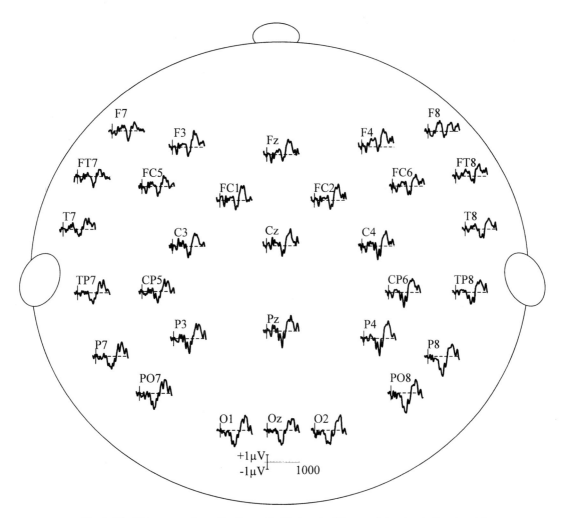

Fig. 2. *The difference waveforms (familiar–unfamiliar) at the different scalp locations in Experiment 1.*

---

[4] For clarity, only difference waveforms are presented.

peak in the difference waveforms corresponded to a vertex-maximal positive peak elicited by nontargets at around 700msec.

The statistical validity of the negative difference was assessed by comparing the mean amplitude of the ERPs elicited by familiar faces and unfamiliar faces separately between 350 and 550msec, and between 550 and 800msec. The analysis of the first period showed that, across all sites[5], the mean amplitude elicited by familiar faces was significantly more negative ($-0.70\mu V$) than that elicited by unfamiliar faces (which was, in fact, positive; $0.12\mu V$) [$F(1,12) = 10.2$, $P < .01$]. There was no effect of hemisphere [$F(1,12) < 1.0$], and none of the interactions were significant. The analysis of the differences observed during the second phase showed a similar pattern. The ERPs elicited by familiar faces between 550 and 800msec were significantly more positive ($2.1\mu V$) than these elicited by unfamiliar faces ($1.4\mu V$) [$F(1,12) = 6.63$, $P < .05$]. The hemisphere effect and all the interactions were not significant ($F < 1.00$ for all comparisons). A more detailed analysis of the familiarity effect on the later components was deferred to the next experiment.

Discussion

The most important result of this experiment was that familiarity with a particular face did not influence the N170. This result supports the hypothesis that the N170 is associated with an early visual mechanism which, although specific for face processing, is not influenced by processes that are directly associated with face identification. Such a mechanism could be the "structural encoder" suggested by Bruce and Young (1986). The structural encoding process is the final stage of the visual analysis and its product is an abstract sensory representation of the face, a representation that is independent of context or viewpoint, corresponding approximately with a 3-D representation in Marr's model (1982). According to Bruce and Young's model, the familiarity of the face is determined by a

different process, one of matching the structural representation with a set of face recognition units. Inasmuch as the N170 is associated with the formation of a sensory representation, the current data suggest that the flow of information between the structural encoding and the face recognition processes is uni-directional, that is, there is no top-down influence on the structural encoding.

It is possible that this hypothesis should, however, be constrained to the conditions of the present experiment, in which face identity was irrelevant for task completion. Indeed, the distinction between the ERPs elicited by familiar and unfamiliar faces found around the N400 latency suggests that, despite being task-irrelevant, face familiarity was probably noticed or, at the very least, implicitly processed. Nonetheless the task-irrelevant distinction between familiar and unfamiliar faces was inconsequential for the N170. Top-down influences on N170 might be evident, however, when the face identity is deliberately processed. Experiment 2 was designed to explore this hypothesis and examine the characteristics of the later differences between the ERPs elicited by familiar and unfamiliar faces.

EXPERIMENT 2

The present experiment was designed to resemble Experiment 1 as much as possible except for using a task that required explicit identification of the faces. For this purpose, faces of famous politicians substituted for the butterflies, and the participants were instructed to silently count the number of politicians. Hence, all the stimuli in this experiment were faces, therefore assumed to generate the N170. The important comparison, however, was between the ERPs elicited by familiar and unfamiliar non-politicians. These two type of faces were equivalent in regard to their task relevance and were included in the same response category. Yet, because the process of matching the sensory representations with the face recognition units may be different for familiar and unfamiliar faces, and in

---

[5] The midline electrodes were excluded from this analysis to allow possible interhemispheric differences to emerge.

addition familiar faces should be able to activate specific semantic information whereas unfamiliar faces cannot, we expected conspicuous differences between the ERPs elicited by these two face categories. In particular, we predicted that they would differ during a latency period consistent with the N400—a potential that has been associated with the activation of semantic information (for a review see Kutas & Van Petten, 1988), as well as by faces (Barrett & Rugg, 1989; Bentin & McCarthy, 1994).

To summarise the questions addressed in this experiment were: (1) Would the difference between processing familiar and unfamiliar faces be reflected in the N170, suggesting top-down influence on the process of structural encoding when face identity is task-relevant? (2) Would the need to identify the faces enhance the difference observed in Experiment 1 between the N400 component elicited by familiar and unfamiliar faces?

Method

Participants

The participants were 24 undergraduates (15 women) who had not participated in the previous experiment. Four of the women were left-handed, by self-report.

Stimuli

The nontarget stimuli were the same faces used in Experiment 1. The familiar faces were media and sport celebrities and movie stars. The target stimuli were faces of politicians.

Task and Procedures

The subjects were instructed to identify and count the politicians. It was assumed that in order to perform this task the subjects would have to attempt to identify each face. The procedures were identical to those used in Experiment 1, except that the EEG was recorded from 48 rather than 30 scalp sites.

Results

The participants' ability to recognise politicians was good, but not perfect. On the average, the participants' count was about 92% accurate. In this experiment, however, we could not efficiently monitor the participants' ability to recognise the politicians because the reported counts might have included not only omissions but also false alarms. Nonetheless, the ERP pattern was mostly clear and consistent across subjects.

Adding recording sites, we obtained a finer grid, which showed that the regions where N170 was most evident extended more posteriorly and laterally than P8 and P7, including the mastoids, the IM locations (midway between the inion and the mastoids), and the parieto-occipital sites (PO7, PO3, PO8, and PO4). At all these sites, the N170 appeared to be larger over the right than the left hemisphere and almost the same for unfamiliar faces and familiar non-politicians (Fig. 3).

This observation was statistically validated by a Familiarity (familiar, unfamiliar) × Site (PO3/4, P7/8, L/R Mast, PO7/8, IM1/2) × Hemisphere (left, right) ANOVA. The dependent variable was the amplitude of the N170, assessed as the most negative amplitude between 140 to 210msec from stimulus onset. Of course, the ERPs elicited by faces of politicians (target stimuli) were not included in this analysis. The ANOVA showed a significant effect of site [$F(4,92) = 11.0$, $P < .001$ G-G Epsilon = 0.47], and a significant effect of hemisphere, revealing that the N170 was larger over right ($- 5.2\mu V$) than over left ($- 3.6\mu V$) hemisphere sites [$F(1,23) = 9.9$, $P < .01$]. The effect of familiarity was not significant [$F(1,23) = 3.0$, $P = .09$], and there were no significant interactions. A post hoc analysis of the site effect showed that the N170 was largest at the lateral parieto-occipital (PO7 and PO8) and mastoid sites and smallest at the medial parieto-occipital sites (PO3 and PO4). The possible effect of attention to face identity was directly examined by comparing the N170 amplitudes in Experiment 1, in which face identity was irrelevant to the task, with those in the present experiment, in which attention had to be allocated to face identity. This analysis was based on a mixed

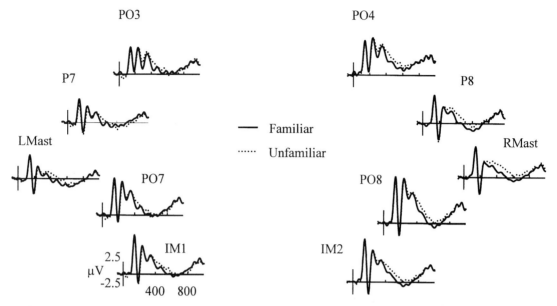

Fig. 3. *The N170 potential at the parieto-temporo-occipital scalp locations in Experiment 2. Larger N170 were recorded over the right than over the left hemisphere, and there was no effect of familiarity.*

model ANOVA in which the Experiment was a between-subjects factor. The results of the ANOVA showed that the N170 was almost the same in both experiments [$F(1,35) < 1.00$], and that the experiment factor did not interact with any of the other factors.

Following the N170, the ERPs elicited by faces of familiar non-politicians differed from those elicited by unfamiliar faces. In contrast to Experiment 1, however, the difference began earlier, at about 250msec, and ended at about 500msec from stimulus onset. During this period the ERPs elicited by familiar faces were more negative than those elicited by unfamiliar faces (Fig. 4). Furthermore, as evident in Fig. 4, the difference between the two conditions was more conspicuous at the central and centro-frontal sites, a distribution more consistent with the distribution of the N400.

The negative potential elicited by familiar faces during the epoch of interest (250–500msec from stimulus onset) included (at least at some sites) 2 distinctive peaks, one at about 300msec and the second at about 425msec from stimulus onset. However, spline interpolations of the potential

scalp distribution and the calculation of the scalp current densities (SCD) at the each of these peaks showed similar patterns. Therefore, the statistical significance of the observed differences was assessed comparing the mean amplitudes of the ERPs elicited by familiar and unfamiliar faces during 250 to 500msec from stimulus onset.

First, in an attempt to reduce the data to a manageable size, the mean averages at the 48 recording sites were collapsed into 4 quadrants: Posterior-right (IM2, O2, PO8, RMast, PO4, P8, P6, P4), Posterior-left (IM1, O1, PO7, LMast, PO3, P7, P5, P3), Anterior-right (TP8, CP6, CP2, T8, C4, FT8, FC6, FC2, F8, F6, F4), and Anterior-left (TP7, CP5, CP1, T7, C3, FT7, FC5, FC1, FT7, F7, F5, F3). These data were analysed by Familiarity (familiar, unfamiliar) × Anterior/Posterior Distribution (anterior, posterior) × Hemisphere (left, right). This analysis revealed that, across all sites, the average amplitude elicited by familiar faces between 250 and 500msec ($-0.14\mu V$) was significantly more negative than that elicited by unfamiliar faces (which was, in fact, positive; $0.47\mu V$) [$F(1,23) = 11.8$, $P < .001$] and that the familiarity

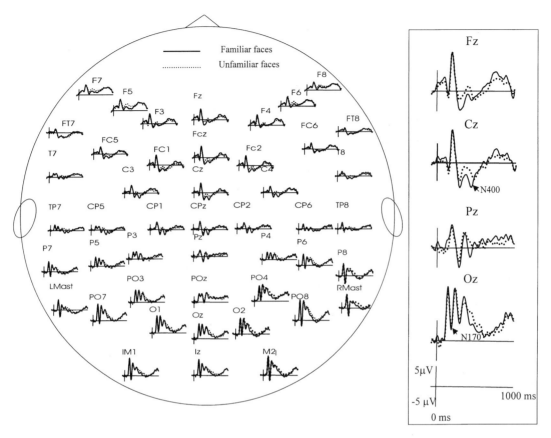

Fig. 4. *ERPs elicited by familiar and unfamiliar faces at all scalp locations in Experiment 2. Note the frontocentral distribution of the face–N400.*

effect significantly interacted with the anterior/posterior distribution [$F(1,23)$ = 4.57, $P < .05$]. Post hoc univariate contrasts showed that the familiarity effect was larger over the anterior (0.76μV) than the posterior quadrants (0.55μV), but was statistically significant over both [$F(1,23$ = 7.7, $P < .05$ and $F(1,23)$ = 32.0, $P < .001$].

Across familiar and unfamiliar faces, the ERPs were more negative over the anterior (– 1.0μV) than the posterior (1.35μV) regions [$F(1,23)$ = 75.9, $P < .001$], and slightly (but not significantly) less positive over the left (0.0μV) than the right (0.3μV) hemisphere [$F(1,23)$ = 1.63, $P = .21$]. No other interactions were significant.

Scrutiny of the individual responses revealed that this pattern was clear in only 16 out of the 24 of participants (Group A). The relationship between

the ERPs elicited by familiar and unfamiliar faces in the other 8 participants (Group B) was less clear, and, at least at some scalp sites, even inverse (i.e. unfamiliar faces were less positive than familiar faces). The difference between the two groups at selected electrode sites is presented in Fig. 5.

Since we assumed that the difference between the two groups might reflect strategic differences in task performance (see following), the familiarity effect was analysed separately for each group. ANOVAs were calculated using only the anterior two quadrants, but the distribution was analysed in detail, using each electrode site as a separate level. Hence the factors were Familiarity (familiar, unfamiliar), site (F7/8, F5/6, F3/4, FT7/8, FC5/6 FC1/2, T7/8, C3/4, TP7/8, CP5/6, CP1/2), and Hemisphere (left, right). These analyses showed that the

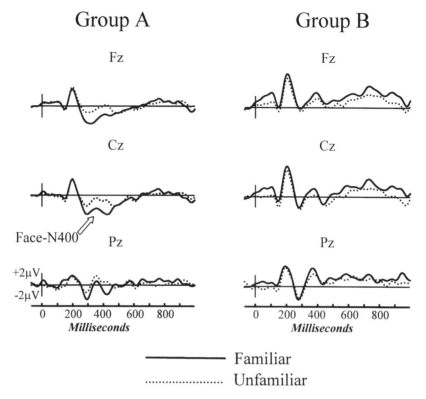

Fig. 5. *N400 modulation in the post hoc determined groups of participants in Experiment 2. Group A included 16 subjects in which the face-N400 was larger for familiar than for unfamiliar faces and Group B included 8 subjects in which this relation was reversed.*

familiarity effect was significant for Group A [$F(1,15)$ = 29.1, $P < .001$] but not for Group B [$F(1,7) < 1.00$]. For both groups the site effect was significant [$F(10,150)$ = 15.21, $P < .001$, G-G Epsilon = 0.28, and $F(10,70)$ = 2.95, $P < .001$, G-G Epsilon = 0.20 for Group A and Group B, respectively]. The interaction between the familiarity and the site effect was significant for Group A [$F(10,150)$ = 3.06, $P < .001$, G-G Epsilon = 0.41], but not for Group B [$F(10,70)$ = 1.58, $P = .22$, G-G Epsilon = 0.34]. There was no effect of hemisphere for either group, and no interactions with the hemisphere effect ($F < 1.00$). Finally, the three-way interaction was also not significant [$F(10,150)$ = 1.15, $P = .34$, and $F(10,70)$ = 1.79, $P = .18$, for Group A and Group B, respectively]. The distribution of the familiarity effect was further analysed in a series of ANOVAs. The overall pattern emerging from these analyses was that the effect was larger at more central than more lateral sites without any effect of the anterior posterior distribution[6].

Discussion

The results of the present experiment supported the hypothesis that the N170 is not susceptible to top-down influences of familiarity, and is probably not associated with a neural mechanism that is directly involved in the process of face recognition or face

---

[6] To recall, only the anterior scalp site was examined in these analyses, which explains the absence of the familiarity × site interaction that was observed in the previous analysis. Details regarding the results of different ANOVAs are available from the first author.

identification. Although face identification must have been attempted in every trial, the N170 elicited by familiar faces was almost identical to that elicited by unfamiliar faces.

Interesting differences were found, however, between the ERPs elicited by familiar and unfamiliar faces starting at about 250msec. From this latency on, all faces elicited a negative potential lasting for about 250msec. This potential was significantly larger (more negative) for familiar than for unfamiliar faces. The centro-frontal scalp distribution of this potential, its time course, and its susceptibility to stimulus familiarity indicate that it might be associated with similar cognitive mechanisms as the N400. Therefore, we will call this potential "face-N400" to distinguish it from the "classical" N400, which has been associated primarily with the semantic processing of words.

Although the familiarity effect was statistically significant across the whole sample, familiar faces elicited a more negative (or less positive) face-N400 in only 16 of the 24 subjects. Among the remainder, seven showed a slightly inverse pattern and for one the mean amplitude across channels was equal for familiar and unfamiliar faces. This pattern might have reflected only random variability among participants but it also could have reflected strategic differences in task performance. A deeper analysis of the latter option was not possible, however, in the present experiment, because using the oddball paradigm we could not monitor the participants' performance sufficiently well. Therefore, a better monitoring of the trial-by-trial performance was attempted in Experiment 3, where subjects were instructed to respond as fast as possible by button-press to each face, categorising it as a politician or a non-politician. This procedure should allow better control of performance. Indeed, such a procedure should usually elicit a P300 for non-politicians as well as for politicians, hence hindering the N400 effects to some extent. On the other hand, on the basis of the knowledge about the latency and scalp distribution of the effect obtained in Experiment 2, we hoped to detect the modulation of the face-N400 on the generally positive-going P300 potential (for such a procedure, see, for example, Bentin, McCarthy, & Wood, 1985).

EXPERIMENT 3

The present experiment was identical with Experiment 2 except that, rather than counting politicians, the participants were instructed to press, on each trial, one button if the presented face was that of a politician and another button if it was not. Unlike a regular face recognition task, this task allows comparison of the ERPs and RTs elicited by familiar and unfamiliar faces within the same response category, that of non-politicians. Hence, differences between the responses to familiar and unfamiliar faces, in performance as well as in ERPs, should reflect primarily stimulus encoding and decision-making factors rather than response selection and execution.

Despite possible interference with ERPs due to speeded motor movements, the availability of overt responses in each trial had several advantages. First, we were able to include in the averaged ERPs only trials in which the face identification was correct. Although, in principle, we were interested in the process rather than in its outcome, each response category might involve different processes, and therefore the inclusion of ERPs elicited by faces that were incorrectly identified might add noise to the averaged response. Second, and more important, we had specific predictions regarding the implication of different performance strategies on the response time.

Within the framework of the Bruce and Young (1986) model the task of detecting politicians could have been accomplished by adopting different strategies. One strategy could be to make a "non-politician" decision for unfamiliar faces on the basis of the negative outcome of the familiarity check, whereas familiar faces should require an additional process of person identification before classifying them to either of the response categories. Such a strategy should have required longer and more extensive processing for familiar than for unfamiliar faces and, therefore, the RTs will be faster for the former stimuli. An alternative strategy, however, might have been to categorise all faces on the basis of fully identifying them (or attempting to do so). This exhaustive identification procedure will, by necessity, end sooner for familiar than for unfamiliar faces and, therefore, a decision will always be reached faster for familiar non-politicians than for unfamiliar faces. If the amplitude of the face-N400 positively correlates with the stimulus processing time, the former performance strategy should lead to larger face-N400 potentials for familiar than for unfamiliar faces, whereas the latter strategy should result in a reversed relation. In the present experiment we examined these hypotheses in two steps. First we examined for each participant whether larger face-N400 potentials are associated with slower responses. Second, if this hypothesis was supported by the data, we examined whether participants who respond more slowly to familiar than to unfamiliar faces are also those who elicit larger face-N400 in response to familiar than to unfamiliar faces and vice versa.

Method

Participants

The participants were 24 right-handed undergraduates (8 men) who had not participated in the former experiments.

Task and Procedure

The stimulus presentation procedure and ERP data collection were identical with those used in Experiment 2. Subjects were instructed to respond on each trial pressing a right-hand button whenever the face of a politician was presented and a left-hand button whenever the presented face was not that of a politician. Speed and accuracy were equally emphasised.

Results

Overt Performance

The RTs and percentage of errors for the different categories of faces are presented in Table 1. The RTs were trimmed for each participant, excluding those that were longer or shorter than 2 SDs from the mean of each condition. The percentage of outliers never exceeded 5% of the trials.

Across all subjects, the RTs were almost identical for all three face categories [$F(2,46) < .001$]. In

Table 1. *RTs (in msec) and Percentage Errors (SEm) in Response to Faces of Politicians, Unfamiliar Faces, and Familiar Non-politicians*

	Unfamiliar	Familiar	Politicians
Mean RT	666 (10.6)	665 (8.2)	661 (7.0)
% errors	2.32(1.2)	3.84 (0.55)	5.65 (0.9)

contrast, the percentage of errors differed across the categories [$F(2,46) = 3.81$, $P < .05$, G-G Epsilon = 0.671]. Post hoc univariate contrasts showed that more errors were made in response to politicians than to non-politicians [$F(1,23) = 5.5$, $P < .05$], whereas the difference between familiar non-politicians and unfamiliar faces was not statistically significant [$F(1,23) = 1.76$ $P = .20$].

This analysis should be interpreted as a demonstration that deciding that a particular face is not the face of a politician is equally fast and accurate for familiar and unfamiliar faces. Nonetheless, considering the two alternative strategies described earlier, two subgroups of participants could be formed on the basis of individual patterns of RTs to non-politicians. Fourteen participants (Group 1) responded faster to unfamiliar (640msec) than to familiar faces (659msec) i.e. they putatively used the familiarity criterion strategy, whereas the other 10 participants (Group 2) responded faster to familiar (674msec) than to unfamiliar faces (701msec) i.e. they putatively used the full identification strategy. The responses of the two groups to politicians was almost the same [657msec for Group 1 and 666msec for Group 2, $t(21) = 0.63$, $P = .55$]. In contrast, the responses to non-politicians were overall significantly slower in Group 2, i.e., those participants who responded faster to familiar than to unfamiliar faces, than in Group 1 [687msec vs. 650msec $F(1,22) = 5.13$, $P < .05$].

ERPs

In an attempt to understand better the pattern of ERP differences between familiar and unfamiliar faces, our major purpose in the present experiment was to examine the extent to which differences in the pattern of reaction times might account for the face-N400 modulation by face-familiarity. We have assumed that the size of the N400 is influenced by the time required to process a stimulus, so that longer processing time is reflected by larger N400s. On the basis of this assumption we predicted that participants for which the face-N400 elicited by familiar faces was larger (more negative) than that elicited by unfamiliar faces would respond more slowly to familiar than to unfamiliar faces, and vice versa.

As a first step we had to demonstrate that, regardless of face familiarity, longer RTs were indeed associated with larger face-N400s. With this purpose in mind, we separately averaged (within subjects) the EEG for trials in which the RTs were faster than the mean (in each condition), and those in which the RTs were slower than the mean. As illustrated in Fig. 6, for both familiar and unfamiliar faces, the ERPs elicited on trials in which the RTs were slower than the mean included a conspicuous negative potential that was absent from the ERPs elicited in trials in which the RTs were faster than the mean. However, the diver-

gence between the two ERPs and the peak of the negative potential elicited by "slow" trials were later than the face-N400 that was described and analysed in Experiment 2. In fact, the current ERP manifestations seemed to be related to a shift in the latency of a late positive ERP component. Therefore, the present RT-influenced negativity and the face-N400 might have been associated with different cognitive mechanisms. With this caveat in mind, we continued our analysis.

Having established an association between the response time and the ERP elicited by faces, and assuming that the RTs reflect to some extent the time required for processing the face, we proceeded with the examination of a possible correlation between the influence of face familiarity on RTs and on ERPs. This was done by examining the ERPs elicited by familiar and unfamiliar faces separately for participants in Group 1 and in Group 2. If the magnitude of the face-N400 was influenced by the time required to identify the faces, it should

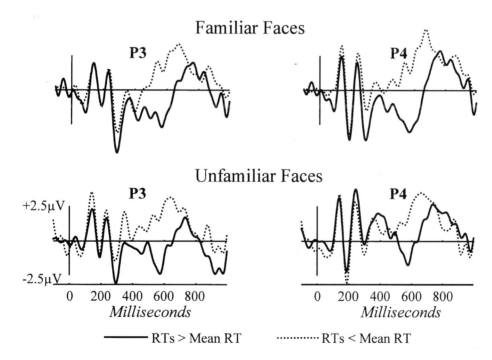

Fig. 6. *ERPs elicited in trials in which the response to the non-politicians was faster than the mean RT, and ERPs in trials in which the response was slower than the mean RT, and the ERPs in trials in which the response was slower than the mean RT in each stimulus category. Note that the latency of the negative potential elicited in slow-RT but not in fast-RT trials was later than that of the face-N400. The effect of the response speed on the ERPs did not interact with face familiarity.*

have been larger for familiar than unfamiliar faces in Group 1 (in which the RTs to familiar faces was longer than to unfamiliar faces) and larger for unfamiliar than for familiar faces in Group 2 (in which the RTs to unfamiliar faces was longer than to familiar faces). This comparison is presented in Fig. 7.

Contrary to our expectations, the ERPs elicited by the two groups during the time range of the face-N400 were similar. ANOVA showed that the mean amplitude elicited by familiar faces across all electrodes ($-1.2\mu V$) was more negative than that elicited by unfamiliar faces ($-0.6\mu V$) [$F(1,22) = 4.48$, $P < .05$], and that there was no interaction between the effect of familiarity and the effect of group [$F(1,22) < 1.0$][7]. As can be seen in Fig. 7, however, an interaction in the expected direction seemed to emerge during a later epoch of the waveforms. During this epoch, a negative-going deflection was evident in the ERPs elicited by familiar faces in Group 1, and by unfamiliar faces in Group 2. Although this was not predicted a priori, we analysed the difference between the mean amplitude elicited by familiar and unfamiliar faces from 500 to 700msec. This analysis revealed that the observed interaction between the familiarity and group effects was statistically significant [$F(1,22) = 5.5$, $P < .05$].

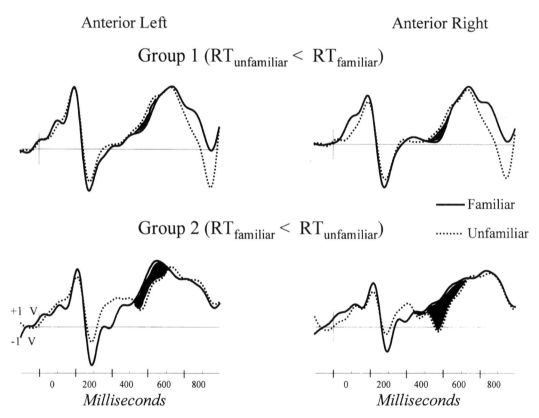

Fig. 7. *Spatial averaging of the ERPs elicited by familiar and unfamiliar faces at the anterior right and anterior left scalp sites in participants who responded faster to unfamiliar than to familiar faces (Group 1) and participants who responded faster to familiar than to unfamiliar faces (Group 2).*

---

[7] A more detailed analysis, with the scalp site as an independent variable, did not reveal any interesting interactions with the factor of group. Therefore, to simplify the presentation these analyses are not presented. They are available upon request from the first author.

Finally, as in the previous experiments, a clear N170 was elicited by all faces. As is evident in Fig. 8, despite the requirement to respond quickly to each stimulus, face familiarity had no effect on either the amplitude or the latency of this potential.

Statistical analysis showed that the amplitudes of the N170 elicited by familiar and unfamiliar faces were similar [$F(1,23) < 1.00$], significantly higher over right (− 8.43μV, averaged over P8, RMast, PO8, PO4, and IM2) than over left (− 5.45μV, averaged over P7, LMast, PO7, PO3, and IM1) hemisphere sites [$F(1,23) = 27.6$, $P < .001$], and different at different sites [$F(4,92) = 2.67$, $P < .05$, G-G Epsilon = 0.55]. The only significant interaction was between the effects of site and hemisphere [$F(4,92) = 3.51$, $P < .05$, G-G Epsilon = 0.58]. Post hoc univariate contrasts showed that the amplitude at PO3 was smaller than at the other left hemisphere sites [$F(4,92) = 5.6$, $P < .001$, G-G Epsilon = 0.6], whereas over the right hemisphere sites the effect was not significant [$F(4,92) = 1.49$, $P = .21$, G-G Epsilon = 0.52].

Because the need to produce speeded responses might have influenced the time course of the brain activity, we analysed the latencies of the N170, using the same design as for the analysis of the amplitudes. This analysis showed that the latency of the N170 was the same in response to familiar and unfamiliar faces (166msec).

Discussion

The purpose of Experiment 3 was to explore the possibility that the difference in the direction of the familiarity effect on the face-N400 potential, which was found in one third of the participants in Experiment 2, revealed an interesting strategic difference in task performance rather than mere noise. This hypothesis was not supported by the results of the present experiment. Although the pattern of the ERPs within subjects was related to the pattern of their RTs (the two variables may have been influenced by the same cognitive process), this correlation was not evident during the face-N400 time range. Hence, the RT data could not provide an objective criterion for predicting the individual differences in the direction of the face-N400 effect. We are therefore left with an ad hoc conclusion that, across participants and accepting some variability, the main effect of familiarity on the ERPs was that familiar faces elicited a more negative face-N400 than unfamiliar faces. This effect will be discussed further in the General Discussion.

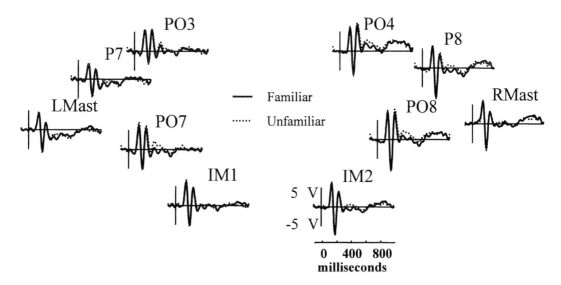

Fig. 8. *The N170 elicited by familiar and unfamiliar faces in Experiment 3. Although face identification was required in each trial and only correct responses were included in the average, there was no effect of face familiarity.*

Although the face-N400 effect could not be predicted by the pattern of the RTs, some evidence for the possible use of different strategies for categorising familiar and unfamiliar faces as non-politicians emerged in the analysis of the RTs. Indeed, across all subjects, familiar and unfamiliar faces were rejected equally quickly and accurately. Yet, comparing subjects who responded more quickly to familiar than to unfamiliar non-politicians with subjects who showed the opposite pattern, we found that the former group responded more slowly overall than the latter. This difference was not an obvious result of the group selection. It is consistent with the hypothesis that the faster rejection of unfamiliar than familiar faces is based on a familiarity cheek at the level of the face recognition units in Bruce and Young's model, whereas faster rejection of familiar than unfamiliar faces is a result of using the identification process at the level of the identity nodes. Although it is speculative, this interpretation is not contradicted by the present data.

Whereas the face-N400 familiarity effect did not correspond with the familiarity effect on RTs, across familiarity, RTs had a robust influence on ERP components elicited later than the N400. A within-subject comparison of the ERPs associated with long and short RTs revealed a distinctive negative component associated with slow but not fast RTs and with a delay in a subsequent positive deflection. This effect is congruent with older findings suggesting that ERPs in general and the latency of the P300 component in particular may reflect the stimulus processing time (e.g. McCarthy & Donchin, 1981), and that it is sensitive to categorical decision strategies as well as the difficulty of discriminating targets from nontargets (e.g. Kutas, McCarthy, & Donchin, 1977). Indeed, as is evident in Fig. 6, the late positive component in trials with long RTs peaked later and had a smaller amplitude than that elicited in trials with short RTs. It is conceivable that this late positive component is the P300, which is usually elicited within this latency range by nontrivial categorical decisions. If so, its latency, as well as the RTs, should be affected by the duration of stimulus processing until it is categorised.

Moreover, the pattern of the late positivity and its variation with the length of the RT were similar for familiar and unfamiliar faces. This similarity suggests that, within each category, there were faces that were more or less easy to categorise and that, in fact, the proportion of "easy" and "difficult" trials was not very different for familiar and unfamiliar faces. It is possible that different strategies are employed by each subject in categorising different faces, and that the choice of strategy in each trial is determined by factors that do not necessarily cut across the a priori determined face familiarity. Of course, given the post hoc nature of this hypothesis, it should remain tentative until directly tested in future research.

GENERAL DISCUSSION

The present study was designed to explore the process of face identification as reflected by ERPs. More specifically, our questions were: (1) Is the face-specific mechanism associated with N170 sensitive to the familiarity of the face? (2) Is the process of face identification reflected by identifiable scalp-recorded ERP components? The results provided clear answers to both questions. Regardless of whether face identity was relevant to the successful completion of the task, neither the amplitude nor the latency of the N170 were modulated by the familiarity of the face, and were similar when attention was directed toward face identification (Experiments 2 and 3) or not (Experiment 1). In contrast to the N170, a later negative component, ranging roughly from 250 to 500msec, was larger in response to familiar than to unfamiliar faces. Unlike the circumscribed posterior temporo-occipital distribution of the N170, the later negative component was recorded at all scalp sites, but it was most conspicuous over the frontal and central regions—a distribution that approximates the distribution of the N400. This distribution as well as theoretical considerations that will be elaborated below lead us to suggest that this negative component is a face-related analogue of the N400, which has been traditionally associated primarily (although not exclusively) with the processing of words.

The insensitivity of the N170 to the familiarity of the face provides additional support for Bentin et al.'s (1996) conclusion that the N170 is associated with an early visual mechanism dedicated to analysing physiognomic information and providing a sensory representation of the face to a higher-level perceptual system. As reviewed in the Introduction, this hypothesis was mainly based on the finding that the N170 is not affected by manipulations known to significantly impair face recognition (such as face inversion and the spatial redistribution of inner components within the face contour (Bentin et al., 1996). Finding that identical N170 potentials are elicited by familiar and unfamiliar faces, regardless of whether viewers intend to identify the faces or not, strongly supports the hypothesis that the brain mechanism with which the N170 is associated is triggered by the presence of a human face in the visual field but is not directly involved in face recognition.

Absence of familiarity effects of the N170 does not imply, however, that structural encoding does not affect the face recognition and face identification processes. This question was not addressed in the present study. Other studies of the N170, however, suggest that efficient identification of faces requires the normal functioning of the structural encoding mechanism (Bentin, et al., 1999). Abnormal N170 patterns were recorded in that study from two patients with considerably impaired ability to identify familiar faces. Specifically, although conspicuous N170s were elicited by faces in both patients, similar negative potentials were elicited by other semantic categories such as hands, animal faces, and items of furniture, as well as nonsense patterns of stimuli. Hence, although a visual structural encoding mechanism was active in these prosopagnostic patients, it was not efficient in selectively streaming this information to the face recognition units.

Integrating the absence of a face familiarity effect on the N170 with previous findings, we suggest that the N170 scalp-recorded potential is associated with a mechanism involved in the formation of sensory representations of faces and streaming these representations to further analysis (by other brain structures) in order to be identified. This mechanism acts on the basic constituents of the face and is not influenced by top-down activity of the face recognition units. Moreover, since the N170 is larger when the inner components are presented without the face contour than when the whole face is presented (Bentin & McCarthy, 1999), there are good reasons to believe that the final integration of the components into a gestalt requires an additional mechanism, possibly reflected by the face-specific activity in the medial parts of the fusiform gyrus, revealed by the fMRI (Kanwisher, et al., 1997; McCarthy et al., 1997; Puce et al., 1995) as well as by intracranial recordings (Allison et al., 1994a, b). Given the orientation of the dipole generating the electrophysiological activity in the fusiform gyrus, its influence on the ERPs recorded over posterior-temporal areas at the scalp is probably small.

The negativity from 250 to 500msec that was modulated by face familiarity in the present study might be associated with the activity of face recognition and face identification mechanisms (Bruce & Young, 1986). According to Bruce and Young's model, the internal representation generated by the structural encoder is tested by a series of face-recognition units, analogous to the logogens in Morton's (1969) model of word recognition. Only if a positive match is achieved at this level, are face identity nodes activated to provide the semantic information relevant to the recognised face. Hence, as is true for lexical access, both familiar and unfamiliar faces should activate the face recognition units, but only familiar faces can fully activate a particular entry in this system. Furthermore, only familiar faces can activate particular nodes in semantic memory. Consequently, any ERP component that is associated with semantic activity should be greater for familiar than for unfamiliar faces. Previous studies have convincingly associated the N400 with the activation of semantic memory.

Initially, the N400 was linked with the processing of semantically anomalous words placed in final sentence position either in reading (Kutas & Hillyard, 1980) or in speech perception (McCallum, Farmer, & Pocock, 1984). It was found that its amplitude can be modulated by the degree of expectancy (cloze probability) as well as the amount of overlap between the semantic characteristics of the expected and the actually presented words (Kutas, Lindamood, & Hillyard, 1984; see also Kutas & Hillyard, 1989). Therefore, it was assumed to reflect a post-lexical process of semantic integration, and to be modulated by the difficulty of integrating the word into its sentential context (e.g. Rugg, 1990). It is unlikely, however, that simple lexical activation is a major factor eliciting or modulating the N400, because closed-class words, although represented in the lexicon, neither elicit nor modulate this component (Nobre & McCarthy, 1994).

This pattern of results suggests that the N400 is not associated with a visual mechanism dedicated to processing of letters, but rather with a higher-level processing system. Moreover, it is probably not elicited exclusively by words because negative waveforms peaking at about 400msec were modulated by the immediate repetition of unfamiliar faces (Bentin & McCarthy, 1994) and other pictorial stimuli (Barrett & Rugg, 1989). Hence, the currently existing evidence indicates that the N400 is elicited only by stimuli that allow deep (semantic) processing. This pattern is consistent with the assumption that the N400 reflects the process of searching for a link between a stimulus and its semantic representation.

The present data suggest that the face-N400 modulated by familiarity was elicited by a similar mechanism of activating the "person identity nodes" by the recognised, familiar structural representation of a face. The fact that it was larger for familiar than for unfamiliar faces is congruent with this hypothesis. As suggested in Bruce and Young's model, described earlier, only familiar faces should activate the semantic person identity nodes, and therefore the semantic processes with which the N400 is associated should be more conspicuous in the ERPs elicited by familiar than by unfamiliar faces. Whether this face-N400 is associated with the same semantic mechanism as the N400 elicited by words (hence nonspecific), or whether it is specific to face processing, should be investigated in future studies.

REFERENCES

Allison, T., Ginter, H., McCarthy, G., Nobre, A.C., Puce, A., Luby, M., & Spencer, D.D. (1994a). Face recognition in human extrastriate cortex. *Journal of Neurophysiology, 71*, 821–825.

Allison, T., McCarthy, G., Belger, A., Puce, A., Luby, M., Spencer, D.D., & Bentin, S. (1994b). What is a face? Electrophysiological responsiveness of human extrastriate visual cortex to human faces, face components, and animal faces. *Society for Neuroscience Abstracts, 20*, 316.

Allison. T., McCarthy, G., Nobre, A.C., Puce, A., & Belger, A. (1994c). Human extrastriate visual cortex and the perception of faces, words, numbers, and colors. *Cerebral Cortex, 5*, 544–554.

Barrett, S.E., & Rugg, M.D. (1989). Event-related potentials and the semantic matching of faces. *Neuropsychologia, 27*, 913–922.

Baylis, G.C., Rolls, E.T., & Leonard, C.M. (1985). Selectivity between faces in the response of a population of neurons in the cortex in the superior temporal sulcus of the monkey. *Brain Research, 342*, 91–102.

Bentin, S., Allison, T., Perez, E., Puce, A., & McCarthy, G. (1996). Electrophysiological studies of face perception in humans. *Journal of Cognitive Neuroscience, 8*, 551–565.

Bentin, S., Deouell, L., & Soroker, N. (1999). Selective streaming of visual information in face recognition: Evidence from developmental prosopagnosia. *NeuroReport, 10*, 823–827.

Bentin, S., & McCarthy, G. (1994). The effect of immediate stimulus repetition on reaction time and event-related potentials in tasks of different complexity. *Journal of Experimental Psychology: Learning, Memory, and Cognition, 20*, 130–149.

Bentin S., & McCarthy, M. (1999). Faces and face-components. ERP evidence for a dual-mechanism for encoding physiognomic information. *NeuroReport, 10*, 823–827.

Bentin, S., McCarthy, G., & Wood, C.C. (1985). Event-related potentials associated with semantic priming. *Electroencephalography and Clinical Neurophysiology, 60*, 343–355.

Benton, A.L. (1980). The neuropsychology of facial recognition. *American Psychologist, 35*, 176–186.

Benton, A.L., & Van Allen, M.W. (1972). Prosopagnosia and facial discrimination. *Journal of Neurological Sciences, 15*, 167–172.

Burton, A.M., Bruce, V., & Johnston, R.A. (1990). Understanding face recognition with an interactive activation model. *British Journal of Psychology*, *81*, 361–380.

Bruce, C.J., Desimone, R., & Gross, C.G. (1981). Visual properties of neurons in a polysensory area in superior temporal sulcus of the macaque. *Journal of Neurophysiology*, *46*, 369–384.

Bruce, V., & Young, A. (1986). Understanding face recognition. *British Journal of Psychology*, *77*, 305–327.

Burton, A.M., Bruce, V., & Hancock, P.J.B. (In press). From pixels to people: A model of familiar face recognition. *Cognitive Science*.

Clark, V.P., Keil, K., Maisog, J.M., Courtney, S.M., Ungerleider, I.G., & Haxby, J.M. (1996). Functional magnetic resonance imaging of human visual cortex during face matching: A comparison with positron emission tomography. *NeuroImage*, *4*, 1–15.

Damasio, A.K., Damasio, H., & Van Hoesen, G.W. (1982). Prosopagnosia: Anatomic basis and behavioral mechanisms. *Neurology*, *32*, 331–341.

De Renzi, E. (1997). Prosopagnosia. In B. Feinberg & M.J. Farah (Eds), *Behavioral neurology and neuropsychology* (pp. 245–255). New York: McGraw-Hill.

Desimone, R. (1991). Face-selective cells in the temporal cortex of monkeys. *Journal of Cognitive Neuroscience*, *3*, 1–8.

Desimone, R., Albright, T.D., Gross, C.G., & Bruce, C.J. (1984). Stimulus selective properties of inferior temporal neurons in the macaque. *Journal of Neuroscience*, *4*, 2051–2062.

Farah, M.J. (1990). *Visual agnosia: Disorders of object recognition and what they tell us about normal vision* (pp. 69–82, 104–111). Cambridge, MA: MIT Press.

Farah, MJ., Klein, K.L., & Levinson, K. (1995). Face recognition and within-category discrimination in prosopagnosia. *Neuropsychologia*, *33*, 661–674.

George, N., Evans, J., Fiori, N., Davidoff, J. (1996). Brain events related to normal and moderately scrambled faces. *Cognitive Brain Research*, *4*, 65–76.

Haxby, J.V., Grady, C.L., Horwitz, B., Salerno, L, Ungerleider, L.G., Mishkin, M., & Schapiro, M.B. (1993). Dissociation of object and spatial visual processing pathways in human extrastriate cortex. In B. Gulyas, D. Ottoson, & P.E. Roland (Eds.), *Functional organisation of the human visual cortex* (pp. 329–340). Oxford: Pergamon Press.

Humphreys, G.W., & Riddoch, M.J. (1987). The fractionation of visual agnosia. In G.M. Humphries & M.J. Riddoch (Eds.), *Visual object processing: A cognitive neuropsychological approach*. Hove, UK: Lawrence Erlbaum Associates Ltd.

Jeffreys, D.A. (1993). The influence of stimulus orientation on the vertex positive scalp potential evoked by faces. *Experimental Brain Research*, *96*, 163–172.

Kanwisher, N., McDermott, J., & Chun, M.M. (1997). The fusiform face area: A module in human extrastriate cortex specialized for face perception. *Journal of Neuroscience*, *17*, 4302–4311.

Kutas, M., & Hillyard, S.A. (1980). Reading senseless sentences: Brain potentials reflect semantic incongruity. *Science*, *207*, 203–205.

Kutas, M., & Hillyard, S.A. (1989). An electrophysiological probe of incidental semantic association. *Journal of Cognitive Neuroscience*, *1*, 38–49.

Kutas, M., Lindamood, T.E., & Hillyard, S.A. (1984). Word expectancy and event-related potentials during sentence processing. In S. Kornblum & J. Requin (Eds.), *Preparatory states and processes*. Hillsdale, NJ: Lawrence Erlbaum Associates Inc.

Kutas, M., McCarthy, G., & Donchin, E. (1977). Augmenting mental chronometry: The P300 as a measure of stimulus evaluation time. *Science*, *197*, 792–795.

Kutas, M., & Van Petten, C. (1988). Event-related brain potential studies of language. *Advances in Psychophysiology*, *3*, 139–187.

Malone, D.R., Morris, H.H., Kay, M.C., & Levin, H.S. (1982). Prosopagnosia: A double dissociation between the recognition of familiar and unfamiliar faces. *Journal of Neurology, Neurosurgery, and Psychiatry*, *45*, 820–822.

Marr, D. (1982). *Vision: A computational investigation into the human representation and processing of visual information*. San Francisco, CA: W.H. Freeman.

McCallum, W.C., Farmer, S.F., & Pocock, P.V. (1984). The effects of physical and semantic incongruities on auditory event-related potentials. *Electroencephalography and Clinical Neurophysiology*, *59*, 477–488.

McCarthy, G., & Donchin, E. (1981). A metric of thought: A comparison of P300 latency and reaction time. *Science*, *211*, 77–80.

McCarthy, G., Puce, A., Gore, J.C. Allison, T. (1997). Face-specific processing in the human fusiform gyrus. *Journal of Cognitive Neuroscience*, *9*, 604–609.

McNeil, J.E., & Warrington, E.K. (1993). Prosopagnosia: A face specific disorder. *Quarterly Journal of Experimental Psychology*, *46A* (1), 10.

Morton, J. (1969). Interaction of information in word recognition. *Psychological Review*, *76*, 165–178.

Moscovitch, M., Behrmann, M., & Winocur, G. (1997). What is special about face recognition? Nineteen experiments on a person with visual object agnosia and dyslexia but normal face recognition. *Journal of Cognitive Neuroscience*, *9*, 555–603.

Nobre, A.C., & McCarthy, G. (1994). Language-related ERPs: Modulation by word type and semantic priming. *Journal of Cognitive Neuroscience*, *6*, 233–255.

Perrett, D.I., Mistlin, A.J., & Chitty, A.J. (1987). Visual neurons responsive to faces. *Trends in Neurosciences*, *10*, 358–364.

Perrett, D.I., Mistlin, A.J., Potter, D.D., Smith, P.A.J., Head, A.S., Chitty, A.S., Broennimann, R., Perrett, D.I., Rolls, E.T., & Caan, W. (1982). Visual neurons responsive to faces in the monkey temporal cortex. *Experimental Brain Research*, *47*, 329–342.

Perrett, D., Rolls, E.T., & Caan, W. (1982). Visual neurons responsive to faces in the monkey temporal cortex. *Experimental Brain Research, 47*, 329–342.

Puce, A., Allison, T., Gore J.C., & McCarthy, G. (1995). Face-sensitive regions in the human extrastriate cortex studied by fMRI. *Journal of Physiology*, *74*, 1192–1199.

Rolls, E.T., & Baylis, G.C. (1986). Size and contrast have only small effects on the responses to faces of neurons in the cortex of the superior temporal sulcus of the monkey. *Experimental Brain Research*, *65*, 38–48.

Rugg, M.D. (1990). Event related potentials dissociate repetition effects of high- and low-frequency words. *Memory and Cognition*, *18*, 367–379.

Saito, H., Yukie, M., Tanaka, K., Hikosaka, K., Fukada, Y., & Iwai, E. (1986). Integration of direction signals of image motion in the superior temporal sulcus of the macaque monkey. *Journal of Neuroscience*, *6*, 145–157.

Sergent, J., Ohta, S., & MacDonald, B. (1992). Functional neuroanatomy of face and object processing: A positron emission tomography study. *Brain*, *115*, 15–36.

Sergent, J., & Signoret, J.L. (1992). Varieties of functional deficits in prosopagnosia. *Cerebral Cortex*, *2*, 275–388.

Tanaka, J.W, & Farah, M.J. (1993). Parts and wholes in face recognition. *Quarterly Journal of Experimental Psychology*, *46A*, 225–245.

Yantis, S. (1998). Control of visual attention. In H. Pashler (Ed.), *Attention* (pp. 223–256). Hove, UK: Psychology Press.

Young, M.P., & Yamane, S. (1992). Sparse population coding of faces in the inferotemporal cortex. *Science*, *256*, 1327–1331.

COGNITIVE NEUROPSYCHOLOGY, 2000, 17 (1/2/3), 55–71

MODELS OF FACE RECOGNITION AND DELUSIONAL MISIDENTIFICATION: A CRITICAL REVIEW

Nora Breen

Macquarie University, and Royal Prince Alfred Hospital, Sydney, Australia

Diana Caine

University of Sydney, and Royal Prince Alfred Hospital, Sydney, Australia

Max Coltheart

Macquarie University, Sydney, Australia

The "two-route model of face recognition" proposed by Bauer (1984) and adopted by Ellis and Young (1990), has become a widely accepted model in studies of face processing disorders, including both prosopagnosia and the delusional misidentification syndromes. We review the origin and application of the two-route model of face recognition in examining both the neuroanatomical pathways and the cognitive pathways to face recognition. With respect to the neuroanatomy, we conclude that face recognition is subserved by a single pathway, the ventral visual pathway, as there is no evidence to suggest that the dorsal visual pathway is capable of visual recognition or of providing an affective response to familiar stimuli. We demonstrate how operation of the ventral visual pathway and its connections to the amygdala can parsimoniously account for the findings in the literature on prosopagnosia and delusional misidentification syndromes. In addition, we propose a cognitive model of face processing stemming from the work of Bruce and Young (1986). Our model involves two pathways subsequent to the system responsible for face recognition: one pathway to a system containing semantic and biographical information about the seen face, and a second pathway to a system responsible for the generation of an affective response to faces that are familiar. We demonstrate how this cognitive model can explain the dissociations between overt and covert recognition observed in prosopagnosia and the Capgras delusion.

The two-route model of face processing, proposed first by Bauer (1984, 1986), has become widely accepted and is much cited in studies of face processing disorders including both prosopagnosia and the delusional misidentification syndromes (Ellis & Young, 1990; Ellis, Young, Quayle, & de Pauw, 1997; Hirstein & Ramachandran, 1997; Schweinberger, Klos, & Sommer, 1995; Sergent & Villemure, 1989; Wacholtz, 1996; Young, Reid, Wright, & Hellawell, 1993). The notion of two routes has referred both to two neuroanatomical visual processing streams and also to two cognitive pathways, and the distinction between the neuroanatomy and the cognitive modelling has not always been clear.

The conflation of these two levels of description—the neuroanatomical and the cognitive—has seemed to imply a neuroanatomical underpinning

Requests for reprints should be addressed to Nora Breen, Neuropsychology Unit, Royal Prince Alfred Hospital, Camperdown, NSW 2050, Australia (Tel: +61 2 9515 7816; Fax: +61 2 9515 7474; Email: norab@npsych.rpa.cs.nsw.gov.au).

The authors thank Andy Young and an anonymous reviewer for detailed and helpful comments on earlier drafts of this paper.

to the cognitive modelling of two separable routes to face recognition. This is problematic, especially if the functions of the relevant neuroanatomical pathways have yet to be fully explicated. Further, as Young (1998, p. 44) has stated, "even though they can be usefully combined, psychological and neurological hypotheses ... have some degree of independence from each other." It is our aim to critically review the origins and application of a two-route model of visual processing in this context. We will examine the evidence for the two routes to face processing, distinguishing between the neuroanatomical pathways that have been described as subserving face recognition and the cognitive processing pathways proposed in cognitive models.

WHAT IS THE EVIDENCE FOR TWO ROUTES TO FACE PROCESSING?

A two-route model of face processing was first proposed by Bauer (1984, 1986), who demonstrated that an autonomic response could sometimes be elicited in prosopagnosic patients (i.e. patients who can no longer recognise familiar faces) in the absence of conscious, "overt" recognition of the same faces. This finding was based largely on work with a prosopagnosic patient LF who, following bilateral occipitotemporal brain damage, was unable to recognise any familiar faces when presented with pictures. However, when the names of five people from the same semantic category were read aloud while LF was looking at the picture, LF had a greater autonomic skin conductance response (SCR) to the correct name compared to the incorrect names. Bauer (1986) refers to the SCR elicited in this patient variously as "electrodermal discrimination," "electrodermal recognition," and "SCR recognition," indicating that he interprets the autonomic response as a measure of unconscious or covert "recognition" of the familiar faces that is separate from conscious overt face recognition. Bauer's (1984, 1986) finding was confirmed by the work of Tranel and Damasio (1985), who also demonstrated covert "recognition" in prosopagnosic

patients as measured by SCR, but using a different methodology.

Bauer proposed that this dissociation between overt visual recognition and autonomic arousal in response to familiar faces indicated two separable face processing routes that could be mapped neuroanatomically; with overt recognition occurring in the "ventral visual-limbic pathway" and covert recognition occurring in the "dorsal visual-limbic pathway." This model was subsequently adopted ingeniously by Ellis and Young to explain Capgras syndrome, a condition in which the patient has a delusional belief that someone they know, usually a relative or close friend, has been replaced by an impostor. Ellis and Young demonstrated that Capgras patients could recognise familiar faces but did not generate an autonomic response to known faces. In other words, in Capgras patients face recognition is normal but the affective response to a familiar person is disturbed.

Ellis and Young (1990) argued that selective damage to the two pathways in face processing could result in one of two deficits, each a mirror image of the other. Specifically, they proposed with Bauer (1984), that the deficit of prosopagnosia, in which face recognition is impaired but the affective response is normal, arose from damage to a primary visual pathway (which they called "ventral"). Conversely, Ellis and Young proposed that the Capgras delusion was due to damage to a secondary affective route (which they called "dorsal") to face recognition, resulting in the patient recognising the misidentified person's face correctly but not receiving any corresponding affective information about that person. Applying the two-route theory to Capgras delusion, Ellis and Young generated the specific prediction, made by no other account, that Capgras patients, who have intact face recognition, would fail to produce an autonomic response to familiar faces. Two independent research groups (Ellis et al., 1997; Hirstein & Ramachandran, 1997) have now reported data consistent with the prediction. This finding has also been taken as confirmation of the two-route theory in that it demonstrates a double dissociation between visual face processing and affective responsiveness to faces.

WHAT CAN THE SCR TELL US?

Although a two-route model of face processing is now widely accepted, the principal evidence for it remains the SCR, a nonspecific physiological response that occurs when a subject is aroused in some way. Arousal has an effect on the sympathetic nervous system, which is measurable as electro-dermal activity in the skin of the fingers. A person can be aroused by many different kinds of stimuli. For example, a person may have a response of arousal and a measurable SCR to a loud tone. This kind of arousal (orientation to an unexpected, non-specific stimulus) is different from the kind of emo-tional arousal (specific affective response) that occurs in response to seeing a familiar face. Since the SCR is no more than a measure of autonomic arousal, interpretation of it in terms of cognitive processing is far from obvious. Potentially it can be read as indicating anything from the mere presence of a new stimulus in the environment to the emo-tional arousal associated with a significant familiar person. In the experimental situation, interpreta-tion of an SCR is dependent on whether or not a different response is elicited to contrasting stimuli. Although most reports interpret the SCR in prosopagnosics to familiar faces as indicating covert "recognition" of familiar faces not recognised overtly, it may represent nothing more than a low level of "discrimination" between familiar and unfamiliar stimuli.

Covert "recognition" has been demonstrated more often, and more robustly, in associative than in apperceptive prosopagnosia (Bauer, 1986; Tranel, Damasio, & Damasio, 1995). Apperceptive prosopagnosia has been defined by Farah (1991, p. 3) as a face recognition disorder "in which perception of faces is grossly abnormal, despite relative preservation of the perception of other types of stimuli." Further, Farah states that "such cases cannot reliably match or describe faces, even by a slow and slavish strategy, and often report

that faces appear distorted." In associative prosopagnosia, faces are not recognised as familiar but are perceived correctly as faces. It is unclear whether the difference between apperceptive and associative prosopagnosia is one of anatomical localisation or of extent of lesion. What needs to be noted is that neither of these is necessarily an all-or-nothing phenomenon.

Bauer (1986) argued that autonomic recogni-tion did not occur in patients with apperceptive def-icits because of an inability to collect visual information sufficient to activate the stored internal representation of the face. To our knowledge, only two prosopagnosics who have been defined as apperceptive have also been reported as demon-strating a SCR to familiar faces (Bauer & Verfaellie, 1988; Tranel et al., 1995). The patient of Bauer and Verfaellie, although described as being an apperceptive prosopagnosic, was 80% accurate on a face match task on which the comparison face was an exact replica of the target, indicating that the face percept was intact. The patient would not meet Farah's (1991) criteria for apperceptive prosopagnosia. The case of Tranel et al. (1995) did produce SCRs to familiar faces but examination of the results shows that the magnitudes of the SCRs were by far the smallest of all the patients tested.

Bauer (1986) found that the actual magnitude of the autonomic responses in the prosopagnosic patients was far smaller than normal controls. In contrast, Tranel and Damasio (1985, 1988) and Tranel et al. (1995) reported two associative prosopagnosic patients (EH-034, DH-1358) who demonstrated relatively normal magnitude SCR when viewing photos of family member's faces and famous faces[1]. It would appear, then, that in at least some cases of associative prosopagnosia, the mag-nitude of the SCR is comparable to that of normals.

The notion that the SCR to familiar faces is reduced by impairment of the normal face recogni-tion pathway does not imply that this is the only mechanism by which autonomic responses are

---

[1] The two patients (EH-034, DH-1358) have relatively normal SCR magnitudes in comparison to the magnitude of control subjects' SCRs to familiar (famous) faces reported by Tranel, Fowles, and Damasio (1985) and Hirstein and Ramachandran (1997).

reduced. A reduced SCR could also result from a general depression of affective responses, as can occur in patients with frontal lobe lesions. For example, Tranel et al. (1995) reported four patients with ventromedial frontal brain damage who failed to generate a SCR to familiar faces, although overt recognition of these faces was intact. Importantly, these patients also failed to respond autonomically to other emotionally charged stimuli, such as pictures of mutilation and social disasters. In these case, as the authors report, "the triggering of central autonomic control nuclei from the ventromedial frontal cortices would be precluded" (Tranel et al., 1995, p. 431).

NEUROANATOMICAL BASIS OF VISUAL FACE PROCESSING

Bauer (1984, 1986) mapped his model of two face processing pathways onto the neuroanatomical model of dorsal and ventral visual streams. He described the ventral "visual-limbic" pathway as involving a pathway from the visual association cortex via the inferior longitudinal fasciculus to the temporal lobe and then to the adjoining limbic system, with the primary limbic "target" structure being the amygdala. He argued that this ventral pathway subserves emotion, memory, and learning functions that are modality-specific to vision. According to Bauer, the second pathway, the dorsal "visual-limbic" pathway, involves projections from the visual association cortex to the superior temporal lobe, then to the inferior parietal lobe, with extensive reciprocal connections with the cingulate gyrus, and subsequent connections with the hypothalamus (see Fig. 1). Bauer stated that the dorsal pathway was responsible for complex attentional functions, emotional arousal, and orientation to stimuli that had motivational significance. The prosopagnosic patient LF had an autonomic response to faces he was not able to recognise overtly and Bauer interpreted the SCR to mean that covert face recognition had occurred. Bauer argued that LF must have gained access to the limbic system via the dorsal pathway. He argued that the dorsal system must contain a mechanism that was

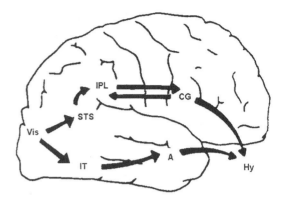

Fig. 1. *Bauer's (1984) diagram demonstrating the ventral visual-limbic pathway and the dorsal visual-limbic pathway in the human brain. The dorsal visual-limbic pathway consists of the visual association cortex (VIS), superior temporal sulcus (STS), inferior parietal lobe (IPL), cingulate gyrus (CG) and hypothalamus (Hy). The ventral visual-limbic pathway consists of the visual association cortex (VIS), the inferior temporal lobe (IT), the amygdala (A), and the hypothalamus (Hy). Some extraneous detail from the original has been omitted. Reprinted from* Neuropsychologia, 22, Bauer, R.M., Autonomic Recognition of Names and Faces in Prospognosia: A Neuropsychological Application of the Guilty Knowledge Test, *pp. 457–469, ©1984, with permission from Elsevier Science.*

capable of covertly detecting the relevance or "significance" of the faces presented, by integrating sensory and limbic input, and that this capability was not dependent on conscious identification.

How did these two routes of visual processing become the "ventral visuo-limbic" and "dorsal visuo-limbic" pathways that Bauer described in his explanation of covert face recognition in prosopagnosic patients? The first account of two visual pathways leading from the occipital lobe to the temporal or parietal lobes respectively was based on anatomical and physiological research on the monkey visual system (Ungerleider & Mishkin, 1982). Ungerleider and Mishkin's lesion studies with monkeys produced dramatic results with respect to the function of the ventral and dorsal pathways. They found that a lesion in the inferior temporal lobe in monkeys produced a deficit that was exclusively visual, and included deficits in discriminating two-dimensional patterns and three-dimensional shapes. This object discrimination deficit was not present when the monkeys received a lesion in the posterior parietal lobe. In contrast, lesions in the posterior parietal lobe in monkeys produced a deficit in their ability to discriminate the locations of objects relative to a landmark object, that is, an inability to determine the object's position in space. Lesions in the inferior temporal lobe did not produce this deficit. Ungerleider and Mishkin integrated the results of their lesion studies with neuronographic, electrophysiological, and functional mapping data and described two independent visual pathways in monkeys: the ventral (occipito-temporal pathway), which is specialised for object perception (identifying *what* an object is), and the dorsal (occipito-parietal) pathway, which is specialised for spatial location (locating *where* an object is). Ungerleider and Mishkin concluded that the dorsal pathway processed only one visual attribute of the stimulus, its spatial location, whereas the ventral pathway processed other visual attributes such as size, shape, orientation, and colour. There is no reference to visual recognition in the dorsal pathway or to visuo-limbic connections of either pathway in this initial description of the two visual pathways (see Fig. 2).

It is curious that Bauer's primary reference in relation to the two visual routes is Bear (1983), rather than the original paper of Ungerleider and Mishkin (1982). In a theoretical article proposing a model for the hemispheric specialisation and representation of "emotion," based largely on work with temporal lobe epilepsy patients, Bear described what he called two "sensorilimbic" connective pathways. One was a dorsal "visuolimbic" system critical for surveillance, attention, and arousal. The other was a ventral system specialised for stimulus identification, learning, and emotional response. In characterising the visual pathways in this way, Bear himself made copious reference to the work of Mishkin (1972) and Ungerleider and Mishkin (1982). His description of the two "sensorilimbic" pathways clearly involved the same structures and tracts, indeed the same pathways, as their two visual pathways.

Because of his specific interest in emotion, however, Bear (1983) focused more closely on the limbic components of the two pathways, to the

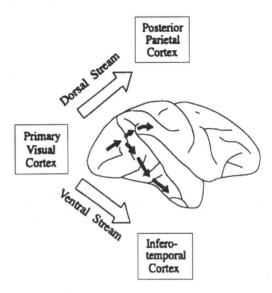

Fig. 2. *An extract of a diagram taken from A.D. Milner and M. Goodale (1995),* The Visual Brain In Action, *demonstrating the dorsal and ventral streams of visual processing in the macaque monkey brain. Reproduced by permission of Oxford University Press.*

point of renaming them as the "visuo-limbic" pathways. Arguing that the right hemisphere was dominant with regard to emotion, Bear drew a clear distinction between the "emotional" functions of the dorsal and ventral visuo-limbic pathways in the right hemisphere. He defined the dorsal pathway as having to do with surveillance and arousal (recognition of threats, pursuit of drive goals), and the ventral pathway as the ventral "learning and emotional response" system. This distinction both preserved and elaborated the separate functions of the ventral and dorsal visual pathways first identified by Ungerleider and Mishkin (1982).

In Bauer's (1984) formulation, the critical distinctions between the two visual pathways, so carefully described and mapped by Ungerleider and Mishkin (1982) and by Bear (1983), are lost. In the first place, Bauer fails to distinguish between the dorsal and ventral pathways with respect to visual processing per se, thereby enabling the notion of "autonomic recognition" via the dorsal visual pathway. The second critical distinction that is lost in Bauer's formulation is that between "arousal" and "affect." Unlike Bear, Bauer does not differentiate between "arousal" and "affect" in his 1984 formulation, thereby enabling him to describe the dorsal pathway as the neuroanatomical substrate of an ill-defined "affective response." These elisions, made initially by Bauer, were subsequently adopted by Ellis and Young (1990), and in our view are crucial to their argument. In their description, the two visual-limbic pathways have become "two routes to face recognition" (Ellis & Young, 1990, p. 244). Their proposal assumes and requires first, that the dorsal pathway is capable of some form of visual recognition, and second, that the dorsal limbic structures are capable of contributing a specific affective response to familiar stimuli. There is considerable evidence that neither of these propositions is correct.

VISUAL RECOGNITION AND THE DORSAL VISUAL PATHWAY

Bauer (1984) argued that prosopagnosia is caused by a complete disruption of the ventral visual pathway, and that covert recognition is therefore only possible because the dorsal visual pathway remains intact. Bauer proposed that the dorsal pathway contains a mechanism that is capable of discriminating "relevance and irrelevance" by integrating limbic and multimodal sensory data and can therefore attach "relevance" to an attended face. Ellis and Young (1990) do not explain how the dorsal pathway enables face recognition, but concentrate instead solely on the affective response they believe is provided by the dorsal limbic structures. However, it is implicit in the arguments of both Bauer and Ellis and Young that the "relevance" or affective response must be attached to a particular face, and hence that face must have been recognised. If, as they all argue, the ventral visual pathway is non-functional, then visual recognition must in some way be taking place in the dorsal visual pathway. However, there is no evidence that the dorsal pathway is capable of visual recognition of either objects or faces.

As we have already mentioned, the pioneering work in the anatomy and function of the two visual pathways was done by Ungerleider and Mishkin

(1982), who argued that the dorsal visual pathway was responsible for the spatial location of an object only, not for object recognition. Milner and Goodale (1995) developed further Ungerleider and Mishkin's description of the respective functions of the two visual pathways. They agreed that there was strong evidence for separate dorsal and ventral visual pathways in the monkey, and proposed that this was also the case in the human visual system. They agreed that object recognition was principally subserved by the ventral visual system. In addition, they extended and elaborated Ungerleider and Mishkin's account of the dorsal visual system. Milner and Goodale proposed that the dorsal visual pathway was responsible for the processing required for visually guided actions, rather than solely for representing the spatial location of objects. Much of the evidence in support of Milner and Goodale's position comes from human case studies. One such case is DF, who was unable to describe the size, shape, or orientation of visual stimuli (visual form agnosia), yet was able to perform visual reaching tasks adequately. This included being able to orient her hand to slots of varying orientation to either place her hand in the slot or to put a piece of paper in the slot. In contrast to this accurate reaching, DF was not able to report the orientation of the slot verbally or to visually or tactually match the orientation using a second slot. Therefore, DF was able to modify the posture of her hand to match the orientation of a slot towards which she was reaching, but was unable to *perceive* the orientation of the slot (Goodale, Milner, Jakobson, & Carey, 1991; Milner & Goodale, 1995; Milner et al., 1991). The opposite pattern was demonstrated in patient RV, who could describe the shape of objects but could not accurately reach for them (optic ataxia) (Goodale et al., 1994). The dissociation in visual function in these two patients supports Milner and Goodale's account of the two visual pathways, with an impairment in the dorsal pathway in RV and in the ventral pathway in DF. Milner and Goodale also raised the possibility that the inferior parietal regions may be involved in many visuospatial cognitive tasks, which would require the integration of information from both visual streams.

More recent work on the two visual pathways has been conducted by Turnbull, Carey, and McCarthy (1997), who have characterised the roles of the ventral and dorsal pathways in terms of viewpoint-independent and viewpoint-dependent processing respectively. This further definition of the processes subserved by the ventral and dorsal visual pathways remains true to Milner and Goodale's overall schema but expands the kinds of spatial information coded in the dorsal stream. That is, Turnbull et al. argue that whereas the ventral pathway, which involves viewpoint-independent processing, is responsible for object recognition, the dorsal pathway, which involves viewpoint-dependent visual processing, involves the ability to appreciate the spatial relations of an object (e.g. rotation from canonical orientation, mirror-image discrimination). Turnbull et al. do argue that in non-optimal viewing conditions, such as when the primary ventral route to object recognition is impaired, viewpoint-dependent visual processing may perhaps reorganise a visual image in order for another attempt to be made at object recognition by the ventral system. They suggest that the viewpoint-dependent visuospatial manipulations that occur in these circumstances most likely take place in the structures of the inferior parietal lobe. In none of this work (Milner & Goodale, 1995; Turnbull et al., 1997; Ungerleider & Mishkin, 1982), has the dorsal visual pathway been attributed with the capacity for object or face recognition.

THE NEUROANATOMICAL SUBSTRATE OF THE SCR TO FAMILIAR FACES

The major component of the dorsal limbic pathway is the cingulate gyrus (Devinsky, Morrell, & Vogt, 1995). In a review article of the role of the anterior cingulate cortex, Devinsky et al. observed that overall it appeared to play a crucial role in initiation,

motivation, attention, and goal-directed behaviours. More specifically, damage to the anterior cingulate can result in disorders of arousal including akinetic mutism, diminished self-awareness and depression, impaired motor initiation, reduced responses to pain and aberrant social behaviour, and complex disorders of autonomic function such as hypothermia and cardiac and respiratory irregularities.

In contrast, it has been demonstrated both in the animal and human literature that the amygdala, a ventral limbic structure that has strong reciprocal connections with the inferotemporal cortex (Milner & Goodale, 1995), has an important role in emotionally significant memories. There are a considerable number of animal studies that have looked at the effects of lesions or electrical or chemical stimulation of the amygdala. A detailed review was provided by Sarter and Markowitsch (1985a, b). It is beyond the scope of this paper to consider all of the studies in detail, but in summary, animal studies suggest that lesions in the amygdala produce deficits in discrimination learning so that, for example, animals with amygdaloid lesions show a decreased responsiveness to changes in rules of reinforcement, especially to withdrawal of positive reinforcement (Sarter & Markowitsch 1985a, b). Sarter and Markowitsch (1985a) argued from this data that the amygdala's role in memory appears to be in attaching information with emotional significance.

There is also strong evidence that the human amygdala has a role in attaching emotional significance to information[2]. Citing studies showing that electrical stimulation of the amygdala can provoke vivid recollections of past emotional experiences, and that such re-experiencing phenomena are confined to activity changes restricted to the amygdala, Sarter and Markowitsch (1985a) proposed that information processed by the human amygdala has a distinct emotional significance, usually related to the life history of the individual.

---

[2] The human amygdala has also been found to have a role in the ability to recognise facial expressions. In particular, Adolphs, Tranel, Damasio, and Damasio (1994, 1995) reported a case of bilateral damage to the amygdala that resulted in the patient being unable to recognise fear in facial expressions. We have not discussed this literature in our paper because we believe that the ability to recognise emotional expressions in a seen face is a different process to the affective response one has to familiar stimuli such as familiar faces.

Further support for the role of the amygdala in emotional memory is provided by Cahill, Babinsky, Markowitsch, and McGaugh (1995), who studied a patient (BP) with Urbach-Wiethe disease, a rare hereditary disorder that produces bilateral brain damage confined to the amygdala. BP was told a short story that was accompanied with a slide show: One part of the story was emotionally neutral (Phase 1) while in the second part emotional events were introduced and graphic pictures shown (Phase 2). Cahill et al. found that control subjects' recall of Phase 2 was consistently superior to that of the relatively unemotional Phase 1 when tested for recall 1 week later. In striking contrast, BP did not show any evidence for enhanced memory of Phase 2 of the story, despite normal memory for Phase 1. BP's self-assessed emotional reaction to the story immediately after exposure to it was no different from controls. Therefore, BP failed to show the normal increase in memory associated with emotional arousal despite a normal self-assessed emotional reaction to the story. These results again support the view that the emotional component of memories is reliant on the function of the amygdala.

More recent evidence that the amygdala, rather than the cingulate, is likely to be the component in the affective response to familiar faces comes from a study of face recognition in six patients with complex partial seizures, who had intracranial electrodes inserted for diagnostic purposes (Seeck et al., 1993). The contact sites of the depth electrodes included the amygdala, hippocampus, parahippocampal gyrus, temporal neocortical areas, the anterior cingulate gyrus, and orbitofrontal and dorsofrontal areas. Patients were shown pictures of familiar and novel faces. The familiar faces were individualised to each patient. The study demonstrated prominent category-related differences between familiar and unfamiliar faces in the medial temporal lobe recordings. The six patients did not show uniform patterns of evoked responses to either novel or familiar faces, but these differences may be explained by seizure-induced alterations of cortical organisation and handedness (three left-handers, two right-handers, one ambidextrous), as suggested by Seeck et al. Nevertheless, a differential evoked response to familiar faces was more frequently obtained in the right than the left hemisphere, while differential responses to familiar faces were obtained at multiple sites of the temporal lobes but not in the dorsolateral frontal cortex or the cingulate gyrus. The right amygdala was the one specific structure most frequently associated with differential evoked responses to familiar as opposed to novel faces.

Although the evidence regarding a significant role of the amygdala in attaching emotional significance to experience is more compelling than that pertaining to any other single component of the limbic system, there is a small amount of evidence that the SCR can occur in the presence of amygdala damage. Tranel and Damasio (1989) reported one case of intact skin conductance in response to viewing familiar items in patient DRB, who had bilateral amygdala damage as a result of herpes simplex encephalitis. This finding may suggest either that the amygdala is not the sole source of the SCR to familiar faces or that other parts of the limbic system may be recruited when there is damage to the amygdala. It should be noted that DRB was only shown familiar items (familiar faces, familiar buildings, familiar furniture, and personal effects), and that when viewing these familiar stimuli DRB had a SCR that was larger than his baseline (resting) SCR. DRB was not assessed with unfamiliar stimuli. As previously discussed, what the SCR signifies is usually inferred by comparing the SCR to different stimuli, for example, familiar versus unfamiliar faces. In the case of DRB, it is unclear whether the SCR to familiar stimuli was simply a response, in a patient with extensive brain damage including both dorsal and ventral components of the limbic system, to being shown a stimulus, rather than a specific affective response to a familiar stimulus.

A SINGLE ANATOMICAL ROUTE TO FACE RECOGNITION

We agree with both Bauer (1986) and with Ellis and Young (1990) that in an unimpaired brain, face recognition is mediated by the ventral visual pathway, a pathway that has been clearly demonstrated to be responsible for face recognition. Further, we argue that much of the available data in both prosopagnosic and Capgras patients can be explained on this basis.

Our proposal is that in normal face recognition, visual recognition is carried out by the ventral temporal lobe structures, a view that is consistent with both established (Ungerleider & Mishkin, 1982) and more recent (Milner & Goodale, 1995; Turnbull et al., 1997) investigations of the functions of the two visual processing streams. In addition, we believe that the affective component of face recognition is most likely to be provided by the connecting ventral limbic structures, most prominently the amygdala. That is, in order to recognise a face as familiar and to generate an affective response to that face, ventral temporal lobe structures match the seen face to a previously stored representation of the face, after which ventral limbic structures contribute the corresponding affective component of the recognition. When there is a disruption to normal face processing, as in prosopagnosia, it is due to a disruption solely in the ventral pathway.

Both apperceptive and associative prosopagnosia can be explained in terms of a breakdown in the ventral visual pathway. In apperceptive prosopagnosia the ventral temporal lobe structures are unable to create an adequate perceptual representation of the seen face, and consequently no information would be passed on to the ventral limbic structures. In associative prosopagnosia, an adequate perceptual representation of the face is made in the ventral temporal lobe structures, but either the strength of that perceptual representation is too weak, or the transmission of that activation to ventral memory stores is too weak to enable conscious recognition of the face. Nevertheless, in associative prosopagnosia, an affective response to a familiar face would occur if sufficient activation of the stored representation of the face were passed on to the ventral limbic structures.

We would predict that in patients with apperceptive prosopagnosia there is less likely to be an autonomic response because of the extent of disruption to the perceptual input of the face. On the other hand, we would expect that in associative prosopagnosic patients, there is more likely to be some activation of the temporal structures responsible for face recognition, although it is insufficient to enable conscious awareness of knowing the face. Nevertheless, this activation may produce a signal in the ventral pathway limbic structures and this is what is recorded on autonomic measures. These predictions are consistent with the literature we have discussed regarding SCR in apperceptive and associative prosopagnosics.

As referred to earlier, recent work by Ellis et al. (1997) found that five patients with the Capgras delusion did not show the normal SCRs to familiar (famous) faces, despite the fact that these faces were overtly recognised. These five patients did demonstrate a normal orienting response to loud tones, which Ellis et al. interpreted as evidence that the reduced skin conduction responses to faces was not the result of such a general reduction in autonomic activity. Ellis et al. interpret the results of this study in the framework of two separate routes for face recognition: a primary "ventral" route subserving overt recognition and a secondary "dorsal" route providing the "orienting response" to familiar faces. However, the findings of their study can also be interpreted within the context of a single ventral neuroanatomical route to face recognition. The Capgras patients demonstrated no difference in their SCR to familiar and nonfamiliar faces, despite good overt recognition of the familiar faces. This could be interpreted in terms of intact ventral temporal visual recognition structures, including access to conscious recognition, but disrupted connections to the ventral limbic structures, or as impairment to the ventral limbic structures themselves, or a combination of these two. The first of these explanations, namely a disconnection between areas of ventral stream visual processing and temporal limbic structures, especially the amygdala, was put forward by Hirstein and Ramachandran (1997) to explain the same SCR findings in their Capgras patient, DS. Their explanation was supported by additional testing with DS that demonstrated accurate recognition of famous faces, indicating intact temporal lobe face recognition structures, and a normal ability to perceive emotions in others and express his own emotions, indicating intact limbic structures.

Ellis et al. (1997) gauged the SCR of their Capgras patients when they listened to a loud tone, to assess whether they were generally hyporesponsive to stimuli from any sense modality, and found their response was the same as controls. The point of measuring habituation to a loud tone was to show that at least some forms of SCR were preserved. It is possible, however, that different structures mediate the SCR to different kinds of stimuli. For example, the SCR to familiar faces is, in our view, more likely to be mediated by the amygdala, whereas the SCR to loud tones is more likely to be mediated by the cingulate. Given that interpretation of the SCR is dependent on the contrast between stimuli, this question could be elucidated, for example, by measurement of these patient's autonomic responses to voices of known and unknown people. Using such a control condition, which included exposure to familiar and unfamiliar stimuli via a sense modality other than vision, would enable one to draw more confident conclusions about the general emotional responsiveness of these patients to familiar people, as well as about whether the hyporesponsiveness was specific to the visual modality. Hirstein and Ramachandran (1997) observed exactly this dissociation between responses in auditory and visual modalities in their patient DS, who was able to recognise his parents when speaking to them on the telephone, thereby demonstrating the specificity of the delusion to the visual modality.

Our proposal of a single neuroanatomical route to face recognition is similar to that proposed by Mesulam (1998), and is consistent with Farah's (1990; Farah, OReilly, & Vecera, 1993) analysis of this literature. Farah emphasises the discrepancy between measures of covert recognition in prosopagnosics and normal subjects, with prosopagnosic patients having weaker SCRs and longer reaction times. Farah argues that the conclusion that can be drawn from these results is that these patients have some degree of covert recognition, not that they have normal recognition when tested covertly. Further, she states (Farah, 1990, p. 80) that this "raises the possibility that the covert measures are just more sensitive measures of the same recognition processes tested overtly, and are

not indexing a true dissociation between conscious and unconscious recognition." That is, Farah proposes that covert tests of recognition are more sensitive to the residual knowledge encoded in a damaged face recognition system than are the overt tests. We agree with Farah's view, as we believe that the autonomic SCRs in prosopagnosic patients with covert recognition results from a low-level response to a familiar face in the ventral pathway recognition structures (so low-level that no conscious recognition takes place), which is then passed on as a low-level input to the ventral limbic structures. We interpret the SCR as a more sensitive—but less specific—measure of the recognition process compared to measures of overt face recognition.

THE COGNITIVE MODELLING OF FACE RECOGNITION

As noted by Young (1998), the question of neuroanatomical pathways subserving a cognitive process is separate from the cognitive modelling of that process. We turn our attention now to the cognitive modelling of face recognition.

Bruce and Young (1986) developed a cognitive model of face processing in which face recognition occurs along a single sequential pathway (see Fig. 3). In the first stage of their model, the seen face is encoded using "descriptions" that are viewer-centred. These descriptions can then be analysed independently for expression, facial speech, and information about sex, age, and race. In the second stage of their model, the seen face, if it is familiar, will contact its representation in the Face Recognition Units (FRU). Familiar faces then activate information held at the third stage of the model, the Person Identity Node (PIN). The PINs contain semantic and biographical information for known people and can be accessed by ways other than face recognition (multi-modal input), including voice and gait. The final stage involves the retrieval of the person's name, which is stored independently of their biographical details.

Ellis and Young (1990) have proposed a two-route model to face recognition, with one

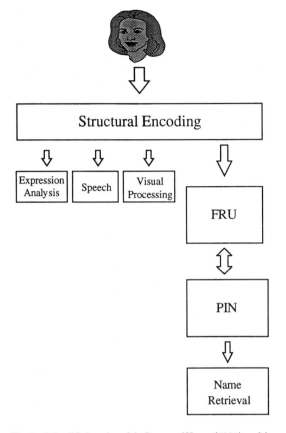

Fig. 3. *A simplified version of the Bruce and Young (1986) model of face recognition. The* Structural Encoding *module encodes information concerning the structure of the seen face. From this module, there are four independent pathways to other aspects of face processing. One pathway leads to* Expression Analysis, *another to* Speech *(analysis of facial movement aspects of speech), a third to* Visual Processing *(analysis for age, sex, race, etc). The fourth independent pathway leads from the* Structural Encoding *module to the* Face Recognition Units (FRU). *At the level of the* FRUs, *the familiarity or otherwise of a face is signalled. Familiar faces then stimulate information held at the* Person Identity Nodes (PIN), *where semantic and biographical information is held. The PINs can be accessed by other sense modalities, such as by voice or gait. Then there is a final pathway from the* PIN *to the* Name Retrieval *module. Reproduced with permission from V. Bruce and A. Young: Understanding Face Recognition, British Journal of Psychology (1986), 77, 305–327, The British Psychological Society.*

route subserving visual recognition of faces (as described by Bruce & Young, 1986) and a separate route subserving an affective component that contributes to familiar face recognition. Ellis and

Young proposed that in prosopagnosic patients with covert recognition, the primary, visual route responsible for overt face recognition is damaged but a secondary, affective route, which provides the affective response for a familiar face is intact. Ellis and Young have proposed that in Capgras patients, conversely, the route to overt face recognition is intact, but there is disconnection or damage within the secondary, affective route.

The two-route model of face processing proposed by Ellis and Young (1990) can be interpreted in two ways. One possibility is that the FRU module is duplicated, with one FRU module located on the visual pathway and one FRU module located on the affective pathway. Alternatively, a two-route model could imply a single route to the FRU module, then a bifurcation subsequent to the FRU module, from which separate pathways lead to the PIN and the affective response. This is an important distinction that has not yet been explicitly addressed.

We agree with the Bruce and Young model up to the point of the FRU module. We propose that the model then bifurcates (see Fig. 4). One pathway leads directly from the FRU module to the PINs. A second pathway leads to an affective response. The stronger the emotional relationship one has with the person whose face is presented, the stronger the affective response that will be activated. Therefore, a very strong affective response would be expected for members of one's immediate family, but only a weak affective response for the local shopkeeper. Like the PINs, the affective response is activated when one is presented with familiar faces, but it is not face-specific. It has multi-modal inputs, so that it could be initiated by a familiar voice or familiar objects (cars, buildings, personal effects, such as a pen) as well as by familiar faces. Therefore, we propose that recognition of a familiar face involves matching the seen face to its stored template at the level of the FRUs and then simultaneous, but independent, activation of the PIN for that person and of an affective response to that person.

In terms of the cognitive model we have proposed, we believe that there is a general arousal/orienting response, which is separate to and different from the affective response to previously known

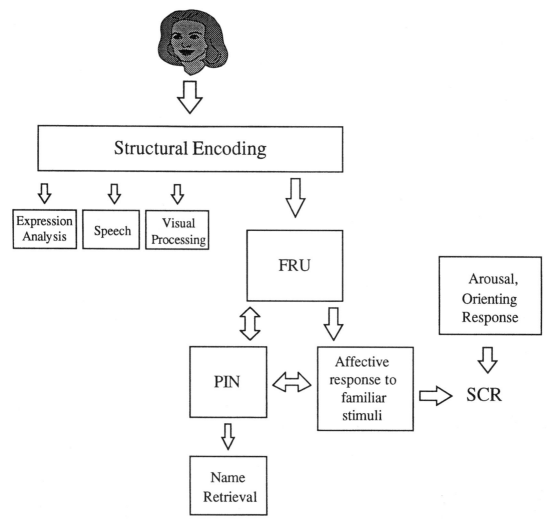

Fig. 4. *Our proposed model of face processing. There are two independent pathways from the* Face Recognition Units (FRU): *one leading to the Person Identity Nodes (PIN), and from there a sequential pathway to* Name Retrieval; *and a second pathway leading to the* Affective Response to Familiar Stimuli. *The* Affective Response to Familiar Stimuli *is measured by the* Skin Conductance Response (SCR). *In addition, the* SCR *is also a measure of the* Arousal or Orienting Response, *which is located in a separate module to the* Affective Response to Familiar Stimuli.

stimuli. The affective response is, in part, a measure of how familiar something is, but the arousal/orienting response is a more primitive response to stimuli in one's environment.

According to our cognitive model, complete ablation at the level of the FRU module or at a level prior to the FRU module, as would occur in apperceptive prosopagnosia, would result in there being no affective response and no conscious recog-

nition of the person. Patients with associative prosopagnosia who demonstrate covert recognition may have a disruption in either one of two places in the model. There may be a disruption, but not complete ablation, at the level of the FRU module that results in only a low level of activation sent along the pathway to the PIN and the pathway to the affective response module. The activation sent to the PIN is so low-level that conscious recognition of the stimuli does not occur. The activation sent to the affective response module is low but still enables an autonomic response to familiar stimuli. Alternatively, covert recognition in patients with associative prosopagnosia may be the result of a disconnection between the FRU module and PINs, but leaving intact the connection from the FRU module to the affective response to familiar stimuli. In this case, the patient would be able to make a decision as to whether the seen face was familiar or not (at the level of the FRUs), but would be unable to access any semantic or biographical information about that person (at the level of the PINs). In this case the dissociation would be between knowing the identity of the seen face and having an affective response to that face (see Fig. 5).

Greve and Bauer (1990), Tranel and Damasio (1988), and Tranel et al. (1995) report cases of

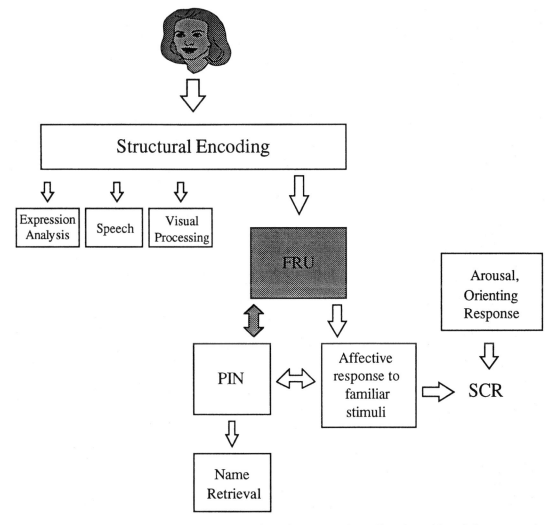

Fig. 5. *Our model of face processing demonstrating the two areas (shaded) that may be disrupted in patients with associative prosopagnosia who demonstrate covert recognition. A disruption, but not complete ablation, of the* FRUs *could result in no overt face recognition, but a signal still being transferred to the* Affective Response to Familiar Stimuli *module and hence a* Skin Conductance Response (SCR) *is produced. Alternatively, a disconnection between the* FRUs *and the* PINs *(at the level of the arrow), but an intact connection between the* FRUs *and the* Affective *Response to Familiar Stimuli* module would also result in no overt face recognition but intact covert recognition.*

"anterograde prosopagnosia," in which patients demonstrate normal overt recognition of faces they knew prior to the onset of their condition, but have no overt recognition of faces to which they have been exposed to subsequent to the onset of the condition. These same patients have demonstrated covert discrimination (as measured by SCR) of familiar faces to which they have only been exposed to in the anterograde period. We can explain these findings within the context of our proposed cognitive model. These patients have intact FRUs for all the faces they knew prior to their brain injury, and this results in normal activation from the FRUs being passed on to both the PIN and the affective response module. Consequently these patients have both overt recognition and a normal affective response to faces that were known to them prior to their brain injury. In contrast, these patients have a problem encoding new faces (i.e. faces that the patients have only been exposed to post brain injury) as FRUs, and the FRU that is formed is degraded. When that new face is encountered again, the corresponding degraded FRU sends only weak activation out to the PIN and the affective response module. The low level of activation in the PIN prevents conscious recognition of that face, but a SCR would occur if enough activation reached the affective response module.

As has been previously discussed, reports of the magnitude of SCR to familiar faces in associative prosopagnosic patients have been variable. Bauer (1986) found that the magnitude of the SCR of associative prosopagnosic patients was far smaller than normal controls, whereas Tranel and Damasio (1985, 1988) and Tranel et al. (1995) reported associative prosopagnosic patients with relatively normal magnitude SCR. These findings can be explained in terms of our proposed cognitive model. If there is a disruption at the level of the FRU module that results in a low level of activation being sent to the PIN and to the affective response module, then we would expect that the magnitude of an SCR to familiar faces would be very small, and this is consistent with Bauer's findings. Alternatively, if there is a disconnection between the FRU module and the PIN, but an intact connection

between the FRU module and the affective response module, we would expect the magnitude of the SCR to be relatively normal, and this is consistent with the findings of Tranel and his colleagues (Tranel & Damasio, 1985, 1988; Tranel et al., 1995).

In Capgras patients who have been found to have intact overt face recognition but no SCR to familiar faces, the model can explain this as the result of intact FRUs, but with a disruption either in the connection between the FRU module and the affective response to familiar stimuli, or in the module of affective response to familiar stimuli itself (see Fig. 6). If the disruption occurred in the connection between the FRU module and the affective response to familiar stimuli, then the patient would still have an intact affective response to familiar stimuli other than faces—for example, to the voice of a familiar person—as the affective response module has multi-modal inputs. Alternatively, if the disruption occurred in the module of affective response to familiar stimuli, then there would be no affective response to familiar stimuli presented in any sensory modality.

We believe that our proposal of a cognitive model bifurcating after the level of the FRU module is a more parsimonious account of face recognition than a model in which the FRU module is duplicated, and that this model is capable of explaining much of the current data.

CONCLUSIONS

Much of the research in prosopagnosia and the delusional misidentification syndromes that we have reviewed has been driven by the assumption that dorsal and ventral neuroanatomical visual processing streams subserve face recognition. We believe, however, that the original two-route theory of face recognition proposed by Bauer (1984, 1986) to explain the autonomic response to familiar faces in prosopagnosia is incorrect. Specifically, we have argued that the dorsal visual pathway, which Bauer claimed provided an alternative route to face recognition, does not have the capacity to identify or recognise faces, and that the dorsal limbic struc-

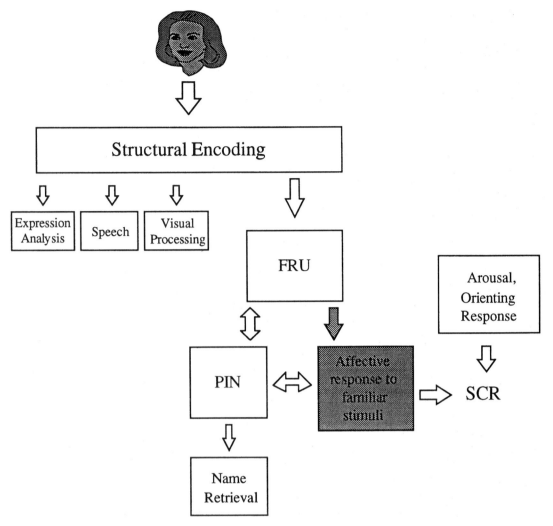

Fig. 6. *Our model of face processing demonstrating the two areas (shaded) that may be disrupted in patients with the Capgras delusion who have overt face recognition but no* SCR *in response to familiar stimuli. This would occur as a result of either a disruption in the connection (arrow) between the* FRUs *and the* Affective Response to Familiar Stimuli *module, or due to damage in the* Affective Response to Familiar Stimuli *module itself.*

tures are not capable of providing an affective response to familiar faces. We have proposed that there is a single anatomical pathway to face recognition: the ventral visual-limbic pathway. Primary visual analysis takes place in the visual cortex of the occipital lobe, face matching and recognition take place in the inferotemporal lobes, and the affective component that accompanies familiar face recognition is provided by the amygdala. We have presented evidence that both face recognition and attachment of an affective response to familiar faces are subserved by the ventral visual-limbic pathway. Further, we have proposed that the double dissociation between reduced autonomic responses to recognised familiar faces in patients with Capgras syndrome, and preserved autonomic responses to familiar faces that are not overtly recognised in patients with associative prosopagnosia, can be explained by varying degrees of damage to the structures in the ventral pathway.

We have proposed a single neuroanatomical route to face processing, one that involves the ventral visual pathway and not the dorsal visual pathway. In contrast, we have presented a two-route cognitive model of face processing. Our cognitive model of face processing can explain the double dissociation between overtly recognising a familiar face but not having an affective response to it and, conversely, having an affective response to a face that is not overtly recognised, in terms of two pathways in the later stages of face processing. In our proposed cognitive model there is a single FRU module, from which there are independent pathways leading to the PINs and to the affective response to previously known faces. Differential damage along these two pathways explains the dissociations between overt and covert face recognition in prosopagnosia and the Capgras delusion.

REFERENCES

Adolphs, R., Tranel, D., Damasio, H., & Damasio, A. (1994). Impaired recognition of emotion in facial expressions following bilateral damage to the human amygdala. *Nature, 375,* 669–672.

Adolphs, R., Tranel, D., Damasio, H., & Damasio, A. (1995). Fear and the human amygdala. *The Journal of Neuroscience, 15*(9), 5879–5891.

Bauer, R. (1984). Autonomic recognition of names and faces: A neuropsychological application of the Guilty Knowledge Test. *Neuropsychologia, 22,* 457–469.

Bauer, R. (1986). The cognitive psychophysiology of prosopagnosia. In H. Ellis, M. Jeeves, F. Newcombe, A. Young, (Eds.), *Aspects of face processing* (pp. 253–267). Dordrecht, The Netherlands: Martinus Nijhoff.

Bauer, R., & Verfaellie, M. (1988). Electrodermal discrimination of familiar but not unfamiliar faces in prosopagnosia. *Brain and Cognition, 8,* 240–252.

Bear, D. (1983). Hemispheric specialization and the neurology of emotion. *Archives of Neurology, 40,* 195–202.

Bruce, V., & Young, A. (1986). Understanding face recognition. *British Journal of Psychology, 77,* 305–327.

Cahill, L., Babinsky, R., Markowitsch, H.J., & McGaugh, J.L. (1995). The amygdala and emotional memory. *Nature, 377,* 295–296.

Devinsky, O., Morrell, M.J., & Vogt, B.A. (1995). Contributions of anterior cingulate cortex to behaviour. *Brain, 118,* 279–306.

Ellis, H.D., & Young, A. (1990). Accounting for delusional misidentifications. *British Journal of Psychiatry, 157,* 239–248.

Ellis, H.D., Young, A.W., Quayle, A.H., & de Pauw, K.W. (1997). Reduced autonomic responses to faces in Capgras delusion. *Proceedings of the Royal Society, London(B), 264,* 1085–1092.

Farah, M.J. (1990). *Visual agnosia.* Cambridge, MA: MIT Press.

Farah, M.J. (1991). Patterns of co-occurrence among the associative agnosias: Implications for visual object representation. *Cognitive Neuropsychology, 8,* 119.

Farah, M.J., O'Reilly, R.C., & Vecera, S.P. (1993). Dissociated overt and covert recognition as an emergent property of a lesioned neural network. *Psychological Review, 100*(4), 571–588.

Goodale, M., Meenan, J., Bulthoff, H., Nicolle, D., Murphy, K., & Racicot, C. (1994). Separate neural pathways for the visual analysis of object shape in perception and prehension. *Current Biology, 4,* 604–610.

Goodale, M., Milner, A., Jakobson, L., & Carey, D. (1991). A neurological dissociation between perceiving objects and grasping them. *Nature, 349,* 154–156.

Greve, K.W., & Bauer, R.M. (1990). Implicit learning of new faces in prosopagnosia: An application of the mere-exposure paradigm. *Neuropsychologia, 28*(10), 1035–1041.

Hirstein, W., & Ramachandran, V.S. (1997). Capgras syndrome: A novel probe for understanding the neural representation of the identity and familiarity of persons. *Proceedings of the Royal Society, London, Series B, 264* (1380), 437–444.

Mesulam, M.-M. (1998). From sensation to cognition. *Brain, 121,* 1013–1052.

Milner, A.D., & Goodale, M.A. (1995). *The visual brain in action.* Oxford: Oxford University Press.

Milner, A.D., Perrett, D.I., Johnston, R.S., Benson, P.J., Jordon, T.R., Heeley, D.W., Bettucci, D., Mortara, F., Mutani, R., Terazzi, E., & Davidson, D.L.W. (1991). Perception and action in "Visual form agnosia". *Brain, 114,* 405–428.

Mishkin, M. (1972). Cortical visual areas and their interaction. In A.G. Karczman & J.C. Eccles (Eds.),

The brain and human behavior. Berlin: Springer-Verlag.

Sarter, M., & Markowitsch, H.J. (1985a). The amygdala's role in human mnemonic processing. *Cortex, 21* (1), 724.

Sarter, M., & Markowitsch, H.J. (1985b). Involvement of the amygdala in learning and memory: A critical review, with emphasis on anatomical relations. *Behavioural Neuroscience, 99* (2), 342–380

Schweinberger, S., Klos, T., & Sommer, W. (1995). Covert face recognition in prosopagnosia: A dissociable function? *Cortex, 31,* 517–529.

Seeck, M., Mainwaring, N., Ives, J., Blume, H., Dubuisson, D., Cosgrove, R., Mesulam, M.M., & Schomer, D. (1993). Differential neural activity in the human temporal lobe evoked by faces of family members and friends. *Annals of Neurology, 34* (3), 369–372.

Sergent, J., & Villemure, J. (1989). Prosopagnosia in a right hemispherectomized patient. *Brain, 112,* 975–995.

Tranel, D., & Damasio, A.R. (1985). Knowledge without awareness: an autonomic index of facial recognition by prosopagnosics. *Science, 228,* 1453–1454.

Tranel, D., & Damasio, A.R. (1988). Non-conscious face recognition in patients with face agnosia. *Behavioural Brain Research, 30,* 235–249.

Tranel, D., & Damasio, H. (1989). Intact electrodermal SCRs after bilateral amygdala damage. *Neuropsychologia, 27*(4), 381–390.

Tranel, D., Damasio, H., & Damasio, A.R. (1995). Double dissociation between overt and covert face recognition. *Journal of Cognitive Neuroscience, 7*(4), 425–432.

Tranel, D., Fowles, D.C., & Damasio, A.R. (1985). Electrodermal discrimination of familiar and unfamiliar faces: A methodology. *Psychophysiology, 22*(4), 403–408.

Turnbull, O.H., Carey, D.P., & McCarthy, R.A. (1997). The neuropsychology of object constancy. *Journal of the International Neuropsychological Society, 3,* 288–298.

Ungerleider, L., & Mishkin, M. (1982). Two cortical visual systems. In D.J. Ingle, M.A. Goodale, & R.J.W Mansfield (Eds.), *Analysis of visual behaviour.* Cambridge, MA: MIT Press.

Wacholtz, E. (1996). Can we learn from the clinically significant face processing deficits, prosopagnosia and Capgras delusion? *Neuropsychology Review, 6*(4), 203–257.

Young, A. (1998). *Face and mind.* New York: Oxford University Press.

Young, A., Reid, I., Wright, S., & Hellawell, D. (1993). Face-Processing impairments and the Capgras delusion. *British Journal of Psychiatry, 162,* 695–698.

COGNITIVE NEUROPSYCHOLOGY, 2000, 17 (1/2/3), 73–87

FACIAL EXPRESSION RECOGNITION BY PEOPLE WITH MÖBIUS SYNDROME

Andrew J. Calder and Jill Keane

MRC Cognition and Brain Sciences Unit, Cambridge, UK

Jonathan Cole

University of Southampton, Southampton General Hospital, UK

Ruth Campbell

University College London, UK

Andrew W. Young

University of York, UK

We present an investigation of facial expression recognition by three people (BC, LP, and NC) with Möbius syndrome, a congenital disorder producing facial paralysis. The participants were asked to identify the emotion displayed in 10 examples of facial expressions associated with each of 6 basic emotions from the Ekman and Friesen (1976) series. None of the three people with Möbius syndrome was significantly impaired on this task. On a second test of facial expression recognition using computer-morphed facial expressions, NC showed a statistically significant impairment, BC a borderline deficit, and LP was unimpaired. However, even when impairments were found, people with Möbius syndrome still recognised many of the facial expressions shown to them. The recognition of facial expressions by people who have never been able to produce such signals on their own faces demonstrates that the ability to produce facial expressions is not a necessary prerequisite of their recognition.

INTRODUCTION

The majority of face research in cognitive psychology has been directed at facial identity recognition, and comparatively few studies have investigated facial expression processing. Instead, facial expression research has tended to feature in the social psychology literature, where the emphasis has been placed on understanding these facial characteristics as emotional signals. Although studies of social signalling are undoubtedly valuable, this means that we currently know little about the *perceptual* representation of facial affect, and the mechanisms used to decode it. Under these circumstances, it is tempting to consider mechanisms involved in facial expression perception as largely analogous to those for facial identity perception, but we should be cautious of adopting this view for a number of reasons. Foremost amongst these is that we not only recognise expressions in other people's faces, we generate them ourselves. Hence, although the mental representation of both facial identity and facial expression will incorporate a visual code (to describe physical structure), facial expressions have the

Requests for reprints should be addressed to Andrew J. Calder, MRC Cognition and Brain Sciences Unit, 15 Chaucer Rd, Cambridge CB2 2EF, UK (Email: andy.calder@mrc-cbu.cam.ac.uk).

We would like to extend our sincere thanks to BC, LP, NC, and their families for giving us their time and assistance. We are grateful to Professor P. Ekman for giving us permission to use pictures from the Ekman and Friesen (1976) Pictures of Facial Affect series. We would also like to thank Gary Jobe for his assistance in preparing figures.

added requirement of a motor-program code (to describe how to produce the expression). Consequently, it is important to consider that there may be some degree of interaction between the visual and motor-program representations of facial affect.

Support for this suggestion comes from a study by Lundqvist and Dimberg (1995). These authors recorded facial muscle EMG reactions in subjects exposed to pictures of facial expressions from the Ekman and Friesen (1976) series. The results showed that the different muscles used to produce these facial expressions were activated simply by viewing them.

It is interesting to consider these findings together with a study by George et al. (1993), which used PET to identify the neural correlates of facial identity and facial expression matching. George et al. found that the facial expression task, but not the facial identity task, was associated with increased blood flow in the inferior frontal gyrus. They note that this same region is damaged in a number of patients with emotional facial paresis (EFP) (Hopf, Muller-Forell, & Hopf, 1992), a facial movement disorder in which the sufferer shows impaired facial muscle movements for spontaneous facial expressions, along with normal volitional facial actions.

The Lundqvist and Dimberg (1995), and George et al. (1993) studies suggest that there is indeed some degree of interaction between the motor programs and visual codes for facial expressions. In view of these findings it is interesting to consider the extent to which one code is dependent on the other.

Of relevance to this discussion is the observation that congenitally blind individuals are able to produce emotional facial expressions (for a review see Galati, Scherer, & Ricci-Bitti, 1997). This strongly suggests that for at least some emotions, the motor-program codes are not dependent on the prior existence of visual representations. However, we currently know very little about the opposite relationship (i.e. is the creation of visual representations of facial expressions dependent on adequate motor representations?). In this present study, then, we address the possible involvement of motor programs in facial expression recognition.

This hypothesis is not dissimilar to the motor theory of speech perception (Liberman, Cooper, Shankweiler, & Studdert-Kennedy, 1967). This predicted that if an individual is unable to generate speech (anarthria), then they should also be totally unable to perceive speech; MacNeilage, Rootes, and Chase (1967) demonstrated that this was not, in fact, the case. However, subsequent work by Bishop and her colleagues has shown that anarthric and dysarthric children with cerebral palsy are impaired on tasks of nonword matching and receptive vocabulary (Bishop, Byers Brown, & Robson, 1990). Bishop et al. suggest that both impairments reflect weak memory for unfamiliar words, brought about by the fact that the speech-impaired children are unable to use (overt or covert) repetition of words as a retention aid. Similarly, then, it also is possible that the process of learning to recognise facial expressions in others is facilitated by producing facial expressions (possibly by mimicking other people's expressions). Möbius syndrome provides a strong test of these hypotheses.

Möbius syndrome is a congenital disorder that causes paralysis of the facial muscles. The facial paralysis is evident in infancy, meaning that adult sufferers have lived their entire lives without being able to produce facial expressions. It follows that if the creation of visual representations of facial expressions is to any degree dependent on the presence of adequate motor representations of the same expressions, then people with Möbius syndrome should have poor and ineffective visual representations. Interestingly, there is already some evidence in the literature that suggests this is so.

Giannini, Tamulonis, Giannini, Loiselle, and Spirtos (1984) published a short investigation of facial expression processing in a person with Möbius syndrome. The authors used a series of videotapes, each showing someone playing a slot machine for different "jackpot" prizes. The task was to use changes in the players' facial expression to estimate which of three jackpots (1¢, 10¢, and 25¢) each person was playing for—the face was the only part of the players' bodies visible in the videos.

Giannini et al. report that the same stimulus materials have been used in a number of previous studies, in which all of the 300 control subjects tested were able to complete the task. However, although the person with Möbius syndrome studied by Giannini et al. was of above-average intelligence (IQ = 132, WAIS), and showed no other perceptual impairments (although details of the actual tests and scores are not reported), she was totally unable to perform this task. Moreover, she informed the experimenters that she could not interpret facial expressions. These findings suggest that the production of facial expressions may indeed be linked to their perception. However, as the Giannini et al. study is a short report of a single facial expression recognition experiment with one individual, we decided that further investigation of facial expression perception in Möbius syndrome is warranted.

We therefore carried out a detailed investigation of face processing in three individuals with bilateral facial paralysis caused by Möbius syndrome. The testing procedure was principally designed to assess their recognition of facial expressions of emotion, but we also included tests of vocal expression recognition and facial identity processing for comparison.

MÖBIUS SYNDROME

Möbius syndrome is a rare congenital disorder whose incidence in the population has not been determined. Symptoms are evident during the first few days of the child's life, and include problems with feeding (sucking, excessive dribbling), a mask-like facial expression while the child is crying, and open eyes during sleep. The mask-like expression continues into adulthood and can create profound difficulties for social interactions with other people—especially strangers who are unfamiliar with this disease (Cole, 1998).

MacDermot, Winter, Taylor, and Baraister (1990) comment that the term Möbius syndrome has been applied to facial paralyses with different aetiologies, and note that four pathological accounts of the clinical symptom have been proposed, (1) hypoplasia or absence of cranial nerves, (2) degeneration of the brainstem nuclei (3) periph-

eral nerve damage, and (4) wasting of skeletal muscle tissue (myopathy). However, MacDermot et al. suggest that the term Möbius syndrome should be reserved for cases that include palsies of the VIth and VIIth cranial nerves, and primary skeletal defects (e.g. club foot, syndactyly, polydactyly, etrodactyly, and missing or deformed fingers); see also Richards (1953) for a similar definition. The patients who participated in the present study met these criteria.

There are 12 pairs of cranial nerves located on each side of the brain stem. The VIIth cranial nerve controls the muscles on the surface of the face that are used to generate facial expressions and lip speech; hence, people with Möbius syndrome are unable to produce facial signals. This leaves them with a mask-like face that is characteristic of the condition. However, the facial paralysis is not always complete, and unilateral or partial facial paralysis is also observed. From a review of 61 reported case studies, Henderson (1939) noted that after the VIIth, the cranial nerve that is most commonly damaged in Möbius syndrome is the VIth, which controls the abduction of the eyes. Palsies of other cranial nerves (usually those proximal to the VIth and VIIth) are also observed, but less frequently.

The majority of Möbius cases are sporadic, but familial reoccurrence is not entirely uncommon, and a genetic link has been suggested. In one genetic study, Kremer et al. (1996) studied a large Dutch family with autosomal dominantly segregating Möbius syndrome; the same family had been described some 40 years earlier by Van der Wiel (1957). Kremer et al.'s study included 31 family members, 20 with Möbius syndrome, 1 obligate carrier, and 10 apparently clear. Linkage analysis located the gene on the long arm of chromosome 3 (3q21q-q22 [GDB]). However, a previous study by Zitter, Wiser, and Robinson (1977) of a similar family group with Möbius members located the relevant gene on chromosome 13 (13q12.2-q13), and further work by Kremer and colleagues has implicated yet another locus. Hence, Kremer et al. conclude that Möbius syndrome is genetically heterogeneous. In relation to this conclusion, it is worth remembering MacDermot et al.'s (1990) observation that there are a number of pathological explanations of "Möbius-type" symptoms.

Case Summaries

Three people with Möbius syndrome agreed to participate in our investigation. They were selected from a larger group of volunteers using a criterion of absence of overall intellectual impairment.

Case 1 BC. BC is a 23-year-old male with Möbius syndrome. He shows a complete bilateral facial paralysis and the absence of eye movements in the horizontal plane. BC also shows congenital malformations of the hands and feet; shortened hands and malformed or absent fingers, with shortening of the foot and malformed toes.

Case 2 LP. LP is a 36-year-old female with Möbius syndrome. She shows a complete bilateral facial paralysis, the absence of eye movements in the horizontal plane and a skeletal deformity of the left hand.

Case 3 NC. NC is a 27-year-old male with Möbius syndrome. He shows bilateral facial paralysis, with a small amount of preserved muscle movement in the lower right quadrant. NC also has no detectable eye movements in the horizontal plane.

Cranial Nerve Examination

To demonstrate formally the nature of the movement problem that characterises Möbius syndrome, BC consented to take part in a cranial nerve examination.

To assist the interpretation of the cranial nerve examination, there follows a short description of the functions of each of the nerves: I [Olfaction] sense of smell and taste—afferent connections from olfactory receptors; II [Optic] visual acuity—afferent connections from the retina; III [Oculomotor] adduction of the eyes—efferent connections to all eye muscles except the oblique and rectus; IV [Trochlear] controls oblique muscles of the eyes; V [Trigeminal] efferent and afferent connections to/from face, nose and tongue; VI

[Abducens] abduction of the eyes, efferent connections to rectus muscles of the eye; VII [Facial] efferent connections to facial muscles used to generate expression and lip speech, afferent connections from taste-buds and anterior part of the tongue; VIII [Auditory-vestibular] afferent connections from the ear controlling hearing and balance; IX [Glossopharyngeal] efferent connections to the throat, afferent connections from the taste-buds and anterior part of the tongue; X [Vagus]: efferent and afferent connections to/from the heart, lungs, thorax, larynx, pharynx, external ear, and abdominal viscera; XI [Spinal accessory] efferent and afferent connections to/from neck muscles; XII [Hypoglossal] efferent connections to tongue muscles.

The results of BC's cranial nerve examination were as follows. (I) normal sense of smell and taste to questioning; (II) normal visual acuity; (III, IV, VI) normal pupil reaction to light both direct and consensual, normal accommodation, normal up and down gaze, no abduction or adduction to either near objects or to following in horizontal plane, normal Bell's phenomena during blink (i.e. upward movement of the eyes), small movement in upper lid with eye closure or upward movement of eyes; (V) normal sensation over V1, V2, V3, normal perceived conjunctival sensation (although this was not tested directly), and normal power in the trigeminal muscles; (VII) no detectable movement of any facial muscle during posed expression or during attempted emotional expression; (VII, IX, X, XI, XII) normal.

INVESTIGATION

Assessments of intelligence and basic visual processing are summarised in Table 1.

Intelligence

Verbal IQ was assessed with the "Spot the word" (version B) task from the Speed and Capacity of Language-Processing test (SCOLP) (Baddeley, Emslie, & Nimmo-Smith, 1992). For this test, the subject is shown a series of word/nonword pairs,

Table 1. *Performance of the Three Participants with Möbius Syndrome (BC, LP, and NC) on a Test of Basic Visual Processing, and Their Verbal Intelligence*

	Möbius Participants		
	BC	LP	NC
VISTECH (VCTS 6000)	Normal	Normal	Normal
Spot the Word	45	49	47
(Max. 60)			
Percentile	50th	50th	50th
Estimated Verbal IQ	107	113	110

and for each pair they are asked to underline the word. The test's authors have shown that performance on this task is highly correlated ($r = .86$) with performance on a more widely used neuropsychological estimate of verbal IQ, the National Adult Reading Test (NART) (Nelson, 1991), and the verbal IQ scores shown in Table 1 are calculated on this basis; as such, each IQ score is associated with a margin of error (± 12). The scores confirm that all three people with Möbius syndrome have IQs in the average to above-average range. Note that this test was used instead of the NART because each trial of the NART requires a precisely articulated verbal response (the test involves reading a list of low-frequency, irregular words, e.g. aisle). The NART was therefore unsuitable for people with Möbius syndrome because their facial paralysis can make it difficult for them to generate certain phonemes, particularly those that depend heavily on lip movements for their precise pronunciation (e.g. "m," "f," "p," and "b"). That said, it should be noted that people with Möbius syndrome do not have damaged vocal chords, hence their speech is, for the main part, readily intelligible.

Basic Visual Processing

The VISTECH VCTS 6000 contrast sensitivity chart was used to confirm that all three participants with Möbius syndrome showed a normal spatial contrast sensitivity function. Consequently, any problems in their face perception would not seem to result from poor vision per se.

Face Processing

We used tests to assess recognition of facial expressions and facial identity. In addition, because the Giannini et al. (1984) study suggested that people with Möbius syndrome may have difficulty in recognising facial expressions, we also included a test of vocal expression recognition for comparison.

Unless otherwise stated, the control data for each test are from 20 people aged 20–39 years.

Facial Identity Processing

Performance on three facial identity processing tasks (unfamiliar face matching; learning unfamiliar faces; recognition of familiar faces) is summarised in Table 2.

Unfamiliar Face Matching. Ability to match unfamiliar faces was assessed with the Benton Test of Facial Recognition (Benton, Hamsher, Varney, & Spreen, 1983). On each trial the subject is shown a target face and array of six faces. The task is to find further examples of the target face amongst the array of six. Changes in head orientation and lighting can occur between the target and array faces. In relation to our own control data for this test, LP and NC showed no evidence of impaired performance (LP 45/50; NC 45/50), while BC showed a mild deficit (BC 41/50, $z = 2.21$, $P < .05$). Note, however, that in relation to the test's published norms, BC's score fell at the lower end of the normal range.

Memory for Unfamiliar Faces. Ability to learn new faces was assessed with Warrington's (1984) recognition memory test for faces. For this test, 50 pictures of unfamiliar faces are presented individually for approximately 3sec each and the subject is asked to say whether each face looks pleasant or unpleasant. Following this, they are shown 50 pairs of faces. Each face pair comprises one of the faces seen in the first section of the test and a new previously unseen face; the subject is asked to select the face that they have seen earlier. LP and BC were significantly impaired (LP 37/50, $z = 2.00$, $P < .05$; BC 38, $z = 1.70$, $P < .05$); NC showed no significant deficit (NC 41/50, $z = 0.79$, $P > .1$).

Table 2. *Individual and Mean Performance (with Standard Deviations) of the Three Möbius Syndrome Participants and Control Subjects on Tests of Face Processing*

		Möbius Participants					Controls	
		BC	LP	NC	Mean	SD	Mean	SD
Benton[a] (Max 54)		41[e]	45	45	43.67	2.31	49.15	3.69
Warrington[b] (Max 50)		38[e]	37[e]	41	36.67	2.08	43.60	3.30
Percentile		5–10	5	25				
Face and Name Recognition[c]								
Faces:	Familiar (Max 30)	29	21[e]	23[d]	24.33	4.16	27.50	3.24
	Occupation (Max 30)	29	21[e]	22[d]	24.00	4.36	27.00	3.53
	Name (Max 30)	29	21	19	23.00	5.29	23.70	4.67
	Unfamiliar (Max 10)	9	9	10	9.33	0.58	9.40	1.07
Names:	Familiar (Max 30)	30	30	30	30.00	0.00	29.70	0.67
	Occupation (Max 30)	30.	28[e]	29	29.00	1.00	29.50	0.71
	Unfamiliar (Max 10)	10	9[f]	10	9.67	0.58	9.90	0.32

[a]Benton's test of face recogniton (unfamiliar face matching). [b]Warrington's test of memory for faces. [c]Familiar face and name recogniton. [d]$z > 1.28$, $.1 > P > .05$. [e]$z > 1.65$, $P < .05$. [f]$z > 2.33$, $P < .01$.

Recognition of Familiar Faces. Identification of familiar faces was assessed with pictures of 30 famous faces and 10 unfamiliar face foils. The faces were presented individually in a pseudorandom order. For each face, participants were asked whether the person was familiar, and if so, to give his or her occupation and name; no feedback was given as to the appropriateness of any responses.

This test was originally produced in 1991, hence, some of the people in the test now have less media exposure. To control for this factor, we collected a new set of control data from 10 subjects, age-matched to our participants with Möbius syndrome.

LP showed impaired recognition of the famous faces as familiar (LP 21/30, $z = 2.01$, $P < .05$) and impaired recall of occupations (LP 21/30, $z = 1.70$, $P < .05$). NC showed a borderline deficit in recognising famous faces as familiar (NC 23/30, $z = 1.36$, $.1 > P > .05$), and a borderline deficit in recalling occupations (NC 22/30, $z = 1.42$, $.1 > P > .05$) . In contrast, BC had no difficulty in recognising the famous faces (29/30), identifying their occupations (29/30), or recalling their names (29/30). None of the people with Möbius syndrome had difficulty in correctly rejecting unfamiliar faces as belonging to people they had not seen before (LP 9/10, $z = 0.37$, $P > .1$; NC 10/10, $z = -0.56$, $P > .1$; BC 9/10, $z = 0.37$, $P > .1$).

The three people with Möbius syndrome were also presented with a control task in which the names of the 30 famous faces used in the above task were presented intermixed with 10 unfamiliar, invented names. They were ask to indicate whether each name was familiar, and if so, to report the persons occupation; no feedback was given as to the appropriateness of any responses. None of the people with Möbius syndrome had difficulty in recognising famous names as familiar (all scored 30/30). LP had some difficulty in recalling occupations (LP 28/30, $z = 2.12$, $P < .01$), whereas NC (29/30) and BC (30/30) did not. Note, that LP's deficit in recalling occupations from names should be interpreted with caution because the controls were performing at ceiling; the actual number of errors made by LP was small. Similarly, although LP showed evidence of a deficit in rejecting unfamiliar names (9/10 correct, $z = 2.85$, $P < .01$), this was based on a single error, which should also be interpreted in the light of the controls' ceiling performance. BC and NC correctly rejected all 10 unfamiliar names.

Summary

None of the three people with Möbius syndrome we investigated had any great difficulty in matching pictures of unfamiliar faces; hence their structural encoding (Bruce & Young, 1986) of faces would appear to be intact. LP was slightly impaired at recognising celebrities' faces as familiar, and recalling the occupations from these faces. However, LP was better at recalling the same celebrities' occupations when presented with their names. Hence, LP's impaired face recognition is not simply due to her being unfamiliar with the people used in the face recognition test. LP was also impaired at learning pictures of unfamiliar faces, as was BC.

Overall, these data indicate that the people with Möbius syndrome show mild impairments in processing facial identity. They did not experience especial difficulties in the Benton face matching task, where the relevant stimuli are constantly in view during testing, but in tasks which involved face memory, some problems were revealed. The source of this deficit is unclear, but could possibly arise from their restricted ability to make horizontal eye movements. Given that there is little work on the role of eye movements in the perception of facial identity, this is clearly a tentative suggestion. However, it is worth noting that Rizzo, Hurtig, and Damasio (1987) have shown that people typically scan the same features (i.e. eyes, nose, mouth, chin, and hairline) when presented with a face. People with Möbius syndrome who have eye movement defects are forced to use head movements instead. Hence, although similar scanpaths could presumably be made by moving the head, significantly more effort and time is involved. Reluctance to make use of this strategy may lead to poor inspection and encoding of faces in everyday life.

Recognition of Facial and Vocal Expressions

Recognition of facial expressions was assessed with two tests. The first test contained prototypical exemplars of facial expressions associated with six basic emotions (happiness, sadness, anger, fear, disgust, and surprise). The second included computer-generated blends or "morphs" of these same six prototypes. Recognition of vocal emotion was assessed with sets of emotional sounds associated with basic emotions. The Möbius and control participants' overall performance of the facial and vocal expressions tasks is summarised in Table 3.

Recognition of Facial Expressions. Photographs of 10 models (6 female, 4 male) were taken from the Ekman and Friesen (1976) series of pictures of facial affect. Each model posed 6 facial expressions corresponding to 6 basic emotions, happiness, sadness, anger, fear, disgust, and surprise; a total of 60 pictures. The 10 models were selected so that each emotion was well recognised in Ekman and Friesen's norms.

For each individual picture, the task was to decide which of six emotion labels (happiness, sadness, anger, fear, disgust, and surprise) best described the facial expression shown; no feedback was given as to the appropriateness of any responses. A list of the six emotion labels was present throughout the test.

Table 3 shows performance, along with the performance of 40 control subjects aged 21–59 years. Although these controls are not matched exactly to the ages of the people with Möbius syndrome (23–36 years), the ranges overlap and there are no grounds for supposing that ability to recognise facial expressions changes markedly across this age range.

None of the overall scores obtained by participants with Möbius syndrome was significantly impaired relative to the controls. However, we would not wish to claim that their recognition is entirely normal on the basis of this test alone. To assess their performance further, they were given a second, possibly more sensitive, test of facial expression recognition that uses computer-blended or "morphed" facial expression images.

Identification of Morphed Facial Expressions. We used the "emotion hexagon" task developed for previous studies (Calder et al., 1996; Sprengelmeyer et al., 1996), which is based on an ordering of the six emotions from the Ekman and Friesen (1976) series by their maximum confusabilities, placing each adjacent to the one it was most likely to be confused with. Morphed images were created for the six continua that lie around the perimeter of the

Table 3. *Individual and Mean Performance (with Standard Deviations) of the Three Möbius Syndrome Participants and Control Subjects on Tests of Facial and Vocal Expression Recognition*

	Möbius Participants					Controls	
	BC	LP	NC	Mean	SD	Mean	SD
Facial Expression Recognition							
Ekman Faces[a] (Max. 60)	47	47	46	46.67	0.58	50.35	5.29
Emotion hexagon[b] (Max. 120)	95[e]	106	83[f]	94.67	11.50	108.33	9.14
Vocal Expression Recognition							
Emotional sounds[c] (Max. 120)	105	103	100	102.67	2.52	98.83	4.45
Emotional prosody[d] (Max. 50)	35	33	29	32.33	3.06	34.30	6.11

[a]Identification of emotion in faces from the Ekman and Friesen series. [b]Identification of emotion in morphed (blended) facial expressions. [c]Identification of emotion in "emotional sounds" (e.g. laughter for happiness, screams for fear, etc.) [d]Recognition of emotion in bisyllabic words, spoken with different emotional prosodies. [e]$z > 1.28$, $.1 > P > .05$. [f]$z > 2.33$, $P > .01$.

resulting hexagon (happiness–surprise, surprise–fear, fear–sadness, sadness–disgust, disgust–anger, anger–happiness), as shown in Fig. 1 (see pp. 82–83).

Photographic-quality continua were made, with five morphed images for each continuum. These were prepared by morphing between two prototype expressions posed by JJ (e.g. happiness and surprise) in proportions 90:10 (i.e. 90% happy 10% surprised for the happiness–surprise continuum), 70:30 (70% happy 30% surprised), 50:50 (50% happy 50% surprised), 30:70 (30% happy 70% surprised), and 10:90 (10% happy 90% surprised). We will refer to these as 90%, 70%, 50%, 30%, and 10% morphs along the appropriate continuum (in our example, happiness–surprise). Details of the image manipulation procedures used to create these images can be found elsewhere (Calder et al., 1996; Sprengelmeyer et al., 1996).

In total, there are 30 images (5 from each of 6 continua). Moving from left to right in Fig. 1, the columns show 90%, 70%, 50%, 30%, and 10% morphs along each continuum. Note that a 90% morph on the happiness–surprise continuum would be the same as a 10% morph on a surprise–happiness continuum, and that the prototype expressions are not shown in Fig. 1. Moving from top to bottom of Fig. 1, the rows show the happiness–surprise continuum (top row), surprise–fear (second row), fear–sadness (third row), sadness–disgust (fourth row), disgust–anger (fifth row), and anger–happiness (bottom row).

The images were presented one at a time, in pseudorandom order (i.e. they were not grouped into the underlying continua). The task was to decide which of the six emotion labels best described the emotion displayed. No feedback was given as to the appropriateness of any responses.

Participants undertook a total of 6 blocks of trials each. In each block, all of the 30 morphed faces were presented once. The first block of trials was discounted as practice, leaving 5 blocks of 30 trials for analysis. Note that the prototype face for each expression was never shown in the experiment; all of the stimuli were morphs.

Figure 2 (see pp. 84–85) shows data pooled across all 3 people with Möbius syndrome (solid line) and data from 40 control subjects aged 20–59 years.

The extent to which the performance of people with Möbius syndrome matched the control data was assessed as follows. The entire hexagonal continuum was divided into six sections corresponding to regions containing morphs that the controls consistently identified with one of the six expression labels. Each expression region comprised four morphs; two of these contained 90% of the target expression and the other two 70%; for example, the surprise section contained the morphs 70% surprised 30% happy, 90% surprised 10% happy, 90% surprised 10% afraid, and 70% surprised 30% afraid. The total number of times the participants with Möbius syndrome identified all of the morphs in each region with the appropriate expression label was calculated, and these values were compared to the mean number of times the control subjects produced the appropriate responses in the same region.

Over all six emotion categories taken together, NC (83/120, $z = 2.77$, $P < .01$) was significantly impaired, BC (95/120, $z = 1.46$, $.1 > P > .05$) showed a borderline deficit, and LP (106/120, $z = 0.25$ $P > .1$) showed no significant deficit. Examining each emotion category separately, all three people with Möbius syndrome showed significantly fewer overall correct responses in at least one of the emotion categories (surprise: BC, LP, and NC, $P > .05$; sadness: NC, $P < .01$; disgust: BC and NC, $P < .05$). The pattern revealed by these statistics (and shown in Fig. 2) is therefore one of patchy but relatively mild deficits affecting the recognition of various emotions.

Recognition of Non-verbal Emotional Sounds. Ten examples of "emotional sounds" associated with the same six basic emotions used in the facial expression tests were presented individually in random order, following the procedure used by Scott et al. (1997). Examples of these sounds were laughter for happiness, crying for sadness, screams for fear, growls for anger, retching for disgust, and gasps of astonishment for surprise. The subject's task was to listen to each sound and indicate the emotion being expressed by making a verbal response; a list of the six emotion labels was available throughout testing. The 60 sounds were presented twice in random order, giving an overall score out of 120. The Möbius and control subjects scores are shown in Table 3. All three participants with Möbius syndrome had no difficulty with this task, performing at control level (LP, 103/120; NC, 100/120; BC, 105/120; controls: mean = 98.83/120, SD = 4.45).

Recognition of Emotional Prosody. This second auditory emotion task was composed of a series of bisyllabic words with neutral emotional meaning (e.g. carpet, sailor, etc.). The words were read by a number of different actors with different emotional intonations corresponding to one of the five basic emotions: happiness, sadness, anger, fear, and disgust; surprise was not used as an emotion in this test because previous work has shown that it is not asso-

ciated with distinctive prosodic features (Murray & Arnott, 1993). There were 10 examples for each emotion category in total. The task was to identify the emotion expressed by selecting one of the five emotion labels listed above; a list of these labels was available throughout testing. Each stimulus was presented once, giving an overall score out of 50, following the procedure used by Scott et al. (1997). The Möbius and control subjects' scores are shown in Table 3. None of the people with Möbius syndrome showed any significant difficulty with this task (LP, 33/50; BC, 35/50; NC, 29/50), despite the control subjects finding it a relatively difficult task to perform (mean = 34.30, SD = 6.11).

Summary

Overall, the results of the two tests of facial expression recognition show that the three people with Möbius syndrome in this present study are considerably better at recognising facial expressions than the person tested by Giannini et al. (1984). Their performance on tests of facial expression recognition was not entirely normal, but it was characterised by relatively mild deficits affecting the recognition of various emotions, rather than the dramatic and selective deficits described in reports using this task with participants with other aetiologies (Calder et al., 1996; Sprengelmeyer et al., 1997b). These findings clearly demonstrate that the production of facial expressions is not a necessary prerequisite of their recognition. People with Möbius syndrome also showed no significant impairments on two tests of vocal expression recognition.

GENERAL DISCUSSION

Our findings show that sufferers from Möbius syndrome show impairments on face processing tasks. However, there was no consistent pattern that characterised the problems shown across all three of our participants, and a number of the deficits we recorded were comparatively mild, often consisting of (statistically significantly) below-control-level performance rather than large numbers of errors or complete inability to perform a particular task. In

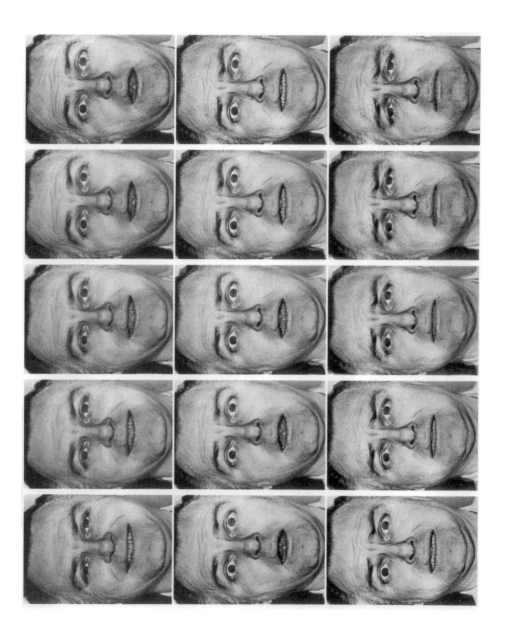

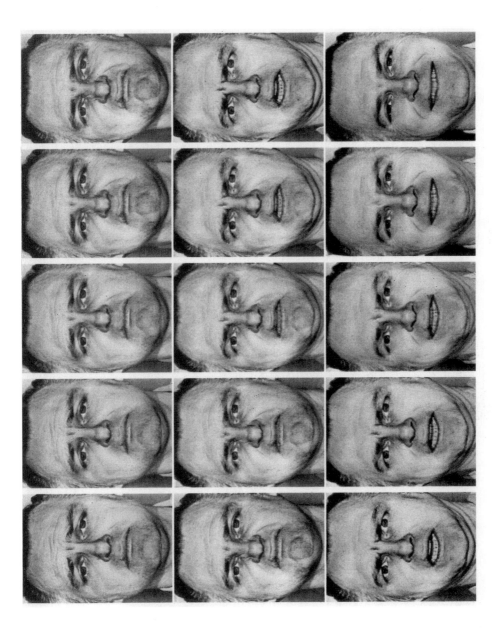

Fig. 1. Morphed expression continua used in the emotion hexagon experiment. Going from left to right, the columns show 90%, 70%, 50%, 30%, and 10% morphs along each continuum. From top to bottom, the continua shown in each row are happiness–surprise (top row), surprise–fear (second row), fear–sadness (third row), sadness–disgust (fourth row), disgust–anger (fifth row), anger–happiness (bottom row).

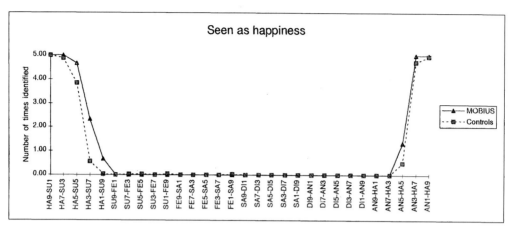

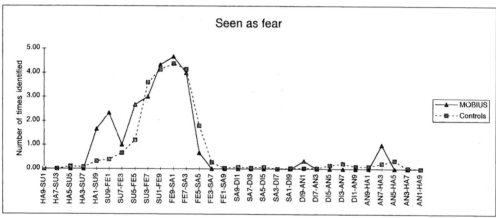

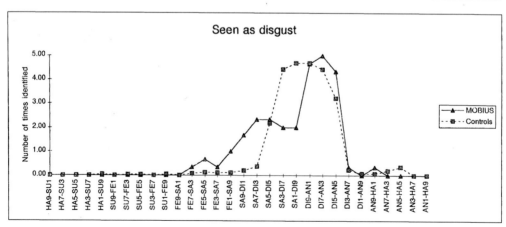

Fig. 2. *Mean correct identification of the morphed images shown in Fig. 1 by three people with Möbius Syndrome, and mean performance of neurologically normal controls. The morphed images shown in Fig. 1 are placed along the x-axis of each graph, running from left to right and top to bottom in Fig. 1; i.e. from 90% happiness 10% surprise (the top left image in Fig. 1; labelled with the convention HA9-SU1*

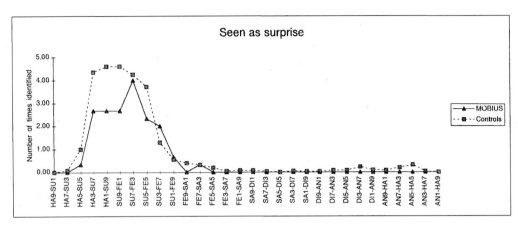

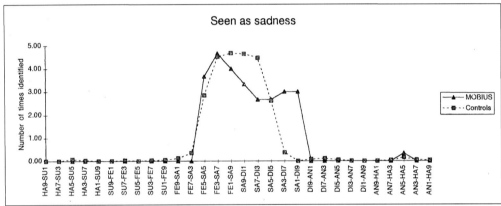

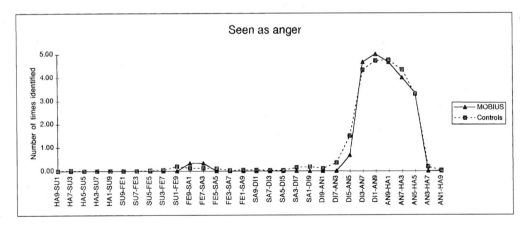

above) to 10% anger 90% happiness (the bottom right image in Fig. 1; labelled AN1-HA9 above). In each graph, the y-axis shows the number of times each image was identified as a particular emotion.

evaluating such problems, it is important to bear in mind that they may at least in part reflect secondary consequences of Möbius syndrome, resulting from eye movement abnormalities that create problems looking at faces, and from the degree of social isolation that often accompanies this personally and interpersonally distressing inability to produce appropriate facial movements. In effect, the nature of their condition means that sufferers of Möbius syndrome will often have less expertise and experience with faces than will neurologically normal people of comparable age.

Given these caveats, we are impressed by the decree of skill in facial expression perception shown by our three participants with Möbius syndrome. All were able to recognise many of the pictures of facial expressions we tested, often at normal or near-normal levels, and with only patchy and inconsistent evidence of any problems.

These findings contrast with the report by Giannini et al. (1984), who a described a woman with bilateral facial paralysis (as a result of Möbius syndrome), who showed a severe deficit in recognising facial expressions. One potential explanation of the different findings of Giannini et al.'s study and our own is that our tests of facial expression recognition are simply not sensitive enough. We think that this is unlikely. The controls' scores on both tests were not at ceiling, and conversations with our participants with Möbius syndrome and their families indicated that none felt that they had difficulty in recognising facial expressions; Giannini et al.'s patient, on the other hand, complained of being totally unable to identify facial expressions. Furthermore, the tests used in our study have proved sensitive enough to pick up selective deficits in recognising individual facial expression categories in previous research (Calder et al., 1996; Sprengelmeyer et al., 1996, 1997a, b). We therefore conclude that the deficit reported by Giannini et al. is not typical of Möbius syndrome.

However, we would not want to claim that the absence of motor-program representations has absolutely no effect on facial expression recognition for people with Möbius syndrome. NC shows a deficit in the morphed facial expression task, and BC's score on this test approaches impaired performance. In addition, Fig. 2 indicates that mean performance of the three Möbius syndrome participants is slightly discrepant for the categories of surprise, sadness, and disgust. These impairments should be considered together with the observation that none of the participants was impaired on the two tests of vocal expression recognition included in our test battery. This means that the facial expression processing deficits we have reported are unlikely to reflect impairments in processing emotional signals regardless of their domain.

In summary, although we should not rule out the idea that subtle deficits in facial expression recognition could be a consequence of having never generated facial signals, our results clearly demonstrate that severely impaired facial expression recognition is *not* characteristic of Möbius syndrome. Hence, our participants claims to be able to interpret other peoples facial expressions are borne out by formal testing.

REFERENCES

Baddeley, A., Emslie, H., & Nimmo-Smith, I. (1992). *Speed and Capacity of Language-Processing Test*. Bury St Edmunds, UK: Thames Valley Test Company.

Benton, A.L., Hamsher, K.S., Varney, N., & Spreen, O. (1983). *Contributions to neuropsychological assessment: A clinical manual*. Oxford: Oxford University Press.

Bishop, D.V.M., Byers Brown, B., & Robson, J. (1990). The relationship between phoneme discrimination, speech production, and language comprehension in cerebral-palsied individuals. *Journal of Speech and Hearing Research, 33*, 210–219.

Bruce, V., & Young, A.W. (1986). Understanding face recognition. *British Journal of Psychology, 77*, 305–327.

Calder, A.J., Young, A.W., Rowland, D., Perrett, D.I., Hodges, J.R., & Etcoff, N.L. (1996). Facial emotion recognition after bilateral amygdala damage: Differentially severe impairment of fear. *Cognitive Neuropsychology, 13*, 699–745.

Cole, J.D. (1998). *About face*. Cambridge, MA: MIT Press.

Ekman, P., & Friesen, W.V. (1976). *Pictures of facial affect*. Palo Alto, CA: Consulting Psychologists Press.

Galati, D., Scherer, K.R., & Ricci-Bitti, P.E. (1997). Voluntary facial expression of emotion: Congenitally blind with normally sighted encoders. *Journal of Personality and Social Psychology, 73*(6), 1363–1379.

George, M.S., Ketter, T.A., Gill, D.S., Haxby, J.V., Ungerleider, L.G., Herscovitch, P., & Post, R.M. (1993). Brain regions involved in recognizing facial emotion or identity: An oxygen-15 PET study. *Journal of Neuropsychology, 5*(4), 384–394.

Giannini, A.J., Tamulonis, D., Giannini, M.C., Loiselle, R.H., & Spirtos, G. (1984). Defective response to social cues in Möbius syndrome. *Journal of Nervous and Mental Disease, 172*(3), 174–175.

Henderson, J.L. (1939). The congenital facial diplegia syndrome: Clinical features, pathology and aetiology. *Brain, 62*, 381–403.

Hopf, H.C., Muller-Forell, W., & Hopf, N.J. (1992). Localization of emotional and volitional facial paresis. *Neurology, 42*, 1918–1923.

Kremer, H., Kuyt, L.P., van den Helm, B., van Reen, M., Leunissen, J.A.M., Hamel, B.C.J., Jansen, C., Mariman, E.C.M., Frants, R., & Padberg, G.W. (1996). Localization of a gene for Möbius syndrome to chromosome 3q by linkage analysis in a Dutch family. *Human Molecular Genetics, 5*(9), 1367–1371.

Liberman, A.M., Cooper, F.S., Shankweiler, D.P., & Studdert-Kennedy, M. (1967). Perception of the speech code. *Psychological Review, 74*, 431–461.

Lundqvist, L.O., & Dimberg, U. (1995). Facial expressions are contagious. *Journal of Psychophysiology, 9*(3), 203–211.

MacDermot, K.D., Winter, R.M., Taylor, D., & Baraister, M. (1990). Oculofacialbulbar palsy in mother and son: Review of 26 reports of familial transmission within the Möbius spectrum of defects. *Journal of Medical Genetics, 27*, 18–26.

MacNeilage, P.F., Rootes, T.P., & Chase, R.A. (1967). Speech production and perception in a patient with severe impairment of somesthetic per-ception and motor control. *Journal of Speech and Hearing Research, 10*, 449–468.

Murray, I.R., & Arnott, J.L. (1993). Toward the simulation of emotion in synthetic speech—A review of the literature on human vocal emotion. *Journal of the Acoustical Society of America, 93*, 1087–1108.

Nelson, H.E. (1991). *National Adult Reading Test (NART): Test manual (revised).* Windsor, UK: NFER-Nelson.

Richards, R.N. (1953). The Mobius Syndrome. *Journal of Bone Joint Surgery, 35A*, 437–444.

Rizzo, M., Hurtig, R., & Damasio, A.R. (1987). The role of scanpaths in facial recognition and learning. *Annals of Neurology, 22*, 41–45.

Scott, S., Young, A.W., Calder, A.J., Hellawell, D.J., Aggleton, J.P., & Johnson, M. (1997). Impaired recognition of fear and anger in speech following bilateral amygdala lesions. *Nature, 385*(16), 254–257.

Sprengelmeyer, R., Young, A.W., Calder, A.J., Karnat, A., Herwig, L., Homberg, V., Perrett, D.I., & Rowland, D. (1996). Loss of disgust in Huntingtons disease: Perception of faces and emotions. *Brain, 119*, 1647–1665.

Sprengelmeyer, R., Young, A.W., Karnat, A., Calder, A.J., Lange, H., Rowland, D., & Perrett, D.I. (1997a). Recogniton of facial expressions of basic emotions in Huntingtons disease. *Cognitive Neuropsychology, 14*, 839–879.

Sprengelmeyer, R., Young, A.W., Pundt, I., Sprengelmeyer, A., Calder, A.J., Berrios, G., Winkel, R., Vollmoeller, W., Przuntek, H., Sortory, G., & Kuhn, W. (1997b). Disgust implicated in obsessive-compulsive disorder. *Proceedings of the Royal Society, London. B, 264*, 1767–1773.

Van der Wiel, H.J. (1957). Hereditary congenital facial paralysis. *Acta Genetica et Statistica Medica, 7*(348A).

Warrington, E.K. (1984). *Recognition memory test.* Windsor: NFER-Nelson.

Zitter, F.A., Wiser, W.C., & Robinson, A. (1997). Three-generation pedigree of a Möbius Syndrome variant with chromosome translocation. *Archives of Neurology, 34*, 437–442.

COGNITIVE NEUROPSYCHOLOGY, 2000, 17 (1/2/3), 89–102

STRUCTURAL ENCODING PRECLUDES RECOGNITION OF FACE PARTS IN PROSOPAGNOSIA

Beatrice de Gelder and Romke Rouw

Cognitive Neuroscience Laboratory, Tilburg University, The Netherlands

The extent and the impact of spared processing of facial stimuli in the prosopagnosic patient LH is examined using the inversion effect and the face context effect. Our study asked how the deficit in individual face recognition is related to two perceptual abilities that are spared in this patient but between which there is interference when both are applied to the face stimulus, i.e. structural encoding of the face and parts-based matching procedures. Three experiments studied this relationship with task demands and stimulus properties designed to trigger the parts-based processes. In the first experiment, human and animal faces are presented upright or inverted with good performance only for the inverted condition. In Experiment 2 normals show a clear face context effect (matching of upright faces easier than scrambled or inverted ones) in the full face matching task whereas in the parts matching task the face superiority effect disappears. In contrast, LH shows a face inferiority effect when matching full faces but also when matching an isolated face part to a face part in a full face context. The results show that structural encoding of the face overrules parts-based procedures that could otherwise be helpful to tell individual faces apart.

Prosopagnosia is a deficit in face recognition (Bodamer, 1947), whereby the face no longer elicits any sense of familiarity although the patient continues to recognise familiar voices or gait. How specific to faces this disorder is, is still controversial, partly because very few cases of prosopagnosia have been studied in such a way that the possibility of at least some mild deficit in other areas like word or object recognition can be entirely excluded (Bruce & Humphreys, 1994; Farah, 1990; Gauthier, Behrmann, & Tarr, in press). The debate is now broadened by contributions from electro-physiological studies (see Jeffreys, 1996) and from brain imaging methods (Gauthier, Tarr, Anderson, Skudlarski, & Gore, 1997; Kanwisher, McDermott, & Chun, 1997a). Recent reports have provided evidence that loss of normal face recognition can manifest itself not just as a loss of the normal pattern of performance—for example, better performance with upright than with inverted faces—but as its opposite, superior performance with inverted in contrast to upright faces (de Gelder, 1999; de Gelder, Bachoud-Levi, & Degos, 1998; Farah, Wilson, Drain, & Tanaka, 1995). In other words, these patients present us with a reversal of the normal pattern. This data suggests that loss of face processing ability is not simply a matter of losing the ability to process a certain category of stimuli (faces) nor of losing a certain processing style (one which targets the stimulus configuration), but that there is an interaction between damaged and intact skills. In order to focus on this interaction we refer to the intact aspects of face processing as "structural encoding" of the face. It is

---

Requests for reprints should be addressed to Beatrice de Gelder, Tilburg University, Department of Psychology, PO Box 90153, 5000 LE Tilburg, The Netherlands (Email: B.deGelder@kub.nl).

We are thankful to two anonymous referees for useful suggestions, to P. Bertelson and B. Rossion for comments on an earlier draft, and to N. Etcoff for bringing us in contact with LH. We thank LH for his collaboration and patience.

important to note that in this paper the term "structural encoding" does not refer specifically to one or another theory of face recognition. The present paper investigates the hypothesis that spared structural encoding renders the patient unable to apply parts and feature-based matching strategies to faces. The robustness and generality of this effect is shown in three experiments.

INTRODUCTION

A perspective common to many studies of prosopagnosia is that the deficit is situated at the within-category level and that face categorisation itself or the ability to make a face decision is intact. In terms of the popular model of Bruce and Young (1986), loss of face recognition ability corresponds to damage to the "face recognition units," leaving intact the earlier stages of face processing. The fact that recognition at the individual or exemplar level is critical for face recognition led to the "individuation" theory of prosopagnosia (Moscovitch, Winocur, & Behrmann, 1997) or the view that prosopagnosia is a deficit of within-category discriminations, defended by Damasio (Damasio, Damasio, & Van Hoesen, 1982; Damasio, Tranel, & Damasio, 1990). Like the model of Bruce and Young, this view assumes that prior to individual identity recognition, visual face processing is intact in prosopagnosics. The concept of structural encoding will be used throughout this paper to refer to this initial face categorisation stage because it is more general than some of the specific notions advanced to explain face processing (see following).

A family of more or less related theories of normal face recognition has focused on within-category processes of face recognition. A common theme is that the whole face is more than the parts, but there is no consensus as to what is exactly meant by "*whole*." One view is that the face initially consists of clearly separate parts or primary features, which when integrated give rise to the second-order features or to recognition of the face as a configuration (the spatial relations between the individual features), as argued by Rhodes and colleagues (Rhodes, 1988; Rhodes, Brake, &

Atkinson, 1993). A stronger claim, made by Farah and collaborators, is that face recognition does not start from the encoding of separate face parts or initial parsing but that the face is represented holistically such that its parts are not represented other than in the whole context (Farah, 1990; Tanaka, & Farah, 1993). Finally, developmentalists have argued that, at the entry level, faces are encoded the same way as any other object by attending to the relations between the parts or to the overall configuration. From there develops the ability to use second-order facial information, which underlies individual face discrimination (Carey & Diamond, 1994; Diamond & Carey, 1986). As Moscovitch et al. (1997) remark, these different theories each address slightly different questions. Nevertheless, fine details aside, each of them suggests just what might be lost in prosopagnosia: loss of configuration-based processes in the sense of Rhodes et al., loss of the face module or of holistic processing in the sens of Farah et al., or loss of face expertise related to second-order representation of individual differences.

A critical question for grasping the differences between these three views concerns what is then spared in prosopagnosia. If second-order or configuration-based processing is lost, is what remains the recognition of isolated face parts? Or, once the face module is lost, are faces processed like objects, in a parts-based way? Or again, is face expertise—or the ability to use second-order relational information—lost but are faces still processed as bundles of first-order relational information just like objects? This latter view is in line with the consensus in the literature that prosopagnosic patients have lost the ability to discriminate between faces but continue to categorise faces normally. Thus, the notion that first-order information is spared and second-order information is lost (in Carey's terms) reflects a certain consensus concerning the pattern of spared and lost skills in prosopagnosia.

Recent studies of prosopagnosic patients have looked at this issue in more detail, complementing traditional clinical tests of intact face decision with behavioural tasks that have shown strong face-specific perceptual processing effects, like the inversion effect, in normal subjects. But studies have revealed a paradox, because some prosopagnosic patients are considerably better at matching inverted than upright faces (de Gelder et al., 1998; Farah et al., 1995).

The Paradox of Inversion Superiority

The inversion effect, first reported by Yin (1969) for normal subjects, has often been referred to as a benchmark for establishing normal face processing (Yin, 1970). Normal subjects are better at recognising, matching, and remembering a pair of faces when these are presented upright than when upside-down (Yin, 1969). Recently Farah et al. (1995) have studied the inversion effect in prosopagnosic patient LH. Following the results obtained with right-hemisphere deficits the prediction was that LH would perform the same way with upright and inverted faces. But instead, LH showed face inversion superiority. We have confirmed this finding and at the same time extended it to objects with agnosic patient AD (de Gelder et al., 1998). Subsequently the same effects were observed with LH (de Gelder, 1999). This reversed face inversion effect cannot be reduced to absence of the normal pattern. This finding challenges the notion that the ability to use second-order relational information is lost and is subsequently compensated for by using intact feature-based routines to discriminate faces.

Instead, the paradox of inversion superiority is that individual face recognition is lost but that some aspects of face processing are still active and interfere with reliance upon general visual routines in order to discriminate individual faces. Thus, when the normal pattern of better performance with upright faces is reversed, more seems to be at stake than just spared face categorisation in the presence of lost second-order or within-category discrimination. Somehow these patients are handicapped by their spared face categorisation and prevented from using intact parts-based processes with faces. The latter are successfully used with inverted faces but are clearly of no use to deal with an upright face. Presumably inverting a face makes it object-like and no longer triggers face-specific processes, therefore giving a chance to part-based routines.

The present study reports experiments designed to test the robustness and generality of this paradox.

Spared Structural Encoding in LH?

The case of patient LH is well suited for examining the relation and the interference between spared first-order categorisation and parts-based processes. Inversion superiority was reported for this patient but there is inconsistency in previous studies of LH concerning the issue of configuration-based processing. An older study by Levine and Calvanio (1989) argues (p.151) that the core of LH's problems with faces is an inability to get "an overview of sufficient features of a stimulus to allow the structuring or crystallisation of a coherent percept" and that LH's disorder is one of "defective visual configural processing." These authors go on (p.161) to propose that "defective configurational processing is characteristic of prosopagnosia." A more recent study by Etcoff, Freeman, and Cave (1991) challenges this view, concluding instead that configural processing is intact in LH. In the two cases the conclusion is based on visuospatial tests and tasks of perceptual closure (for example, Kaniza figures). Neither of these two studies provides data from face or object recognition tasks that specifically addressed the issue of intact visual integration in higher-order visual cognition.

A new paradigm for studying the influence of structural encoding of faces is provided by studies that have investigated the effect of a face context on perception and recognition of a face part. These effects can either manifest themselves as superiority effects or as inferiority effects, depending on whether a memory rather than a visual search is required (Mermelstein, Banks, & Prinzmetal, 1979). The face superiority effect refers to the finding that face parts are recognised better in a normal face context than outside it or in a scrambled face (Homa, Haver, & Schwartz, 1976; Van Santen & Jonides, 1978). This effect is similar to the word superiority effect, where letters are recognised better and faster when presented in the context of a real word than that of a pseudoword (Reicher, 1969). The same effect of context was found in a search task with conjunction of features vs. isolated features (Suzuki & Cavanagh, 1995). A similar effect was reported in studies examining the whole face advantage, as improved performance of recognising whole faces vs. face parts was not found with scrambled faces (Tanaka & Farah, 1993). Recently Gauthier and Tarr (1997) and Tanaka and Gauthier (1997) have studied this part/whole advantage for objects other than faces in an effort to pull apart the importance of stimulus configuration (which is either parts-based or referred to as "holistic" in the sense of Farah and collaborators) and that of expertise with the stimulus domain. These studies provided evidence for holistic processing of cars, houses, cells, and "greebles".

There are two aspects to structural encoding of faces that are central to our experiments. Since face superiority does not occur when the face configuration is lost because the face parts are scrambled (Mermelstein et al., 1976), the effect is related to presence of the normal face *configuration*. Moreover, since the effect disappears or is strongly reduced when a normally configured face is inverted, the face context effect also depends on *canonical orientation*. A reversed effect of that found in normals would be consistent with the previous reports of inversion superiority. If, moreover, the contrast between normal and scrambled faces also yields the reverse pattern of that found in normals, we have significantly expanded the scope of the previous findings and thereby pointed to structural encoding as the common factor explaining inversion superiority as well as context inferiority.

The goal of Experiment 1 is to see whether structural encoding of the face overrules LH's part-based strategies. If LH's performance still reflects inversion superiority, this would testify to the strong dominance of structural encoding, more specifically the role of canonical orientation. We then need to test, with a new paradigm based on the face context effect, whether his spared structural encoding still dominates explicitly induced internal part-based processes (Experiment 3). Experiment 2 was run with normal subjects in order to establish that the pattern of results typical for the face context effect obtains with our novel materials and testing procedure. These results are also useful as control data for LH.

Case Presentation

Prosopagnosic patient LH is a 48-year-old minister and social worker, who suffered a severe closed head injury in an automobile accident at the age of 18. What follows is a brief summary of the aspects relevant for the present study, since the case has been reported in the literature on previous occasions beginning with Teuber (1968). LH has bilateral lesions affecting visual association cortices and the subjacent white matter. These sites include the right temporal lobe, the left subcortical occipitotemporal white matter, and bilateral parieto-occipital regions (see Levine, Calvanio, & Wolfe, 1980; Levine, Warach, & Farah, 1985, for details of visual testing). Spatial perception was untouched by his injuries. LH performed flawlessly on a standard test of judging the orientation of lines (Benton, Hamsher, Varney, & Spreen, 1978). He has no discernible language deficits. Writing is normal but reading is slow. Copying of objects and complex drawings is excellent. LH was 85% accurate on the object decision task, judging 87% of the objects as real and only 11% of the nonobjects as real (Etcoff et al., 1991).

LH's most striking deficit concerns faces. He is unable to recognise any familiar face. Recognition of individuals via other channels such as their voices remains intact, as does his retention of biographical information. LH scored 36/54 on the Benton-Van Allen face matching task (Benton & van Allen, 1968), a result that qualifies as impaired. On matching of identical faces he was 100% accurate, but when test and target differed on lighting and appeared fragmented and silhouetted he scored only 54% correct.

EXPERIMENT 1. DOES INVERSION SUPERIORITY GENERALISE TO NONHUMAN FACES?

Animal faces present stimuli that share the basic configuration and orientation with human faces but differ in the internal and external face parts (eyes, mouth, but also hair, ears, shape of head, etc). Prosopagnosia extends sometimes to nonhuman faces for which the patient previously had a particular expertise (Bornstein, Sroka, & Munitz, 1969). Sometimes prosopagnosics regain animal face recognition while human face recognition remains impaired (Bruyer, et al., 1983; McNeil & Warrington, 1993). Prior to his accident LH had no particular expertise with animals, nor was he particularly knowledgeable about a specific species. We reasoned that using animal faces would enhance the use of part-based strategies. If so, his performance would be the same for upright as for inverted stimuli. We chose a task that consisted of normal human faces (man, woman) as well as animal faces (cow, monkey) and images generated by blending these in order to obtain a stimulus continuum, enabling us to use a task of categorical perception. From the literature on categorical perception it is well known that the more subjects are acquainted with the stimuli the more their perception is driven by the underlying categories rather than by peripheral stimulus aspects (Repp, 1984). The stimuli were presented to normal subjects in an earlier study (Campbell, Pascalis, Coleman, Wallace, & Benson, 1997). Campbell et al. found a normal inversion effect in a two-alternative forced-choice matching task (2AFC), although normals could still identify inverted stimuli as belonging to a specific category. If overall similarity in configuration between human and animal faces determines the course of processing then LH might not be able to take advantage of the very obvious differences between parts of the face that easily allow discrimination between a pair of adjacent stimuli. In that case LH would show inversion superiority for animal and human faces alike.

Materials and Procedure

Two sets of 15 pictures each were obtained as follows. Starting from 3 natural photographs (a female face, a monkey face, and a cow face for the first series and a male face, a monkey face, and a cow face for the second series), 12 intermediate stimuli were created with a morphing program (see Campbell et al., 1997, for details). The morphing went through four intermediate steps from one kind of face into

the other (from male or female face to monkey face and to cow face). Within each series, pairs of adjacent stimuli were probes in a 2AFC task, with either the one or the other as the target. This resulted in 30 trials, each with a different probe. For testing LH, laser prints of the computer images were used. The probe was shown for 4sec, followed by the two alternatives. LH responded by pointing to the left or the right picture. In a separate testing session, these same probes were used in an identification task. LH made a forced choice between one of the three stimuli categories.

Results

Performance on this task was 60% (18/30) correct choices (see Table 1), which does not differ reliably from chance performance ($\chi^2 = 0.61$, $P > .25$). In a separate testing session some weeks later the same stimuli were presented upside-down. LH was 83% (25/30) correct on this test, which is reliably better than chance performance ($\chi^2 = 7.5$, $P < .01$) and superior to the performance on the normally oriented stimuli ($\chi^2 = 4.02$, $P < .05$). Given the limited number of trials for the unmodified stimuli, a comparison between the three face categories could not be made. Interestingly, on trials using stimuli exactly in between categories (40%–60% of the two anchor points), inverting the stimuli yielded the most improvement in performance (from 5/9, 44% error to 0% error).

In the forced-choice identification task, we analysed trials with the normal human, cow, or monkey images only (57%). LH performed at ceiling with the human faces (100%), reasonably well (71%) with the cow faces, and at chance (30%) with the monkey faces. His bad performance with the monkey faces was due to consistently classifying these faces as human. However, the cow faces were mistakenly classified as monkey faces.

Table 1. *Patient LH's Percentage Correct on a Simultaneous Matching Task With Animal Faces*

	Upright	Inverted
% correct	60	83

More accurate on inverted than upright: $\chi^2 = 4.02$, $P < .05$.

Discussion

The question raised in Experiment 1 was whether LH would show better performance with inverted presentation (inversion superiority) for human as well as for animal faces. The animal faces have the same schematic configuration as human faces but are more discriminable because of numerous internal and external details. Using the blended stimuli should encourage parts-based processing in LH. However, the data show that LH performs at chance level with all upright stimuli but he is clearly much better when the faces are presented upside-down. This generalised face inversion superiority effect suggests that structural encoding of the face overrules the ability to attend to the local details, which is so clearly manifest in LH's performance with upside-down faces. Various aspects of this result require comment.

The first thing worth noting is that this result confirms the inversion superiority for human faces previously observed for LH (Farah et al., 1995) and AD (de Gelder et al., 1998). The finding also adds to evidence in favour of theories arguing that upright and inverted faces are dealt with by separate mechanisms, also called dual-route models (Moscovitch et al., 1997). The fact that LH's performance shows the same pattern whether the faces are animal or human suggests that the critical factor is the structural encoding of the face and not expertise with the stimulus class. Animal faces have only a schematic configuration in common with human faces and differ from each other and from human faces in many local details. The presence of this configuration in its normal orientation appears to be enough to interfere with the application of parts-based strategies to the upright stimuli. Our results are consistent with the findings by Gauthier et al. (1997) and Tanaka and Gauthier (1998), showing that expertise with the stimulus category is not a significant factor in determining holistic encoding. Although our notion of structural encoding is weaker, the findings clearly converge.

The present result cannot be explained by referring to loss of the ability to perceive second-order configuration, characteristic of prosopagnosic patients. Undoubtedly LH, like other pro-

sopagnosic patients, has lost the use of second-order configuration information or the typical ability to tell apart individual faces, and his chance performance with upright faces confirms that once more. But the crucial aspect of our results is the relationship between poor performance with upright and good performance with inverted stimuli. This pattern cannot be explained by reference to loss of the ability to use second-order information nor by reference to intact parts-based strategies. Neither of these explanations can account for the difference in performance between the upright and the inverted condition, since both these explanations suggest that upright and inverted faces are dealt with in the same fashion. Instead, these results testify to the influence on later processes of LH's spared ability of structural encoding. As we noted in the Introduction, we have adopted the notion of structural encoding to refer to the perceptual stage of encoding the face structure but cannot at this stage favour a view that structural encoding is entirely the same as making a category decision, or that it either precedes, parallels, or follows upon it.

The next experiment with LH (Experiment 3) looks into the influence of structural encoding more closely. It used a new paradigm, that of the face context effect, which requires whole-based and parts-based matching processes. This paradigm allows us to look at the effect of orientation (like Experiment 1) but also to study the impact of the configuration by comparing normal and scrambled faces. Also, the stimulus set could be controlled such that any difference between one face and another was strictly limited to either the eyes or the mouth.

EXPERIMENT 2. INNER FACIAL FEATURES: FACE CONTEXT EFFECTS FOR MATCHING FULL FACES AND PARTS-BASED MATCHING IN NORMALS

Experiments 2 and 3 are designed to study directly whether structural encoding of faces is intact, by using the face inversion effect and the face superiority effect with new materials and a new task. A set of face materials was constructed, each one based on the same natural-looking facial contour. Thus, in contrast with Experiment 1, stimuli did not provide any external cues and attention was focused entirely on the inner face parts. These stimuli should encourage featural processing as they can be differentiated only by close examination of the eyes or the mouth (see Appendix A for an example). Two tasks were designed: matching of whole faces and matching of an isolated face part to its corresponding face part presented in a whole-face context. Both tasks are presented in a simultaneous matching paradigm with three conditions: upright, scrambled, and inverted. The comparison of upright and scrambled performance is relevant for understanding the role of configuration, and comparing upright vs. inverted presentation also informs about the role of canonical orientation. A simultaneous matching task was chosen in order to focus on structural encoding as it takes place in perception. To further encourage parts-based comparison based on visual search, a 2AFC task was preferred over a same/different decision.

Experiment 2 presented these tasks to normal subjects and was performed because of the novelty of the tasks and of the materials.

Subjects

Twenty students from Tilburg University participated as subjects in two simultaneous matching tasks.

Materials

A black-and-white computer-edited prototype face of photographic quality of a young male served as the framework. One of a set of six pairs of eyes and six mouths were put in this facial contour, making for six different faces. These faces could be presented upright or inverted. A face presentation covered approximately 2° of visual angle. Further, an equal number of scrambled faces was made by interchanging the position of eyes and mouth. Thus, there are three conditions: inverted, normal, and scrambled faces.

Method and Results

Order of the two tasks and the two blocks (normal-inverted-scrambled, or scrambled-inverted-normal) was balanced between subjects. In between the two tasks subjects were given another task with different stimuli, which lasted for about 15 minutes.

Experiment 2A: Matching Full Faces

For each condition (upright, inverted, and scrambled) 60 face pairs were made: 30 "different" and 30 "same." Each subject was presented with all conditions. Presentation was blocked and a block consisted of 18 "same" and 18 "different" trials, presented in random order. A trial started with a fixation cross for 500msec. Then two whole faces were presented simultaneously until a response was made.

As expected with unconstrained viewing time, subjects' performance was almost flawless. However, the pattern of latencies for the different conditions is revealing. In task 1 (whole-to-whole matching), there was an overall effect of presentation $[F(2,18) = 18.13, P < .001]$. The normal presented faces were responded to faster than either the scrambled faces $[F(1,19) = 40.04, P < .001]$ or the inverted faces $[F(1,19) = 13.54, P < .002]$. Separate anaylsis revealed that the normal presentation advantage was significant for both the "same" trials $[F(2,18) = 9.11, P < .002]$ and the "different" trials $[F(2,18) = 23.79, P < .001]$.

Experiment 2B: Matching Face Parts to the Corresponding Part in Full Faces

The same subjects performed a simultaneous matching task, this time involving faces and facial parts. Stimuli were the same whole faces and face parts (six eyes and six mouths). There were three blocks of trials corresponding to three presentation conditions: upright, inverted, and scrambled. Each subject was presented with each of 108 trials: 18 eye and 18 mouth trials for each presentation block. A trial consisted of a fixation cross for 800msec, followed by a simultaneous presentation of a whole face at the top and two parts at the bottom of the screen. Subjects indicated by a key press which of the two parts (left or right) was present in the whole face.

Again, errors were too few to reveal any effects in accuracy. Latencies showed a main effect of Eye–mouth [$F(1,19) = 16.15$, $P = .001$] and an Eye–mouth × Presentation interaction [$F(2,38) = 3.8$, $P = .021$], but no main effect of Orientation. Accordingly, the difference in response times between normal and inverted, or normal and scrambled, faces is not significant (see Table 2).

Discussion

The results of Experiment 2A show that in this novel design with normal subjects, using a simultaneous matching task, performance with normal faces is clearly superior to that with inverted or scrambled faces. Thus, both the face superiority and the face inversion effect obtain with these materials and are found even with unlimited viewing time. These results further show that with stimuli differing from each other exclusively in the internal parts of the face, there was still an effect of face configuration even if both the stimulus properties and the simultaneous matching presentation could have induced visual search for the critical part. In that case the difference between the upright condition would have disappeared and latencies would have been the same for the three conditions. This is exactly what happened in Experiment 2B, where the context effect is no longer observed.

The pattern of an advantage of matching normal whole faces over scrambled faces in the whole-face matching task but not in the parts matching task is

Table 2. *Normal RTs and Percentage Correct at Simultaneous Matching of Upright, Scrambled, or Inverted Faces with Whole Faces (Experiment 2A) or With Face Parts (Experiment 2B)*

	Upright	Scrambled	Inverted
Whole–whole			
Mean RT(msec)	1393	1623*	1621**
% correct	97.8	96.9	85.6
Whole–parts			
Mean RT(msec)	1785	1782	1869
% correct	98.3	98.1	96.7

Faster response to upright faces: * $P < .002$; ** $P < .001$.

consistent with the results of Davidoff and Donnelly (1990) and Farah et al. (1998). The former authors found an object (faces and chairs) superiority effect for whole but not part probes, unless the presentation times were very short. This is consistent with our findings, which indicate that in the parts matching task but not in the whole faces matching task some kind of featural or parts-based analysis was used. The fact that an attentional manipulation can overrule face superiority is consistent with the results of an fMRI study on the effect of attention on the activation of the face area in the brain (Wojciulik, Kanwisher, & Driver, 1998).

EXPERIMENT 3. INNER FACIAL FEATURES: FACE SUPERIORITY FOR WHOLE FACE AND PART TO WHOLE MATCHING IN PATIENT LH

LH was presented with the same two tasks as normals (see Experiment 2). Experiment 3 asks whether his ability to focus on stimulus parts will reduce influence of the face configuration observed in Experiment 1. If so, he would not show the face superiority effect of normal subjects in Experiment 2A and he should be able to overcome the effect of configuration and orientation if the task demands explicitly require this (Experiment 2B).

Experiment 3A: Method and Results

Stimuli were the same faces, differing only in internal features, as described in Experiment 2. Laser prints of the stimuli were used for presentation with LH. In the first task, two whole faces were presented. A stimulus pair was shown for as long as it took LH to given an answer (same or different judgement). Instructions were explained by two examples of each condition. Presentation was blocked with sets containing 18 normal, scrambled, or inverted faces. There was a total of 12 blocks alternating, divided over 2 presentation sessions with some weeks in between.

Performance with upright faces did not differ significantly from chance: 31/72 (43.1%). Performance improved in the scrambled face condition: 49/72, 68.1%, both compared with upright presentation ($\chi^2 = 8.14$, $P < .005$) and from chance ($\chi^2 = 4.84$, $P < .05$). Performance on inverted faces was good: 62/72 (86.1%), much better than chance performance ($\chi^2 = 21.6$, $P < .001$) and upright presentation performance ($\chi^2 = 27.32$, $P < .001$).

Experiment 3B: Method and Results

In a separate testing sessions the same task as Experiment 2B was presented. Performance with upright faces was at chance 18/48 (37.5%). Performance in the scrambled condition 32/48 (66.7%) improved from upright ($\chi^2 = 7.06$, $P < .01$), but was just slightly better than chance ($\chi^2 = 2.74$, $P < .1$). Presenting the faces inverted strikingly improved performance (38/48, 79.1%), differing both from chance performance ($\chi^2 = 8.92$, $P < .005$) and from upright performance ($\chi^2 = 15.46$, $P < .001$) (see Table 3).

Discussion

Unlike normal subjects, LH does not benefit from the normal upright presentation to match faces faster than is done in either the scrambled or the inverted condition. His pattern of results is thus the opposite of the face superiority shown by normals (Experiment 2A) and amounts to a face *inferiority* effect. In Experiment 3A, performance with upright faces was at chance, a result that confirms that LH has lost normal processing of faces and cannot rely on a compensation strategy of attending

Table 3. *Patient LH Percentage Correct on Simultaneous Matching of Upright, Scrambled, or Inverted Faces with Whole Faces (Experiment 3A) or With Face Parts (Experiment 3B)*

% Correct	Upright	Scrambled	Inverted
Whole–whole	43.1	68.1**	86.1***
Whole–parts	37.5	66.7*	79.1***

Scores are significantly improved in scrambled or inverted condition compared with upright condition: *$P < .01$; **$P < .005$; ***$P < .001$.

to a specific face part. The comparison of upright and inverted faces shows that LH is very good at matching inverted faces. This aspect of the results confirms that the normal inversion effect is replaced by inversion superiority and replicates previous observations (de Gelder, 1999; de Gelder et al., 1998; Farah et al., 1995) and Experiment 1 of the present study.

The results of Experiment 3 consolidate and extend the original finding in significant ways. The present inversion superiority is obtained with face stimuli that differ only in internal parts. Loss of face processing due to prosopagnosia is thus not a consequence of a shift in the reliance on external vs. internal cues or reliance on external cues to the detriment of internal ones. Such a pattern was observed with normal older subjects. These subjects showed the same inversion superiority as reported there but, when tested with stimuli that differed only in internal face parts, the normal pattern of better performance with upright than with inverted faces reappeared. Loss of face skills as a consequence of normal ageing is thus different from its manifestation in prosopagnosia (de Gelder, Rossion, & Pourtois, 1998). Next, the original face superiority result was not simply due to noncanonical orientation of the stimuli. Disturbing the face context by scrambling the parts raised LH's performance considerably and indicates that the presence of the critical face structure is what triggers that interference on parts-based matching.

In Experiment 3B LH again performs very poorly when having to match a part of a face to the corresponding part in a full upright face. For LH, unlike for normal subjects, the facial context continues to influence part recognition even though it is noninformative in the task. Only when the face configuration is lost as a consequence of scrambling or the canonical orientation is lost due to inversion is structural encoding no longer triggered, and LH can make efficient use of his skills in matching parts.

This result is in line with the goals of a previous study using the face superiority effect to ascertain residual intact face processing in prosopagnosics (Davidoff & Donnelly, 1990), but the outcome with LH is different. The authors correctly note that if prosopagnosia were a disorder specific only for recognition of familiar faces, prosopagnosics would show a normal face superiority effect. Instead, their patient KD does not show face superiority and thus proves their point that some prosopagnosics have problems with structural encoding and cannot achieve an integrated representation of a face stimulus (compromising subsequent processes of identity recognition). In contrast, LH's inversion superiority and face inferiority is evidence that his problems do not have their origin in a difficulty with achieving an integrated face representation. With respect to that issue, the present study shows that having intact structural encoding of faces is not sufficient for subsequent personal identity recognition and may actually constitute an obstacle for alternative compensation strategies.

GENERAL DISCUSSION

The influence of spared structural encoding of faces in a prosopagnosic patient is examined using the inversion effect and the face context effect. Starting from the inversion superiority previously reported, the study asked how the deficit in individual face recognition is related to two perceptual abilities that are spared in this patient but between which there is interference when both are applied to the face stimulus: structural encoding of the face and parts-based matching procedures. Three experiments studied this relationship with task demands and stimulus properties designed to trigger the parts-based processes. In Experiment 1, human and animal faces are presented upright or inverted, with good performance only for inverted condition. In Experiment 2 normals show a clear face context effect (matching of upright faces is easier than matching scrambled or inverted ones) in the full face matching task, whereas in the parts matching task the face superiority effect disappears. In contrast, LH shows a face inferiority effect when matching full faces and when matching an isolated face part to a part in a full face context. The results show that structural encoding of the face overrules parts-based procedures that could otherwise be

helpful to tell individual faces apart. Our experiments show that even when task demands and stimulus properties are designed to boost an alternative routine this is overruled by spared structural encoding of the face. Paradoxically, the degree of face impairment of prosopagnosic patients thus seems to predict the extent to which compensation strategies can be successful. In the case of LH, spared structural encoding does lead to worse performance by inhibiting parts-based procedures. Our results stress the need to examine in detail the initial stages on which subsequent personal identity recognition depends. This perceptual stage of structural encoding may be impaired, as for example in the patients reported by Davidoff and Landis (1990), or it may be intact as for LH.

The notion of spared structural encoding as the locus of inhibition was already hinted at by McNeil and Warrington (1993) at the end of their study of WJ. This patient is severely prosopagnosic and has not recovered any recognition of human faces. Nevertheless, he is perfectly able to recognise the faces of his sheep and he can tell apart different unfamiliar examples in a recognition memory task. The authors note that apparently WJ does not seem able to use the strategies he employs with sheep to compensate for his deficit with human faces. They go on to make two important suggestions. First, WJ's deficit might consist of a disconnection between the structural encoding stage and the face recognition nodes of the Bruce and Young model. Second, they suggest that this deficit might "prevent the development of alternative methods of perceptual encoding" (McNeil & Warrington, 1993, p.9). This suggestion of an interference from intact processes is supported by the present results.

In this study we have not looked at inversion superiority for objects. Our previous results with both LH and AD provide evidence that inversion superiority also obtains in these two patients for matching of objects. As we argued previously, this implies that structural encoding is critical not only for faces but also for some object categories. Our finding of an inversion superiority for some nonface stimuli is actually consistent with the recent report by Farah, Wilson, Drain, and Tanaka (1998). These authors now propose what in fact amounts to a relative version of their original claims about face specificity, whereby the inversion effect is *relatively* strongest for faces and faces are processed *relatively* more holistically than other objects.

Our findings have implications for what the theories of face processing we reviewed suggest to be the critical loss in prosopagnosia. The pattern of lost vs. spared processing routines does not correspond to the conventional view that whatever is face-specific is lost and whatever is object-specific is spared. Neither does our study support the view that first-order abilities are spared and second-order ones (in the sense of Carey and collaborators) lost. Moreover, it suggests that first- and second-order information is not independent. On the other hand, Farah's notion of a damaged face module (Farah et al., 1995) is not entirely satisfactory because it does not provide room for sorting out what is lost and what could be spared for an inhibitory role of spared structural encoding. Our results add to the evidence provided by Moscovitch et al. (1997), showing that a sharp division between face-specific or whole-based procedures and object-specific or parts-based procedures is not entirely satisfactory. Our results with LH make a point similar to theirs in a different way, by showing an influence of whole-based on parts-based routines which results in an inhibition of the latter by the former.

Inversion superiority has only been reported in a couple of patients so far. Given the number of case studies available and the widespread view that these patients can still see faces as a separate visual category, this is surprising. A question for future research is to understand why only some prosopagnosic patients seem to show this phenomenon (de Gelder, Rouw, & Rossion, 1999). A critical factor may be the extent of preserved face processing abilities in prosopagnosics. The two patients for whom we have now reported inversion superiority do not suffer from the kind of agnosia that has been labeled integrative agnosia (Humphreys & Riddock, 1987), where the patient manages the see parts of an object but fails to integrate them into a whole. Our conjecture is that in such patients inversion superiority will not be observed. However, it is worth noting that only a few studies of prosopagnosics have addressed this issue with the use of experimental tasks that are more demanding than clinical batteries. How strong is the evidence for intact face decisions in prosopagnosia and what conclusions about spared skills does it warrant? In conventional screening of face problems, a face recognition battery like the Warrington Face Recognition Test (relying heavily on memory for faces) or the face test by Benton and van Allen (1968) or a face decision task are used (for instance, Schweich & Bruyer, 1993). If it is indeed the case that prosopagnosics can make intact category assignments for faces, they should perform at ceiling on a face decision task. But as shown in the last study, out of nine prosopagnosic patients only three performed like controls, two were borderline, and the remaining four failed to tell faces from nonfaces. The question can still be raised as to what the performance of the three good subjects tells about structural encoding? Davidoff and Landis (1990) argued convincingly that evidence from performance on the Benton test or on a face decision task is not sufficiently convincing to establish intact structural encoding. Usually in a face decision task the stimuli (normal, scrambled, incomplete faces) are presented under unconstrained viewing conditions, which allows for maximal contribution from general problem-solving strategies. Patients can combine intact spatial knowledge of the canonical face format and apply general visual strategies based on features, as in object recognition. It is thus entirely possible to arrive at a correct facial decision without encoding the facial structure in the course of perception. From this vantage point, an important question for future research is whether prosopagnosics can make face decisions based on structural encoding in the course of perception, as contrasted with being able to use it off-line in order to make explicit, conscious decisions about stimulus category.

Finally, more detailed information is needed about the specific loci of, on the one hand, the patient's lesions and, on the other, areas involved in treating upright vs. inverted faces and other objects in normal subjects (Kanwisher, Tong, & Nakayama, 1998). But we cannot exclude at present that inversion superiority for faces in prosopagnosia results from a more complex combination of spared and lost abilities.

REFERENCES

Assal, G., Favre, C., & Anderes, J.P. (1984). Non-reconnaissance d'animaux familiers chez un paysan: Zooagnosie ou prosopagnosie pour les animaux. *Revue Neurologique, 140,* 590–584.

Benton, A.L., Hamsher, K.S., Varney N.R., & Spreen. O. (1978). *Facial recognition: Stimulus and multiple choice pictures.* New York: Oxford University Press.

Benton, A.L., & van Allen, M.W. (1968). Impairment in facial recognition in patients with cerebral disease. *Cortex, 4,* 344–358.

Bodamer, J. (1947). Die prosop-Agnosie. *Archiv für Psychiatrie und Nervenkrankheiten, 179,* 6–53.

Bornstein, B., Sroka, M., & Munitz, H. (1969). Prosopagnosia with animal face agnosia. *Cortex, 4,* 344–358.

Bruce, V., & Humphreys, G.W. (Eds.) (1994). *Object and face recognition.* Hove, UK: Lawrence Erlbaum Associates Ltd.

Bruce, V., & Young, A.W. (1986). Understanding face recognition. *British Journal of Psychology, 77,* 305–327.

Bruyer, R., Laterre, C., Seron, X., Feyereisen, P., Strypstein, E., Peirrard, E., & Rectem, D. (1983). A case of prosopagnosia with some preserved covert remembrance of familiar faces. *Brain and Cognition, 2,* 257–284.

Campbell, R., Pascalis, O., Coleman, M., Wallace, S.B., & Benson, P.J. (1997). Are faces of different species perceived categorically by human observers? *Proceedings of the Royal Society London B, 264,* 1429–1434.

Carey, S., & Diamond, R. (1994). Are faces perceived as configurations more by adults than by children? *Visual Cognition, 1,* 313–348.

Damasio, A.R. (1990). Category-related recognition defects as a clue to the neural substrates of knowledge. *Trends in Neuroscience, 13,* 95–98.

Damasio, A.R., Damasio, H., & Van Hoesen, G.W. (1982). Prosopagnosia: Anatomical basis and behavioural mechanisms. *Neurology, 32,* 331–341.

Damasio, A.R., Tranel, D., & Damasio, H. (1990). Face agnosia and the neural substrates of memory. *Annual Review of Neuroscience, 13,* 89–109.

Davidoff, J., & Donnelly, N. (1990). Object superiority: A comparison of complete and part probes. *Acta Psychologica, 73,* 225–243.

Davidoff, J., & Landis, T. (1990). Recognition of unfamiliar faces in prosopagnosia. *Neuropsychologia, 28 (11),* 1143–1161.

de Gelder, B. (1999). *Inversion superiority in prosopagnosia extends to objects.* Manuscript submitted for publication.

de Gelder, B., Bachoud-Levi, A.C., & Degos, J.D. (1998). Inversion superiority in visual agnosia may be common to a variety of orientation polarised objects besides faces. *Vision Research, 38,* 2855–2861.

de Gelder, B., Rossion, B., & Pourtois, G.R.C. (1998). Normal face recognition is lost with age. *39th Annual Meeting of the Psychonomic Society,* 19–22 November.

de Gelder, B., Rouw, R., & Rossion, B. (1999). *Early stages of face processing: Contrasting acquired and developmental prosopagnosia.* Manuscript submitted for publication.

de Gelder, B., Teunisse, J.P., & Bertelson, P. (1993). *In search of a lost effect: Face superiority and its normal or impaired development.* International Conference on face Processing. Cardif, September 21–23.

Diamond, R., & Carey, S. (1986). Why faces are and are not special. An effect of expertise. *Journal of Experimental Psychology, 115,* 107–117.

Etcoff, N.L., Freeman, R., & Cave, K.R. (1991). Can we lose memories of faces? Content-specificity and awareness in a prosopagnosic. *Journal of Cognitive Neuroscience, 3,* 25–41.

Farah, M.J. (1990). *Visual agnosia. Disorders of object recognition and what they tell us about normal vision.* Cambridge, MA: MIT Press.

Farah, M., Wilson, K., Drain, H., & Tanaka, J. (1995). The inverted face inversion effect in prosopagnosia: Evidence for mandatory, face-specific perceptual mechanisms. *Vision Research, 35 (14),* 2089–2093.

Farah, M.J., Wilson, K.D., Drain, M., & Tanaka, J.N. (1998). What is "special" about face perception? *Psychological Review, 105 (3),* 482–498.

Gauthier, I., & Tarr, M.J. (1997). Becoming a "Greeble" expert: Exploring mechanisms for face recognition. *Vision Research, 37,* 1673–1682.

Gauthier, I., Tarr, M.J., Anderson, A.W., Skudlarski, P., & Gore, J.C. (1999). Activation of the middle fusiform "face area" increases with expertise in recognizing novel objects. *Nature Neuroscience, 2 (6),* 568–573.

Homa, D.B., Haver, B., & Schwartz, T. (1976). Perceptibility of schematic face stimuli: Evidence for a perceptual gestalt. *Memory and Cognition, 4,* 176–285.

Humphreys, G.W., & Riddoch, M.J. (1987). *To see but not to see.* Hove, UK: Lawrence Erlbaum Associates Ltd.

Jeffreys, D.A. (1996). Evoked potential studies of face and object processing. *Visual Cognition, 3,* 1–38.

Kanwisher, N., McDermott, J., & Chun, M. (1997a). The fusiform face area: A module for the visual representation of faces. *Journal of Neuroscience, 17,* 4302–4311.

Kanwisher, N., Tong, F., & Nakayama, K. (1998). The effect of face inversion on the human fusiform face area. *Cognition, 68,* B1–B11.

Kanwisher, N., Weinrib, O., Tong, F., & Nakayama, K. (1997b). Response of the human fusiform face area to facelike stimuli. *Society of Neurosciences Abstracts, 23,* 2229.

Levine, D.N., & Calvanio, R. (1989). Prosopagnosia: A defect in visual configural processing. *Brain and Cognition, 10,* 149–170.

Levine, D.N., Calvanio, R., & Wolfe. E. (1980). Disorders of visual behaviour following bilateral posterior cerebral lesions. *Psychological Research, 41,* 217–234.

Levine, D.N., Warach, J., & Farah, M.J. (1985). Two visual systems in mental imagery: Dissociation of "what" and "where" in imagery disorders due to bilateral posterior cerebral lesions. *Neurology, 35,* 1010–1018.

McNeil, J., & Warrington, E. (1993). Prosopagnosia: A face-specific disorder. *Quarterly Journal of Experimental Psychology: Human Experimental Psychology, 46A(1),* 1–10.

Mermelstein, R., Banks, W., & Prinzmetal, W. (1979). Figural goodness effects in perception and memory. *Perception and Psychophysics, 26(6),* 472–480.

Moscovitch, M. Winocur, G., & Behrmann, M. (1997). What is special about face recognition: Nineteen experiments on a person with visual object agnosia and dyslexia but normal face recognition. *Journal of Cognitive Neuroscience, 9,* 555–604.

Reicher, G.M. (1969). Perceptual recognition as a function of meaningfulness of stimulus material. *Journal of Experimental Psychology, 81,* 274–280.

Repp, B.H. (1984). Categorical perception: Issues, methods, findings. *Speech and Language: Advances in Basic Research and Practise, 10,* 234–275.

Rhodes, G. (1998). Looking at faces: First-order and second-order features as determinants of facial appearance. *Perception, 17,* 43–63.

Rhodes, G., Brake., S., & Atkinson, A.P. (1993). What's lost in inverted faces? *Cognition, 47,* 25–57.

Riddoch, J.M., & Humphreys, G.W. (1987). A case of integrative visual agnosia. *Brain, 110,* 1431–1462.

Schweich, M., & Bruyer, R. (1983). Heterogeneity in the cognitive manifestations of prosopagnosia: The study of a group of single cases. *Cognitive Neuropsychology, 10* (6), 529–547.

Suzuki, S., & Cavanagh, P. (1995). Facial oganisation blocks accesses to low-level features: An object inferiority effect. *Journal of Experimental Psychology: Human Perception and Performance, 21* (4), 901–913.

Tanaka, J.W., & Farah, M.J. (1993). Parts and wholes in face recognition. *Quarterly Journal of Experimental Psychology, 46A,* 225–245.

Tanaka, J.W., & Gauthier, I. (1997). Expertise in object and face recognition. *The Psychology of Learning and Motivation, 36,* 83–125.

Tarr, M.J., Gauthier, I., & Behrmann, M. (1998). *Measuring prosopagnosic patients' recognition sensitivity and bias for faces and objects using ROC curves.* Cognitive Neuroscience Society Annual Meeting, san Francisco, CA April 5–7.

Teuber, H.L. (1968). Alteration of perception and memory in man. In L. Weiskrantz (Ed.), *Analysis of behavioural change.* New York: Harper & Row.

Tranel, D., Damasio, A.R., & Damasio, H. (1988). Intact recognition of facial expression, gender and age in patients with impaired recognition of face identity. *Neurology, 38,* 690–696.

Valentine, T. (1989). Upside-down faces: A review of the effect of inversion upon face recognition. *British Journal of Psychology, 79,* 471–491.

Van Santen, J.P.H., & Jonides, J. (1978). A replication of the face-superiority effect. *Bulletin of Psychonomic Society, 12,* 378–388.

Wojciulik, E., Kanwisher, N., & Driver, J. (1988). Modulation of activity in the fusiform face area by covert attention: An fMRI study. *Journal of Neurophysiology, 79,* 1574–1579.

Yin, R.K. (1969). Looking at upside-down faces. *Journal of Experimental Psychology, 81,* 141–145.

Yin, R.K. (1970). Face recognition by brain-injured patients. A dissociable ability? *Neuropsychologia, 8,* 395–402.

Young, A.W., Hellawell, D., & Hay, D.C. (1987). Configural information in face perception. *Perception, 16,* 747–759.

APPENDIX A

Experiment 2A and 3A: Matching Whole Faces

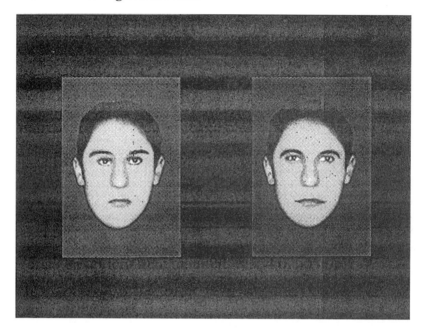

Experiment 2B and 3B: Matching Whole Faces to Face Parts

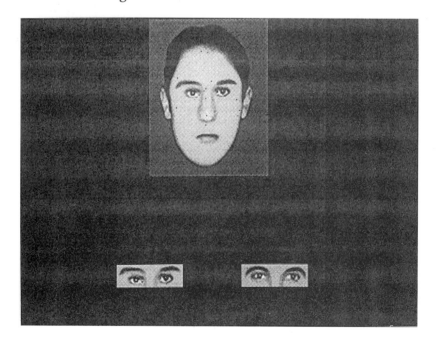

COGNITIVE NEUROPSYCHOLOGY, 2000 17 (1/2/3), 103–116

ATTENTIONAL MODULATIONS OF EVENT-RELATED BRAIN POTENTIALS SENSITIVE TO FACES

Martin Eimer

University of Cambridge, UK

Event-related brain potentials (ERPs) were recorded in response to centrally and peripherally presented faces and chairs under conditions where one stimulus category was attended and the other unattended. It was studied whether selective attention affects ERP components sensitive to the presence of faces. When compared with chairs, faces elicited larger N1 amplitudes at lateral temporal electrodes and a midline positivity in the same latency range. The latter effect was only found for central faces. Attention to centrally presented faces was reflected in enhanced posterior N1 amplitudes. This effect may be related to an attentional modulation of processing within face-specific brain areas. It was not elicited by chairs or peripheral faces. Beyond 200msec post-stimulus, a category-unspecific attentional negativity was found at all recording sites for centrally and peripherally presented face and nonface stimuli.

INTRODUCTION

Evidence from numerous sources suggests that the perception of faces is qualitatively different from the perception of other types of objects. Whereas object recognition is assumed to proceed by decomposing objects into component parts on the basis of low-level edge and contour features (Biederman, 1987; Marr & Nishihara, 1978), face recognition seems to be based on more holistic representations. Object recognition is efficient with line drawings (Biederman & Ju, 1988), whereas face identification is impaired with line drawings as compared with photographs (Davies, Ellis, & Shepherd, 1978). Face recognition is more affected by object inversion than is the recognition of other object classes (face inversion effect: Valentine, 1988; Yin, 1969), which led Diamond and Carey (1986) to argue that face recognition depends on an analysis

of prototypical configurations of face components. Farah (1991) suggested that different types of representations underlie face and object recognition. In object recognition, representations are employed where wholes are decomposed into multiple simple parts, whereas face recognition depends on representations of complex wholes without part decomposition. Recent evidence for this comes from a neuropsychological case study of Moscovitch, Winocur, and Behrmann (1997), who studied a patient with severe object agnosia and dyslexia, with face recognition apparently spared. This patient performed normally in recognising photographs of famous people and caricatures, and in judging family resemblance. In contrast, when inverted or fractured faces were shown, recognition and perceptual matching performance was impaired. This suggests that a "holistic" face recognition system operates effectively in isolation upon

Requests for reprints should be addressed to Martin Eimer, Department of Experimental Psychology, University of Cambridge, Downing Street, Cambridge CB2 3EB, UK (Email: me209@cam.ac.uk).

This research has been supported by the Max-Planck-Institute for Psychological Research, Munich, and by a grant from the Human Frontier Science Program (HFSP). The author wants to thank Renate Tschakert, Monika Fahn, and Verena Pritschow for their help in conducting the experiment.

upright (but not inverted) faces, and detects face identity by analysing the configuration of facial features.

If the processes underlying face and object recognition are qualitatively different, there may be brain areas exclusively devoted to the processing of faces. Evidence for this has been found in electrophysiological and brain imaging studies. Face-specific cells have been located in the macaque temporal cortex in the inferior temporal gyrus and on the banks and the floor of the superior temporal sulcus. These cells respond strongly to faces, but not to other types of objects (Perrett, Rolls, & Caan, 1982). Some cells respond equally well to filtered images of faces that do not share any spatial frequencies, to face images with changed or removed surface colours, and to images with different contrast levels, suggesting that they are truly face-selective, instead of responding to visual features common to all faces. The configuration of face components is critical for some face cells; their activity is reduced when face components are rearranged, or when only single facial components are presented (Desimone, Albright, Gross, & Bruce, 1984). Further evidence for the existence of face-specific brain areas comes from functional imaging studies in humans. In a PET study, Sergent, Ohta, and MacDonald (1992) found a bilateral, right predominant activation of the fusiform gyrus, of bilateral medial temporal areas, and of the right parahippocampal region in a face discrimination task. Kanwisher, McDermott, and Chun (1997) compared fMRI activity during passive viewing of faces or objects and located a fusiform region that was selectively activated when faces were presented. A similar pattern emerged when faces were compared to houses, scrambled faces, or hands. Since this "fusiform face area" responded to three-quarter views of faces with hair concealed, its activity seems largely viewpoint independent and is likely to be involved in face recognition rather than head detection.

If there is a brain region devoted to the processing of faces, an obvious question is whether this region will be automatically activated by the presence of face stimuli, or whether its activity is modulated by endogenous factors like selective attention. If face-specific brain areas were activated pre-attentively, face stimuli should presumably pop out in visual search tasks against a background of nonface stimuli. Kuehn and Jolicoeur (1994) and Nothdurft (1993) tested this by presenting face targets simultaneously with a variable number of nonface distractors. Reaction time increased steeply with the number of distractors, indicating serial search. In contrast to the detection of low-level visual features, the detection of faces seems to require attention. Consistent with this, Wojciulik, Kanwisher, and Driver (1998) recently found attentional effects on face-specific fMRI activity of the fusiform face area (FFA). With retinal stimulation held constant, FFA activity was stronger when subjects were engaged in a face-matching task than when they had to match houses (see also Clark et al., 1997).

In the present experiment, event-related brain potentials (ERPs) were recorded from normal subjects in response to attended or unattended face and nonface stimuli. Previous studies found ERP modulations specifically related to the presence of faces, although these results are not fully consistent. Allison et al. (1994) recorded ERPs to faces and nonface stimuli intracranially and found that faces elicited a large-amplitude negativity with a latency of about 200msec in the left and right fusiform and inferior temporal gyri. Electrical stimulation of these areas resulted in a temporary inability to name familiar faces. Jeffreys (1996) reported a face-specific positive potential with a latency of 160msec that was maximal at Cz ("positive potential", VPP). A VPP was obtained in response to foveal faces, but not to faces presented with a horizontal distance of 3° or more from fixation. Bötzel, Schulze, and Stodick (1995) also found a VPP, and an additional negative peak at lateral temporal electrodes (T5, T6) in the same latency range. Based on dipole analyses, they suggested that the VPP may reflect hippocampal activity, whereas the lateral temporal negativity may be generated in the fusiform and lingual gyri. George, Evans, Fiori, Davidoff, and Renault (1996) observed positive potentials at midline sites and temporal negativities in response to faces as well as scrambled faces. In contrast to Bötzel et al. (1995), they argued that these effects are caused by a single neural generator in the parahippocampal and fusiform gyri that is oriented in a way that produces a polarity reversal at the scalp surface between T5/T6 and Cz. Bentin, Allison, Puce, Perez, and McCarthy (1996) also recorded ERPs to face and nonface stimuli and found that faces elicited a negative potential with a latency of 170msec (N170) at lateral posterior temporal sites and a frontocentral positivity of slightly longer latency (P190). No N170 was triggered by cars, hands, furniture, or animal faces, nor, in contrast to George et al. (1996), by scrambled faces. According to Bentin et al. (1996), the N170 and the VPP are most likely to be caused by different generators, although their functional relationship is still unclear. Attentional modulations of these face-specific ERP components have not yet been investigated.

In the present experiment, ERPs were recorded in response to single centrally or peripherally presented face and nonface stimuli (chairs). Examples of these stimuli are shown in Fig. 1. The subjects' task was to attend to faces or chairs in order to detect target stimuli within this category (immediate repetitions of items in parts A and C, predefined target items in part B). Attention instructions were varied between blocks. In parts A and B, all stimuli were presented at fixation. In part C, stimuli were delivered in the left or right visual field centred about 3.5° horizontally displaced from fixation. In contrast to the Wojciulik et al. (1998) fMRI study, where attended and unattended stimuli appeared at different locations, so that some of the observed effects may have been due to location-specific sensory gating processes, all face and chair stimuli were presented in random sequence at fixation or unpredictably in the left or right visual field. Chairs were chosen as nonface items because within-category discrimination difficulties for face and nonface stimuli needed to be be approximately equal. Similar to faces, the chairs employed in this study differed only with respect to the properties and configuration of their component parts.

The subsequent analyses consisted of two steps. First, ERPs elicited by face and nonface stimuli were compared to find out whether ERP components are selectively sensitive to the presence of faces. Based on results of previous ERP studies, faces were expected to elicit enhanced negativities at lateral temporal electrodes and an enlarged positivity (VPP) at midline electrodes with a latency of 150–180msec post-stimulus. Such effects may, however, be restricted to faces presented at fixation, as Jeffreys (1996) found no VPP component for lateralised faces. Second, ERPs elicited in blocks where the respective stimulus category (face or chair) was relevant were compared to ERPs elicited by faces or chairs in blocks where the other category was relevant. If attention affected the processing of face stimuli within face-specific brain regions, this could be reflected in systematic attentional modulations of face-specific ERP responses. No such attentional effects should be observed for nonface (chair) stimuli. If attention affected object identification in an unspecific way, similar attentional modulations should be observed for face and nonface stimuli. An additional analysis was conducted in part B, where subjects had to detect a predefined target item. ERPs to male and female nontarget faces were compared between blocks where a face of the same sex or the opposite sex served as target. Differences between these waveforms would reflect effects of attention directed to male or female faces.

METHODS

Subjects

Thirteen paid volunteers participated in the experiment. One of them had to be excluded because of excessive eye blink activity. Thus 12 subjects (10 female), aged 19–36 years (mean age: 27.4 years) remained in the sample. All subjects were right-handed and had normal or corrected-to-normal vision.

Stimuli and Apparatus

Subjects were seated in a dimly lit, electrically shielded, and sound attenuated cabin, with response buttons under their left and right hands. A computer screen was placed 110cm in front of the subject's eyes and the screen centre was positioned on the subject's horizontal straight-ahead line of sight. The stimuli were photographs of faces and chairs that were digitally scanned, processed by graphics software, and presented on a computer monitor in front of a white background (see Fig. 1 for examples). Fifteen images of chairs, and 9 images of male and female faces (resulting in a total of 18 face photographs) were used. All face images showed a frontal view, with eyes positioned in the middle of the image. Chair and face stimuli occupied a visual angle of approximately $3° \times 4.5°$. All stimuli were presented for 200msec, and successive stimulus presentations were separated by intertrial intervals of 1200msec. In the peripheral presentation condition (part C, see following), a small fixation cross (subtending a visual angle of about $0.2° \times 0.2°$) was continuously present at the screen centre. In parts A and B, all stimuli were presented at the centre of the screen. In part C, stimuli were presented in random order on the left or right side of the screen, with a horizontal distance of 3.5° from central fixation to the centre of the stimulus.

Procedure

The experiment consisted of 16 experimental blocks, divided into 3 experimental parts (A, B, and C). The order in which these parts were delivered was balanced across subjects. In all blocks, a sequence of 80 nontarget stimuli (faces and chairs) and a variable number of potential targets were presented and subjects were instructed to respond with a left or right button press to infrequently delivered relevant target items. Nontarget stimuli were selected randomly for each trial, and a total number of 20 male faces, 20 female faces, and 40 chairs was presented as nontargets. Part A consisted of four blocks, and the subjects' task was to attend to a stimulus category (faces or chairs) that was specified prior to the start of each block, in order to respond with a left-hand or right-hand button press to immediate repetitions of stimuli that belong to the relevant category. Repetitions of stimuli from the irrelevant category were to be ignored. Each of the four possible combinations of attended category

(faces, chairs) and response side (left, fight) was realised in one block. In each block, 20 immediate stimulus repetitions occurred, with an average of 10 repetitions within the relevant category. Part B consisted of eight blocks, and the subjects' task was to remember a stimulus presented to them on the screen prior to the start of each block. A response was required whenever this stimulus was encountered in the course of a block. In four blocks the to-be-attended stimulus was a chair, in two blocks it was a male face, and in the remaining two blocks it was a female face. This critical stimulus was presented between 8 and 12 times in each block (10 presentations on the average), and subjects had to press the left or right button in blocks, respectively. Part C was identical to part A, except that all stimuli were presented horizontally displaced and in random order in the left or right visual field. Subjects were told that the position of a stimulus was irrelevant for their task of detecting immediate repetitions within the designated stimulus category.

Subjects were instructed to respond as quickly and accurately as possible to relevant target stimuli, to withhold responses to all other stimuli, and to maintain central eye fixation during the trials. To make subjects familiar with these task requirements and to ensure that all stimuli were encountered at least once before the start of the experimental blocks, one training block was run prior to each experimental part.

Recording

EEG was recorded with Ag-AgCl electrodes from Fz, Cz, Pz, T5, O1, T6, and O2 (according to the 10–20 system). EEG was measured relative to a reference electrode positioned on the tip of the nose. Horizontal EOG was recorded bipolarly from electrodes at the outer canthi of both eyes, vertical EOG was recorded from electrodes above and beside the right eye. Electrode impedance was kept below 5 kΩ. The amplifier bandpass was 0.10–40Hz. EEG and EOG were sampled with a digitisation rate of 200Hz, and stored on disk. The latency of manual responses (if present) was measured on each trial.

Fig. 1. *Examples of chair and face stimuli used in the present experiment.*

Data Analysis

EEG and EOG were epoched off-line into periods of 700 msec, starting 100msec prior to the onset of a stimulus, and ending 600msec, after stimulus onset. Trials with eyeblinks (vertical EOG exceeding 60 μV in the 600msec interval following imperative stimulus onset) or lateral eye movements (horizontal EOG exceeding ±30 μV in the 600 msec interval following stimulus onset), response errors, or overt responses on nontarget trials were excluded from analysis. For the ERP analysis, only the data from nonrepetition trials (parts A and Q and nontarget trials (parts B) were analysed. EEG was averaged separately for the three experimental parts for all combinations of stimulus type (male, female, chair) attended category (attend face vs. attend chair), and stimulus side (left vs. right, part C). For part B, separate averages were computed for blocks where a male or a female face served as target stimulus. For all analyses except one, averages obtained to male and female face stimuli were collapsed.

All measures were taken relative to the mean voltage of the 100msec interval preceding stimulus onset. ERP effects of experimental variables were determined by conducting repeated measures analyses of variance on ERP mean amplitude values within three post-stimulus time windows (P1: 90–120msec; N1: 135–180msec; Nd: 200–260msec). Repeated measures ANOVAs were conducted separately for centrally presented stimuli (parts A and B) and laterally presented stimuli (part C) on ERP mean amplitude measures obtained at midline and lateral posterior sites. P1 effects were only analysed for lateral posterior electrodes. The following factors were included: stimulus category (face vs. chair), attention (attend face vs. attend chair), electrode location (temporal vs. occipital for lateral sites; frontal vs. central vs. parietal for midline sites), and recording side (left vs. right for lateral sites). For centrally presented stimuli, experimental condition (part A vs. part B), was included as a factor; for laterally presented stimuli, stimulus position (left vs. right) was included. When appropriate, additional ANOVAs were conducted for a single stimulus category or electrode location. For the ERPs elicited by faces in part B, an additional

analysis was conducted to investigate effects of attention directed to male or female faces. Reaction times (RTs) obtained in response to target stimuli were submitted to a repeated measures ANOVA with attention (attend face vs. attend chair) and experimental part (A, B, and C) as factors. Greenhouse-Geisser adjustments to the degrees of freedom were performed when appropriate.

RESULTS

Behavioural performance

RTs to target stimuli were 487msec, 488msec, and 534 msec in parts A, B, and C, respectively. These differences were reflected in an effect of experimental part $[F(2,22) = 7.62; P < .008; \varepsilon = 0.738]$. Additional t-tests revealed significant differences between the RTs obtained for peripheral targets (part C) and for central targets (parts A and B). RTs did not differ significantly for face and chair targets (488 vs. 487msec, 525 vs. 542 msec, for centrally and peripherally presented faces and chairs, respectively). Incorrect responses to nontarget stimuli were observed in less than 0.4% of all trials. Subjects missed 2.9%, 1%, and 6.1% of the targets in parts A, B, and C, respectively.

Event-related Brain Potentials: Centrally Presented Stimuli (Parts A and B)

Figure 2 (top) shows ERPs elicited by non-target faces and chairs at midline and lateral posterior sites, collapsed over parts A and B. The resulting face–chair difference waveforms are shown in Fig. 2 (bottom, solid lines) together with the difference waves obtained in the lateral presentation condition (part C). At lateral posterior sites, P1 amplitudes were slightly larger for faces than for chairs $[F(1,11) = 6.45; P < .027]$, and an interaction between stimulus category and electrode location was obtained $[F(1,11) = 8.17; P < .016]$. Further analyses revealed that this P1 amplitude difference was significant at occipital electrodes $[F(1,11) = 9.12; P < .012]$, but not at temporal sites. In the NI interval, mean amplitudes to face

Centrally Presented Stimuli

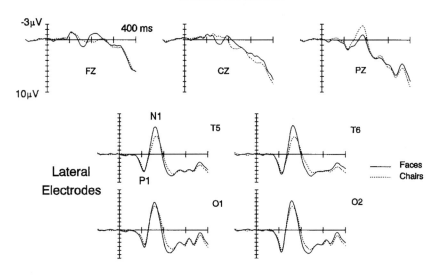

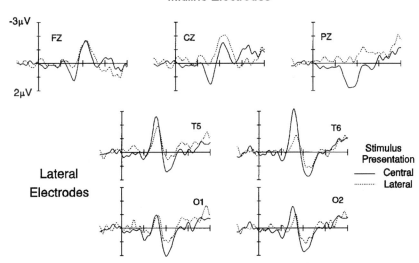

Fig. 2. *Top: Grand–averaged ERPs recorded at midline and lateral posterior electrodes in response to faces (solid lines) and chairs (dashed lines) in the central presentation conditions (parts A and B). Bottom: Difference waveforms obtained by subtracting ERPs to chairs from ERPs to faces in the central presentation conditions (parts A and B, solid lines) and the lateral presentation condition (part C, dashed lines).*

stimuli were more positive than ERPs to chairs at midline sites [$F(1,11)$ = 24.11; $P < .001$]. At lateral sites, the effect of stimuli category approached significance [$F(1,11)$ = 4.05; $P < .069$), and was accompanied by a significant category × electrode location interaction [$F(1,11)$ = 27.79; $P < .001$]. As can be seen from Fig. 2, faces elicited an enlarged NI as compared to chairs, and this effect was larger at temporal sites. Subsequent analyses revealed a significant effect of stimulus category at temporal electrodes [$F(1, 11)$ = 10.79; $P < .007$] but not at occipital sites.

Figure 3 (top) shows ERPs elicited by face stimuli in blocks where faces were attended or unattended. Difference waveforms resulting from subtracting ERPs to unattended stimuli from attended-stimuli ERPs separately for faces and chairs are shown in Fig. 3 (bottom). All waveforms were collapsed over parts A and B. No effect of attention was obtained in the NI interval at midline electrodes. At lateral posterior sites, a main effect of attention approached significance [$F(1,11)$ = 3.77; $P < .078$], and an interaction between stimulus category and attention was obtained [$F(1, 11)$ = 5.94; $P < .033$]. As can be seen in Fig. 3, an enhanced negativity in the N1 time range was elicited at lateral electrodes by attended as compared to unattended faces. No such enhancement was present for chairs. This was confirmed by additional analyses of ERPs obtained at lateral posterior sites that were conducted separately for each stimulus category. For faces, attention affected N1 amplitude significantly [$F(1,11)$ = 7.16; $P < .022$], and no interaction between attention and electrode location was obtained [$F(1,11)$ < 1]. In contrast to the category-specific N1 effect that was largely restricted to temporal electrodes, the attentional N1 effect on face ERPs was present at temporal and occipital sites (see Fig. 3, bottom). No significant effects of attention were found in the N1 time range ERPs to chairs.

In the Nd interval (200–260msec), attention affected ERP amplitudes at midline electrodes as well as at lateral sites [$F(1,11)$ = 11.67; $P < .006$; and $F(1,11)$ = 16.27; $P < .002$, respectively], with enhanced negativities observed when a stimulus category was relevant. At midline sites, these effects

were larger for faces than for chairs (see Fig. 3, bottom), as evidenced by a stimulus category × attention interaction [$F(1,11)$ = 10.09; $P < .009$] This interaction failed to reach significance at lateral posterior sites. At midline sites, an additional interaction between attention and electrode location was obtained [$F(2,22)$ = 5.31; $P < .038$; $\varepsilon = 0.544$], indicating that enhanced negativities for attended stimuli were larger at Cz and Pz than at Fz (Fig. 3, bottom). An interaction between experimental condition and attention that was significant at midline sites and almost significant at lateral electrodes [$F(1,11)$ = 5.04; $P < .046$; and $F(1,11)$ = 4.73; $P < .052$, respectively] indicated that these attentional effects tended to be larger in part B than in part A. Apart from this, no other interactions involving experimental condition and stimulus category and/or attention were obtained.

Figure 4 compares ERPs elicited by male and female nontarget faces when a same-sex or a different-sex face served as target. ERPs elicited by face stimuli of the attended sex were more negative than ERPs for unattended-sex faces, but these effects started later than the ERP effects of attention directed to faces as a category. No significant effects were found in the P1, N1, and Nd measurement window. An additional analysis was conducted on mean amplitude values obtained between 230msec and 300msec post-stimulus. An effect of attention to sex was found at lateral electrodes [$F(1,11)$ = 9.39; $P < .011$], and subsequent analyses revealed significant differences between attended-sex and unattended-sex faces at all four lateral sites. At midline electrodes, this effect failed to reach significance [$F(1, 11)$ = 3.29; $P < .097$].

Event-related Brain Potentials: Laterally Presented Stimuli (Part C)

Figure 5 (top) shows ERPs elicited by nontarget faces and chairs at midline and posterior sites ipsilateral and contralateral to the visual field of stimulus presentation. Face–chair difference waves are shown in Fig. 2 (bottom, dashed lines) together with the difference waves obtained in the central presentation condition. No effect of stimulus category on P1 amplitude was present. In contrast to

ERPs to Face Stimuli

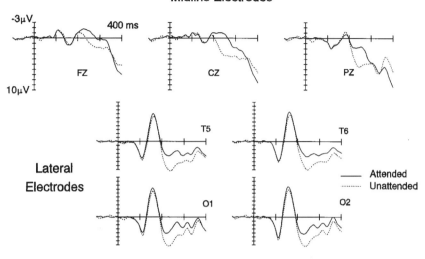

Attended - Unattended Difference Waves

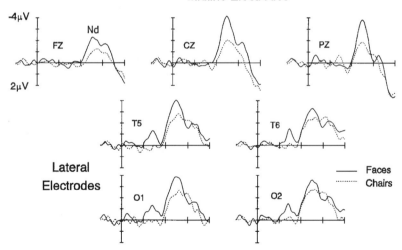

Fig. 3. *Top: Grand-averaged ERPs recorded at midline and lateral posterior electrodes in the response to attended faces (solid lines) and unattended faces (dashed lines) in the central presentation conditions (parts A and B). Bottom: Difference waveforms obtained by subtracting ERPs to unattended stimuli from ERPs to attended stimuli in the central presentation conditions (parts A and B) separately for faces (solid lines) and chairs (dashed lines).*

ERPs to Face Stimuli

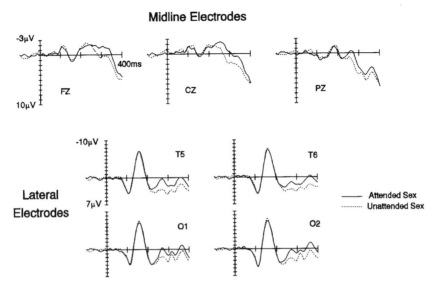

Fig. 4. *Grand-averaged ERPs recorded in response to faces at midline and lateral posterior electrodes in part B in blocks where faces served as targets, displayed separately for faces of the the same sex as the target (attended sex: solid lines) and faces of the opposite sex as the target (unattended sex: dashed lines).*

the results obtained with central stimuli, no significant differences between faces and chairs were found in the N1 interval at midline electrodes, but face-specific N1 modulations similar to the central presentation conditions were present at lateral posterior electrodes (Fig. 2, bottom). A category × electrode location interaction [$F(1,11) = 22.93$; $P < .001$] was obtained. N1 amplitude was significantly larger for faces than for chairs at temporal sites [$F(1,11) = 6.08$; $P < .031$], while this effect was not significant at occipital electrodes. A category × recording side × stimulus side interaction ($F(1,11) = 7.54$; $P < .019$] indicated that this temporal face-specific effect was larger contralateral to the visual field of stimulus presentation (Fig. 5, top).

ERPs elicited by attended and unattended faces are shown in Fig. 5 (bottom). No significant attentional effects were found in the N1 interval. In the Nd interval, a main effect of attention at midline electrodes [$F(1,11) = 6.5$; $P < .027$] was accompanied by a category × attention interaction [$F(1,11) = 10.67$; $P < .008$ reflecting enhanced

negativities for attended-category stimuli that were more pronounced with faces than with chairs. At lateral electrodes, a main effect of attention [$F(1,11) = 17.82$; $P < .001$] was present and no additional interaction was obtained.

DISCUSSION

The aim of the present study was twofold: First, we wanted to study differential effects of face and nonface stimuli on ERP waveforms, both for centrally presented and for lateral stimuli. Second, we wanted to investigate whether such effects would be modulated by selective attention. With respect to the first issue, the present results confirmed and extended previous findings. When compared with chairs, faces elicited an enhanced negativity at lateral temporal electrodes (T5, T6) and an enhanced positivity at midline sites in the N1 latency range (135–180msec post-stimulus). The latter effect was observed for centrally presented faces, but not when faces were presented laterally. Jeffreys (1996)

Laterally Presented Stimuli

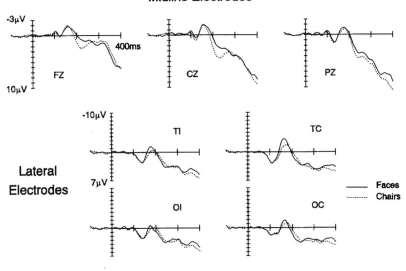

ERPs to Face Stimuli

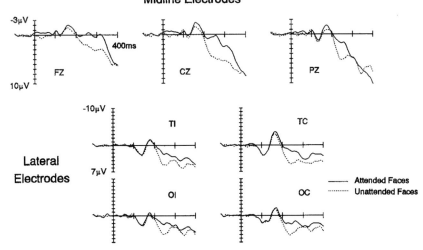

Fig. 5. *Top: Grand-averaged ERPs recorded at midline and lateral posterior electrodes in response to faces (solid lines) and chairs (dashed lines) in the lateral presentation condition (part C). Bottom: Grand-averaged ERPs recorded at midline and lateral posterior electrodes in the response to attended faces (solid lines) and unattended faces (dashed lines) in the lateral presentation conditions (part C). Lateral posterior ERPs are shown for temporal and occipital electrodes ipsilateral (TI, OI) and contralateral (TC, OC) to the visual field of stimulus presentation.*

reported a failure to obtain face-specific ERP effects (VPPs) for peripherally presented faces. Since his analysis was restricted to midline electrodes, he apparently missed the fact that similar to faces presented at fixation, peripheral faces elicit enhanced lateral temporal N1 amplitude. However, this effect seems to be considerably smaller for peripheral than for foveal faces (Fig. 2, bottom). The present study thus demonstrated that face-specific ERP modulations can be obtained in response to peripherally presented stimuli. The fact that face-specific temporal N1 enhancements were elicited by peripheral faces in the absence of any midline VPP may be seen as evidence against the idea that these two ERP effects reflect a unitary generator.

The face and nonface (chair) stimuli employed in the present study were presumably not completely equivalent with respect to their low-level visual features, which may explain why a slightly larger occipital P1 component was elicited by faces as compared to chairs in the central presentation condition (Fig. 2, top). It is, however, unlikely that such differences are responsible for the face-specific ERP effects observed in the present experiment. The effects reflected in the face–chair difference waveforms are very similar to face-specific ERP effects reported in previous studies where all sorts of different nonface stimuli were employed (Bentin et al., 1996; Bötzel et al., 1995; George et al., 1996). It is thus unlikely that these effects are primarily due to our specific choice of nonface stimuli. In subsequent, yet unpublished experiments in our lab, face ERPs were compared to ERPs elicited by different stimulus types (houses, objects, landscapes, human hands), and face-specific ERP effects were obtained that were highly similar to the effects reported here.

The second aim of the present study was to find whether face-specific ERP modulations are affected by selective attention. ERP effects of attention were present in the Nd time range (200–260msec) for faces and for chairs in the central and peripheral presentation conditions. In this interval, an enhanced negativity was elicited by items of the relevant category at midline and at lateral posterior electrodes. This effect is likely to reflect an attentional selection negativity (Harter & Guido, 1980). Broadly distributed negativities are usually found in ERP studies of attentional selectivity and are presumably related to the detection and representation of task-relevant stimulus attributes (see Näätänen, 1990). The fact that similar Nd effects were observed for faces and chairs indicates that the underlying processes are not specifically related to face processing. Attention directed to male or female faces affected ERP waveforms obtained in part B in a similar way. Enhanced negativities were obtained for attended-sex faces beyond 230msec post-stimulus. This effect, which was significant at lateral posterior electrodes, may reflect the detection of features that differentiate between male and female faces (e.g. hair style).

Prior to these Nd effects, an attentional modulation of the N1 component was obtained at lateral posterior electrodes in the central presentation conditions. In contrast to the longer-latency effects of selective attention, this modulation was restricted to face ERPs, and was absent in the attended-unattended difference waveforms for chairs (Fig. 3, bottom). Since the lateral posterior N1 has been repeatedly shown to be selectively sensitive to face stimuli, the observation that its amplitude is affected by selective attention directed to or away from faces may be interpreted as further evidence for an attentional modulation of processing in face-specific brain areas, in line with the fMRI effects reported by Wojciulik et al. (1998). As an alternative, one could argue that the N1 amplitude differences between "detect faces" and "detect chairs" blocks are not specific to face processing, but rather reflect differences in task difficulty. For several reasons, this is not very likely. First, RTs were not significantly different for face and for chair targets. Second, if the N1 effects were an unspecific reflection of task difficulty, one should predict analogous effects for ERPs elicited by chairs, which was clearly not the case. Third, differential task requirements between conditions typically manifest themselves in ERP waveforms as sustained negativities with durations of at least 100–200msec. The posterior face-specific attention effects observed in the present experiment were clearly more transient in nature (Fig. 3, bottom). More problematic for the idea that the attentional NI modulations obtained for centrally presented faces reflect the impact of selective attention on the processing of face-specific brain areas is the fact that these effects were equally large at temporal and occipital electrodes, whereas the face-specific ERP modulations were distributed temporally. Further experiments using more dense electrode arrays will be necessary to investigate the scalp distribution of these effects in more detail.

There were several other notable findings regarding the effects of category-specific attention on ERP waveforms. First, the two attentional manipulations for centrally presented items in parts A and B (detect repetitions of faces or chairs vs. detect face or chair targets) yielded equivalent attentional effects. There were no interactions involving experimental condition, except for the fact that attentional Nd effects beyond 200msec post-stimulus were larger in part B. Second, although centrally presented faces elicited enhanced N1 amplitudes at lateral temporal electrodes and a broadly distributed VPP at midline sites, early attentional effects were completely absent at midline sites. This apparent dissociation in the sensitivity of face-specific ERP components to attentional manipulations may be taken as additional evidence that the temporal negativities and the VPP do not reflect a unitary neuronal source. Third, no significant effect of selective attention on lateral posterior N1 amplitude was found for laterally presented faces. While this may indicate that selective attention affects the processing of foveal and peripheral faces differentially, such a conclusion may be premature. Similar to the fMRI activations reported by Wojciulik et al. (1998), face-specific effects were considerably smaller for lateral than for central stimuli (see Fig. 2, bottom). It is possible that any superimposed attentional modulations were simply too small to be reliably detected on the basis of the relatively small number of trials collected in part C.

In summary, the present experiment found enhanced NI amplitudes at lateral temporal sites and a broadly distributed VPP at midline electrodes specifically elicited by centrally presented faces. The former, but not the latter, effect was also pres-ent for peripheral faces. Selective attention was reflected in a category-unspecific Nd effect starting around 200msec post-stimulus, and in an earlier modulation of the lateral posterior N1 that was only observed for centrally presented faces. This effect may be related to a selective attentional modulation of processing within face-specific brain areas.

REFERENCES

Allison, T., Ginter, H., McCarthy, G., Nobre, A.C., Puce, A., Luby, M., & Spencer, D.D. (1994). Face recognition in human extrastriate cortex. *Journal of Neurophysiology, 71*, 821–825.

Bentin, S., Allison, T., Puce, A., Perez, E., & McCarthy, G. (1996). Electrophysiological studies of face perception in humans. *Journal of Cognitive Neuroscience, 8*, 551–565.

Biederman, I. (1987). Recognition-by-components: A theory of human image understanding. *Psychological Review, 94*, 115–147.

Biederman, I., & Ju, G. (1988). Surface versus edge-based determinants of visual recognition. *Cognitive Psychology, 20*, 38–64.

Bötzel, K., Schulze, S., & Stodiek, S.R.G. (1995). Scalp topography and analysis of intracranial sources of face-evoked potentials. *Experimental Brain Research, 104*, 135–143.

Clark, V.P., Parasuraman, R., Keil, K., Kulansky, R., Fannon, S., Maisog, LM., Ungerleider, L.G., & Haxby, J.V. (1997). Selective attention to face identity and color studied with fMRL *Human Brain Mapping, 5*, 293–297.

Davies, G.M., Ellis, H.D., & Shepherd, J.W. (1978). Face recognition accuracy as a function of mode of representation. *Journal of Applied Psychology, 63*, 180–187.

Desimone, R., Albright, T.D., Gross, C.G., & Bruce, C. (1984). Stimulus selective properties of inferior temporal neurons in the macaque. *Journal of Neuroscience, 4*, 2051–2062.

Diamond, R., & Carey, S. (1986). Why faces are and are not special: An effect of expertise. *Journal of Experimental Psychology: General, 115*, 107–117.

Farah, M.J. (1991). Patterns of co-occurrence among the associative agnosias: Implications for visual object recognition. *Cognitive Neuropsychology, 8*, 1–19.

George, N., Evans, J., Fiori, N., Davidoff, L., & Renault, B. (1996). Brain events related to normal and moderately scrambled faces. *Cognitive Brain Research, 4,* 65–76.

Harter, M.R., & Guido, W. (1980). Attention to pattern orientation: Negative cortical potentials, reaction time, and the selection process. *Electroencephalography and Clinical Neurophysiology, 49,* 461–475.

Jeffreys, D.A. (1996). Evoked potential studies of face and object processing. *Visual Cognition, 3,* 1–38.

Kanwisher, N., McDermott, J., & Chun, M.M. (1997). The Fusiform Face Area: A module in human extrastriate cortex specialized for face perception. *Journal of Neuroscience, 17,* 4302–4311.

Kuelm, S.M., & Jolicoeur, P. (1994). Impact of quality of the image, orientation, and similarity of the stimuli on visual search for faces. *Perception, 23,* 95–122.

Marr, D., & Nishiliara, H.K. (1978). Representation and recognition of the spatial organization of three-dimensional shapes. *Proceedings of the Royal Society of London, B200,* 269–294.

Moscovitch, M., Winocur, D., & Behrmann, M. (1997). What is special about face recognition? Nineteen experiments on a person with visual object agnosia and dyslexia but normal face recognition. *Journal of Cognitive Neuroscience, 9,* 555–604.

Näätänen, R. (1990). The role of attention in auditory information processing as revealed by event-related brain potentials and other brain measures of cognitive function. *Behavioral and Brain Sciences, 13,* 201–288.

Nothdurft, H.-C. (1993). Faces and facial expressions do not pop out. *Perception, 22,* 1287–1298.

Perrett, D.I., Rolls, E.T., & Caan, W. (1982). Visual neurons responsive to faces in the monkey temporal cortex. *Experimental Brain Research, 47, 329–342.*

Sergent, J., Ohta, S., & MacDonald, B. (1992). Functional neuroanatomy of face and object processing. A positron emission tomography study. *Brain, 115,* 15–36.

Valentine, T. (1988). Upside-down faces: A review of the effect of inversion upon face recognition. *British Journal of Psychology, 79,* 471–491

Wojciulik, E., Kanwisher, N., & Driver, J. (1998). Covert visual attention modulates face-specific activity in the human fusiform gyrus: fMRI study. *Journal of Neurophysiology, 79,* 1574–1578.

Yin, R.K. (1969). Looking at upside-down faces. *Journal of Experimental Psychology, 81,* 141–145.

EARLY COMMITMENT OF NEURAL SUBSTRATES FOR FACE RECOGNITION

Martha J. Farah and Carol Rabinowitz
University of Pennsylvania, Philadelphia, USA

Graham E. Quinn and Grant T. Liu
University of Pennsylvania and Children's Hospital of Philadelphia, USA

We present evidence of a striking failure of plasticity in the neural substrates of face recognition, which suggests that the distinction between faces and other objects, and the localisation of faces relative to other objects, is fully determined prior to any postnatal experience. A boy who sustained brain damage at 1 day of age has the classic lesions and behavioural profile of adult-acquired prosopagnosia. He has profoundly impaired face recognition, whereas his recognition of objects is much less impaired. This implies that the human genome contains sufficiently explicit information about faces and nonface objects, or visual features by which they can be distinguished, that experience with these categories is not necessary for their functional delineation and differential brain localisation.

INTRODUCTION

Localisation of function as a long history of controversy in neuropsychology. Since the 19th century neuropsychologists have debated whether the neural substrates of psychological functions are specialised and segregated or multipurpose and shared (Feinberg & Farah, 1997). Recent advances in theory and methods have helped to resolve the issue in favour of a high degree of localisation. Information-processing theories from cognitive psychology have guided task analyses, which are crucial for testing localisation because they allow the relevant individual psychological functions, rather than whole tasks, to be localised. Functional neuroimaging has expanded the domain of evidence that can be used to test localisation, from behavioural impairments in brain-damaged patients to regional patterns of activity in normal brains. As a result of these developments, we now have strong evidence that many higher functions are carried out in localised neural substrates.

Face recognition constitutes a particularly interesting case of a localised brain function. It might seem implausible that face recognition would be segregated in the brain from other forms of object recognition, given the apparent similarity of the two processes. This intuition calls our attention to the distinct functional and anatomical aspects of the issue. The hypothesis that face recognition is a localised function of the brain can be thought of as two hypotheses bundled together. One of these concerns the functional organisation of the visual system, and is the hypothesis that face and object

Requests for reprints should be addressed to M.J. Farah, Department of Psychology, University of Pennsylvania, 3815 Walnut St., Philadelphia, PA 19104-6196, USA (Fax: 215-898-1982; Email: mfarah@cattell.psych.upenn.edu).

The authors thank Idit Trope and Patricia White for their discussion of this case and access to the results of IQ testing, and Mark Johnson, Nancy Kanwisher, and two anonymous referees for helpful comments on an earlier draft of this paper. We also thank Adam and his mother for their time, effort, and generous cooperation. This research was supported by NIH grants R01NS34030, R01-AG14082, and K02-AG0056.

recognition are distinct in that they are carried out by separate systems. The other concerns the localisation per se of face recognition, and is the hypothesis that face and object recognition are functions of physically segregated populations of neurons.

A growing body of evidence supports the hypothesis that face recognition is functionally distinct and segregated from object recognition in the brain. Prosopagnosia, the impairment of face recognition after brain damage, can leave object recognition relatively intact (Farah, Levinson, & Klein, 1995; McNeill & Warrington, 1994). Conversely, some object agnosics have relatively spared face recognition (Feinberg, Schindler, Ochoa, Kwan, & Farah, 1994; Moscovitch, Winocur, & Behrmann, 1997). This double dissociation between face and object recognition implies that the two abilities are functionally distinct, in that either one can proceed without the other, and also implies that they are anatomically segregated, in that focal brain damage can selectively impair either one. Although inferences from brain-damaged patients concerning localisation are constrained by the size and systematic placement of the lesions, it would appear that object recognition is most dependent on left ventromedial temporo-occipital cortex (Feinberg et al., 1994), whereas ventral temporo-occipital areas of both hemispheres are necessary for face recognition, with some degree of greater specialisation on the right (DeRenzi, Perani, Carlesimo, Silveri, & Fazio, 1994).

Converging evidence for the anatomical segregation of face and object recognition comes from recent neuroimaging studies. A number of PET and fMRI studies have found distinct areas of activation during face and object recognition (e.g. Kanwisher, McDonald, & Chun, 1997; Sergent, Ohta, & McDonald, 1992). Although the precise localisation for face recognition is not consistent across these studies, the ventral temporo-occipital region is almost universally implicated.

As the issue of the localisation of face recognition reaches a resolution, another issue is raised: How might this localisation come about? Is the functional distinction between faces and other objects, and their segregation in neural tissue, fully determined at birth by genetic encoding, such that

visual experience with faces and other objects is not necessary? Or does our genetic endowment for face and object recognition require interaction with a visual environment containing stimuli from these categories in order for the normal organisation of face and nonface object recognition to be expressed?

Studies of an earlier stage of visual perception suggest that experience plays a significant role in determining localisation of function. Research with cats, monkeys, and humans has shown that lesions of primary visual cortex have relatively little effect when sustained early in life (see Payne, Lomber, MacNeil, & Cornwell, 1996, for a review). This implies that the localised functions of a mature primary visual cortex are not entirely specified genetically; in an immature brain other systems have at least a partial capacity to carry out these functions. Is the same true of the ventral temporo-occipital regions that normally take on the function of face recognition in the mature brain? Or is the unique commitment of this area for face recognition present at birth?

To answer these questions, we must observe the effects of early damage to the cortical areas necessary for face recognition. The most relevant case reported to date is that of a prosopagnosic girl, who sustained brain damage at the age of 14 months (Young & Ellis, 1989). From this case we can conclude that by 14 months of age, the delineation of faces as a separate category of visual patterns, and the localisation of face recognition, are effectively complete. However, 14 months' worth of experience with faces allows for considerable learning-based changes in brain organisation.

How early would brain damage need to occur, in order for there to be reasonable certainty that brain organisation and localisation had been only minimally affected by experience? Morton and Johnson (1991) have put forward a two-process theory of infant face perception, according to which early face perception is driven by innate factors, and later face perception results from the interaction of these innate factors with a learning-based system. Their research suggests that the learning-based system begins functioning at about 2 months of age. From the vantage point of Morton and Johnson's work, then, the onset of brain damage at 14 months is too late to disentangle many of the factors in question. In order to evaluate the role of experience versus innate factors in the functional delineation and localisation of face recognition, a subject is needed whose brain damage occurred well before 2 months of age, ideally as a newborn. In the present paper we describe such an individual.

SUBJECT

Adam is a 16-year-old boy who, after a normal gestation and delivery, developed Group B streptococcal meningitis at 1 day of age. Following this diagnosis, the only developmental deficit noted was a lack of visual interest. This was presumed to be the result of infarction of the posterior cerebral arteries,

a common occurrence in such cases. Later visual field testing suggested bilateral homonymous hemianopia, denser on the right than on the left, and denser inferiorly than superiorly.

Further confirmation of damage in the territories of the posterior cerebral arteries came from a CT scan performed at age 6 years, shown in Fig. 1, which reveals bilateral occipital and occipitotemporal lesions. These lesions, typical of prosopagnosia acquired in adulthood, clearly encompass more brain tissue than just the small "face area" identified in neuroimaging studies (e.g. Kanwisher et al., 1997). The present case study will therefore leave open the possibility of plasticity on a very local scale, with the function of one small part of the fusiform gyrus being taken over by another small neighbouring region of the same gyrus. However, Adam's relatively preserved object recognition

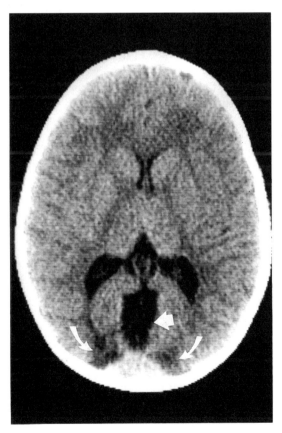

Fig. 1. *Axial CT scan of the brain, taken when the subject was 6 years of age, showing bilateral occipital (wide arrow) and occipitotemporal (curved arrow) infarctions.*

provides evidence against the form of plasticity most relevant to the issue of how face and object recognition come to be implemented separately in the brain, as the parts of visual association cortex that are able to support object recognition could not do the same for face recognition.

Adam's neurologic development has been normal except for problems with vision and visual recognition. At age 9 he was referred to a neuro-ophthalmologist because of his difficulty with face recognition. His most recent ophthalmologic exam showed esotropia, amblyopia of the left eye, and visual field abnormalities. Best corrected acuity is 20/80 for distance and 20/40 for near vision in the right eye and counting fingers vision in the left. Goldman kinetic perimetry performed at age 12 demonstrated a left central homonymous hemianopia and an incomplete right homonymous hemianopia with macular sparing. Although there were areas in the right visual field that appeared defective only for the left eye, this seemed attributable to the patient's concentration and cooperation with the procedure. Aside from some degree of incongruity in the right visual field, the results of perimetry were consistent with bilateral posterior lesions.

Adam's recognition abilities for both objects and faces appear more impaired than one would expect on the basis of these elementary visual deficits, with face recognition disproportionately impaired relative to object recognition. His performance on object and face processing tasks, described in detail here, conforms to the pattern of a classic prosopagnosic.

Adam has had a normal childhood in most respects, attending a combination of special education and mainstream classes at his local public school. On recent neuropsychological testing his verbal IQ was 101 and his performance IQ was 68.

INVESTIGATIONS OF OBJECT AND FACE RECOGNITION

The goal of the following investigations is to assess Adam's ability to recognise objects and faces, and to compare his pattern of performance with that of typical adult-onset prosopagnosia.

Object Recognition

Adam shows no discernable object agnosia with real objects in everyday life, but he does have some difficulty with photographs of objects. Line drawings pose a considerably greater problem, and when they are misidentified it is often for a visually similar item. The detrimental effect of going from realistic to more impoverished depictions of objects is typical of associative visual agnosics, including prosopagnosics (see Farah, 1990, for a review). In contrast, this pattern is not seen in other syndromes affecting high-level vision, such as optic aphasia. Another feature of Adam's performance that is seen in most cases of adult prosopagnosia is a difference between recognition of living and nonliving things (Farah, 1990); Adam is worse at recognising pictures of animals and plants than pictures of nonliving things.

Recognition of Photographs of Objects. Thirty colour photographs of inanimate objects were cut out of magazines and mounted on index cards. They included common household objects (e.g. cooking pot, keys), vehicles (e.g. plane, bicycle), and toys (e.g. balloon, skateboard). With 4 seconds to view each picture, he named 26/30, or 87%, of them correctly. He made errors on the teapot (calling it a "watering can"), the wooden stool ("a painting easel"), the screws (calling them "drill bits") and the rolls of toilet paper (calling them "rolls of tape"). All of these errors involve a visual resemblance between the object and his answer.

Recognition of Line Drawings of Objects. Stimuli were selected from the Snodgrass and Vanderwart (1980) corpus of line drawings, depicting a variety of common objects, buildings and other large outdoor objects, body parts, animals, and plants. Each drawing in the corpus is rated for complexity, familiarity, name frequency, and a number of other properties. We used the same subset of 85 drawings selected by Funnell and Sheridan (1992) in their study of semantic memory impairment, 43 of which depicted living things and 42 of which depicted nonliving things. Living and nonliving things in this subset were roughly equated for complexity, familiarity, and name frequency. The drawings were mounted on index cards and presented to Adam for 4sec each, with instructions to name each picture. He was asked to name each picture a total of six times without feedback, twice on each of three occasions.

Averaging over the six trials with each picture, Adam correctly named an average of 31.3/42, or 75%, of nonliving things, and 17/43, or 40%, of living things. This suggests that Adam has a mild or moderate visual object agnosia for nonliving things. Although exceptions may exist (e.g., DeRenzi, 1986), this is generally the rule in prosopagnosia. For example, case LH, a prosopagnosic who has been studied by a number of research groups because of the highly selective nature of his face recognition impairment (e.g. Etcoff, Freeman & Cave, 1991; Farah et al., 1995; Levine & Calvanio, 1989) named 84% of the same subset of drawings on which Adam obtained 75% correct. Another similarity to many adult prosopagnosics, including case LH, is that Adam performs worse with pictures of living things. For example, when tested on the same pictures of living things used with Adam, LH named an average of only 52% correctly.

The nature of Adam's errors in drawing recognition, as in photograph recognition, was invariably visual. For example, he misidentified celery as rope, a cigar as a crayon, and a broom as a spatula.

Face Recognition

In everyday life, Adam is profoundly impaired at face recognition. This was the problem that originally caused his mother to seek the help of a neuro-ophthalmologist. In group situations, for example in the school cafeteria, Adam generally waits until he is addressed to speak, because he is able to recognise voices but not faces. His mother reports that he never greets his school friends if he sees them unexpectedly out of context, for example on a shopping trip. In short, his prosopagnosia is profound, and has an enormous effect on his everyday life.

Like most prosopagnosics, Adam's face recognition impairment seems disproportionate to his elementary visual abilities, even when those elementary abilities are tested with photographs of faces. He has no trouble identifying the individual features of a face, and given sufficient time, can match identical photographs of faces quite accurately. However, when the camera angle or lighting changes between two photographs of the same face, his most diligent attempts at matching fail. This pattern is typical of prosopagnosia (Farah, 1990; Shuttleworth, Syring, & Allen, 1982).

The goals of the tests we performed were to establish his face recognition impairment with a set of famous faces to which he had ample exposure, and to assess his face perception ability with a standardised face matching task.

Recognition of Photographs of Faces. The Famous Faces test that has been used with many adult amnesics and prosopagnosics (Albert, Butters, & Levin, 1979) is not appropriate for a person Adam's age because he will never have encountered pictures of many of the people depicted. One source of famous faces to which Adam has been exposed is the TV show *Baywatch*. Adam's mother told us this is his favourite show, and that for the past 1½ years Adam has watched it for 1 hour every day. Luckily, the show has seven stars, and the studio kindly provided us with a press packet containing numerous photographs. We assembled a set of 10 clear, portrait-style colour photographs of the *Baywatch* cast, which we intermixed with 30 other photographs. Ten of the other pictures were clear magazine photographs of famous individuals with whom Adam was familiar (Tim Allen, Jim Carrey, Connie Chung, Bill Clinton, Newt Gingrich, Whitney Houston, Mick Jagger, Farrah Fawcett-Majors, Cybill Shepherd, and John Travolta), and the remaining 20 were magazine photographs of nonfamous faces.

Adam was shown these faces for as long as he wished to view them, and was told that some faces were famous and some were not. For each face he was asked who the person was, and was encouraged to guess even if he was not sure. He was unable to identify a single face, and refused to guess. We acknowledge that his refusal to guess could merely reflect an extremely conservative response bias, rather than an impairment in face recognition. However, on other tasks he showed himself willing to make errors, including both object picture naming and the face matching task to be described next. On these grounds, as well as his failure to demonstrate face recognition in everyday life, we suggest that a response bias account of his performance in this task is unlikely to be correct.

Matching of Faces. We used the Benton Test of Facial Recognition (Benton & van Allen, 1972), a standardised test in which black-and-white photographs of unfamiliar faces must be matched. When matching identical photographs, Adam proceeded in a slow and careful manner, comparing individual features of the faces and frequently commenting on the difficulty of the task and the specific features that he was finding helpful for a given face. Despite his abnormal approach, he obtained a perfect score on these trials. The slow but successful feature-based strategy is a common finding in associative prosopagnosia (Farah, 1990; Newcombe, 1979), and suggests that his elementary visual deficits are not responsible for his face recognition impairment. Also like a typical associative prosopagnosic, he performed poorly on trials in which angle and lighting varied, obtaining only 11 out of 21 correct. His overall score of 36 falls in the severely impaired range on this test.

GENERAL DISCUSSION

In every way that we have been able to observe, Adam appears to be a typical prosopagnosic. Anatomically, his lesions affect ventral occipito-temporal cortex bilaterally, as is the case with most adult prosopagnosics, and resulted from the most common aetiology of prosopagnosia in adults, namely bilateral infarction of the posterior cerebral arteries. His visual recognition impairments show a degree of selectivity comparable to most adult prosopagnosics. Although his object recognition is far from perfect, it is considerably better than his face recognition. In everyday life he is unable to

recognise faces, whereas his object recognition ability is fully adequate for activities of daily living. We have also reported four ways in which the qualitative nature of his object and face recognition is similar to typical adult prosopagnosics. First, the more impoverished the visual stimulus (as with line drawings relative to photographs and photographs relative to real objects), the worse his performance. Second, living things are more difficult for him than nonliving things. Third, when errors of recognition are made, the wrong answer tends to be visually similar to the correct answer. Fourth, when faces are successfully matched, it is by virtue of a laborious, feature-by-feature strategy.

Adam differs from the typical prosopagnosic in one major way: His brain damage was sustained as a newborn, long before he had ever recognised a face. The fact that face recognition ability in this individual could not be supported by other, intact parts of the brain (for example the parts of the brain that enable him to recognise objects), has direct implications for the mechanisms by which face recognition comes to be localised in the brain. Specifically, it suggests that prior to visual experience, we are destined to carry out face and object recognition with different neural substrates. This in turn implies that some distinction between face and object recognition, and the anatomical localisation of face recognition, are explicitly specified in the genome. Whatever role environmental factors play in the normal unfolding of separate face and object recognition systems, some factor distinguishing between faces and nonface objects and their separate brain localisations does not require experience with stimuli from these different categories.

REFERENCES

Albert, M.C., Butters, N., & Levin, J. (1979). Temporal gradients in the retrograde amnesia of patients with alcoholic Korsakoff's disease. *Brain, 36,* 876–879.

Benton, A.L. & Van Allen, M.W. (1972). Prosopagnosia and facial discrimination. *Journal of Neurological Sciences, 15,* 167–172.

De Renzi, E. (1986). Current issues in prosopagnosia. In H.D. Ellis, M.A. Jeeves, F. Newcombe, & A. Young (Eds.), *Aspects of face processing*. Dordrecht, The Netherlands: Martinus Nijhoff.

De Renzi, E., Perani, D., Cariesimo, G.A., Silveri, M.C., & Fazio, F. (1994). Propopagnosia can be associated with damage confined to the right hemisphere—An MRI and PET study and a review of the literature. *Neuropsychologia, 32,* 893–902.

Etcoff, N.L., Freeman, R., & Cave, R. (1991). Can we lose memories of faces? Content specificity and awareness in a prosopagnosic. *Journal of Cognitive Neuroscience, 3,* 25–41.

Farah, M.J. (1990). *Visual agnosia: Disorders of object recognition and what they tell us about normal vision.* Cambridge, MA: MIT Press/Bradford Books.

Farah, M.J., Levinson, K.L., & KIein, K.L. (1995). Face perception and within-category discrimination in prosopagnosia. *Neuropsychologia, 33,* 661–674.

Feinberg, T.E., & Farah, M.J. (1997). The development of modern behavioural neurology and neuropsychology. In T.E. Feinberg & M.J. Farah (Eds.), *Behavioural neurology and neuropsychology* (pp. 3–24). New York: McGraw-Hill.

Feinberg, T.E., Schindler, R.J., Ochoa, E., Kwan, P.C., & Farah, M.J. (1994). Associative visual agnosia and alexia without prosopagnosia. *Cortex, 30,* 395–411.

Funnell, E., & Sheridan, J. (1992). Categories of knowledge? Unfamiliar aspects of living and nonliving things. *Cognitive Neuropsychology, 9,* 135–154.

Kanwisher, N., McDermott, J., & Chun, M.M. (1997). The fusiform face area: A module in human extrastriate cortex specialised for face perception. *Journal of Neuroscience, 17*(11), 4302–4311.

Levine, D., & Calvanio, R. (1989). Prosopagnosia: A defect in visual configural processing. *Brain and Cognition, 10,* 149–170.

McNeil, J.E., & Warrington, E.K. (1993). Prosopagnosia: A face-specific disorder. *Quarterly Journal of Experimental Psychology: Human Experimental Psychology, 46A,* 1–10.

Morton, J., & Johnson, M.H. (1991). CONSPEC and CONLERN: A two-process theory of infant face recognition. *Psychological Review, 98(2),* 164–181.

Moscovitch, M., Winocur, G., & Behrmann, M. (1997). What is special about face recognition? Nineteen experiments on a person with visual object agnosia and dyslexia but normal face recognition. *Journal of Cognitive Neuroscience, 9,* 555–604.

Newcombe, F. (1979). The processing of visual information in prosopagnosia and acquired dyslexia: Functional versus physiological interpretation. In D.J. Oborne, M.M. Gruneberg, & J.R. Eiser (Eds.), *Research in psychology and medicine*. London: Academic Press.

Payne, B.R., Lomber, S.G., MacNeil, M.A., & Cornwell, P. (1996). Evidence for greater sight in blindsight following damage of primary visual cortex early in life. *Neuropsychologia, 34,* 741–774.

Sergent, J., Ohta, S., & MacDonald, B. (1992). Functional neuroanatomy of face and object processing. *Brain, 115,* 15–36.

Shuttleworth, E.C., Syring, V., & Allen, N. (1982). Further observations on the nature of prosopagnosia. *Brain and Cognition, 1,* 307–322.

Snodgrass, J.G., & Vanderwart, M. (1980). A standardised set of 260 pictures: Norms for name agreement, image agreement, familiarity, and visual complexity. *Journal of Experimental Psychology: Human Learning and Memory, 6,* 174–215.

Young, A.W., & Ellis, H.D. (1989). Childhood prosopagnosia. *Brain and Cognition, 9*(1), 16–47.

IS FACE RECOGNITION NOT SO UNIQUE AFTER ALL?

Isabel Gauthier

Department of Diagnostic Radiology, Yale School of Medicine, New Haven, CT, USA

Nikos K. Logothetis

Max Planck Institute for Biological Cybernetics, Tuebingen, Germany

In monkeys, a number of different neocortical as well as limbic structures have cell populations that respond preferentially to face stimuli. Face selectivity is also differentiated within itself: Cells in the inferior temporal and prefrontal cortex tend to respond to facial identity, others in the upper bank of the superior temporal sulcus to gaze directions, and yet another population in the amygdala to facial expression. The great majority of these cells are sensitive to the entire configuration of a face. Changing the spatial arrangement of the facial features greatly diminishes the neurons' response. It would appear, then, that an entire neural network for faces exists which contains units highly selective to complex configurations and that respond to different aspects of the object "face." Given the vital importance of face recognition in primates, this may not come as a surprise. But are faces the only objects represented in this way? Behavioural work in humans suggests that nonface objects may be processed like faces if subjects are required to discriminate between visually similar exemplars and acquire sufficient expertise in doing so. Recent neuroimaging studies in humans indicate that level of categorisation and expertise interact to produce the specialisation for faces in the middle fusiform gyrus. Here we discuss some new evidence in the monkey suggesting that any arbitrary homogeneous class of artificial objects—which the animal has to individually learn, remember, and recognise again and again from among a large number of distractors sharing a number of common features with the target—can induce configurational selectivity in the response of neurons in the visual system. For all of the animals tested, the neurons from which we recorded were located in the anterior inferotemporal cortex. However, as we have only recorded from the posterior and anterior ventrolateral temporal lobe, other cells with a similar selectivity for the same objects may also exist in areas of the medial temporal lobe or in the limbic structures of the same "expert" monkeys. It seems that the encoding scheme used for faces may also be employed for other classes with similar properties. Thus, regarding their neural encoding, faces are not "special" but rather the "default special" class in the primate recognition system.

INTRODUCTION

The current debate on whether faces are "special" or not (Farah, 1996; Tovée, 1998) is firmly rooted in research on humans. The evidence that face recognition in humans may be qualitatively different from the recognition of other objects comes from brain lesion studies (e.g. Farah, Levinson, & Klein, 1995a; Moscovitch, Winocur, & Behrmann, 1997; Yin, 1969), behavioural studies (e.g. Farah, Wilson, Drain, & Tanaka, 1998; Young, Hellawell, & Hay, 1987) and neuroimaging studies (Clark et al.,

Requests for reprints should be addressed to Nikos K. Logothetis, Max Planck Institute for Biological Cybernetics, Spemannstr. 38, 72076 Tuebingen, Germany (Tel: +49 7071 601-650; Fax: +49 7071 601-660; Email: nikos.logothetis@tuebingen.mpg.de).

1996; Kanwisher, McDermott, & Chun, 1997; McCarthy, Puce, Gore, & Allison, 1997; Puce, Allison, Gore, & McCarthy, 1995; Sergent, Ohta, & MacDonald, 1992; Sergent & Signoret, 1992). In parallel, we have known of the existence of "face cells" in the monkey brain for many years (Gross, Bender, & Rocha-Miranda 1969). Monkeys' face-recognition performance is remarkably similar to that of humans (Bruce, 1982; Hamilton & Vermeire, 1983; Lutz, Lockard, Gunderson, & Grant, 1998; Mendelson, Haith, & Goldman-Rakic, 1982; Nahm, Perret, Amaral, & Albright 1997; Rosenfield & Van Hoesen, 1979; Wright & Roberts, 1996). It is not surprising, therefore, that a great deal of neural tissue is devoted to the processing of facial information in this species, too. However, perhaps because the techniques are so different, evidence from the animal and human literatures is not fully integrated. The physiological evidence from animal research may considerably enrich the debate and offer information that is lacking in humans because of technical and ethical constraints. On the other hand, the monkey and human work may be difficult to compare because of large methodological differences. Here we briefly review the issues that are most debated regarding the possibility of face-specific mechanisms in humans and we consider relevant evidence from some recent neurophysiological work in the monkey.

During the last 15 years, the interpretation of virtually every piece of evidence for a face-specific system in humans has been contested. Newborns show a preference for facelike patterns (Johnson & Morton, 1991; Valenza, Simion, Macchi Cassia, & Umilta, 1996): However, this preference appears to depend on a crude subcortical mechanism termed CONSPEC, whereas cortical circuits specialised for identifying faces (CONLERN) and responsible for adult-like face recognition are thought to arise at around 2 months of age, presumably through repeated exposure to faces (Morton & Johnson, 1991; Simion, Valenza, Umilta, & Dalla Barba, 1998). A stronger inversion effect was found for faces (i.e., face recognition is more dramatically impaired by inversion than the recognition of other objects, Yin, 1969) but this effect was replicated

with dog experts (Diamond & Carey, 1986) and later on with handwriting experts (Bruyer & Crispeels, 1992). Faces seemed to be processed in a more configural (or "holistic") manner than other objects (Farah, 1996; Farah et al., 1995b; Young et al., 1987) but these configural effects have now been replicated with subjects trained to expertise with novel objects (Gauthier & Tarr, 1997; Gauthier, Williams, Tarr, & Tanaka, 1998). Patients with a selective deficit for faces (prosopagnosia; Bodamer, 1947) have been reported (De Renzi, 1986; Farah et al., 1995a), but recent evidence suggests that past studies have failed to control adequately for the dramatic impairment shown by such patients in the discrimination of visually similar nonface objects (Gauthier, Behrmann, & Tarr, 1999b; see also Damasio, Damasio, & Van Hoesen, 1982). A prosopagnosic patient was found to be significantly better with inverted faces than upright faces, contrary to the inversion effect obtained with normal control subjects (Farah et al., 1995a). This was interpreted as evidence for a face-specific recognition module until another prosopagnosic patient (de Gelder, Bachoud-Levi, & Degos, 1998) showed the same "reversed" inversion effect for...shoes! In neuroimaging, the existence of a cortical area that responds preferentially to faces in the right fusiform gyrus has been well established (Kanwisher et al., 1997; McCarthy et al., 1997; Sergent & Signoret, 1992). Recent studies (Gauthier & Tarr, 1997; Gauthier et al., this issue) indicate that the same area can be activated for nonface objects when they are processed at a specific (or subordinate) level (e.g. *Honda* rather than *car*) and that relatively short-term expertise with novel objects can also recruit the "face area" (Gauthier, Tarr, Anderson, Skudlarski, & Gore, 1999a).

The question of a special status for faces is complicated by the fact that "special" does not mean the same thing for everybody. Hay and Young (1982) dissociated two different aspects of this question: first, the possibility of a specific part of the brain processing faces (specificity), and second, the issue of whether or not faces are recognised in a qualitatively different way (uniqueness). We will consider how neurophysiological evidence in monkeys may inform the debate on each of these issues. First, however, we offer a summary of the anatomy of face recognition in the monkey and discuss the response properties of face cells in different cortical areas (for more details, see Logothetis & Sheinberg, 1996; or Logothetis, 1998).

THE ANATOMY OF THE FACE RECOGNITION SYSTEM IN THE MONKEY

The cortical pathway that originates in the primary visual cortex and stretches through the extrastriate areas V2 and V4 to the temporal cortices is known to be involved in pattern perception and recognition. In this pathway, the hierarchically highest association area that is exclusively visual is the inferior temporal cortex (IT).

Based on cytoarchitectonic criteria (Von Bonin & Bailey, 1947) and later also on the deficits that follow focal lesions (Iwai & Mishkin, 1969), IT was initially subdivided into a posterior (TEO) and anterior (TE) part. On the basis of both cytoarchitectonic and myeloarchitectonic criteria and of afferent cortical connections, the area TE was later subdivided further into five more or less parallel, rostrocaudally oriented cortical sectors termed areas TE1, TE2, TE3, TEm, and TEa (Seltzer & Pandya, 1978). Input to the area TE comes primarily from the area TEO (Desimone, Fleming, & Gross, 1980; Distler, Boussaoud, Desimone, & Ungerleider, 1993; Shiwa, 1987; Webster, Ungerleider, & Bachevalier, 1991), but also directly from V4 (Shiwa, 1987). Areas TE and TEO possess many other sparser inputs, send feedback projections to other visual areas and medial temporal lobe structures, and project to areas in prefrontal cortex, the limbic system, and to a large number of subcortical structures (see Logothetis, 1998).

Not surprisingly, many of the TE and TEO subdivisions contain cells that have different physiological properties. The area TEO has a coarse visuotopic organisation. Its receptive fields are larger than those of the neurons in area V4

(Boussaoud, Desimone, & Ungerleider, 1991). The cells here respond to moderately complex patterns (K. Tanaka, 1996). The areas TEa, TEm, and TE1-3 are primarily visual and can be activated by stationary stimuli of various complexity (Baylis, Rolls, & Leonard, 1987). Areas in the anterior-dorsal part of STS show sensitivity to motion, whereas cells in the areas TPO, PGa, and IPa are multimodal.

Face cells were discovered by Charles Gross at the beginning of the 1970s (Gross et al., 1969; Gross, Roche-Miranda, & Bender, 1972). In their seminal studies the authors reported a few cells that responded best to complex shapes, such as hands, trees, and human and monkey faces, providing the first evidence for a neurophysiological correlate for Konorski's gnostic (Konorski, 1967). A large number of investigations confirmed and extended these initial findings. Face neurons have been found mainly in the inferotemporal areas TEa and TEm (lower bank of the STS—within an area also called IT) as well as in areas TPO1 and TPO2 (upper bank of the STS—also called superior temporal sensory area or STP) (Baylis et al., 1987; Desimone, Albright, Gross, & Bruce, 1984). Face cells tend to cluster in small patches of 0.5 to 2.5mm across. Face selective cells were also found outside of the STS in the amygdala (Rolls, 1992), the ventral striatum, which receives a projection from the amygdala (Williams, Rolls, Leonard, & Stern 1993), and the inferior convexity of the prefrontal cortex (Wilson, Ó Scalaidhe, & Goldman-Rakic, 1993; Ó Scalaidhe, Wilson, & Goldman-Rakic, 1997).

RELATION TO THE ANATOMY OF FACE RECOGNITION IN MAN

The presence of face cells in several parts of the monkey brain may appear inconsistent with the predominant story in the human of a single "face area" in the right fusiform gyrus (Kanwisher et al., 1997; McCarthy et al., 1997). However, cortical responses to faces in humans are not limited to the right fusiform gyrus. In PET studies, several regions have been implicated in face processing, in areas of the occipital, temporal, and frontal lobes, although the control conditions in many of these studies make it difficult to know whether the responses are highly selective to faces (see Ungerleider, 1995, for a review). In fMRI studies of face recognition, the fusiform "face area" is often identified using a functional definition (Gauthier et al., this issue; Kanwisher et al., 1997; McCarthy et al., 1997). In such a design, a comparison of passive viewing for faces vs. nonface objects is used by experimenters to define in each subject the part of the fusiform gyrus that is highly selective for faces. The strongest activation in this case is typically an area within the right fusiform gyrus. However, several other areas are routinely found to be more activated for faces than objects, including areas within the left fusiform gyrus, bilateraly in the anterior fusiform gyrus (Gauthier et al., 1999a; Sergent & Signoret, 1992), the left posterior inferior temporal gyrus (Gauthier et al., this issue), and in the medial occipital lobe (Gauthier, personal observation). Recently, Puce, Allison, Bentin, Gore, and McCarthy (1998) have identified an area of the human superior temporal sulcus (STS) that responds to gaze direction and mouth movements.

The multiplicity of areas that show some degree of selectivity for faces in both the human and monkey makes the task of finding homologue regions particularly difficult. (This is not just a problem limited to high-level visual areas—see Kaas, 1995.) Because of the unavailability of cytoarchitectonic and connectivity data in humans, the evidence is mostly restricted to the functional properties of different areas. Given this limited information, we will consider two possible homologies between the human and monkey face processing systems. The first is a region in the STS of both humans and monkeys, which appears to be important for the processing of eye gaze and other facial expressions. The second is an area of the fusiform gyrus in humans and its putative homologue in areas TEa and TEm, which may be important for the identification of individual faces.

FACE CELLS IN THE UPPER BANK OF STS

In general, cells that respond to facial expressions and gaze direction are mostly located in the upper bank and fundus of the STS (Hasselmo et al., 1989; Perrett, Hietanen, Oram, & Benson, 1992; Perrett et al., 1991). Most of these face neurons were found to be 2 to 10 times more sensitive to faces than to simple geometrical stimuli or three-dimensional objects (Perrett, Oram, Hietanen, & Benson 1994; Perrett, Rolls, & Caan, 1979, 1982). They show considerable translation and position invariance, but their response is affected when a three-dimensional head is rotated around the vertical axis (they are somewhat insensitive to rotations in the picture plane). A detailed analysis by Perrett and his colleagues (Perrett et al., 1985, 1994) revealed a total of five types of cells in STS, each maximally responsive to one view of the head. The five types of cells were separately tuned for full face, profile, back of the head, head up, and head down. In addition, two subtypes have been discovered that respond only to left profile or only to right profile, suggesting that these cells are involved in visual analysis rather than representing specific behavioural or emotional responses. The viewpoint selectivity of these neurons is preserved independently of very large changes in lighting. For instance, a cell may respond more to a front view than a profile view regardless of whether the faces are illuminated from a front, top, bottom, or side light source (Hietanen, Perrett, Oram, Benson, & Dittrich, 1992). Masking out or presenting parts of the face in isolation revealed that different cells respond to different features or subsets of features. For most cells in the upper bank of the STS, different faces fail to elicit differentiated activity of the cells, suggesting that this cell population was encoding the object "face" rather than specifying the presence of particular faces. However, a small proportion (10%) of the view-selective face cells in this area appear to show some sensitivity to differences between individual faces (Hietanen et al., 1992).

Lesion experiments in monkeys (Heywood & Cowey, 1992) first revealed that removal of the cortex in the banks and floor of the rostral STS of monkeys results in deficits in the perception of gaze directions and the facial expression, but not in face identification. A later study (Eacott, Heywood, Gross, & Cowey, 1993) found that similar lesions can result in a marked impairment in learning novel visual discriminations (rather than for performing preoperatively learned discriminations as in the 1992 study), but this deficit was not selective for face or eye gaze discriminations.

Perrett and colleagues (1992) have suggested that STS face cells may signal "social attention," or the direction of another individual's attention, information clearly crucial in the social interactions of primates. A possible human homologue for this population of face cells has recently been described by Puce et al. (1998). These authors found that an area in the human STS (posterior portion of the straight segment of the STS) is involved in the perception of gaze direction and mouth movements, but not the perception of comparable nonfacial motion. Puce et al. also note that a number of neuroimaging studies have reported activation in adjacent areas for the perception of different types of biological motion (e.g. lip-reading or body movements).

FACE CELLS IN THE LOWER BANK OF STS

In general, face-selective neurons responsive to the identity of faces are found in a region straddling the lower lip of the STS, in areas TEa/m (Hasselmo, Rolls, & Baylis 1989; Young & Yamane, 1992). These face cells generalise over retinal position but are sensitive to orientation and size to a larger extent than cells in the upper bank of the STS. They show the same type of orientation tuning as Elaborate cells (K. Tanaka, Saito, Fukada, & Moriya, 1991), which respond to moderately complex features such as a vertically striped triangle. To the extent that Elaborate cells may be thought of as shape primitives appropriate to represent nonface objects, the face cells interspersed among them may

be thought of as features appropriate to the representation of different faces.

Hasselmo et al. (1989) studied face cells with a set of nine stimuli consisting of three different monkeys each displaying three different expressions. Neurons were found to respond to either dimension independently of the other. Interestingly, cells responding to expressions clustered in the STS whereas cells responding to identity clustered in area TE. Cells in area TEm showed effects of both dimensions. A quantitative study using correlation analysis between the quantified facial features and the neurons' responses showed that anterior IT face neurons can detect combinations of the distances between facial parts such as eyes, mouth, eyebrows, and hair (Young & Yamane, 1992). These cells show a remarkable redundancy of coding characteristics, as becomes evident from the fact that two dimensions were already found to be enough to explain most of the variance in a population of studied neurons. For example, all the width measurements, such as the width of the eyes or the mouth, the interocular distance, etc., covary with the general width of the face. Moreover, the neurons responsive to faces exhibited graded responses with respect to the face stimuli, with each cell appearing to participate in the representation of many different faces (Young & Yamane, 1992). In comparison, a population of face neurons in the upper bank of STS also exhibited a graded representation of the face stimuli but this population seemed to encode familiarity with the faces (and possibly some other social properties of the stimuli, such as dominance) rather than their physical characteristics. Face-selective neurons are remarkably sensitive to changes in facial configuration, and their response diminishes significantly if facial features are reduced or their spatial relationship is changed. Faces are not the only objects that elicit selective responses in this area. For instance, some cells in inferotemporal cortex also respond to the sight of the entire human body or of body parts (Wachsmuth, Oram, & Perrett, 1994). About 90% of these neurons responded to the human body with responses being selective for certain views, whereas the rest responded equally well to any view of the stimulus. An intriguing finding, which may lead one to question the simplistic view of "social" face cells in the upper bank of the STS and identity face cells in the lower bank of the STS, is that of cells in area TEa that seem to code for actions. These cells were selectively activated for different instances of certain actions of the hand (e.g. only for manipulate, pick, or tear), and for many of the cells, the responses were independent of the object acted upon (Perrett et al., 1989).

In summary, face cells respond to faces significantly more than to any other visual stimulus (they respond at least twice as much, and often more, to faces compared to the best nonface stimuli). Although they show considerable position and translation invariance, they also exhibit selectivity for rotations in depth or in the picture plane. Most importantly, they appear to encode holistic information, as the entire configuration of a face is often critical for the neuron to discharge action potentials. At this point, population of face cells in TEa/m (lower bank of STS) represents the most likely homologue of the human fusiform face area, since these cell populations are thought to provide distributed representations about face identity (Rolls & Tovée, 1995; Young & Yamane, 1992).

METHODOLOGICAL ISSUES

A few technical aspects of single-cell recording may be worth pointing out to some readers who may primarily be familiar with brain imaging techniques in humans. A limitation of single-cell recording is that researchers are limited to recording from only a small part of the brain at any one moment (in contrast to brain imaging techniques with poorer spatial resolution but a much larger field of view). In addition, there is no way to record systematically from a large and representative sample of neurons of a given brain area: One is more or less dropping a microphone slowly into a pool of firing cells until a single voice can be heard and isolated as an individual cell. Then, an experiment can begin in which the response of the cell is examined under a variety of conditions (for instance, its response to various visual stimuli). The experiment with this particular cell can proceed until the cell is lost (usually because of cell injury), in which case the experimenter can start looking for another "subject." These technical aspects are important because they limit some of the interpretation of the findings obtained by single-cell recording. That is, to characterise the response of a brain area that would be very homogeneous and would contain cells with identical properties, interrogating just a small number of them would be sufficient. Unfortunately, most brain areas are not homogeneous: In particular, the organisation of IT has been shown to be strongly modular. For instance, the preferred stimuli of different cells within a small cortical column of cells tend to be similar and there is a wide range of optical stimuli for different cortical columns in the same area. Even in areas TEa and TEm, only about 20% of the cells respond to faces. This makes it difficult to record from a large number of face cells. Given that faces are only one of the several categories that an animal may encounter, 20% is a very large representation and this could be due to the particular importance of faces to primates. The approach taken in the experiments described later on is to provide monkeys with extensive training at discriminating members of a particular object category. As the category gains importance for the monkey and as an animal becomes capable of very fine discriminations, this may lead to a more important representation of this category in IT.

Another methodological constraint is that the measured selectivity of any cell depends directly on the set of stimuli that it is confronted with. It is possible faces are over-represented in the sets of stimuli used in many experiments. As an example, Mikami, Nakamura, and Kubota (1994) report having used 411 photographs of human faces, 308 photographs of monkey faces, and 35 nonface objects as stimuli. They found that 45% of stimulus-selective neurons (responding to less than 20% of the stimuli tested) responded to human faces, 29% to a monkey face, 7% to food, 9% to a nonfood object, and 10% to simple geometric shapes. It is difficult to know what to make of these numbers given the biased representation of faces in the stimulus set.

NEURONS SELECTIVE FOR COMPLEX VIEWS OTHER THAN FACES

Face cells may be greatly represented within IT because faces are one of the few categories of visually similar objects that a monkey needs to discriminate. Consistent with this idea, more face cells in lab-reared monkeys are found to respond to human faces than monkey faces and cells often show better responses to familiar than unfamiliar humans (Mikami et al., 1994). This anecdotal evidence suggests that experience in discriminating visually similar objects of a novel category could lead to more neurons being devoted to this category. Logothetis and Pauls (1995) and Logothetis, Pauls, and Poggio (1995) addressed this question by generating expert monkeys on two different object classes. They used the same wire-like and spheroidal objects (Fig. 1) that had been studied previously in human psychophysical experiments (Buelthoff & Edelman, 1992; Edelman & Buelthoff, 1992).

The animals were trained to recognise novel objects presented from one view and were then tested for their ability to generalise recognition to views generated by rotating the objects mathematically around arbitrary axes. More specifically, successful fixation of a central light spot was followed by the *learning phase*, during which the monkeys were allowed to inspect an object, the *target*, from a given viewpoint arbitrarily called the *zero view* of the target. The learning phase was followed by a short fixation period, after which the *testing phase* started. Each testing phase consisted of up to 10 trials. The beginning of a trial was indicated by a low-pitched tone, immediately followed by the presentation of the test stimulus, a shaded, static view of either the target or a *distractor*. Target views were generated by rotating the object one of four axes: the vertical, the horizontal, the right oblique, or the left oblique. Distractors were other objects from the same or a different class. Two levers were attached to the front panel of the monkey chair, and reinforcement was contingent upon pressing the right lever each time the target was presented. Pressing the left lever was required upon presentation of a distractor.

After the monkeys mastered the task, they were tested for generalising recognition with a variety of objects, including pictures of real objects (e.g. cars, airplanes, fruits), and wire-like and spheroid objects. In contrast to real objects, the recognition of the novel objects was strictly view-dependent. The monkey could correctly identify the views of the target around the trained view, whereas its performance dropped to chance levels for disparities larger than approximately 40° of rotation in depth. For many wire-like objects the animal's recognition was found to exceed criterion performance for views that resembled "mirror-symmetrical," two-dimensional images of each other, due to accidental lack of self-occlusion. Initially, the animal's generalisation of recognition was also view-dependent for rotations in the picture plane. However, in the latter case recognition performance improved, and in a few sessions it became rotation-invariant.

Recording from the anterior inferotemporal cortex (mostly in the upper bank of the anterior medial temporal sulcus) during this recognition task revealed a number of cells that were highly selective to familiar views of these recently learned objects (Logothetis & Pauls, 1995; Logothetis et al., 1995). These cells exhibit a selectivity for objects and viewpoints that is similar to that found in face cells. The response of many object-selective neurons was invariant for translations within the foveal region (centre 5°) and large changes in size (often by a factor of four in a linear dimension).

To determine the features driving the neural responses, Jon Pauls developed a method in our laboratory of eliminating, scrambling, or occluding the displayed wire segments (Pauls, 1997). By systematically reducing the complexity of the stimulus with this technique, Pauls found that some cells were actually selective to a simple feature such as an angle, rather than to the entire wire configuration. In sharp contrast to such cells, however, other wire-selective neurons exhibited extreme sensitivity to alterations of the stimulus configuration. In other words, reduction of the stimulus was impossible without significantly reducing the unit's response. Almost all view-selective neurons were recorded around the anterior mediotemporal sulcus (Fig. 3).

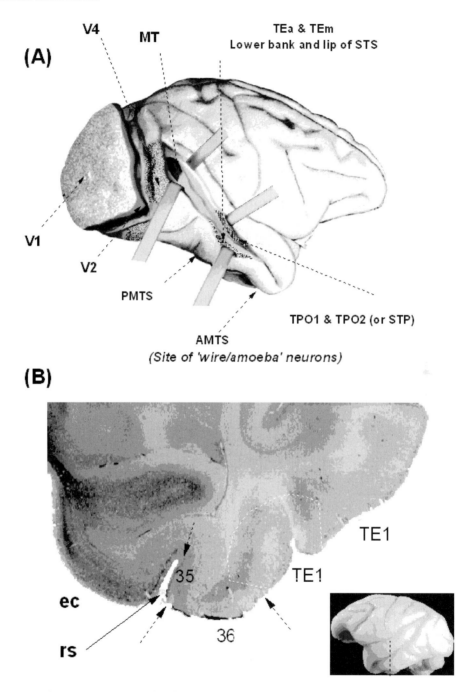

Fig. 1. *Lateral view of a monkey's brain and location of the wire-selective neurons. A. Lateral view with the superior temporal sulcus (STS) opened up to illustrate various visual areas in the temporal pathway. V1, primary (striate) cortex; V2, V4, second and fourth visual areas; MT (or V5) middle temporal visual area; PMTS, posterior mediotemporal sulcus; AMTS, anterior mediotemporal sulcus; TEa/m areas within the inferotemporal cortex; TPO1/2 areas within the STS. B. Histological slice showing the anatomical site in which the wire/amoeba selective neurons were found: ec, entorhinal cortex, 35/36 areas 35 and 46 respectively (perirhinal cortex); rs, rhinal sulcus. The vertical line depicts the position of the coronal section shown in (B). The arrows depict approximately the borders of the corresponding areas.*

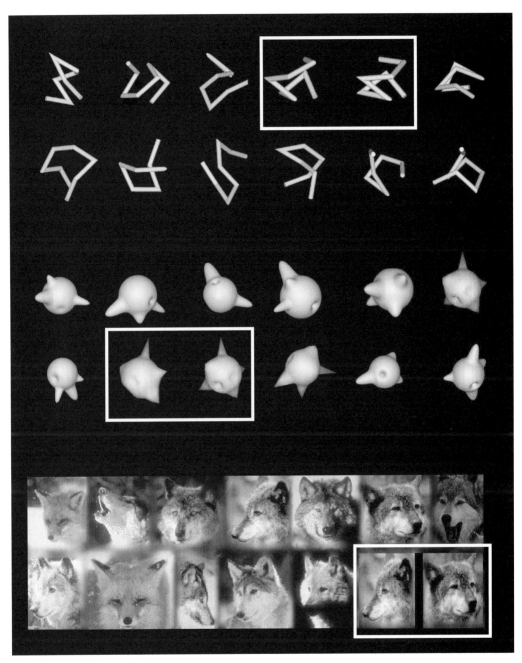

Fig. 2. *The wire- and amoeba-like objects used to study the neural representations that may be employed for recognising objects at the subordinate level. The exemplars of both classes are different barring the two within each white rectangle, which are two views of the same objects 90° apart. Recognising individual exemplars of these classes is not unlike recognising individual exemplars of other homogeneous natural classes. The wolves in the last row are all different barring those within the white rectangle. Again, the latter are two views of the same animal 90° apart. In each case, identification of a member requires excessive practice.*

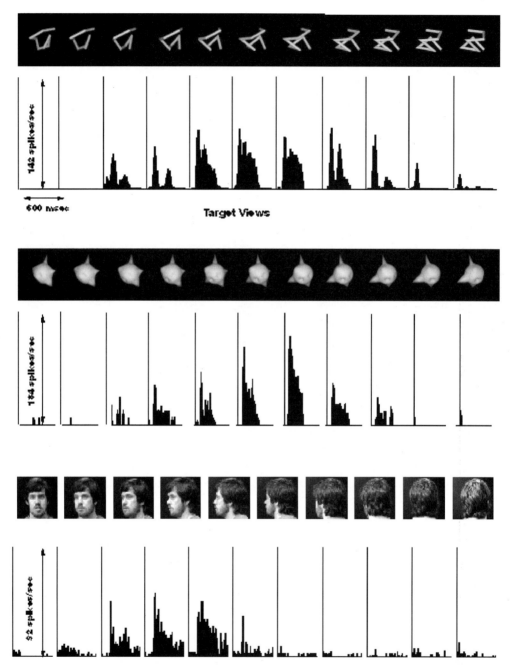

Fig. 3. *Responses of single units in the inferior temporal cortex of the monkey. The upper row shows responses to wire-like objects and the middle row to amoeba-like objects. The neuron responds best to a recently learned object–view and its response diminishes as the object is rotated in depth. For objects that the monkey could recognise from all vantage points more than one unit was found that responded to different views of the same object. Systematic decomposition of the wire objects showed that while some neurons could also be activated by parts of the object (e.g. an angle), others required the entire configuration, strongly diminishing their response even when only a single wire-segment was removed (Pauls, 1997). The bottom row shows responses of a face-selective neuron recorded in the upper bank of the STS. "Wire" and "amoeba" cells display view tuning similar to that of the face cells.*

IS FACE PROCESSING UNIQUE?

The finding of "expert" cells in monkeys trained to discriminate among amoebas and wires suggest that face recognition may find its homologue in the brain under the right circumstances. In Hay and Young's (1982) framework, one way in which faces may be special is that they could be represented in a different manner to nonface objects. In humans, evidence for unique face processing comes from a number of behavioural effects that are obtained with faces but not with nonface control stimuli such as houses and even inverted faces. Most of these behavioural effects measure some aspect of what is called holistic or configural processing. Simply stated, face recognition is often found to be more sensitive than nonface recognition to the disruption of the configuration of features: for instance, moving the eyes slightly apart or inverting the entire face so that relations such as "top of" or "right of" are changed (for reviews, see Farah, 1996; J.W. Tanaka & Gauthier, 1997). Evidence against face processing being unique comes from experiments where the same configural effects are obtained with nonface objects when subjects are experts with these categories (Diamond & Carey, 1986; Gauthier & Tarr, 1997; J.W. Tanaka & Gauthier, 1997). This suggests that configural sensitivity is not restricted to faces and that it is the particular experience with an object category, rather than its superficial properties, which determines the processing of its exemplars. Here, we consider whether IT cells may be thought to represent faces in a different way to other objects.

Face Cells Show a High Degree of Selectivity to the Face Category

Face cells in anterior IT are sensitive to configuration of features (Young & Yamane, 1992) and may be mediating the configural sensitivity that is a hallmark of upright face recognition. In a paper discussing face specificity in humans, Farah et al. (1998) cite the existence of face cells as converging evidence for faces being represented in a different fashion, because "the selectivity and strength of such responses [to nonface objects] are weaker [than to faces]". In a recent review article, Tovée (1998) notes that face cells are resistant to a stimulus simplification protocol (K. Tanaka, 1997) whereas the selectivity of most other IT cells can be reduced to rather simple stimuli. Tovée argues that "The 'specialness' of the face processing system will rest upon the determination of whether the face processing cells in IT have no functional equivalent counterparts for object processing, either in IT or elsewhere."

The single-cell recording experiments described in this paper may provide some evidence for nonface object cells that are the functional equivalent of face cells. A remarkable similarity exists between the properties of the face cells and those of the wire- or amoeba-selective neurons recorded from expert monkeys (Logothetis & Pauls, 1995; Logothetis et al., 1995). The latter type of neurons show selectivity to complex configurations that cannot be reduced without diminishing the cells' response to specific views and to views that appear to be mirror symmetrical. They also exhibit position and scale invariance, and are clustered in a specific brain location. This evidence is consistent with the possibility that the responses of IT cells are built from experience and adapted to the interactions of an animal with objects. In most cases, animals need to recognise most objects at a categorical level (e.g. cage, ball, tree) and faces at the exemplar level. However, if animals need to treat other objects like faces and discriminate visually similar exemplars, a number of cells within IT may begin to represent the features that are best suited to this task.

Face Cells Represent Face Identity in a Sparse Fashion

Several authors (Rolls & Tovée, 1995; Young & Yamane, 1992) have suggested that IT face cells may be representing face identity using sparse coding. On a continuum from "grandmother" representations (where a single cell represents a single object) to highly distributed processing (in which a very large number of cells contribute to the representation, each one carrying an infinitely small amount of useful information), sparse coding constitutes a case where the firing of each neuron strongly biases the probability of a response to an object. Face cell populations are thought to use sparse rather than distributed coding because each face cell at least carries a lot of information at the level of the stimulus class, responding more to any face than to nonface stimuli. Within the class of faces, however, the cells respond to many of the faces in a more distributed fashion. This type of representation has been suggested to be ideal for the discrimination of faces (Rolls & Tovée, 1995). Note that such conclusions are based on what is called information theoretic analyses, in which face-selective cells are first selected and later shown to provide more information about faces than about nonface stimuli. A comparable analysis for nonface objects would first require the selection of a population of cells that respond best to a certain class of nonface objects than to other stimuli. As discussed previously, this may be impractical for nonface categories of no particular relevance to an animal but may be feasible after an animal has been trained to discriminate among visually similar objects.

Some authors emphasise the similarities between face cells and other IT cells selective for elaborate features. For instance, Perrett and Oram (1993) note that in the anterior temporal cortex, both face cells and Elaborate cells do not generalise across orientation and size (whereas face cells in STP do). In both cases a rotation of 90° in the picture plane reduces the response by more than 50%. However, other authors have contrasted the apparent sparse coding for faces to the more distributed coding by which nonface objects appear to be represented. K. Tanaka (1997) has suggested that nonface objects are represented by distributed coding over a large number of IT columns, each containing cells selective for moderately complex features. In this framework, each shape primitive carries very little information about the identity of the object and the representation of nonface objects may be argued to be qualitatively different from that of faces, in that it would be considerably more distributed.

Recently, however, Kobatake, Wang, and Tanaka (1998) have trained monkeys to recognise 28 moderately complex stimuli (mostly combinations of 2 simple geometric shapes, these stimuli were less homogeneous than wires or amoebas) and found a greater proportion of cells responsive to the trained stimuli in trained than untrained monkeys. Furthermore, many of these cells responded to multiple members of the training stimuli, not unlike face cells. The discriminations learned by the monkeys may be supported by sparse representations and the number of cells that respond to a certain object may be partly determined by an animal's experience with this category (see also Booth & Rolls, 1998). However, experience with a visually homogeneous class of objects (e.g. the wires and ameobas) may be necessary to build up a population of cells that will generalise to novel exemplars of the category. When humans are trained with several objects of an homogeneous category, their expertise generalises to novel exemplars (for instance, configural sensitivity is found for untrained objects—Gauthier & Tarr, 1997). Given the similarity of behavioural performance in object recognition tasks between man and monkey (Logothetis & Pauls, 1995), we can hypothesise that expertise in monkeys would also generalise to novel exemplars of a trained class. However, such generalisation could be expected in monkeys trained with ameobas and wires, but not necessarily for animals trained with less homogeneous stimulus sets.

IS FACE PROCESSING SPECIFIC?

Even if we found that faces and objects are represented by common mechanisms in IT, faces could still be special in that they could be processed in a distinct and separate neural system. It may be that *specificity* (Hay & Young, 1982) in the location of cells for any object category is not a sufficient criterion to designate this category "special" (Tovée, 1998), presumably because specificity would not be unique to a single category (i.e. if face cells are separated from wire cells, then wire cells are also separated from face cells). However, regardless of the debate on faces, to consider the spatial organisation of object-selective cells is essential to the understanding of the temporal cortex organisation.

The area where wire and amoeba cells were found, the AMTS, is anterior to area TE and more ventral than areas where face cells are typically found in other studies. What this means is somewhat difficult to interpret, given the methodological constraints of single-cell recording. As in any single-cell study where there is no prior knowledge of precisely where selective responses are expected, Logothetis and colleagues (Logothetis & Pauls, 1995; Logothetis et al., 1995) recorded systematically from posterior to anterior areas of the temporal lobe, moving to a new area after a week or so of fruitless explorations. Once a first wire- or amoeba-selective cell was found in AMTS, the researchers kept on recording in this area without going back to more posterior regions. In addition, the AMTS was not systematically tested with faces in this experiment. In other words, the current evidence suggests that populations of expert object cells are found in a different area than populations of face cells with comparable properties, but this evidence is not as strong as it would be if it came from a neuroimaging experiment in which all areas of the visual system had been equally sampled at all time-points.

Evidence that face processing may be segregated from object processing in the human brain mainly comes from two different sources. The first is evidence from patients with selective deficits in face processing (De Renzi, 1986; Farah et al., 1995a). The selectivity of face agnosia is controversial, as many prosopagnosic patients also report difficulties with other visually similar categories (Bornstein, Sroka, & Munitz, 1969; Damasio et al., 1982; Shuttleworth, Syring, & Norman, 1982). Even in the case of patients who believe that their deficit applies only to faces, recent work has revealed a more general impairment for subtle, subordinate-level discriminations (Gauthier et al., 1999b). A second source of evidence comes from neuroimaging studies in which activation in the middle fusiform gyrus is found when subjects are viewing faces as opposed to nonface objects (Kanwisher et al., 1997; McCarthy et al., 1997; Sergent & Signoret, 1992). To address this evidence and inspired by the fact that prosopagnosic patients often have difficulties discriminating objects within the same category, Gauthier et al. (1998) compared brain activation when normal subjects verified the

subordinate identity of a picture (e.g. *pelican*) vs. the basic level (e.g. *bird*). They found activation in ventral temporal areas described as face-sensitive in prior studies. In this issue, a new study (Gauthier et al., this issue) verified that subordinate-level processing of nonface objects activates the small area that can be defined as face-specific in each subject. Thus, the presentation of faces is not necessary to engage what is often called the "face area." This region can be differentially engaged when the same nonface object is recognised at the subordinate vs. the basic level. However, faces appear to activate only a portion of ventral cortex dedicated to subordinate-level processing. These studies, which suggest that subordinate level processing accounts for *some* of the activation in the face area, are not necessarily incompatible with other work suggesting that *not all* of the activation in the face area can be accounted for by subordinate-level classification (Kanwisher et al., 1997). What may be happening is that the former studies focus on the fact that there is difference between basic level and subordinate level recognition of nonface objects in the face area, whereas the latter studies account for a different part of the data, pointing out that there is still more evidence for subordinate-level recognition of faces than subordinate-level recognition of nonface objects. A recent fMRI study (Gauthier et al., 1999a) has revealed that expertise with subordinate-level discrimination of novel objects (similar training experience as the monkeys in Logothetis & Pauls, 1995; Logothetis et al., 1995) leads to increased activation localised in the "face area." This suggests that the interaction of two factors, level of categorisation and expertise, may interact to produce the specialisation for faces found in the middle fusiform face area. In the next section, we consider how what we know of the monkey visual system can help resolve the role of these two factors.

Level of Categorisation and Expertise

Given the importance of level of categorisation demonstrated in behavioural (J.W. Tanaka & Taylor, 1993) and fMRI studies in humans (Gauthier et al., 1998, this issue), one may ask whether there is any evidence that this factor is important in determining the responses of IT cells. Unfortunately, no single-cell recording study has compared the responses of cells to the same stimuli when animals are requested to recognise it at different levels of abstraction. However, Logothetis and Pauls (1995) have trained monkeys to recognise objects either at the basic level (among distractors differing largely in shape, such as a wire vs. an amoeba) or at the subordinate level (for instance, discriminating between two wires). They found that the animals' behavioural performance was viewpoint-dependent in the case of subordinate-level judgements and viewpoint-independent in the case of basic-level judgements. This suggests that level of categorisation may at least have a similar importance for monkey and human visual recognition.

Two recent studies provided monkeys with experience with certain objects and later found cells to be responsive to many of these trained objects (Booth & Rolls, 1998; Kobatake et al., 1998). However, these studies differ in an important way from the wire-frame and amoeba study by Logothetis and colleagues: The different objects did not belong to what would be considered the same "basic-level" category (Rosch, Mervis, Gray, Johnson, & Boyes-Braem, 1976). This is because they do not share common parts and could be discriminated by the presence of a single feature (e.g. the way that the presence of eyes is diagnostic to detect a face) or simple relationships between parts (e.g. as for the presence of a nose underneath two eyes). In comparison, objects from homogeneous categories share common parts as well as the first-order configuration of these parts (Diamond & Carey, 1986; Rhodes & McLean, 1990). They can only be distinguished using subtle differences in the shape of their parts or subtle differences in the configuration of their parts (e.g. distances between different face features). It is expertise discriminating between objects of such homogeneous categories that is thought to mediate behavioural configural effects and the increased recruitment of the fusiform face area (Gauthier & Tarr, 1997; Gauthier et al., 1999a). Again, there is yet no direct comparison using physiological measurements of the difference between basic and subordinate level processing of objects, but the expertise of monkeys

discriminating between wires and amoebas may be most relevant to the debate on face recognition in humans.

In humans, recent fMRI results suggest that expertise with novel objects (Greebles) can recruit the middle fusiform face area (Gauthier et al., 1999a). However, at least one area, in the lateral occipital gyrus, showed a strong expertise effect, with more activation for Greeble experts than novices, and even more for Greebles than for faces. This lateral occipital gyrus area did not behave like the fusiform face area in all conditions: In particular, this region responded more to inverted than to upright faces, whereas the face area responded more to upright than to inverted faces. Thus, there may be a complex system of areas within the temporal lobe that is modified by experience with objects. This is consistent with the existence of face cells in many areas of both the human and the monkey brain. Similarly, AMTS may not be the only area of expert monkeys where wire and amoeba cells can be found. At this point, it is likely that further advances in comparing the man and monkey systems will require the addition of novel techniques such as functional MRI in monkeys (Logothetis, Guggenberger, Peled, & Pauls, 1999) to those already available in both species.

CONCLUSIONS

Both humans and monkeys are extremely good at recognising faces, a fact that is hardly surprising in view of the vital importance that face recognition has for the primate. An important neural system exists in both species for the processing of facial information. In the human behavioural literature, starting with Diamond and Carey's (1986) landmark study of dog expertise, a consensus has grown that nonface categories of objects can be processed in the same way as faces given similar task constraints and subject expertise. However, in human neuropsychological and neuroimaging studies, there is still an ongoing debate regarding the possibility that faces may be special.

Interestingly, the single-cell recording literature also converges to suggest that faces are not represented by IT cells in a unique fashion. Several authors, including C.G. Gross (1992), the pioneer in the domain of face cells, have suggested that face cells may appear more specialised than other IT cells only because face recognition happens to be an extremely demanding subordinate recognition task, and for nonhuman primates it may be the only identification task performed in life. Clearly, such an hypothesis leads to the prediction that a similar specialisation may also arise when the identification of members of other classes becomes the critical task at hand. This was tested in recent single-cell recording experiments. A remarkable similarity was found between the properties of the face cells and those of the wire- or amoeba-selective neurons recorded from expert monkeys (Logothetis & Pauls, 1995; Logothetis et al., 1995). The latter type of neurons show selectivity to complex configurations that cannot be reduced without diminishing the cells' response to specific views and to views that appear to be mirror-symmetrical. They exhibit position and scale invariance, and are clustered in a specific brain location. Since recordings have only been made in the inferotemporal cortex and mostly in AMTS, it is not currently known whether selectivity to these objects might not also be found in other brain structures.

Such results are consistent with behavioural and fMRI studies in humans showing that novel objects are processed in a more configural manner with expertise and can increasingly recruit parts of the ventral temporal lobe. However, whereas fMRI results in humans suggests that the very same areas are recruited for faces and nonface objects, single-cell studies in monkeys point to specialisation of different areas. These techniques are very different and it is important to note that fMRI could provide more convincing evidence than single-cell data for a *dissociation* between the location of face and object expert processing. On the other hand, the better spatial resolution of single-cell recording could provide stronger support for an *association* in location (e.g. if the very same cells were found to mediate expert representations of different categories). Paradoxically, the current data in fMRI suggests an association whereas single cell recording suggests a dissociation, albeit only in the location of

face and wire/amoeba cells within the anterior temporal lobe. Therefore, for both sources of evidence the interpretation should be cautious. In any case, faces are not unique with regard to the type of neural activity that can be recorded in a monkey's brain when the animal is coping with other classes of objects in the same manner with which it deals with faces.

REFERENCES

Baylis, G.C., Rolls, E.T., & Leonard C.M. (1987). Functional subdivisions of the temporal lobe neocortex. *Journal of Neuroscience, 7*, 330–342.

Bodamer, J. (1947). Die Prosopagnosie. Die Agnosie des Physiognomieerkennes. *Arch Psychiatr Nervenkr, 179*, 6–54.

Booth, M.C.A., & Rolls, E.T. (1998). View-invariant representations of familiar objects by neurons in the inferior temporal visual cortex. *Cerebral Cortex, 8*, 510–523.

Bornstein, B., Sroka, H., & Munitz, H. (1969). Prosopagnosia with animal face agnosia *Cortex, 5*, 164–171.

Boussaoud, D., Desimone, R., & Ungerleider, L.G. (1991). Visual topography of area TEO in the macaque. *Journal of Comparative Neurology, 306*, 554–575.

Bruce, C.J. (1982). Face recognition by monkeys: Absence of an inversion effect. *Neuropsychologia, 20*, 515–521.

Bruyer, R., & Crispeels, G. (1992). Expertise in person recognition. *Bulletin of the Psychonomic Society, 30*, 501–504.

Buelthoff, H.H., & Edelman, S. (1992). Psychophysical support for a two-dimensional view interpolation theory of object recognition. *Proceedings of the National Academy of Sciences USA, 89*, 60–64.

Clark, V.P., Keil, K., Maisog, J.M., Courtney, S.M., Ungerleider, L.G., & Haxby, J.V. (1996). Functional magnetic resonance imaging of human visual cortex during face matching: A comparison with positron emission tomography. *Neuroimage, 4*, 1–15.

Damasio, A.R., Damasio, H.C., & Van Hoesen, G.W. (1982). Prosopagnosia: Anatomic basis and behavioral mechanisms. *Neurology, 32*, 331–341.

de Gelder, B., Bachoud-Lévi, A.C., & Degos, J.D. (1998). Inversion superiority in visual agnosia may be common to a variety of orientation-polarised objects besides faces. *Vision Research, 38*, 2855–2861.

De Renzi, E. (1986). Slowly progressive visual agnosia or apraxia without dementia. *Cortex, 22,* 171–180.

Desimone, R., Albright, T.D., Gross, C.G., & Bruce, C.J. (1984). Stimulus-selective properties of inferior temporal neurons in the macaque. *Journal of Neurosciences, 4,* 2051–2062.

Desimone, R., Fleming, J.F.R., & Gross, C.G. (1980). Prestriate afferents to inferior temporal cortex: An HRP study. *Brain Research, 184,* 41–55.

Diamond, R., & Carey, S. (1986). Why faces are and are not special: An effect of expertise, *Journal of Experimental Psychology: General, 115,* 107–117.

Distler, C., Boussaoud, D., Desimone, R., & Ungerleider, L.G. (1993). Cortical connections of inferior temporal area TEO in macaque monkeys. *Journal of Comparative Neurology, 334,* 125–150.

Eacott, M.J., Heywood, C.A., Gross, C.G., & Cowey, A. (1993). Visual discrimination impairments following lesions of the superior temporal sulcus are not specific for facial stimuli. *Neuropsychologia, 31,* 609–619.

Edelman, S., & Buelthoff, H.H. (1992). Orientation dependence in the recognition of familiar and novel views of 3D objects. *Vision Research, 32,* 2385–2400.

Farah, M.J. (1996). Is face recognition 'special'? Evidence from neuropsychology. *Behavioural Brain Research, 76,* 181–189.

Farah, M.J., Levison, K.L., & Klein, K.L. (1995a). Face perception and within-category discrimination in prosopagnosia. *Neuropsychologia, 33,* 661–674.

Farah, M.J., McMullen, P.A., & Meyer, M.M. (1991). Can recognition of living things be selectively impaired? *Neuropsychologia, 29,* 185–193.

Farah, M.J., Wilson, K.D., Drain, H.M., & Tanaka, J.W. (1995b). The inverted face inversion effect in prosopagnosia: Evidence for mandatory, face-specific perceptual mechanisms. *Vision Research, 35,* 2089–2093.

Farah, M.J., Wilson, K.D., Drain, M., & Tanaka, J.N. (1998). What is "special" about face perception? *Psychological Review, 105,* 482–498.

Gaffan, D., & Heywood, C.A. (1993). A spurious category-specific visual agnosia for living things in human and nonhuman primates. *Journal of Cognitive Neuroscience, 5,* 118–128.

Gauthier, I., Behrmann, M., & Tarr, M.J. (1999). Can face recognition really be dissociated from object recognition? *Journal of Cognitive Neuroscience, 11,* 349–370.

Gauthier, I., & Tarr, M.J. (1997). Becoming a "Greeble" expert: Exploring the face recognition mechanism. *Vision Research, 37,* 1673–1682.

Gauthier, I., Tarr, M.J., Anderson, A.W., Skudlarski, P., & Gore, J.C. (1999a). Activation of the middle fusiform "face area" increases with experience in recognizing novel objects. *Nature Neuroscience, 2,* 568–573.

Gauthier, I., Tarr, M.J., Moylan, J., Anderson, A.W., Skudlarski, P., & Gore, J.C. (this issue). Does visual subordinate-level categorization engage the functionally-defined fusiform face area? *Cognitive Neuropsychology, 16,* 143–163.

Gauthier, I., Williams, P., Tarr, M.J., & Tanaka, J.W. (1998). Training "Greeble" experts: A framework for studying expert obect recognition processes. *Vision Research, 38,* 2401–2428.

Gross, C. (1992). Representation of visual stimuli in inferior temporal cortex. *Philosophical Transactions of the Royal Society of London, B, 335,* 3–10.

Gross, C.G., Bender, D.B., & Rocha-Miranda, C.E. (1969). Visual receptive fields of neurons in inferotemporal cortex of the monkey. *Science, 166,* 1303–1306.

Gross, C.G., Roche-Miranda, C.E., & Bender, D.B. (1972). Visual properties of neurons in inferotemporal cortex of the macaque. *Journal of Neurophysiology, 35,* 96–111.

Hamilton, C.R., & Vermeire, B.A. (1983). Discrimination of monkey faces by split-brain monkeys. *Behavioural Brain Research, 9,* 263–275.

Hasselmo, M.E., Rolls, E.T., & Baylis, G.C. (1989). The role of expression and identity in the face-selective responses of neurons in the temporal visual cortex of the monkey. *Behavioural Brain Research, 32,* 203–218.

Hay, D.C., & Young, A.W. (1982). The human face. In A.W. Ellis (Ed.), *Normality and pathology in cognitive function.* London: Academic Press.

Heywood, C.A., & Cowey, A. (1992). The role of the "face-cell" area in the discrimination and recognition of faces by monkeys. *Philosophical Transactions of the Royal Society of London–Series B: Biological Sciences, 335,* 31–37.

Hietanen, J.K., Perrett, D.I., Oram, M.W., Benson, P.J., & Dittrich, W.H. (1992). The effects of lighting conditions on the responses of cells selective for face views in the macaque temporal cortex. *Experimental Brain Research, 89,* 157–171.

Iwai, E., & Mishkin, M. (1969). Further evidence on the locus of the visual area in the temporal lobe of the monkey. *Experimental Neurology, 25,* 585–594.

Johnson, M.H., & Morton, J. (1991). *Biology and cognitive development: The case of face recognition.* Oxford: Basil Blackwell.

Kaas, J.H. (1995). Progress and puzzles. *Current Biology*, 5, 1126–1128.

Kanwisher, N., McDermott, J., & Chun, M.M. (1997). The fusiform face area: A module in human extrastriate cortex specialised for face perception. *Journal of Neuroscience, 17*, 4302–4311.

Kobatake, E., Wang, G., & Tanaka, K. (1998). Effects of shape-discrimination training on the selectivity of inferotemporal cells in adult monkeys. *Journal of Neurophysiology, 80*, 324–330.

Konorski, J. (1967). *Integrative activity of the brain. An interdisciplinary approach.* Chicago: University of Chicago Press.

Logothetis, N.K. (1998). Object vision and visual awareness. *Current Opinion in Neurobiology, 8*, 536–544.

Logothetis, N.K., Guggenberger, H., Peled, S., & Pauls, J. (1999). Functional imaging of the monkey brain. *Nature Neuroscience, 2*, 555–562.

Logothetis, N.K., & Pauls, J. (1995). Psychophysical and physiological evidence for viewer-centered object representations in the primate. *Cerebral Cortex, 5*, 270–288.

Logothetis, N.K., Pauls, J., Buelthoff, H.H., & Poggio, T. (1994). View-dependent object recognition in the primate. *Current Biology, 4*, 401–414.

Logothetis, N.K., Pauls, J., & Poggio, T. (1995). Shape representation in the inferior temporal cortex of monkeys. *Current Biology, 5*, 552–563.

Logothetis, N.K., & Sheinberg, D. (1996). Visual object recognition, *Annual Review of Neuroscience, 19*, 577–621.

Lutz, C.K., Lockard, J.S., Gunderson, V.M., & Grant, K.S. (1998). Infant monkeys' visual responses to drawings of normal and distorted faces. *American Journal of Primatology, 44*, 169–174.

McCarthy, G., Puce, A., Gore, J.C., & Allison, T. (1997). Face-specific processing in the fusiform gyrus, *Journal of Cognitive Neuroscience, 9*, 605–610.

Mendelson, M.J., Haith, M.M., & Goldman-Rakic, P.S. (1982). Face scanning and responsiveness to social cues in infant rhesus monkeys. *Developmental Psychology, 18*, 222–228.

Mikami, A., Nakamura, K., & Kubota, K. (1994). Neuronal responses to photographs in the superior temporal sulcus of the rhesus monkey. *Behavioural Brain Research, 60*, 1–13.

Morton, J., & Johnson, M.H. (1991). CONSPEC and CONLERN: A two-process theory of infant face recognition. *Psychological Review, 98*, 164–181.

Moscovitch, M., Winocur, G., & Behrmann, M. (1997). What is special in face recognition? Nineteen experiments on a person with visual object agnosia and dyslexia but normal face recognition. *Journal of Cognitive Neuroscience, 9*, 555–604.

Nahm, F.D., Perret, A., Amaral, D.G., & Albright, T.D. (1997). How do monkeys look at faces. *Journal of Cognitive Neuroscience, 9*, 611–623.

Ó Scalaidhe, S.P., Wilson, F.A.W., & Goldman-Rakic, P.S. (1997). Areal segregation of face-processing neurons in prefrontal cortex. *Science, 278*, 1135–1138.

Pauls, J. (1997). *The representation of 3-dimensional objects in the primate visual system.* Unpublished dissertation number 1–162. Baylor College of Medicine.

Perrett, D.I., Harries, M.H., Bevan, R., Thomas, S., Benson, P.J., Mistlin, A.J., Chitty, J.K., Hietanen, J.K., & Ortega, J.E. (1989). Frameworks of analysis for the neural representation of animate object and actions. *Journal of Experimental Biology, 146*, 87–113.

Perrett, D.I., Hietanen, J.K., Oram, M.W., & Benson, P.J. (1992). Organisation and functions of cells responsive to faces in the temporal cortex. *Philosophical Transactions of the Royal Society of London B: Biological Science, 335*, 23–30.

Perrett, D.I., & Oram, M.W. (1993). Neurophysiology of shape processing. *Image and Visual Computing, 11*, 317–333.

Perrett, D.I., Oram, M.W., Harries, M.H., Bevan, R., Hietanen, J.K., Benson, P.J., & Thomas, S. (1991). Viewer-centred and object-centred coding of heads in the macaque temporal cortex. *Experimental Brain Research, 86*, 159–173.

Perrett, D.I., Oram, M.W., Hietanen, J.K., & Benson, P.J. (1994). Issues of representation in object vision. In M.J. Farah, G. Ratcliff (Eds.), The neuropsychology of high-level vision: Collected tutorial assays, (pp 33–62). Hillsdale NJ: Lawrence Erlbaum Associates Inc.

Perrett, D.I., Rolls, E.T., & Caan, W. (1979). Temporal lobe cells of the monkey with visual responses selective for faces. *Neuroscience Lettr Suppl, S3*, S358.

Perrett, D.I., Rolls, E.T., & Caan, W. (1982). Visual neurones responsive to faces in the monkey temporal cortex. *Experimental Brain Research, 47*, 329–342.

Perrett, D.I., Smith, P.A., Potter, D.D., Mistlin, A.J., Head, A.S., Milner, A.D., & Jeeves, M.A. (1985). Visual cells in the temporal cortex sensitive to face view and gaze direction. *Proceedings of the Royal Society of London–Series B: Biological Sciences, 223*, 293–317.

Puce, A., Allison, T., Bentin, S., Gore, J.C., & McCarthy, G. (1998). Temporal cortex activation in humans viewing eye and mouth movements. *Journal of Neuroscience, 18*, 2188–2199.

Puce, A., Allison, T., Gore, J.C., & McCarthy, G. (1995). Face-sensitive regions in human extrastriate cortex studied by functional MRI. *Journal of Neurophysiology, 74*, 1192–1199.

Rhodes, G., & McLean, I.G. (1990). Distinctiveness and expertise effects with homogeneous stimuli: Towards a model of configural coding. *Perception, 19*, 773–794.

Rolls, E.T. (1992). Neurophysiology and functions of the primate amygdala. In J.P. Aggleton (Ed.),The amygdala (pp 143–165). New York: Wiley-Liss.

Rolls, E.T., & Tovée, M.J. (1995). Sparseness of the neuronal representation of stimuli in the primate temporal cortex. *Journal of Neurophysiology, 73*, 713–726.

Rosch, E., Mervis, C.B., Gray, W.D., Johnson, D.M., & Boyes-Braem, P. (1976). Basic objects in natural categories. *Cognitive Psychology, 8*, 382–439.

Rosenfield, S.A., & Van Hoesen, G.W. (1979). Face recognition in the rhesus monkey. *Neuropsychologia, 17*, 503–509.

Seltzer, J.B., & Pandya, D.N. (1978). Afferent cortical connections and architectonics of the superior temporal sulcus and surrounding cortex in the rhesus monkey. *Brain Research, 149*, 1–24.

Sergent, J., Ohta, S., & MacDonald, B. (1992). Functional neuroanatomy of face and object processing. A positron emission tomography study. *Brain, 115*, 15–36.

Sergent, J., & Signoret, J.L. (1992). Functional and anatomical decomposition of face processing: Evidence from prosopagnosia and PET study of normal subjects. *Philosophical Transactions of the Royal Society of London B, 335*, 55–62.

Shiwa, T. (1987). Corticocortical projections to the monkey temporal lobe with particular reference to the visual processing pathways. *Arch Ital Biol, 125*, 139–154.

Shuttleworth, E.C., Syring, V., & Norman, A. (1982). Further observations on the nature of prosopagnosia. *Brain and Cognition, 1*, 307–322.

Simion, F., Valenza, E., Umilta, C., & Dalla Barba, B. (1998). Preferential orienting to faces in newborns: A temporal-nasal asymmetry. *JEP: HPP, 24*, 1399–1405.

Tanaka, J.W., & Gauthier, I. (1997). Expertise in object and face recognition. In R.L. Goldstone, P.G. Schyns, & D.L. Medin (Eds.), *Psychology of learning and motivation*. San Diego, CA: Academic Press.

Tanaka, J.W., & Taylor, M. (1991). Object categories and expertise: Is the basic level in the eye of the beholder? *Cognitive Psychology, 23*, 457–482.

Tanaka, K. (1996). Inferotemporal cortex and object vision. *Annual Review of Neuroscience, 19*, 109–139.

Tanaka, K. (1997). Mechanisms of visual object recognition: Monkey and human studies. *Current Opinion in Neurobiology, 7*, 523–529.

Tanaka, K., Saito, H., Fukada, Y., & Moriya, M. (1991). Coding visual images of objects in the inferotemporal cortex of the macaque monkey. *Journal of Neurophysiology, 66*, 170–189.

Tovée, M.J. (1998). Is face processing special? *Neuron, 21*, 1239–1242.

Ungerleider, L.G. (1995). Functional brain imaging studies of cortical mechanisms for memory. *Science, 270*, 769–775.

Valenza, E., Simion, F., Macchi Cassia, V., & Umilta, C. (1996). Face preference at birth. *JEP:HPP, 22*, 892–903.

Von Bonin, G., & Bailey, P. (1947). *The neocortex of macaca mulatta*. Urbana, IL: University of Illinois Press.

Wachsmuth, E., Oram, M.W., & Perrett, D.I. (1994). Recognition of objects and their component parts: Responses of single units in the temporal cortex of the macaque. *Cerebral Cortex, 4*, 509–522.

Webster, M.J., Ungerleider, L.G., & Bachevalier, J. (1991). Connections of inferior temporal areas TE and TEO with medial temporal-lobe structures in infant and adult monkeys. *Journal of Neuroscience, 11*, 1095–1116.

Williams, G.V., Rolls, E.T., Leonard, C.M., & Stern, C. (1993). Neuronal responses in the ventral striatum of the behaving macaque. *Behavioural Brain Research, 55*, 243–252.

Wilson, F.A.W., Ó Scalaidhe, S.P., & Goldman-Rakic, P.S. (1993). Dissociation of object and spatial processing domains in primate prefrontal cortex. *Science, 260*, 1955–1958.

Wright, A.A., & Roberts, W.A. (1996). Monkey and human face perception: Inversion effects for human faces but not for monkey faces or scenes. *Journal of Cognitive Neuroscience, 8*, 278–290.

Yin, R.K. (1969). Looking at upside-down faces, *JEP, 81*, 141–145.

Young, A.W., Hellawell, D., & Hay, D. (1987). Configural information in face perception. *Perception, 10*, 747–759.

Young, M.P., & Yamane, S. (1992). Sparse population coding of faces in the inferotemporal cortex. *Science, 256*, 1327–1331.

COGNITIVE NEUROPSYCHOLOGY, 2000, 17 (1/2/3), 143–163

Does Visual Subordinate-level Categorisation Engage the Functionally Defined Fusiform Face Area?

Isabel Gauthier

Yale University, New Haven, CT, USA

Michael J. Tarr

Brown University, Providence, RI, USA

Jill Moylan, Adam W. Anderson, Pawel Skudlarski, and John C. Gore

Yale University, New Haven, CT, USA

Functional magnetic resonance imaging was used to compare brain activation associated with basic-level (e.g. bird) and subordinate-level (e.g. eagle) processing for both visual and semantic judgements. We localised the putative face area for 11 subjects, who also performed visual matching judgements for pictures and aurally presented words. The middle fusiform and occipital gyri were recruited for subordinate minus basic visual judgements, reflecting additional perceptual processing. When the face area was localised individually for each subject, analyses in the middle fusiform gyri revealed that subordinate-level processing activated the individuals face area. We propose that what is unique about the way faces engage this region is the focal spatial distribution of the activation rather than the recruitment of the face per se. Eight subjects also performed semantic judgements on aurally presented basic- and subordinate-level words. The parahippocampal gyri were more activated for subordinate-level than basic-level semantic judgements. Finally, the left posterior inferior temporal gyrus was activated for subordinate-level judgements, both visual and semantic, as well as during passive viewing of faces.

INTRODUCTION

Recent neuroimaging studies have contributed to our understanding of part of the human visual system where objects appear to be coded as objects (rather than as simple features as in primary visual cortex). For instance, experiments comparing "objects" to "nonobjects" such as scrambled features or textures have identified an area in the lateral occipital gyrus that responds preferentially to any stimulus, novel or familiar, which has a clear three-dimensional interpretation (Kanwisher, Chun, McDermott, & Ledden, 1996; Kanwisher, Woods, Iacoboni, & Mazziota, 1997b; Malach et al., 1995; Schacter et al., 1995). Other neuroimaging studies have focused on comparisons between particular object categories, leading to a modular view of human inferotemporal cortex in which there are regions dedicated to the recognition of distinct object categories such as faces or letter strings. For example, inspired by the neuropsychological literature on prosopagnosia (face recognition deficits

Requests for reprints should be addressed to Isabel Gauthier, Psychology Department, 502 Wilson Hall, Vanderbilt University, Nashville, TN 37240, USA (Email: isabel.gauthier@vanderbilt.edu).

This work was supported by NSF award to MJT (SBR 9615819).

following brain insults), several studies have compared faces to nonface objects. Results of these studies suggest that part of the middle fusiform gyrus is dedicated to face recognition (Haxby et al., 1994; Ishai, Ungerleider, Martin, Maisog, & Haxby, 1997; Kanwisher, McDermott, & Chun, 1997a; McCarthy, Puce, Gore, & Allison, 1997; Puce, Allison, Asgari, Gore, & McCarthy, 1996; Puce, Allison, Gore, & McCarthy, 1995; Puce, Allison, Spencer, Spencer, & McCarthy, 1997).

In a recent paper (Gauthier, Anderson, Tarr, Skudlarski, & Gore, 1997), we proposed that many studies have failed to control for a critical difference between faces and nonface objects: That of the level of categorisation at which such stimuli are typically recognised. Rosch, Mervis, Gray, Johnson, and Boyes-Braem (1976) presented evidence that familiar objects are first recognised at a level of abstraction referred to as the "basic" level (or "entry" level, when defined independently for each object as the level at which contact is made first in semantic memory, Jolicoeur, Gluck, & Kosslyn, 1984). Objects in different basic-level categories (e.g. chair or bicycle) generally differ in their parts and configuration and so are easily discriminable (Tversky & Hemenway, 1984). In contrast, recognising objects at the "subordinate" level (e.g. desk chair vs. arm chair) requires additional time and perceptual processing (Jolicoeur et al., 1984), relying more heavily on multiple perceptual dimensions such as shading, texture, colour, surface detail, pigmentation, and spatial arrangement of features (Bruce & Humphreys, 1994).

Within this framework, faces are typically recognised at a very subordinate level (the exemplar level, e.g. Jill's or Isabel's face, or "this particular individual" for an unfamiliar face) whereas most other objects are typically recognised at the basic level. Based on this observation, Gauthier et al. (1997) tested the possibility that this difference in categorisation level contributed to the activation obtained when faces and objects are compared. The hypothesis is that, especially when subjects *passively* view a stream of faces and nonface objects, they are more likely to process faces than objects at the subordinate level. This may be so for at least two reasons: The presentation of several objects exclusively

from the same category may encourage such subordinate-level processing and a lifetime of experience recognising faces at the this level may lead subjects to do so automatically, regardless of the task.

In Gauthier et al. (1997), a picture was presented together with a basic-level or subordinate-level word and participants were asked to verify whether the picture matched the word. After removal of the contribution of semantic processing of the word using a double-subtraction (see the Semantic task described later in this paper), a region of the fusiform and inferotemporal cortex similar to that described in prior studies as face-sensitive was found to be selectively engaged by subordinate-level processing for nonface objects. However, a limitation of this finding is that each individual's putative face area occupies only a small portion of the group-defined face-sensitive region (Allison et al., 1994). It is therefore possible that face recognition and subordinate-level categorisation engage mutually exclusive areas within this region in each individual but that they average to the same area across a group of subjects. The present study was designed to address this limitation by measuring for the same individuals both the activation for passive viewing of faces minus objects and the activation for a manipulation of categorisation level for nonface objects. Again, we believe that the latter manipulation contributes to the faces minus objects effect.

Since our first study manipulating categorisation level, two neuroimaging studies have equated subordinate-level processing of nonface objects with face processing (Kanwisher et al., 1997a; McCarthy et al., 1997). Both studies led to the conclusion that the activation for faces could not be accounted for by a category-level manipulation. However, methodological issues may limit the strength of this interpretation. First, McCarthy et al. compared passive viewing of faces and flowers appearing on a continuously changing background of nonsense patterns or nonface objects. Both faces and flowers, when shown on a background of nonsense patterns, engaged the right fusiform gyrus. When compared to a baseline of nonface objects, faces, but not flowers, produced activation in this area. The authors concluded that faces are treated differently to other objects, in a specialised brain area. However, flowers as a control stimulus class and passive viewing instructions may not be optimal for engaging subordinate-level processing. Unlike faces, which share common parts and configuration, most flowers have very distinctive and unique features, such as the number and shape of the petals. Face-like subordinate-level processing is likely to be engaged by those object categories that have been termed "homogeneous classes." These are defined as categories that share a configuration of features so that common points can be located on every member of the class; exemplars from homogeneous classes can be averaged together to produce another instance of the same category (Diamond & Carey, 1986; Rhodes & McLean, 1990). Thus, whereas a composite of faces progresses towards a prototype as the number of exemplars averaged together increases (Levin, 1996; Rhodes, Brennan, & Carey, 1987), the same effect cannot be obtained with flowers of various species in that they differ widely in appearance (e.g. tulip, rose, and daisy). As a second concern, passive viewing of exemplars from a single category in the context of other objects is less likely to automatically engage subordinate-level processing (unless perhaps with expert subjects). Finally, McCarthy et al. (1997) quantified the activation in the comparison with nonface objects by thresholding individual activation maps at a relatively high threshold, the same used for the comparison with nonsense patterns, and then counting activated voxels. Faces differ from common objects along more dimensions (conceptual category, homogeneity of the class, default level of categorisation, degree of expertise) than do flowers (conceptual category, homogeneity of the class). Therefore, the activation for faces compared to objects may be stronger than that for flowers. A lower threshold might reveal a peak of activation for flowers among objects in the putative face area. Thus, the selection of a high threshold on individual activation maps may produce an artificial floor effect that could compromise the interpretation of a task comparison. In contrast, the quantification method used in the present study, that of summing the percentage signal change or t-values for voxels over a very low threshold in a region of interest (ROI), does not have this limitation. This method

has been found to be less dependent on ROI size than on voxel count and rather insensitive to the threshold value (Constable et al., 1998).

In a second study, Kanwisher, McDermott, and Chun (Kanwisher et al., 1997a) compared activation during "one-back" judgements for consecutive repetitions of identical stimuli for faces and hands and found significantly more activation for faces than hands as compared to a fixation baseline. In contrast to McCarthy et al. (1997), this study used a homogeneous class of stimuli and required subjects to process subordinate-level information. A face area ROI was also defined in each subject, and the signal change for other comparisons was evaluated in this ROI regardless of threshold. However, an important difference is that the one-back task includes only a small proportion of matching trials as compared to a task such as that used by Gauthier et al. (1997), which included 50% matching trials (see Dill & Fahle, 1998; Farell, 1985; for differences between same and different trials). In order to convince themselves that they are not seeing a repetition, subjects need only notice a single featural difference. On the other hand, in order to give a "same" response, subjects need to have searched more thoroughly for differences and found none: "Same" responses are thus more likely to recruit configural processing than are "different" responses. In addition, whereas Kanwisher et al. (1997a) found more activation for faces than hands in the face area, it may still be the case that the hand task activates the face area to a significant degree, because it requires subordinate-level processing. The fact that the hand task does not engage the face area as much as the face task could reflect a difference in difficulty based on within-class similarity (which cannot be equated across classes) or a difference in the subjects' level of expertise for each class, as well as possible preference of this area for faces.

To summarise, both McCarthy et al. (1997) and Kanwisher et al. (1997a) found activation for faces to be *stronger* than that obtained for nonface objects and rejected level of categorisation as an important factor in interpreting the specialisation of the putative face area. However, although categorisation level may not be sufficient to account for *all* of the specificity in the face area, it remains possible that some of the activation in the face area, when faces are compared to objects at the basic level, may be due to subordinate-level processing (as it is engaged automatically for faces but not for objects). Thus, although categorisation level may be only one of the several organising principles for the inferior temporal cortex, it may be of somewhat greater importance in that it appears to play a role early in development (Rosch, 1976) and has universal influence (in contrast to the more idiosyncratic role of expertise with particular object categories). Subordinate-level processing could thus account for a coarse specialisation in the middle fusiform and inferior temporal gyri, while expertise (with faces or other categories) may further refine this specialisation.

The present study was designed to revisit the question of whether a significant part of the activation found in the face area can be attributed to subordinate-level processing. What is new, however, is that here the putative face area is defined functionally in *individual* subjects (Kanwisher et al., 1997a). Other manipulations from our earlier study remain relatively unchanged. As before, we isolate subordinate-level processing by manipulating the categorical level of a word (basic or subordinate) matched to identical objects. In Gauthier et al. (1997), a double-subtraction method was used to isolate this process, as it was important to control for the visually presented subordinate-level words being longer on average than the basic-level words. Here we used aurally presented words, so that a single-subtraction design was possible. Although we define the face area using passive viewing of faces minus objects, as in Kanwisher and colleagues' work, our approach varies in that we investigate not only the activation within this ROI, but also in the rest of the ventral temporal cortex and especially in ROIs bordering the face area. In contrast, many recent studies (Kanwisher et al., 1997a; Kanwisher, Tong, & Nakayama, 1998; Tong, Nakayama, Moscovitch, Weinrib, & Kanwisher, 1998) investigating the response in the face area restrict their analyses to a small region of the fusiform gyrus generally defined using passive viewing of faces minus objects. Such an analysis would not distinguish, for instance, whether subordinate-level processing

leads to activation of a small magnitude but precisely centred on the face area or to a larger activation that is not as precisely focused.

A second goal was to explore further the neural basis of categorisation at different levels of abstraction. The preponderance of experiments investigating the inferotemporal cortex in terms of stimulus preferences may lead to a skewed picture of the organisation of this region. Crucially, implicit task manipulations may reside within stimulus manipulations (e.g. passive viewing of faces may imply a different level of categorisation than passive viewing of objects), whereas when the same stimulus is presented and the task is varied, any difference obtained must be attributed to the task manipulation. The importance of such endogenous mechanisms is well illustrated in experiments where attention is shifted between dimensions (e.g. colour vs. motion; Zeki, Watson, Friston, & Frackowiak, 1991) or between an identity and a location task (Haxby et al., 1994; Moscovitch, Kapur, Kohler, & Houle, 1995) with the same stimulus. It is our belief that experiments investigating the role of endogenous factors that recruit in different cortical areas are needed to understand the neural basis of visual object recognition. Here, we aim to test what extent an endogenous manipulation alone can activate the "face area". This will provide an estimate of the maximum possible contribution of the level of categorisation effect when comparing faces to objects (if an explicit endogenous manipulation cannot engage the face area, it is unlikely that an implicit manipulation can do so).

In addition to the primary goals stated, we hoped to pursue the hypothesis advanced in Gauthier et al. (1997), that early visual areas may be recruited by subordinate-level semantic judgements because subordinate words provide a more specific basis for detailed visual imagery. By using aurally presented words, the present study controls for the possibility that this effect in the original study was due to greater visual stimulation for subordinate-level words in that they were on average longer than the basic-level words.

As in Gauthier et al. (1997), we used an empirical definition of basic and subordinate levels, using object and name pairings that were selected by

Gauthier et al. so that name verification times were significantly slower at the subordinate level than at the basic level[1]. Moreover, semantic judgements on the same basic-level and subordinate-level words also showed a basic-level advantage in response times, although not as large as the advantage found for visual judgements (Gauthier, unpublished data). Indeed, some of the basic-level advantage in response time for picture naming and even name-verification may be due to nonperceptual factors such as name frequency, name length, and order of learning (Johnson, Paivio, & Clark, 1996). However, we believe that our object–name pairings require additional *perceptual processing* for subordinate judgements.

METHOD

Subjects

Fourteen neurologically normal subjects (all right-handed) took part in the study (approved by the Yale University Human Investigation Committee). Eleven subjects performed the Localiser and the Visual task (five males, six females) and eight performed the Semantic Task (five males, three females). Three subjects participated in all three tasks in the same session.

Materials and Procedure

The same 72 images of objects as in Gauthier et al. (1997) were used, except that words were presented aurally (see Appendix A). The words were recorded on a Macintosh computer by a female native English speaker using SoundEdit Pro Software (Macromedia, San Francisco). Here, the Semantic task was not designed as a control for the Visual task. Therefore, 38 basic-level words and 38 subordinate-level words, not directly matched with the words used in the Visual task, were used in the Semantic task (see Appendix B).

In the Visual task, participants performed name-verification judgements in which they decided whether a greyscale image of an object matched an aurally presented word (responding Yes or No by pressing one of two buttons). On each trial, a word was presented through headphones while an object appeared simultaneously and remained on the screen for 2750msec with an intertrial interval of 750msec. Nine 21.3sec epochs showed Basic and Subordinate trials in alternation (order counterbalanced between runs, 4 runs per subject) for a total of 192sec. Identical sets of images were shown during the Basic and Subordinate epochs, in a randomised order, and the only difference between the two conditions was the level of categorisation of the aurally presented word (either basic as in "bird" or subordinate as in "sparrow"). Seventy-two pictures were repeated an average of three times each during the experiment (an *average* of 1.5 times at each level, with either matching or nonmatching labels). In the Semantic task, the same design as in the Visual task was used, except that subjects were asked to close their eyes and judge whether each of the words presented aurally described an object that could move by its own power (stimulus onset asynchrony of 3500msec—identical to the Visual task). Words were randomised within each level and each word was repeated an average of 2.8 times during the experiment (there were four runs per subject). In order to define face-selective areas individually, a Faces minus Objects Localiser task was performed using 90 greyscale faces (all cropped in the same oval shape) as well as 90 greyscale images of common nonface objects, with no overlap with the subordinate-level lists used in Visual and Semantic tasks. In each run for this task, 26 faces or 26 objects were flashed, each for 750msec within 9 alternating epochs of 21.3sec. Stimuli were projected on a screen at the subjects' feet within a square region of approximately 4 × 4 degrees of visual angle. This resulted in each image being shown once in each run. Subjects were told to fixate on the centre of the screen during the entire run for both visual tasks, although there was no fixation cross on the screen

---

[1] Judgements were timed starting from onset of the presentation of the picture following the presentation of the word.

during the presentation of pictures. The experiments were conducted using RSVP software (Williams & Tarr, undated).

fMRI Scan Acquisition

Imaging was performed on a 1.5 Tesla Signa scanner (GE Medical Systems, Waukesha, WI), with Instascan echo planar imaging capabilities (Advanced NMR Systems, Wilmington, MA). A single shot, gradient echo, echo-planar pulse sequence was used to acquire 64 by 128 voxel images over a field of view of 20 by 40cm. Imaging parameters were T_E = 60msec, T_R = 1500msec, flip angle 60 degrees, slice thickness 7mm. Six contiguous axial-oblique slices were imaged during each repetition time interval. The image plane was aligned along the longitudinal extent of the temporal lobe, with the lowest slice capturing the inferior occipital gyrus and the lowest portion of the temporal poles. This slice orientation was chosen to maximise resolution in the fusiform gyrus (in-plane resolution = 3.125 × 3.125mm, through-plane resolution = 7mm). Each run produced 128 images per slice. Image data were corrected for motion using the SPM 96 software (Wellcome Department of Cognitive Neurology, London). Changes in image intensity were analysed on a voxel-by-voxel basis: Maps of t-values were created for each pair of conditions compared and corrected for a low-frequency drift in the signal with an estimated 2sec haemodynamic lag taken into account. In addition, the two images (per slice) that occurred at the beginning of each epoch were discarded because at this point, the rising signal for the starting task would be confounded with the declining signal for the task that just ended. The t-maps were superimposed on T1-weighted anatomical images of the corresponding slice. No statistical significance is attributed to these activation maps, which are then used as raw data for further analyses in ROIs.

For averaging purposes, anatomical landmarks were defined in T1-weighted axial-oblique and midline sagittal images of each subject (they consisted of, in the oblique plane, the outer edges of the brain, the optic chiasma, and the anterior edge of the cerebral aqueduct, and in the sagittal plane, the superior and inferior edges of the brain, the optic chiasma, and the most posterior point of the fourth ventricle). Functional and anatomical images were transformed by piece-wise linear warping in 12 brain subvolumes to register the results for each subject in a common coordinate system. The transformed functional maps were then combined across subjects using a median value for each voxel and thresholded to obtain composite functional maps.

Anatomically Defined Regions of Interest

For analyses on anatomically defined areas, regions of interest (ROIs) were drawn a priori on the standardised anatomical images (Plate 2, see colour section situated between pages 160 and 161), based on a comparison of the average and individual anatomy with several human brain atlases (H. Damasio, 1995; Duvernoy, 1991; Talairach & Tournoux, 1988). No ROIs were defined in the first and last standard slices because several subjects had no equivalent original slice and to avoid artefacts caused by the motion correction algorithm. Skew-corrected t-values were summed in each ROI (Skudlarski, Constable, & Gore, 1999), and normalised for ROI size and amount of activation in all ROIs in a given hemisphere: A value of 1 therefore indicates that an ROI has a density of activation that is identical to the mean activation in the hemisphere, and higher values signify higher-than-average densities. No probabilistic value is attributed to the t-maps or the density values in individual subjects. Rather, the statistical significance of effects is determined by their representation in the group sample.

RESULTS

Analyses on Anatomically Defined ROIs

Plate 2 (see colour section) shows the median activation maps for the subtractions of the Subordinate minus the Basic condition for both the Visual and

Table 1. *Mean Density of Activation for Each ROI in the Visual (N = 11) and Semantic (N = 8) Tasks*

ROI (ROI No.)	Visual		Semantic	
	S–B	*B–S*	*S–B*	*B–S*
amg (16)	1.22	.81	1.06	.98
antFG (11)	1.05	R(1.27) L (.79)	1.35	1.07
antITG (2)	.89	1.17	1.14	.82
antMTG (12)	1.19	1.60	1.27	1.04
cun (8)	.84	2.07**	*1.05*	1.34*
hipp (14)	.83	1.38	1.02	1.41
infOG (5)	2.66**	.46	1.02	1.54*
latOG (9)	2.70**	.49	*1.15*	1.12
linG (7)	.85	*1.81***	*1.56*	1.13
midFG (10)	*1.56***	.86	1.26	1.24
parahippG (3)	1.28	.81	*1.29***	1.06
postFG (6)	2.20**	.67	1.32*	1.18
postITG (4)	*R (.75) L (1.47**)*	1.22	R(.81) L (1.41)	R(.77) L(1.69)
postMTG (13)	1.70**	1.19	1.44	1.12
supOG (15)	2.00**	.95	1.39	.97
tPol (1)	.96	1.05	1.05	1.10

Results are split by hemisphere only when the laterality effect was significant by paired *t*-tests, *P* < .05. Significance only indicated for densities > 1. Italic with **: a priori tests, *P* < .05. Italic without asterisk: a priori tests, n.s. **: post hoc, *P* < .01/number of post hoc tests. *: post hoc, *P* < .05. (df = 10 for the Visual task and 7 for the Semantic task).

S: subordinate; B: Basic; amg: amygdala; antFG: anterior fusiform gyrus; antITG: anterior inferior temporal gyrus; antMTG: anterior middle temporal gyrus; cun: cuneus; hipp: hippocampus; infOG: inferior occipital gyrus; latOG: lateral occipital gyrus; linG: lingual gyrus; midFG: middle fusiform gyrus; parahippG: parahippocampal gyrus; postFG: posterior fusiform gyrus; postITG: posterior inferior temporal gyrus; postMTG: posterior middle tempral gyrus; supOG: superior occipital gyrus; tPol: temporal poles.

the Semantic tasks. Table 1 gives the mean density of activation for each ROI for each comparison.

Single-sample *t*-tests (Sheskin, 1997) were performed for each cell of the table to assess whether the mean density in each ROI was significantly higher than the average hemisphere activation density[2]. A priori hypotheses were formulated based on the results of Gauthier et al. (1997) and the corresponding tests were performed at the .05 level per comparison. These hypotheses concerned five ROIs for the Visual task, three expected to be associated with subordinate level (midFG, postITG, postMTG), and two with basic level (cun, linG, both visible in the composite images in Gauthier et al.) and for ROIs expected to be associated with subordinate level for the Semantic task (cun, latOG, midFG, linG). For all other ROIs, the probability of committing a Type I error was minimised by dividing an α-level of .05 by the number of post hoc ROIs, independently for each task (for Visual Subordinate minus Basic, .05/13 = .0038, and Basic minus Subordinate, .05/14 = .0036; for Semantic Subordinate minus Basic, .05/12 = .0042 and Basic minus Subordinate, .05/16 = .0031). Effects that did not reach the corrected α-level but were significant at the .05 level are reported as such, so that they can form the basis of hypotheses for future studies.

---

[2] Because the two sides of each subtraction (Subordinate minus Basic and Basic minus Subordinate) are not independent for each task, densities significantly lower than 1 are not reported. In most cases where this happened, the density for the other side of the subtraction was significantly higher than 1.

Visual Subordinate Minus Basic

The Visual Subordinate minus Basic comparison revealed activation in the middle and posterior fusiform gyri (midFG and postFG), the left postITG, the entire occipital gyri (infOG, latOG, supOG) as well as the posterior middle temporal gyri (postMTG, see Plate 2 in the colour section situated between pages 160 and 161).

The activations in midFG and post ITG replicate the findings from the double subtraction in Gauthier et al. (1997), as can be seen in Fig. 1. This activation overlaps with that described in many studies as the group-averaged face sensitive area (Puce et al., 1995, 1996, 1997; Sergent et al., 1992). Below, we use the Faces minus Objects comparison to localise individual subject's face area. We then investigate whether the association between the face area and subordinate-level processing (Gauthier et al.) can be replicated in individually defined face areas (which vary in location from subject to subject). Activation in the occipital lobe (postFG and OG) was anticipated by the composite results for the single (Subordinate minus Basic) subtraction for the Visual task in Gauthier et al., although it did not reach significance in that study.

This difference in OG activation, stronger here than in the prior study, may be the major difference between the double- and single-subtraction designs. We address the extensive recruitment of the visual system by subordinate-level processing in the final discussion. These consistent results obtained by comparing subordinate-level to basic-level judgements with fMRI here and in our prior study may be contrasted to the results of a similar comparison with PET by Kosslyn, Alpert, and Thompson (1995), who found only a single area in the ventral pathway (left BA 19) that was more active for Subordinate minus Basic visual judgements.

The postMTG activation most likely reflects the recruitment of the secondary auditory cortex by the longer subordinate-level words (similar, albeit nonsignificant activation is found in the homologous comparison for the Semantic task).

Visual Basic Minus Subordinate

Whereas Gauthier et al. (1997) found no significant activation for basic *over* subordinate visual judgements (in contrast to the additional activation obtained for subordinate over basic), the subject-

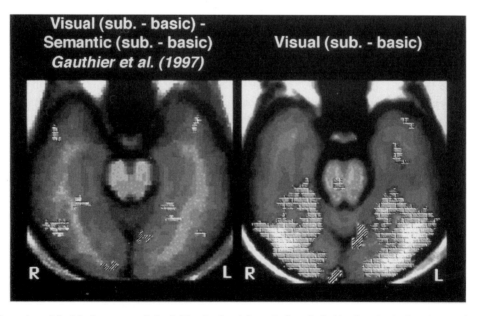

Fig. 1. *Comparison of slice 3 in the present study for the Visual task and the results from the double subtraction in Gauthier et al. (1997). The horizontal brick texture shows the result of the indicated subtractions.*

average composite map for the double subtraction suggested some activity in presumptive retinotopic visual cortex. A strikingly similar pattern is found here in the Visual single subtraction (Basic minus Subordinate) in both the cuneus and lingual gyri (see Fig. 1). These two areas are the only ones that survive our criterion for statistical significance. Thus, despite the differences in design between the two experiments (single vs. double subtraction, auditory vs. visual presentation of the words), there is a close correspondence in the activation patterns seen for the basic minus subordinate comparison. It is worth noting, however, that inspection of the individual activation maps suggests that at least some of this activation may be taking place in large vessels, although it is difficult to know without angiography, not performed in this study. The pattern is similar to that sometimes obtained when subtracting from a fixation baseline, suggestive of draining vessels.

Greater visual cortex activation for basic-level over subordinate-level recognition is inconsistent with almost all accounts of object categorisation. Models typically postulate that the basic (or entry) level is necessarily accessed before access to the subordinate level (Jolicoeur et al., 1984; Kosslyn et al., 1995) or that subordinate-level judgements require a higher criterion than basic-level judgements (without attributing a special status to basic-level categories). The assumption is that more features must be verified to distinguish among objects at the subordinate level as compared to objects at the basic level (G. Murphy & Smith, 1982; G.L. Murphy, 1991). Consequently, no additional processing would be predicted for making basic-level judgements relative to subordinate-level judgements. Because our finding would require a major revision of object recognition theories and given our uncertainty as to its source, we favour a cautious interpretation.

Semantic Subordinate Minus Basic

The Semantic Subordinate minus Basic comparison revealed significant activation in the parahippocampal gyri (parahippG). Early visual areas such as the linG and the postFG show higher than average densities of activation but are not sig-

nificant. Therefore, our results provide little support for Gauthier et al.'s (1997) hypothesis that subordinate-level words may recruit early visual cortex through visual imagery. However, postMTG, activated for visual subordinate judgements presumably because of longer subordinate-level words on average, also shows nonsignificant but higher than average density of activation. This suggests that the reduced statistical power in the Semantic task relative to the visual task (8 vs. 11 subjects) may have contributed to our null result and that the same issue should be addressed in a larger study. It should be noted that the lingual gyrus was more strongly activated during Semantic than Visual subordinate-level judgements [$F(1,17) = 5.05, P < .05$].

Semantic Basic Minus Subordinate. No region was expected to be specifically recruited by basic-level semantic judgements and none showed activation surviving our corrected α-level. However the infOG came close ($P < .0004$) and also showed stronger activation for Semantic than Visual basic-level judgements [$F(1,17) = 28.0, P < .0001$].

Visual vs. Semantic Judgements

Given the many differences between the Visual and Semantic conditions (different number of subjects, different words, basic and subordinate words conceptually related in the Visual task, as they described the same images, but not in the Semantic task), only a qualitative summary (rather than a quantitative analysis) of the regions engaged in the two experiments will be reported here.

Common Areas

The postMTG, significantly recruited for subordinate visual judgements and only showing numerically above-average density of activation for semantic subordinate judgements, is thought to reflect secondary auditory cortex activation caused by the longer subordinate-level words (Binder et al., 1997). The left posterior inferior temporal gyrus was significantly engaged by both visual and semantic subordinate-level judgements. Binder et al. investigated cerebral linguistic areas involved in making semantic judgements upon the presentation of aurally presented animal names (relative to pitch-based decisions about tones). Consistent with the present results, Binder et al. also found activation of the left inferior temporal gyrus and suggested a role in comprehension at a linguistic/semantic level. Interestingly, the words and tones in this study were equated in duration (unlike our subordinate-level and basic-level words), suggesting that a linguistic component may be sufficient to engage this area.

Differentially-engaged Areas. Subordinate-level visual judgements engaged the midFG gyrus, consistent with the double-subtraction results reported by Gauthier et al. (1997). The entire OG (inferior, lateral and superior—predominantly BA 19) was also engaged for subordinate visual but not semantic judgements. This is consistent with the demonstration by Jolicoeur et al. (1984) that picture recognition at the subordinate level requires more perceptual processing than recognition of the same picture at the basic level. The parahippG was specifically engaged by subordinate-level semantic judgements. This area was also activated in the Semantic task using animal names in Binder et al. (1997), who suggested that processing at a semantic level may have enhanced storage of episodic memories (Craik & Lockhart, 1972; Zola-Morgan, Squire, Amaral, & Suzuki, 1989). The parahippocampus has been implicated in the encoding of novel material (Gabrieli, Brewer, Desmond, & Glover, 1997; Stern et al., 1996), but our Semantic task involved no novelty manipulation. However, the subordinate-level words clearly had lower word frequencies and it is possible that this factor could lead to a pseudo-novelty effect.

The absence of common activation for basic-level visual and semantic judgements is consistent with the hypothesis that there is no additional semantic/linguistic component involved in processing basic-level words as compared to subordinate-level words (that is, the comprehension of the word "pelican" includes the comprehension of the concept "bird"). This is because the only shared feature in the Visual and Semantic tasks is the auditory presentation of words. Therefore, any component that would be mediated solely by language process-

ing should be common to both tasks. Of course, differences may occur in brain areas not covered by our slices.

Results for Faces Minus Objects in Anatomically Defined ROIs

The normalised density of activation (sum of t-values over $t = 0.1$, normalised by the sum of t-values in all ROIs in a given hemisphere) for the Localiser task (Faces minus Objects and Objects minus Faces) in each anatomically defined ROI (Plate 2) was compared by t-test to a baseline of 1 (average density in the hemisphere). For Faces minus Objects, two ROIs (midFG and postITG) were predicted a priori to be activated and statistical significance was assessed at an α-level of .05. Alpha was corrected for all other ROIs (.0035 for 14 ROIs in Faces minus Objects, .0031 for 16 ROIs in Objects minus Faces). For Faces minus Objects, activation density in the midFG was not significantly higher than the average (mean = 1.065, n.s.). Figure 2 shows that the group-average "face area" is located within the midFG ROI but is only a small portion of this ROI: A measure of activation based on density is highly sensitive to the fit between the ROI size and activation size. Furthermore, Fig. 2 also illustrates that some of the midFG surrounding the putative face area is actually more activated for objects than faces (mean = 1.77, [$t(10) = 3.70$, $P < .004$]. There was a significant effect of hemisphere in post ITG [$F(1,10) = 5.15$, $P < .05$], with density of activation higher than average in the left hemisphere only [right = 1.19, n.s.; left = 1.66, $t(10) = 2.89$, $P < .02$). The left postITG activation is of particular interest given that this same area appeared to be engaged for both Visual and Semantic subordinate judgements. The left-side activation in the postITG for Faces minus Objects can hardly be attributed to a linguistic difference (in fact, nonface objects might have been expected to lead to stronger naming responses than unfamiliar faces).

For the Faces minus Objects comparison, only one additional ROI (cuneus) showed higher than average activation but did not pass our corrected α criterion [mean = 2.23, $t(10) = 2.94$, $P < .02$]. The density of activation in the right parahippG (visible

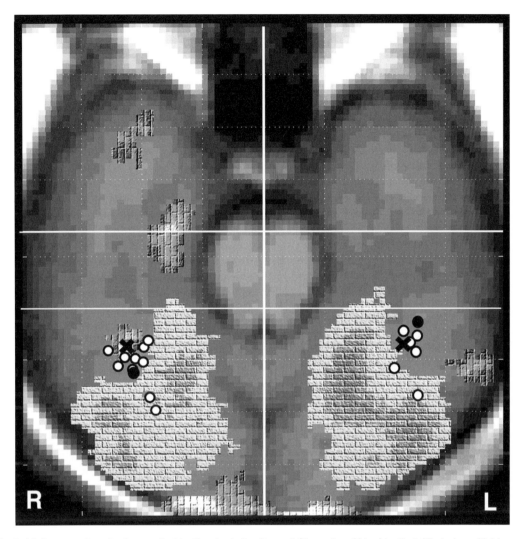

Fig. 2. *Median composite activation map for 11 subjects in the Localizer task (Faces minus Objects) in slice 3. The horizontal brick texture shows the voxels more activated for faces while the vertical brick texture indicates voxels more activated for non-face objects. The threshold is t = 0.1 for Faces minus Objects and t = 0.5 for Objects minus Faces, with a cluster size of 20 voxels. Black Xs indicate the centre of the average definition for the face area in each hemisphere. The criterion for lateralisation (see text) led to three subjects being right-lateralised, one subject being left-lateralised, six bilateral subjects, and one with no face area for the average definition. For the individual definition, this led to four subjects being right-lateralised and seven being bilateral. Centres of individual face areas in each hemisphere are shown with white-filled circles, the black-filled circles show the face area in slice 2 for a bilateral subject.*

in Fig. 2) was not significantly higher than 1 (mean = 1.12, n.s.) but there was a significant effect of Hemisphere in the hippocampus ROI, stronger on the right [right = .99; left = .56; $F(1,10) = 7.32$, $P < .02$]. Four additional ROIs were more activated bilaterally for objects than faces: the left infOG

[mean = 3.22, $t(10) = 4.31$, $P < .002$], the latOG [mean = 4.74, $[t(10) = 4.93$, $P < .0006$], the postFG [mean = 3.93, $t(10) = 9.67$, $P < .0001$] and the supOG [mean = 3.75, $t(10) = 5.14$, $P < .0004$].

The fact that the density of activation was significant in the midGF for the Visual Subordinate minus Basic comparison, whereas it was not in the Faces minus Objects comparison, can be explained by the much wider focus of activation in the Visual task than the Localiser. To address this issue, in the next section we introduce a technique in which we positioned a small ROI on the putative face area in the average as well as the individual results for the Localiser task, the purpose being to compare the activation in the Visual task for these two definitions; in doing so, we also verify that there is a local peak of activation in the midFG for the Faces minus Objects comparison.

COMPARISON OF AVERAGE AND INDIVIDUAL DEFINITIONS OF THE FACE AREA

Definitions of the Face Area ROI

Because of the known variability in the location of the face area, Gauthier et al. (1997) used a large ROI, which should have included most subjects' face areas based on results from intracranial recordings and fMRI (Allison et al., 1994; Puce et al., 1995, 1996). The caveat of this technique, as shown in the previous section, is that such a large ROI is also likely to include cortical areas that are actually more responsive to the presentation of nonface objects than faces.

Here we compare two different definitions of the face area. In the *average* definition, a small ROI is centred on the face area of a composite map for the 11 subjects. If such a group-average definition is found to be an efficient way of localising the face area within a restricted region, it has the advantage that only a limited number of Localiser images are required of any subject in an experiment. This is important if a group-average definition is to be used in further imaging studies—the number of images that can be obtained from one subject in one session is limited. In contrast, when sufficient data for a Localiser task is gathered in each subject (here for instance, we took as many images for the Localiser task for the Visual task), an *individual* definition of the functional face area can be used. This method has proven useful in prior studies but it has never

been compared with an average definition (Kanwisher et al., 1997a; Gauthier, Tarr, Anderson, & Gore, 1999).

The centre of the *average* face area was positioned in the Localiser task, for the midFG foci in each hemisphere (Slice 3) that showed the strongest activation for Faces minus Objects in the median composite for all subjects (see Fig. 2). *Individual* face area ROIs were centred on the strongest midFG focus (or postFG in some subjects) encountered in the Localiser task for each subject, in each hemisphere independently. All ROIs were localised without regard to the activation in the Visual task.

Apart from the two different ways of positioning ROIs, the same procedure was used to quantify activation according to both definitions. A grid composed of a central box-ROI of 5 × 5 voxels surrounded by four adjacent boxes of the same size (see Fig. 2) was centred on the average and individual face areas. This ROI was defined in standardised (pseudo-Talairach) space and each voxel was 1.3mm × 1.7mm in plane (about 5.4 of the original voxels which were 3.125mm × 3.125mm each). The size of our face area ROI is thus comparable (and even smaller) to that defined in published studies (Kanwisher et al., 1997a, 1998). The size of the box was chosen to match the size of the face area in the Localiser task. The individual definition includes on average 23 out of 25 standardised voxels with signal higher for faces than objects. A larger area includes more voxels with a signal change in the other direction (objects > faces), while a smaller area leads to a less focused "face area", with activation for Faces minus Objects spilling to contiguous ROIs. In each of these box-ROIs, the per cent signal change was summed for voxels for the Faces minus Objects and the Visual Subordinate minus Basic comparisons. This measure is similar to that of Kanwisher et al. (1997a).

The Localiser results for some subjects showed bilateral activation in the midFG whereas for others the activation was more strongly lateralised. In order to define a single face area in each individual, the data for each subject were obtained only from the dominant hemisphere (for the Localiser task) or from both hemispheres combined if the Localiser activation was bilateral. For both the individual and average definitions, subjects were defined as "lateralised" if they had at least 50% more voxels showing higher signal for faces than objects in one hemisphere than in the other. Because laterality was determined for each definition separately, a subject may be lateralised in one definition and bilateral in the other (see Fig. 2). Summed per cent signal change was measured in each of the five box-ROIs and averaged across hemisphere for bilateral subjects and only in the dominant hemisphere for lateralised subjects.

Results

The data were first combined across hemispheres for "bilateral" subjects, and a mean was computed for each box-ROI. Mean summed activation in each box-ROI for the individual and average definitions of the face area are shown in Fig. 3. For each definition, an ANOVA was performed on the summed activation with Task (Visual Subordinate minus Basic vs. Faces minus Objects) and ROI (1–5) as within-subjects factors.

For the average definition, none of the main effects was significant, nor was the interaction between ROI and Task (F < 1). There was no difference between the different box-ROIs for Faces minus Objects nor for Subordinate minus Basic,

even using the powerful Least Significant Difference (LSD) post hoc test (using $P < .05$). LSD tests showed a higher signal change for Faces minus Objects than Subordinate minus Basic judgements in box ROIs 1 and 4.

For the individual definition, only the main effect of ROI was significant [$F(4,10) = 2.75$, $P < .05$]. The Task by ROI interaction was not significant [$F(4,40) = 1.53$, n.s.]. LSD tests showed more activation in box-ROI 3 (face area) than all other box-ROIs for Faces minus Objects but no difference between box-ROIs for Subordinate minus Basic. The only task differences occurred in box-ROIs 1 and 4, with a stronger signal change for Subordinate minus Basic than for Faces minus Objects. Having defined ROI based on the Localiser results, we maximised the amount of activation in this area for the Faces minus Objects comparison: A regression to the mean would disadvantage the Visual task, playing against our hypothesis.

We also compared directly the individual and average definitions in each box-ROI, for each of the two tasks. The only significant difference occurred in the box-ROI 3 (face area) for Faces minus Objects, where the individual definition led to a stronger summed signal change than the average definition [mean difference = 4.3, $t(10) = 3.56$, $P = .005$]. Thus, the individual definition leads to both stronger and more focused activation in the

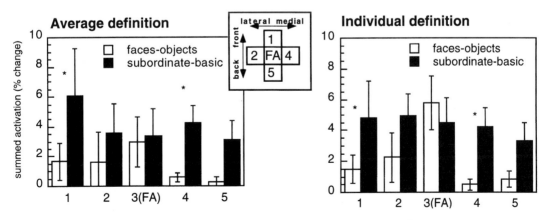

Fig. 3. *Summed per cent signal change in each 5 × 5 standardized voxel square ROI (a volume of .38cm³) for the average and individual definitions of the face area, for data combined across hemisphere for "bilateral" subjects and that from the dominant hemisphere in "lateralised" subjects. Asterisks indicate significant paired t-tests.*

face area for Faces minus Objects. This is not surprising, because it is optimised for each subject. However, it is worth pointing out that a mean individual definition is more similar to each individual face area, which typically shows a strong and focused peak of activation, and thus may be necessary in order to investigate the spatial distribution of the activation.

DISCUSSION

Categorisation Level in Visual and Semantic Processing

Categorisation level was found to be an important determinant for the recruitment of several occipital and temporal areas in both visual and semantic judgements. Our results are consistent with Jolicoeur et al. (1984) in that subordinate-level judgements required additional perceptual processing relative to basic-level judgements. Subordinate-level visual judgements engaged a much larger portion of the ventral pathway than their basic-level counterparts, including a large part of the fusiform gyri as well as the ventral and lateral aspects of the occipital gyri.

We also tested the hypothesis formulated by Gauthier et al. (1997), that subordinate-level semantic judgements may recruit early visual areas because of visual imagery. In Gauthier et al. this effect could have been the result of the differential word length in the Semantic task when subordinate-level and basic-level words were visually presented. Here, by using aurally presented words and asking subjects to close their eyes, the additional length of the subordinate-level words was carried in the auditory domain (presumably causing postMTG activation). This reduced the extent of activation as compared to the visual presentation. We obtained no strong evidence of early visual activation by semantic subordinate-level judgements. This result, however, should be considered cautiously because of two caveats: a possible lack of statistical power as well as the fact that the lingual gyrus was significantly more activated for Semantic than Visual subordinate-level judgements.

Finally, the recruitment of the left postITG in all three of the comparisons used in this study came as somewhat of a surprise. Both our Visual and Semantic Subordinate minus Basic comparisons could lead to differential linguistic/semantic processing. This would be consistent with the activation of the left inferior temporal gyrus in a study by Binder et al. (1997) for semantic judgements on animals' names when compared to judgements on tones. However, passive viewing of faces should not evoke any more linguistic/semantic processing than that of nonface objects, but the postITG was also recruited, only in the left hemisphere, in our Faces minus Objects comparison. We originally postulated that subordinate-level visual judgements would share perceptual processing with that of faces even during passive viewing of the latter. It is possible that the common denominator in all of our tasks, as well as Binder et al.'s study, is an aspect of visual processing that is elicited by concrete nouns more than by tones and by subordinate-level more than by basic-level judgements, regardless of whether they rely on perception or on mental images. In order for this to be resolved, a stronger test of visual imagery for subordinate semantic judgements is required.

The Role of Categorisation Level in Face Recognition

The single subtraction design used here was successful in replicating, within individual subjects, the pattern of results obtained by Gauthier et al. (1997). The present results also extend our earlier findings, providing additional information on the role of categorisation level in the comparison between faces and objects. Consistent with Gauthier et al., the anatomically defined mid-fusiform gyrus was found to be engaged by visual subordinate-level judgements with nonface objects. An individual functional definition of the face area was found to be preferable to an anatomical definition or to an average functional definition for measuring the focal signal change for faces minus objects. Critically, subordinate-level processing recruited the face area using both an average and an individual definition. This is evidence against the hypothesis that the subordinate-level activation isolated by Gauthier et al. (1997) could be mutually exclusive from the face area within individual subjects.

Subordinate-level processing elicited activation of a magnitude comparable to that obtained for Faces minus Objects in the individually defined face area, *as well as* in surrounding ventral temporal cortex. Therefore, categorisation level, a dimension that we argue is often confounded with stimulus-class membership in experimental designs, could potentially account for the *magnitude* of the activation in the face area but not for the specificity in spatial distribution. In other words, the face area is a subset of the region of midFG cortex that is implicated in subordinate-level processing of objects. In reality, it is unlikely that level of categorisation can account for the entire magnitude of the faces minus objects effect, given that studies that compared face and object processing at the subordinate level obtained stronger activation for faces (Kanwisher et al., 1997a; Tong et al., 1998, but see our earlier discussion regarding a "1-back" task with rare target repetitions).

Before we accept the hypothesis that categorisation level accounts for the magnitude of activation in the face area, several issues need to be addressed. First, is this not merely the result of a difficulty effect? And if it is, what is the relation between difficulty and face recognition? Second, even if some of the Faces minus Objects effects are due to a level of categorisation difference, what accounts for the spatial specificity of the activation pattern?

There is no doubt that there is a difficulty effect intrinsic to our level of categorisation manipulation: We selected our stimuli so that each picture would be matched faster to its basic-level name than its subordinate-level name (Gauthier et al., 1997). The basic-level advantage is crucial to categorisation work (Rosch, 1978; Rosch et al., 1976; Tanaka & Taylor, 1991) and it would be meaningless to attempt to equate level of difficulty between basic and subordinate-level judgements. Consider that objects can often be categorised at the basic level merely by the presence of single features or configurations of features (e.g. the presence of wings is highly diagnostic of the category "bird"),

whereas objects within the same basic-level category share parts and their configuration (e.g. all cars have wheels, a bumper, and headlights in the same relative configuration). On the other hand, some perceptual dimensions have been found to be more important to the processing of subordinate-level tasks (including faces) as compared to basic-level tasks, for example, shading, texture, colour, surface detail, pigmentation, and the specific spatial arrangement of features (see Bruce & Humphreys, 1994, for review).

In this context, the activation of most of the ventral pathway obtained here for Subordinate minus Basic can be viewed as the result of the additional visual attention or more complex processing required for subordinate-level judgements. However, this does not mean that the fusiform and occipital gyri play the same undifferentiated role. Some evidence comes from Gauthier et al. (1997), who used a visual semantic control condition in which subordinate-level and basic-level words, matched in many respects (including a difficulty effect) with those used in the visual task, were presented visually (rather than aurally). When this Semantic Subordinate minus Basic control (which includes a difference in difficulty) was subtracted from the Visual Subordinate minus Basic comparison, what remained of the ventral temporal lobe activation was only the fusiform-ITG region. In addition, one can consider the effect of brain lesions in different parts of the visual system. Lesions anywhere in the ventral visual pathway can produce visual recognition impairments that may be worse for subordinate than basic-level recognition, again simply because subordinate-level judgements are more difficult. However, a recent study (Gauthier, Behrmann, & Tarr, 1999) reveals that prosopagnosic patients (prosopagnosia tends to be associated with fusiform damage [A.R. Damasio, Damasio, & Hoesen, 1982; A.R. Damasio, Tranel, & Damasio, 1990]) may be normal at basic-level recognition but show an increasing impairment as the recognition task becomes increasingly subordinate (e.g. discriminating a chair, a pelican, or a duck from another duck). In other words, although a level-of-categorisation manipulation leads to a significant difficulty effect in normal subjects (who respond more slowly the more subordinate the comparison), prosopagnosic patients show a disproportionate sensitivity. Many studies report that prosopagnosic patients have configural processing difficulties (Arguin, Bub, & Dudek, 1996; Davidoff, Matthews, & Newcombe, 1986; Levine & Calvanio, 1989; Rentschler, Treutwein, & Landis, 1994; Williams & Behrmann, 1998), so it appears that for the most part, they can see local features but cannot integrate them to discriminate visually similar objects. Subordinate-level recognition probably requires additional processing of local features as well as combining them into more global configurations. Thus, it is possible that the additional occipital lobe activation for subordinate-level matching is due to additional featural processing and the additional fusiform activation to the additional configural processing.

Our initial claim was that the often-used Faces minus Objects task includes, among other things, a subordinate-level effect. How can this hold, when Faces minus Objects does not include a difficulty effect (given the absence of a task) nor lead to increased activation of the occipital lobe? It may be worth distinguishing two ways in which tasks may differ in difficulty. On the one hand, a given task may require more complex or additional computational steps, causing subjects to perform it more slowly and less accurately than another task. On the other hand, two tasks may include comparable computational demands but subjects may have much more experience solving one task than another, in practice making it less difficult (similar to an automaticity effect). Expertise in visual recognition leads to what has been called a "basic-level shift" (Tanaka & Gauthier, 1997; Tanaka & Taylor, 1991): While novices take longer identifying a robin as a robin than as a bird, expert birders are equivalently fast at both levels. Although we do not understand what mediates this shift or what neural substrates support such a shift, we do know that experts use configurational clues more than novices. Thus, expertise leads to well-established behavioural effects (configural processing) that are similar to those obtained with faces (Diamond & Carey, 1986; Gauthier & Tarr, 1997; Gauthier, Williams, Tarr, & Tanaka, 1998).

Such configural processing may be reflected in a relative shift of the burden of processing from early visual areas to the midFG. In other words, it is possible, and consistent with the behavioural literature, that the relative absence of occipital lobe activation for faces (as compared to subordinate-level matching for nonface objects) reflects an expertise shift in difficulty. Faces recognised at the subordinate level may require configural processing similar to that necessary for subordinate-level object matching (and presumably performed in the midFG), but expert subjects may be more efficient in earlier computational steps that feed in the midFG and/or they may have learned to use relatively fewer processing resources than novices. Indeed, a recent experiment (Gauthier et al., 1999) demonstrated that when subjects are experts with a category of novel objects ("Greebles"), identity matching of upright minus inverted Greebles as well as passive viewing of Greebles minus Objects both produce focal activation comparable in spatial extent to that obtained with faces. Thus, the combination of categorisation level and expertise appears to provide a plausible explanation for the strong focal activation obtained when faces are compared to nonface objects.

One piece of evidence that may be hard to reconcile with our conclusions is the behavioural pattern exhibited by patient CK (Moscovitch, Winocur, & Behrmann, 1997). CK has selectively spared face recognition abilities, but fails at subordinate-level (even basic-level in some cases) recognition of nonface objects. Such results are consistent with nonexpert subordinate-level processing requiring much of the ventral pathway as well as the midFG. However, anecdotal evidence suggests that CK has lost his expertise in recognising toy soldiers, *inconsistent* with his face recognition abilities being spared because of expertise (although it is possible that knowledge of toy soldiers has more to do with local features—colours of uniforms, shape of hats, types of weapons, flags—than with configural cues). Ideally, we would want to know what would have happened if CK had premorbidly been an expert with objects, such as Greebles, that have been shown to produce behavioural configural effects and recruit the face area in experts. Obviously, this particular question cannot be answered.

Our experiments tested directly what was already implicit in the neuroimaging literature: There is nothing unique about faces activating the fusiform gyrus, since many other tasks also do so (Kanwisher et al., 1997a; Lang et al., 1998; Schacter et al., 1995). In this study, however, we have established that midFG activation for nonface objects includes the face area even when measured in individual subjects. We have also demonstrated that an endogenous manipulation of categorisation level, using identical pictures of nonface objects, can lead to a signal change in the face area of a magnitude comparable to that of passive viewing of faces minus objects. Our results point to what may be special about the way faces activate the midFG: For each individual, faces lead to spatially focused activation in a small part of the fusiform gyrus. Categorisation level does not seem to be able to account for this spatial specificity. Rather than focusing only on this small area of the cortex (Kanwisher et al., 1997a, 1998; Tong et al., 1998), neuroimaging research may have to consider how the activation in the entire ventral pathway is modulated by different object categories, tasks, and levels of expertise. We may arrive at new and productive hypotheses by rephrasing the question "Why is the face area so strongly engaged by faces?" into "Why is the surrounding cortex so weakly engaged by faces?". Our results also highlight the importance of controlling for categorisation level in making comparisons across stimulus classes. Consider the proposal by McCarthy et al. (1997) that face-specific processing can only be isolated if the "general" object recognition system is occupied by concurrent object processing. To demonstrate this point, these authors devised a stimulus presentation design in which faces (or flowers) would appear periodically at one of several locations while nonface objects would occupy the other positions randomly. However, in light of our findings, it appears that there is a confound in this design—nonface objects (for instance the objects presented during passive viewing in our Localiser task) are *not* processed automatically at the subordinate level (Jolicoeur et al., 1984; Rosch et al., 1976; Schultz et al., 1997; Tanaka & Gauthier, 1997). Therefore, the background objects presented in this study in all likelihood *did not* "occupy" general subordinate-level processes to any significant degree. Moreover, it is unlikely that flowers are processed at the subordinate level without specific instructions to this effect.

The current debate on whether the putative face area is or is not a face-specific module has focused on contrasting two types of evidence. First, that the "face area" is engaged more strongly by faces than any other type of nonface objects. Second, that under some circumstances (e.g. expertise, subordinate-level processing), nonface objects may recruit the same area. This debate may be doomed to remain unresolved in that even if faces turn out to consistently engage a specific part of the midFG more than other objects, it would still be unclear what factors produce such specialisation. Thus, we suggest that a more profitable course is to explore how the "face area" becomes specialised by resolving the conditions under which nonface objects can also activate this area.

REFERENCES

Allison, T., Ginter, H., McCarthy, G., Nobre, A., Puce, A., Luby, M., & Spencer, D.D. (1994). Face recognition in human extrastriate cortex. *Journal of Neurophysiology, 71*(2), 821–825.

Arguin, M., Bub, D., & Dudek, G. (1996). Shape integration for visual object recognition and its implications in category-specific visual agnosia. *Visual Cognition, 3*(3), 221–275.

Binder, J.R., Frost, J., Hammeke, T., Cox, R.W., Rao, S.M., & Prieto, T. (1997). Human brain language areas identified by functional magnetic resonance imaging. *Journal of Neuroscience, 17*(1), 353–362.

Bruce, V., & Humphreys, G. (1994). Recognizing faces and objects. *Visual Cognition, 1*, 141–180.

Constable, R., Studlarski, P., Mencl, E., Pugh, K.R., Fulbright, R., Lacadie, C., Shaywitz, S.E., & Shaywitz, B.A. (1998). Quantifying and comparing ROI activation patterns in functional brain MR imaging: Methodology considerations. *Magnetic Resonance Imaging, 16*, 289–300.

Craik, F.I.M., & Lockhart, R.S. (1972). Levels of processing: A framework for memory research. *Journal of Verbal Learning and Verbal Behaviour, 11,* 671–684.

Damasio, A.R., Damasio, H., & Hoesen, G.W.V. (1982). Prosopagnosia: Anatomical basis and behavioral mechanisms. *Neurology, 32,* 331–341.

Damasio, A.R., Tranel, D., & Damasio, H. (1990). Face agnosia and the neural substrates of memory. *Annual Review of Neuroscience, 13,* 89–109.

Damasio, H. (1995). *Human brain anatomy in computerized images.* New York: Oxford University Press.

Davidoff, J.B., Matthews, W.B., & Newcombe, F. (1986). Observations on a case of prosopagnosia. In H.D. Ellis, M.A. Jeeves, F. Newcombe, & A. Young (Eds.), *Aspects of face processing* (pp. 279–290). Dordrecht, The Netherlands: Martinus Nijhoff.

Diamond, R., & Carey, S. (1986). Why faces are and are not special: An effect of expertise. *Journal of Experimental Psychology: General, 115*(2), 107–117.

Dill, M., & Fahle, M. (1998). Limited translation invariance of human visual pattern recognition. *Perception and Psychophysics, 60*(1), 65–81.

Duvernoy, H.M. (1991). *The human brain. Surface, three-dimensional sectional anatomy and MRI.* Wien: Springer-Verlag.

Farrell, B. (1985). "Same"–"different" judgements: A review of current controversies in perceptual comparisons. *Psychological Bulletin, 98*(3), 419–456.

Gabrieli, J.D.E., Brewer, J.B., Desmond, J.E., & Glover, G.H. (1997). Separate neural bases of two fundamental memory processes in the human medial temporal lobe. *Science, 276,* 264–266.

Gauthier, I., Anderson, A.W., Tarr, M.J., Skudlarski, P., & Gore, J.C. (1997). Levels of categorization in visual object studied with functional MRI. *Current Biology, 7,* 645–651.

Gauthier, I., Behrmann, M., & Tarr, M.J. (1999a). Can face recognition really be dissociated from object recognition? *Journal of Cognitive Neuroscience, 11,* 349–370.

Gauthier, I., & Tarr, M.J. (1997). Becoming a "Greeble" expert: Exploring the face recognition mechanism. *Vision Research, 37*(12), 1673–1682.

Gauthier, I., Tarr, M.J., Anderson, A., & Gore, J. (1999b). Activation of the middle fusiform "face area" increases with experience in recognizing novel objects. *Nature Neuroscience, 2,* 568–573

Gauthier, I., Williams, P., Tarr, M.J., & Tanaka, J.W. (1998). Training "Greeble" experts: A framework for studying expert object recognition processes. *Vision Research, 38,* 2401–2428.

Haxby, J.V., Horwitz, B., Ungerleider, L.B., Maisog, J.M., Pietrini, P., & Grady, C.L. (1994). The functional organization of human extrastriate cortex: A PET/RCBF study of selective attention to faces and locations. *The Journal of Neuroscience, 14,* 6336–6353.

Ishai, A., Ungerleider, L.G., Martin, A., Maisog, J.M., & Haxby, J.V. (1997). fMRI reveals differential activation in the ventral object vision pathway during the perception of faces, houses, and chairs. *NeuroImage, 5,* S149.

Johnson, C.L., Paivio, A., & Clark, J.M. (1996). Cognitive components of picture naming. *Psychological Bulletin, 120*(1), 113–139.

Jolicoeur, P., Gluck, M., & Kosslyn, S.M. (1984). Pictures and names: Making the connection. *Cognitive Psychology, 16,* 243–275.

Kanwisher, N., Chun, M.M., McDermott, J., & Ledden, P.J. (1996). Functional imaging of human visual recognition. *Cognitive Brain Research, 5,* 55–67.

Kanwisher, N., McDermott, J., & Chun, M.M. (1997a). The fusiform face area: A module in human extrastriate cortex specialized for face perception. *Journal of Neuroscience, 17,* 4302–4311.

Kanwisher, N., Tong, F., & Nakayama, K. (1998). The effect of face inversion on the human fusiform face area. *Cognition, 68*(1), B1–11.

Kanwisher, N., Woods, R., Iacoboni, M., & Mazziota, J. (1997b). A locus in human extrastriate cortex for visual shape analysis. *Journal of Cognitive Neuroscience, 9,* 133–142.

Kosslyn, S.M., Alpert, N.M., & Thompson, W.L. (1995). Identifying objects at different levels of hierarchy: A positron emission tomography study. *Human Brain Mapping, 3,* 107–132.

Lang, P.J., Bradley, M.M., Fitzsimmons, J.R., Scott, J.D., Moulder, B., & Nangia, V. (1998). Emotional arousal and activation of the visual cortex: An fmri analysis. *Psychophysiology, 35*(2), 199–210.

Levin, D.T. (1996). Classifying faces by race: The structure of face categories. *Journal of Experimental Psychology: Learning, Memory and Cognition, 22,* 1364–1382.

Levine, D.N., & Calvanio, R. (1989). Prosopagnosia: A defect in visual configural processing. *Brain and Cognition, 10,* 149–170.

Malach, R., Reppas, J., Benson, R., Kwong, K., Jiang, H., Kennedy, W., Ledden, P., Brady, T., Rosen, B., & Tootell, R. (1995). Object-related activity revealed by functional magnetic resonance imaging in

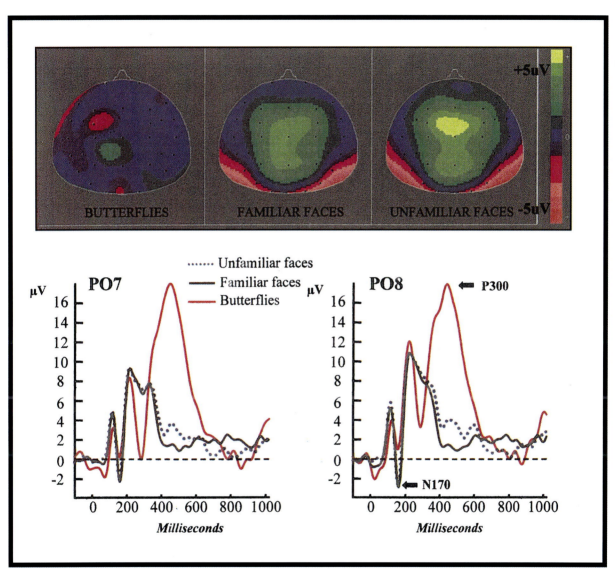

Plate 1 (Bentin and Deouell). *Upper panel: Scalp spline interpolations of the potentials elicited by familiar faces, unfamiliar faces, and butterflies at 164msec—the peak latency of the N170. Lower panel: The ERPs elicited by butterflies (targets) and by familiar and unfamiliar faces (distractors) in Experiment 1, at PO8 (right hemisphere) and PO7 (left hemisphere).*

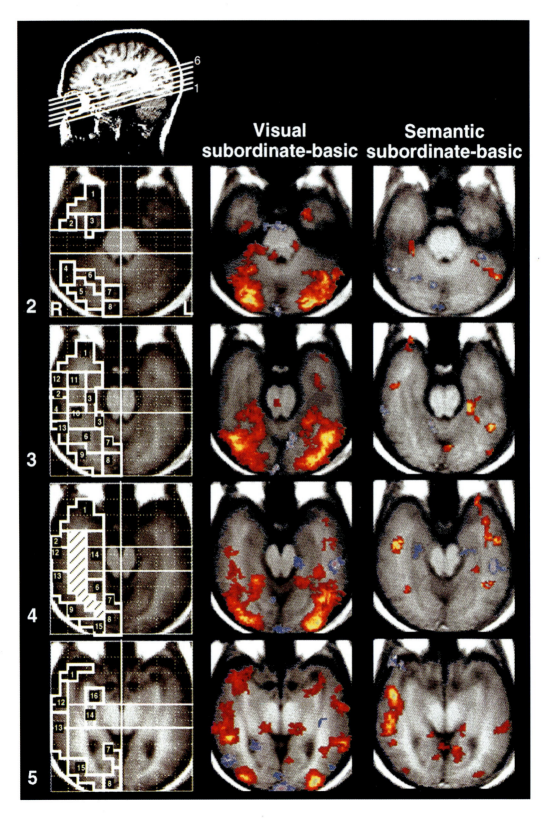

Plate 2 (Gauthier et al., caption opposite).

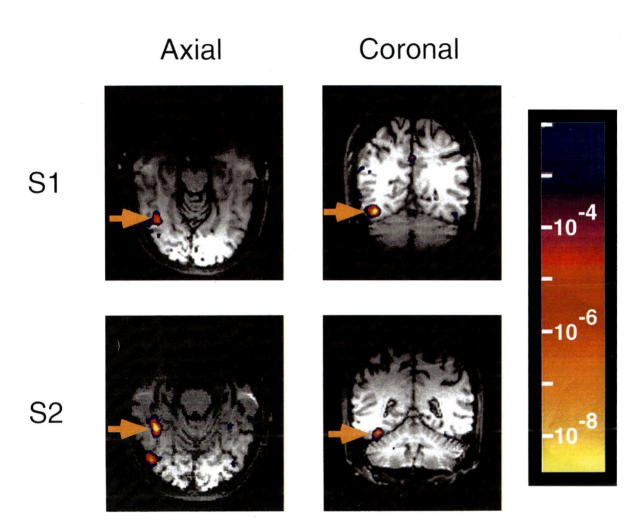

Plate 3 (Tong et al.). *Axial and coronal slices showing the fusiform face area (FFA) in two subjects. Arrows point to the FFA, which included all contiguous voxels in the fusiform gyrus that showed significant differences in activity to faces minus objects or faces minus houses (P < .0001 uncorrected on a Kolmogorov–Smirnov test, see adjacent colour scale) on functional localiser scans. Note that the right hemisphere is shown on the left side in all images and vice versa.*

Plate 2 (opposite: Gauthier et al.). *Regions of interest defined anatomically, mapped on composite anatomical images for 11 subjects. 1, temporal poles; 2, anterior inferior temporal gyrus; 3, parahippocampal gyrus; 4, posterior inferior temporal gyrus; 5, inferior occipital gyrus; 6, posterior fusiform gyrus; 7, lingual gyrus; 8, cuneus; 9, lateral occipital gyrus; 10, middle fusiform gyrus; 11, anterior fusiform gyrus; 12, anterior middle temporal gyrus; 13, posterior middle temporal gyrus; 14, hippocampus; 15, superior occipital gyrus; 16, amygdala. Median composite image for the Visual (N = 11) and the Semantic (N = 8) Subordinate minus Basic comparisons, in four different slices through the temporal lobe. Red to yellow voxels show the voxels more activated for Subordinate than Basic level while blue to purple voxels indicate voxels activated for Basic than Subordinate level. The maps are thresholded at a t-value of 0.25 and a cluster filter of 11 voxels.*

human occipital cortex. *Proceedings of the National Academy of Sciences, USA, 18,* 8135–8139.

McCarthy, G., Puce, A., Gore, J., & Allison, T. (1997). Face-specific processing in the fusiform gyrus. *Journal of Cognitive Neuroscience, 9*(5), 605–610.

Moscovitch, M., Kapur, S., Kohler, S., & Houle, S. (1995). Distinct neural correlates of visual long-term memory for spatial location and object identity: A positron emission tomography study in humans. *Proceedings of the National Academy of Sciences, USA, 92,* 3721–3725.

Moscovitch, M., Winocur, G., & Behrmann, M. (1997). What is special in face recognition? Nineteen experiments on a person with visual object agnosia and dyslexia but normal face recognition. *Journal of Cognitive Neuroscience, 9*(5), 555–604.

Murphy, G., & Smith, E. (1982). Basic-level superiority in picture categorization. *Journal of Verbal Learning and Verbal Behaviour, 21,* 120.

Murphy, G.L. (1991). Parts in object concepts: Experiments with artificial categories. *Memory and Cognition, 19,* 423–438.

Puce, A., Allison, T., Asgari, M., Gore, J.C., & McCarthy, G. (1996). Face-sensitive regions in human extrastriate cortex studied by functional MRI. *Neurophysiology, 74*(3), 1192–1199.

Puce, A., Allison, T., Gore, J.C., & McCarthy, G. (1995). Differential sensitivity of human visual cortex to faces, letter strings, and textures: A functional magnetic resonance imaging study. *Neurophysiology, 74*(3), 1192–1199.

Puce, A., Allison, T., Spencer, S.S., Spencer, D.D., & McCarthy, G. (1997). Comparisons of cortical activation evoked by faces by intracranial field potentials and functional MRI: Two case studies. *Human Brain Mapping, 5,* 298–305.

Rentschler, I., Treutwein, B., & Landis, T. (1994). Dissociation of local and global processing in visual agnosia. *Vision Research, 34,* 963–971.

Rhodes, G., Brennan, S., & Carey, S. (1987). Identification and ratings of caricatures: Implications for mental representations of faces. *Cognitive Psychology, 19,* 473–497.

Rhodes, G., & McLean, I.G. (1990). Distinctiveness and expertise effects with homogeneous stimuli: Towards a model of configural coding. *Perception, 19,* 773–794.

Rosch, E. (1976). Basic objects in natural categories. *Cognitive Psychology, 8*(3), 382–439.

Rosch, E. (1978). Principles of categorization. In E. Rosch & B.B. Lloyd (Eds.), *Cognition and categorization* (pp. 27–48). Hillsdale, NJ: Lawrence Erlbaum Associates Inc.

Rosch, E., Mervis, C.B., Gray, W.D., Johnson, D.M., & Boyes-Braem, P. (1976). Basic objects in natural categories. *Cognitive Psychology, 8,* 382–439.

Schacter, D.L., Reiman, E., Uecker, A., Polster, M.R., Yun, L.S., & Cooper, L.A. (1995). Brain regions associated with retrieval of structurally coherent visual information. *Nature, 376,* 587–590.

Schultz, R.T., Gauthier, I., Fulbright, R., Anderson, A.W., Lacadie, C., Skudlarski, P., Tarr, M.J., Cohen, D.J., & Gore, J.C. (1997). Are face identity and emotion processed automatically? *Neuroimage, 5*(4), S148.

Sergent, J., Ohta, S., & MacDonald, B. (1992). Functional neuroanatomy of face and object processing. *Brain, 115,* 15–36.

Sheskin, D.J. (1997). *Handbook of parametric and nonparametric statistical procedures.* Boca Raton, FA: CRC Press.

Skudlarski, P., Constable, R.T., & Gore, J.C. (1999). ROC analysis of statistical methods used in functional MRI. *Neuroimage, 9,* 311-329.

Stern, C.E., Corkin, S., Gonzalez, R.G., Guimaraes, A.R., Baker, J.R., Carr, C.A., Sugiura, R.M., Vedantham, V., & Rosen, B.R. (1996). The hippocampal formation participates in novel picture encoding: Evidence from functional magnetic resonance imaging. *Proceedings of the National Academy of Sciences, USA, 93*(16), 8660–8665.

Talairach, J., & Tournoux, P. (1998). *Co-planar stereotaxic atlas of the human brain: 3-dimensional proportion system: An approach to cerebral imaging.* Stuttgart: G. Thieme.

Tanaka, J.W., & Gauthier, I. (1997). Expertise in object and face recognition. In R.L. Goldstone, P.G. Schyns, & D.L. Medin (Eds.), *Psychology of learning and motivation* (Vol. 36, pp. 83–125). San Diego, CA: Academic Press.

Tanaka, J.W., & Taylor, M. (1991). Object categories and expertise: Is the basic level in the eye of the beholder? *Cognitive Psychology, 23,* 457–482.

Tong, F., Nakayama, K., Moscovitch, M., Weinrib, O., & Kanwisher, N. (1998). *Response properties of the human fusiform face area.* Unpublished manuscript, Harvard University.

Tversky, B., & Hemenway, K. (1984). Objects, parts, and categories. *Journal of Experimental Psychology: General, 113,* 169–193.

Williams, P., & Behrmann, M. (1998). *Acquisition and recognition of novel entry-level object categories in prosopagnosic patients*. Paper presented at the 69th annual meeting of the Eastern Psychological Association, Boston, MA.

Williams, P., & Tarr, M.J. (undated). *RSVP: Experimental control software for MacOS*. [Online]. Available: http://psych.umb.edu/rsvp/ [1998, September 9th].

Zeki, S., Watson, J.D., Friston, K., & Frackowiak, R. (1991). A direct demonstration of functional specialization in human visual cortex. *Journal of Neuroscience, 11*(3), 641–649.

Zola-Morgan, S. Squire, L.R., Amaral, D.G., & Suzuki, W.A. (1989). Lesions of perirhinal and parahippocampal cortex that spare the amygdala and hippocampal formation produce severe memory impairment. *Journal of Neuroscience, 9*, 4355–4370.

APPENDIX A

List of Words Used in the Visual Task

Picture (Sub Matching)	Sub Distractor	Basic Matching	Basic Distractor	Picture (Sub Matching)	Sub Distractor	Basic Matching	Basic Distractor
Acoustic guitar	Electric guitar	Guitar	Phone	Lounge chair	Beach chair	Chair	Phone
Alarm clock	Mantle clock	Clock	Chair	Mantle clock	Alarm clock	Clock	Chair
Ant	Bee	Insect	Bird	Motorboat	Dinghy	Boat	Chair
Beach chair	Classroom chair	Chair	Dog	Mug	Tea cup	Cup	Chair
Bee	Fly	Insect	Car	Payphone	Rotary phone	Phone	Piano
Biplane	Boeing	Plane	Dog	Pelican	Sparrow	Bird	Dinosaur
Blue Whale	Beluga	Whale	Phone	Picnic table	Coffee table	Table	Guitar
Boeing	Bomber	Plane	Clock	Pine	Cedar	Tree	Hat
Bomber	Seaplane	Plane	Car	Police car	Honda	Car	Shoe
Camaro	Station wagon	Car	Tree	Poster bed	Bunkbed	Bed	Boat
City bus	School bus	Bus	Boat	Racing car	Honda	Car	Clock
Classroom chair	Lounge chair	Chair	Boat	Recliner	German Shepherd	Dog	Chair
Coffee table	Dining table	Table	Insect	Rotary phone	Touchtone phone	Phone	Car
Cruiser	Galleon	Boat	Car	Sandal	Sneaker	Shoe	Bus
Daisy	Rose	Flower	Car	School bus	Tour bus	Bus	Bird
Deck chair	Folding chair	Chair	Plane	Seaplane	Triplane	Plane	Car
Desk chair	Recliner	Chair	Car	Sneaker	Sandal	Shoe	Bus
Dinghy	Speedboat	Boat	Chair	Sparrow	Eagle	Bird	Fish
Dining table	Picnic table	Table	Piano	Speedboat	Cruiser	Boat	Piano
Diplodocus	Triceratops	Dinosaur	Bird	Station wagon	Lamborghini	Car	Bottle
Duck	Pelican	Bird	Car	T-rex	Diplodocus	Dinosaur	Table
Dumptruck	Tractor trailer	Truck	Whale	Tabasco bottle	Wine bottle	Bottle	Boat
Eagle	Jay	Bird	Dinosaur	Tea cup	Mug	Cup	Plane
Electric piano	Upright piano	Piano	Insect	Thunderbird	Police car	Car	Dog
Executive chair	Beach chair	Chair	Bird	Top hat	Cap	Hat	Table
Ferrari	Police Car	Car	Bus	Touchtone phone	Payphone	Phone	Table
Flamingo	Duck	Bird	Chair	Tour bus	City bus	Bus	Bird
Fluted glass	Water glass	Glass	Bird	Tractor trailer	Dumptruck	Truck	Whale
Fly	Ant	Insect	Piano	Triceratops	T-rex	Dinosaur	Fish
Folding chair	Lounge chair	Chair	Glass	Triplane	Bomber	Plane	Bed
Galleon	Motor boat	Boat	Truck	Tuna	Piranha	Fish	Cup
German shepherd	Retriever	Dog	Shoe	Upright piano	Electric piano	Piano	Plane
Goose	Eagle	Bird	Flower	Volkswagen	Thunderbird	Car	Bottle
Honda	Ferrari	Car	Bus	Water glass	Fluted glass	Glass	Bus
Jay	Pelican	Bird	Truck	Wine bottle	Tabasco bottle	Bottle	Car
Lamborghini	Camaro	Car	Insect				

APPENDIX B

Lists of Words Used in the Semantic Task

Basic	Subordinate	Basic	Subordinate	Basic	Subordinate	Basic	Subordinate
Automobile	Black bear	Bowl	Grand piano	Helicopter	Picnic basket	Pants	Siamese
Baby	Boxing glove	Box	Grizzly	Horse	Pingpong table	Pig	Ski goggles
Bag	Cobra	Bat	Hammerhead	House	Polar bear	Plant	Soda bottle
Basket	Cockatoo	Boat	Jeep	Knife	Pool table	Rabbit	Sunglasses
Bear	Corvette	Door	Ketchup bottle	Lamp	Pterodactyl	Rocket	Swan
Bell	Crane	Elephant	Lab coat	Leaf	Raincoat	Shark	Tow truck
Bike	Dagger	Fan	Maple leaf	Light	Rattlesnake	Ship	Traffic light
Bike[a]	Dalmation	Glasses	Mouthwash bottle	Motorcycle	Sailboat	Snake	Tricycle
Bone	Desk lamp	Glove	Oil lamp	Mouse	Seagull	Train	Victorian Chair
Book	Flash light	Gun	Owl				

[a]Repeated due to experimenter's error.

COGNITIVE NEUROPSYCHOLOGY, 2000, 17 (1/2/3), 165–186

AGE-RELATED CHANGES IN THE NEURAL CORRELATES OF DEGRADED AND NONDEGRADED FACE PROCESSING

Cheryl L. Grady and A. Randy McIntosh

Rotman Research Institute, Baycrest Centre for Geriatric Care, University of Toronto, Canada

Barry Horwitz and Stanley I. Rapoport

National Institute on Aging, Bethesda, USA

In order to explore the neural correlates of age-related changes in visual perception of faces, positron emission tomographic scans were obtained on young and old adults while they were engaged in tasks of nondegraded and degraded face matching. Old adults were less accurate than were young adults across all face matching conditions, although the age difference was greatly reduced when degraded performance was adjusted for nondegraded performance. The interaction of age and degree of degradation on performance measures was not significant. Brain activity patterns during nondegraded face matching were similar in the two groups with some differences in parietal and prestriate cortices (greater activity in young adults) and in prefrontal cortex, thalamus, and hippocampus (greater activity in old adults). Increases in activity related to increasing degradation of the faces were seen mainly in prefrontal cortices in both age groups. Despite this similarity in the brain response to face degradation, there were striking differences between groups in the correlations between brain activity and degraded task performance. Different regions of extrastriate cortex were positively correlated with behavioural measures in the two groups (fusiform gyrus in the young adults and posterior occipital regions in old adults). In addition two areas where older adults showed greater activity during nondegraded face matching, thalamus and hippocampus, also showed positive correlations with behaviour during the degraded tasks in this group, but not in the young group. Thus, although the elderly are not more vulnerable to the effects of increasing face degradation, the brain systems involved in carrying out these visual discriminations in young and old adults are not the same. These results are consistent with the idea of functional plasticity in face processing over the life span.

INTRODUCTION

Older individuals have changes in the visual system that affect contrast sensitivity and other aspects of vision (e.g. Spear, 1993). These changes, most of which are thought to be of central rather than peripheral origin (Burton, Owsley, & Sloane, 1993; Spear, Moore, Kim, Xue, & Tumosa, 1994), affect older adults' ability to detect or discriminate faces, as indexed by an increase in contrast necessary for discrimination to take place in elderly subjects (Owsley, Sekuler, & Boldt, 1981; Sekuler &

Requests for reprints should be addressed to Cheryl L. Grady, Rotman Research Institute, Baycrest Centre for Geriatric Care, 3560 Bathurst St., Toronto, Ontario M6A 2E1, Canada (Tel: (416) 785-2500 ext. 3525; Fax: (416) 785-2862; Email: cgrady@rotman-baycrest.on.ca).

This work was supported by the National Institute on Aging (intramural program) and the Medical Research Council of Canada (grant # MT14036). The authors would like to thank David Mangot and Richard Desmond for their technical assistance.

Owsley, 1982). The reduced ability of the elderly to simply discriminate faces is smaller in magnitude than the age-related difference found in the ability to remember faces (Bartlett & Leslie, 1986; Bartlett, Leslie, Tubbs, & Fulton, 1989; Grady et al., 1995) but perceptual changes could have an adverse effect on memory for visual stimuli of all types, including faces. The purpose of the current experiment was to examine performance and brain activity in older adults during degraded face perception tasks under the assumption that understanding of higher-order processes such as face memory will not be complete unless we also understand age-related changes in lower-level perceptual function.

Perception of visual stimuli, including faces, declines as they are degraded or blurred (e.g. Frazier & Hoyer, 1992; Harmon, 1973; Harmon & Julesz, 1973; Hellige, 1976). The effect of ageing on the perception of degraded stimuli has been examined in the context of incomplete or degraded pictures of common objects and in masking experiments, but not for degraded faces. Older adults are less accurate than younger adults at identifying fragmented pictures (Danziger & Salthouse, 1978), although the age-related reduction in degraded perception can be minimised if the older adults are able to view nondegraded versions of the stimuli prior to viewing the degraded version (Whitfield & Elias, 1992). The evidence for an increased vulnerability to stimulus degradation in the elderly is inconsistent. Some have found that the age-related difference in discrimination increases as fragmentation increases (Frazier & Hoyer, 1992), whereas others have reported no interaction of age and amount of stimulus degradation (Cremer & Zeef, 1987). Byrd and Moscovitch (1984) have reported that when masking is used to degrade perceptual representations of words, the type of mask used will determine whether age-related differences in identification will be found. That is, masks that merely add homogeneous noise to the visual stimuli may not differentially affect older adults but masks with more structure or patterns that would interfere more directly with object perception would result in a reduction in older adults' performance. There also is some evidence that perception of degraded stimuli is better when stimuli are presented to the right

hemisphere than when they are presented to the left hemisphere (Hellige, 1976; Jonsson & Hellige, 1986; Michimata & Hellige, 1987), but this asymmetry appears not to be affected by ageing (Byrd & Moscovitch, 1984; Dollinger, 1995). These behavioural results suggest that the discrimination ability of elderly observers under degraded viewing conditions may or may not be worse than that of their younger counterparts depending on the task demands.

The neural correlates of face perception in the elderly have not been studied in detail. One previous experiment found activation of areas in the fusiform gyrus during a face matching task in both young and old adults (Grady et al., 1994), consistent with the specialisation of these ventral visual areas for object perception (Haxby et al., 1994; Kanwisher, McDermott, & Chun, 1997; Sergent, Ohta, & MacDonald, 1992; Ungerleider & Mishkin, 1982). However, the older individuals, in comparison to the young adults, showed less activation of medial parts of visual cortex and greater activation in prefrontal cortex (Grady et al., 1994). In addition, face perception in these older adults was accompanied by increased feedback from prefrontal cortex to the occipitotemporal regions (Horwitz et al., 1995; McIntosh et al., 1994), suggesting an age-related alteration in the functional connectivity involved in face processing. In terms of degraded perception, we found in a previous study of degraded face discrimination in young adults (Grady et al., 1996) that there was a linear increase of activity in right prefrontal cortex as face degradation increased, along with a decline in activity in the occipitotemporal visual regions involved in face processing. An additional study of degraded picture identification in humans using event-related potentials found increasing negativity at 400msec as the pictures became more incomplete (Stuss, Picton, Cerri, Leech, & Stethem, 1992), which was maximal over the frontal lobes. Thus, a direct relationship between stimulus discriminability and activity in both prefrontal cortex and visually responsive regions has been noted, and both these regions are affected by ageing.

In the current experiment we examined whether this relationship between face degradation and brain activity would be altered in older adults. We hypothesised that older adults would be less accurate at discriminating the degraded faces and that the accompanying brain activity would reflect this difference, perhaps showing a smaller change in activity with increasing degradation or a more bilateral pattern of prefrontal activity similar to that seen in older subjects performing other types of cognitive tasks (Cabeza et al., 1997a; Cabeza, McIntosh, Tulving, Nyberg, & Grady, 1997b). Contrary to our expectations, we found that older adults showed a brain response to increasing face degradation that was indistinguishable from that seen in young adults, but that the relation between brain activity and the behavioural response was quite different in the two groups.

METHODS

Ten young adults (mean age ± SD, 25 ± 3 yrs) and 10 old adults (66 ± 4 yrs) participated in the experiment. There were five males and five females in each group, and all participants, with the exception of one young female, were right-handed. All subjects were screened for health status to rule out any diseases that would compromise cerebral function (Duara et al., 1984), and none was taking any medication. The data from the young subjects have been published previously (Grady et al., 1996). All subjects with less than 20/20 vision uncorrected wore glasses during the scan, either their usual corrective lenses, or lenses custom-made to correct their vision for the viewing distance used during the scanning session (55cm).

The face stimuli used in this experiment (Grady et al., 1996) consisted of black-and-white photographs that had been altered by replacing a percentage of the image pixels with random gray values. The amount of degradation varied from none to 70% (i.e. 0%, 20%, 40%, 50%, 60%, 70%). All matching tasks utilised a forced-choice, two-alternative format, with each stimulus array consisting of three faces, one on the top of the array (the sample face) and two on the bottom (the choice faces). Subjects were instructed to press a button with their right or left thumb to indicate whether the correct match was on the right or left side of the stimulus display. During the degraded conditions, only the two choice faces were altered. The tasks were subject-paced and the instructions emphasised accuracy rather than response speed. The control stimulus was a visual "noise" image that was the same size as the faces and similar in contrast and complexity (Grady et al., 1994). During the control tasks the noise pattern was presented using the same stimulus array that was used in the face matching tasks, with the noise pattern placed in each of the three stimulus positions. Subjects were instructed to alternate right and left hand responses with successive presentations of the control stimulus.

Participants underwent eight scans in total, two nonface control task scans (one at the beginning and one at the end of the scanning session), and the six face matching conditions. Each scan consisted of an injection of 37.5 mCi of $H_2^{15}O$ and was separated from the following scan by 12 minutes. Scans were performed on a Scanditronix PC2048-15B tomograph (Uppsala, Sweden), which has a reconstructed resolution of 6.5mm in both transverse and axial planes. Emission data were corrected for attenuation by means of a transmission scan obtained at the same levels as the emission scans. Head movement during the scans was minimised by using a thermoplastic mask that was moulded to each subject's head and attached to the scanner bed. Each task started 1 minute prior to isotope injection and continued throughout the scanning period. Scanning began when the radioactive count rate reached a threshold value in the brain, and continued for 4 minutes. Blood flow was calculated using a rapid least squares method (Carson et al., 1987; Holden et al., 1981).

Accuracy of face matching (per cent correct) and reaction time for correct responses were analysed with repeated measures ANOVAs with group as the independent factor and level of degradation as the within-subject factor. Both raw behavioural measures and measures adjusted for nondegraded face matching performance (using a ratio with nondegraded performance as the denominator) were analysed.

PET data were registered, spatially normalised to the Talairach and Tournoux atlas coordinate system (Talairach & Tournoux, 1988), and smoothed (to 10mm) using SPM95 (Frackowiak & Friston, 1994). The rCBF values were then proportionally scaled (each voxel to global flow for each subject). To examine brain activity during nondegraded face matching, compared to the control task, and the effect of increasing degradation on brain activity, rCBF was analysed using Partial Least Squares (McIntosh, Bookstein, Haxby, & Grady, 1996). Partial Least Squares (PLS) is a multivariate analysis that operates on the covariance between brain voxels and the experimental design to identify a new set of variables (so-called Latent Variables or LVs) that optimally relate the two sets of measurements. Two PLS analyses were carried out for both age groups combined to examine task effects and task by group interactions—one analysis that contrasted the nondegraded face matching task with the two control tasks, and one that contrasted the six face matching conditions (degraded and nondegraded). Prior to the PLS analyses, the overall group effect, which often is confounded by errors in registration between groups, was removed. To accomplish this, the rCBF value in each voxel for each subject was adjusted by regressing out the group main effect from each voxel, leaving only the residual variance due to the response of the brain to the tasks. We then used PLS to analyse the correlation of the brain voxel values with orthogonal contrasts coding for task and group by task interactions. Weights, which are either positive or negative and are known as saliences, are computed for each brain voxel and represent the contribution of that voxel to a given LV. Using these saliences, "brain scores" are then computed for each subject, which indicate the degree to which the pattern of activity identified by a LV is expressed in each subject in each condition. Plotting these brain scores by condition for each LV shows how rCBF in the brain areas that are identified by that LV changes across the experimental conditions.

Statistical significance was assessed by means of a permutation test (Edgington, 1980; McIntosh et al., 1996) to assign a probability value to each LV as a whole. In the permutation test the data are randomly scrambled 500 times and the PLS analysis is recalculated to determine how frequently the scrambled data results in larger amounts of covariance accounted for than the original LVs, thus allowing an exact probability to be obtained for each LV. To determine the stability and reliability of the patterns identified by the LVs, the standard error of the saliences at each voxel were estimated through bootstrap resampling (Efron & Tibshirani, 1986). For PLS, this method provides an assessment of the precision of saliences (Sampson, Streissguth, Barr, & Bookstein, 1989). Saliences with values greater than twice their estimated standard error, i.e. with a salience/SE ratio $\geq$ 2.0, were considered stable (Sampson et al., 1989), since these ratios are roughly analogous to Z scores (a Z score of 1.96 has $P < .05$, two-tailed). The local maximum of each stable region was defined as the voxel with the largest ratio within a 2cm cube centred on that voxel. Locations of these maxima are reported in terms of brain region, or gyrus, and estimated Brodmann area (BA) as indicated in the Talairach and Tournoux atlas.

A similar PLS analysis was used to examine the covariance between the behavioural measures and rCBF. For this analysis the adjusted behavioural measures (ratios to nondegraded performance) were used, so that only the degraded conditions were included (20%–70%). To make the brain values comparable to the behavioural ratios, the rCBF value at each voxel in each degraded condition was divided by the value at that voxel in the nondegraded condition. This type of PLS analysis is carried out on the correlation matrix of rCBF and behavioural measures rather than the task contrasts used for the analysis described above (Schreurs et al., 1997). Both behavioural measures (i.e. accuracy and RT) were included in this analysis so that we could determine whether rCBF was similarly or differentially correlated with these two measures within and across conditions. The saliences resulting from this analysis were submitted to the bootstrap procedure as described earlier. The behavioural PLS was carried out on the young and old adults separately, and only the first LV from each analysis will be presented here.

RESULTS

Behaviour

Performance by young and old adults on the face-matching tasks is shown in Table 1. There was a significant main effect of group on task accuracy ($F = 26.4$, $P < .001$), as well as a significant main effect of degradation ($F = 60.2$, $P < .001$). The interaction of degradation and group was not significant. Since the older adults were less accurate on the nondegraded face condition, the accuracy results also were analysed after the accuracy for each of the degraded conditions was divided by the accuracy in the nondegraded condition. The significant effects of task and group on these ratio values remained, although the group effect was much reduced in size (task $F = 40.6$, $P < .001$; group $F = 4.8$, $P < .05$). The only significant effect on reaction time was that of degradation condition, both for the raw measures ($F = 29.0$, $P < .001$), and for the ratio-adjusted RT measures ($F = 17.5$, $P < .001$).

Task-related Changes in rCBF

Comparison of rCBF during the nondegraded face-matching task with that during the control task was carried out to assess age-related differences in baseline face perception in the absence of any manipulation of the stimuli. The first brain activity pattern identified by this analysis ($P < .0001$) revealed a number of brain areas with differential activity during face matching vs. the control tasks in both young and old adults (Fig. 1A and Table 2A). Increased rCBF in the areas with positive salience on this LV (seen in white in Fig. 1A) characterised the face matching conditions (i.e. those conditions in which subjects had positive brain scores), whereas increased activity in those areas with negative salience characterised the control tasks (those conditions in which subjects had negative brain scores). The areas with increased activity during face matching included bilateral extrastriate cortex, extending into the anterior fusiform gyrus in the right hemisphere, bilateral premotor cortex, right ventral prefrontal cortex, and left dorsolateral

Table 1. *Performance on the Face Matching Tasks*

			Degradation Level			
	0	*20%*	*40%*	*50%*	*60%*	*70%*
Young Adults						
Raw Values[a]						
Accuracy (*SD*)	99 (1)	95 (5)	89 (7)	86 (8)	81 (10)	71 (10)
RT (*SD*)	2385 (839)	3087 (1039)	3615 (1664)	4053 (1588)	4912 (1734)	5546 (1958)
Adjusted[b]						
Accuracy (*SD*)		0.96 (0.04)	0.90 (0.06)	0.86 (0.08)	0.81 (0.09)	0.72 (0.09)
RT (*SD*)		1.31 (0.19)	1.49 (0.30)	1.73 (0.49)	2.11 (0.56)	2.50 (1.08)
Old Adults						
Raw Values[a]						
Accuracy (*SD*)	90 (4)	83 (7)	74 (8)	69 (11)	69 (8)	58 (6)
RT (*SD*)	2681 (824)	3171 (1195)	3286 (1183)	3622 (1662)	4651 (1558)	5022 (1954)
Adjusted[b]						
Accuracy (*SD*)		0.93 (0.06)	0.83 (0.11)	0.77 (0.13)	0.77 (0.09)	0.65 (0.06)
RT (*SD*)		1.17 (0.19)	1.25 (0.32)	1.33 (0.33)	1.75 (0.52)	1.97 (0.89)

[a]Raw values: Accuracy is per cent correct, reaction time (RT) is in msec. [b]Adjusted for baseline face matching.

A. Face Matching v. Control

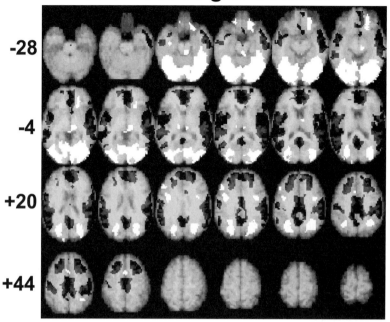

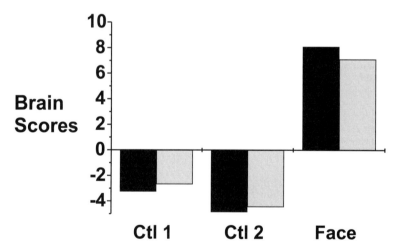

Fig. 1. *Pattern of task contrasts and brain areas contributing to this pattern for two LVs from the comparison of nondegraded face matching to the control tasks (brain areas meeting the bootstrap criterion of salience/SE ≥ 2.0 are shown). The images at the top of the figure show the brain regions (plotted on a standard MRI) with positive saliences (shown in white) and negative saliences (shown in black) on the LVs. In this figure (and in figures following) the right side of the brain is shown on the right side of the images. The numbers to the left of each row of brain images indicate the level in mm relative to the AC–PC line of the leftmost image in each row. The graphs at the bottom of the figure show the mean brain scores plotted for each of the task conditions for young and old subjects separately. These scores are analogous to factor scores in a principle component analysis. The first LV shown on the left of the figure (A) identifies brain regions with greater activity during*

B. Task by Group Interaction

face matching or during the control. Increased rCBF in brain areas with positive saliences is found in those conditions where the mean brain score is positive (face matching), whereas the opposite pattern holds for regions with negative salience. On the right side of the figure is shown the third LV (B) which identified a task by group interaction. Regions with positive salience (resulting in positive brain scores) showed increased activity in young subjects during face matching, whereas regions with negative salience (resulting in negative brain scores) showed increased activity in older adults during face matching. The second LV from this analysis identified a time effect (i.e. from the first control task to the second which was always the last scan in the sequence) and is not presented here.

Table 2. *Local Maxima of Regions with Differential Activity in Non-degraded Face Matching vs. Control*

Region, Gyrus	Hem	BA	X	Y	Z
A. Face > Control					
Prefrontal					
GOb	R	11	16	18	−20
	L	11	−12	34	−20
GFm	L	9	−48	22	32
Premotor (GPrC)	R	6	26	2	28
	L	6	−36	−6	28
Thalamus	R		10	−24	−4
	L		−14	−22	4
Parietal (LPi)	R	7/40	32	−58	40
	L	40	−24	−56	36
Extrastriate					
GF	R	19	28	−74	−4
	R	37	34	−62	−20
	R	37	40	−38	−20
	L	19	−34	−70	−12
GL	L	18	−6	−78	−20
Pcu	R	7/19	22	−70	32
	L	18	−28	−72	20
B. Control > Face					
Prefrontal					
GFd	R	9	6	46	32
	L	10	−10	58	12
GFi	R	45	50	18	8
GFs	R	8	18	26	44
	L	8	−18	26	44
Cingulate (GC)	R	32	8	36	0
	M	24	2	−14	40
	L	23	−6	−56	12
Premotor (GPrC)	R	6	44	2	8
	L	6	−40	−6	8
Sensory (GPoC)	R	3	46	−20	40
	L	3	−56	−8	24
Temporal (GTm)	R	22	42	−34	4
	R	21	46	−10	−12
	L	21	−50	−38	−4
	L	39	−48	−62	20

Coordinates from regions (seen in Fig. 1) of at least 30 contiguous voxels. Coordinates and estimated Brodmann's areas from Talairach and Tournoux (1988).

X (right/left): Negative values are in the Left Hemisphere; Y (anterior/posterior): Negative values are posterior to the zero point (located at the anterior commissure); Z (superior/inferior): Negative values are inferior to the plane defined by the anterior and posterior commissures.

Abbreviations: BA = Brodmann's area; Cu = cuneus; GC = cingulate gyrus; GF(s,m,i,d) = frontal gyrus (superior, middle, inferior, medial); GF = fusiform gyrus; GH = parahippocampal gyrus; GL = lingual gyrus; GOb = orbitofrontal gyrus; GOi = inferior occipital gyrus; GOm = middle occipital gyrus; GPoC = postcentral gyrus; GPrC = precentral gyrus; Gsm = supramarginal gyrus; GT(s,m,i) = temporal gyrus (superior, middle, inferior); GTT = transverse temporal gyrus; Hem= hemisphere; LPi = inferior parietal; Mid= midline (≤5 mm from 0 point in X dimension); Pcu = precuneus.

prefrontal cortex (Table 2A). Increased activity also was seen during nondegraded face matching in bilateral parietal cortex and the posterior thalamus. Increased activity during the control tasks compared to face matching was found in anteromedial prefrontal cortex, cingulate gyrus, middle and inferior temporal cortex, sensorimotor cortex, and perisylvian regions (Fig. 1A and Table 2B). This pattern of activity characterised both young and old adults.

Another LV from this analysis (*P* = .004) identified a task by group interaction (Fig. 1B). Young adults had greater activity during face matching relative to the control task, compared to older adults, in a number of right-hemisphere regions, including ventral premotor, ventral prefrontal, and superior temporal cortices. Bilateral activity in posterior extrastriate and parietal cortices also was greater in the young group during baseline face matching (Table 3A). The older group, on the other hand, showed greater activity during face matching, compared to younger adults, in mostly left hemisphere areas, such as prefrontal and temporal cortices, including the hippocampus, the insula, and the posterior thalamus (Fig. 1B and Table 3B). Bilateral activity during face matching was greater in old adults in anterior portions of the fusiform gyri, and dorsal premotor areas in the region of the frontal eye fields (Paus, 1996). In fact, most of the regions where young adults showed more activity during face matching in this interaction were in the right hemisphere, whereas most of the regions where old adults had greater activity were in the left hemisphere (Table 3). Some of the regions identified by this LV, such as right auditory cortex, where young adults showed greater activity during face matching, and posterior cingulate, where old adults showed greater activity, actually had reduced activity during face matching compared to the control task (compare the right and left images in Fig. 1). Thus, these group differences in activity patterns in these areas may reflect a difference in "deactivation" during the control task rather than an increased "activation" during face matching.

The analysis that examined the effect of increasing face degradation on rCBF resulted in one LV that was significant by permutation test (*P* < .0001).

Table 3. *Local Maxima of Regions with Task x Group Interaction (Non-degraded Face Matching vs. Control: Face > Control)*

Region, Gyrus	Hem	BA	X	Y	Z
A. Young Adults					
Prefrontal (GFi)	R	11/47	38	24	−12
Cingulate (GC)	R	24	20	2	48
Motor/Premotor	R	4	56	−6	24
(GPrC)	R	6	34	−8	28
Temporal (GTs)	R	42/22	46	−18	4
Parietal					
Gsm	R	39	28	−56	28
	L	40	−26	−58	36
LPi	L	40	−42	−46	36
Extrastriate					
GL	L	18	−8	−74	−8
GOm	R	19	30	−74	12
B. Old Adults					
Prefrontal					
GOb	L	11	−24	22	−8
GFd	L	10	−8	56	−8
	L	9	−16	48	16
GFi	L	45	−44	18	20
Premotor					
GPrC	R	6	36	6	44
GFm	L	6	−52	−8	40
Insula	L		−40	8	4
	L		−38	−20	4
Thalamus	L		−10	−16	16
Midbrain	M		2	−28	−20
Cingulate	M	23	−4	−56	28
Temporal					
GTm	L	37	−50	−60	0
	L	39	−40	−60	20
GH	L	36	−32	−14	−20
Hipp	L		−22	−36	−4
Extrastriate					
GF	R	19	26	−70	−4
	R	37	38	−40	−12
	L	20	−48	−24	−20

Coordinates from regions (seen in Fig. 1) of at least 30 contiguous voxels. Coordinates and Brodmann's areas from Talairach and Tournoux (1988). Abbreviations are the same as in Table 2.

Table 4. *Coordinates of Local Maxima that Show Linear Changes in rCBF with Increasing Face Degradation in Young and Old Adults*

Region, Gyrus	Hem	BA	X	Y	Z
A. Increase					
Prefrontal					
GOb	L	25	−12	14	−16
GFd	R	9	14	46	24
	L	10	−16	44	−8
GFi	L	45/46	−46	40	20
GFm	R	8/9	20	34	36
	R	8	28	20	44
Cingulate (GC)	L	32	−12	36	8
Insula	R		28	−14	16
Sensory (GPoC)	R	3	48	−18	44
Temporal (GTT)	R	41/42	40	−32	16
Parietal (LPi)	L	39	−56	−56	24
Extrastriate					
GF	L	18	−22	−102	−12
GTi	R	37	58	−48	−8
B. Decrease					
Extrastriate					
GOi	L	18	−46	−76	−8
GOm	R	18	22	−84	16
	L	18	−22	−82	16
GF	R	19/37	28	−60	−16
	L	19	−22	−62	0
Cu	M	18	−2	−82	16

Coordinates from regions (seen in Fig. 2) of at least 30 contiguous voxels. Coordinates and Brodmann's areas from Talairach and Tournoux (1988). Abbreviations are the same as in Table 2.

This LV identified brain regions that showed a linear change in activity in response to increasing degradation of the faces (Fig. 2). Regions with increased activity (Table 4A) included an extensive area of right dorsolateral prefrontal cortex, smaller areas of medial and lateral prefrontal cortex in the left hemisphere, and a region encompassing the right insula and auditory region. Several small areas of increase also were seen in extrastriate cortex, mainly in posterior and ventral regions. Decreases in brain activity with increasing face degradation were found in ventral and dorsal extrastriate cortex bilaterally, including medial prestriate regions (Table 4B). This pattern of rCBF change in response to face degradation was the same for both young and old adults (Fig. 2).

Correlations of rCBF and Behaviour

The analysis of rCBF and behaviour was carried out only on the degradation conditions (20–70%) using the behavioural and rCBF measures that had been adjusted for the effect of the nondegraded

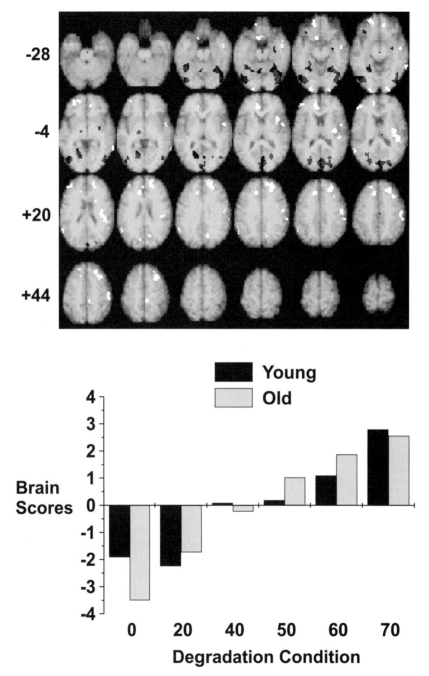

Fig. 2. *Pattern of task contrasts and brain areas contributing to this pattern for the significant LV from the analysis contrasting all of the face matching tasks. Conventions are the same as in Fig. 1. The image at the top of the figure shows the brain regions with linear increases (positive saliences, shown in white) and decreases (negative saliences, shown in black) in rCBF as face degradation increased. In the graph at the bottom of the figure, the increase in brain scores from negative to positive can be seen for both young and old adults. This graph shows that the lower levels of degradation were characterised by increased activity in regions with negative salience (e.g. extrastriate cortex) whereas higher levels of degradation were characterised by increased activity in regions with positive salience (e.g. right prefrontal cortex).*

condition. Although *across* degradation conditions accuracy decreased and RT increased, *within* each condition there was a positive association between the adjusted measures for accuracy and RT in the young adults (correlations ranged from .41 to .84), and also in the old adults (although the correlations were somewhat lower, ranging from .13 to .60). Thus, one might expect that within each condition rCBF would be correlated similarly with both behavioural measures, i.e. either positively correlated with both or negatively correlated with both. The first LVs from the PLS analyses of rCBF and behavior showed just such a result in that a set of brain regions was identified where activity correlated positively with both accuracy and RT. In addition, these correlations were found to be similar across the conditions, indicating a common relation between brain activity and discrimination performance regardless of level of degradation. We will focus on those regions identified in the behavioural analysis that also showed differential activity during face matching compared to the baseline condition or showed a modulation of activity with increasing degradation, i.e. that reflected changes in stimulus input as well as behavioural output.

The results of the behavioural analysis are best assessed by examining the correlations between the behavioural measures and the brain scores from the analysis. Since the brain scores give an indication of the total contribution of all the brain areas participating in each LV, the relation of these scores to performance shows how increases or decreases of rCBF are related to behaviour. The first LV for both young and old adults (seen in Figs. 3 and 4, respectively) identified brain areas that had positive correlations of brain scores with both accuracy and RT measures over all the face matching conditions (range from .50 to .91 in young adults and from .13 to .97 in old adults). The scatterplots of brain scores and behavioural measures seen in Figs. 3 and 4 indicate that increased rCBF in the regions shown in white at the top of the figures (positive saliences resulting in more positive brain scores) was associated with an increase in both accuracy and RT (the 20% and 70% conditions are shown in the figures as representative of the associations seen across all conditions). Conversely, increased rCBF in the

regions shown in black in Figs. 3 and 4 (negative saliences resulting in more negative brain scores) was correlated with a decrease in both behavioural measures.

The only regions where increased rCBF in young adults was associated with increased accuracy and RT (that also corresponded to regions with a task effect) were in extrastriate cortex, mainly in the right fusiform gyrus (Table 5A). All of these areas were similar in location to regions of extrastriate cortex that showed both increased activity in nondegraded face matching, compared to the control task, and a decrease in activity as face degradation increased (compare Fig. 3 to Fig. 1A). Several areas showed an association between increased rCBF and reductions in both accuracy and response times across all levels of degradation. These areas included regions of perisylvian cortex (Table 5B), and all showed decreased activity in nondegraded face matching compared to the control tasks (compare Fig. 1A and Fig. 3).

The first LV from the brain-behaviour analysis of the older adults identified brain regions with a common pattern of correlations across the conditions, similar to that seen in the young adults (Fig. 4), but the brain areas identified by this pattern were not the same as those seen in LV1 from the young group. The older group showed a correlation between increased rCBF in bilateral extrastriate cortex and both behavioural measures, as did the young group, but the extrastriate regions in the older adults were more posterior. In addition to extrastriate cortex, increased activity in the thalamus, posterior cingulate, and hippocampus was associated with increased accuracy and response times across all degraded conditions in the old adults (Table 5A). The occipital and thalamic areas were activated during face matching compared to the control tasks (compare Fig.1A and Fig. 4), and the left thalamus also was more active during face matching in the old adults compared to the young adults (compare Fig.1B and Fig. 4). In addition, the left hippocampal region showed more activation during face matching in the old adults compared to the young adults (see Figs. 1 and 4) as well as a positive correlation with behaviour. Four regions showed an association between increased

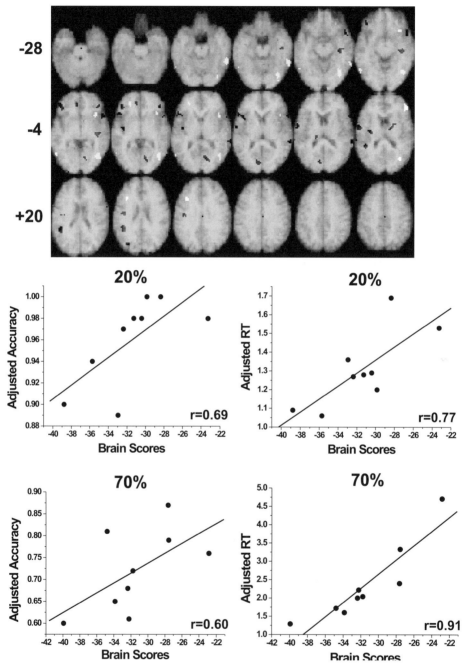

Fig. 3. *The first LV from the behavioural correlation analysis of the young subjects' data (regions meeting the bootstrap criterion of salience/ SE ≥ 2.0). The images at the top show the brain regions with positive (in white) and negative saliences (in black) on this LV on a standard MRI. Numbers indicate level of images relative to the AC– PC line as in Fig. 1. Plots of brain scores vs. accuracy and response time for the 20% and 70% conditions are shown at the bottom of the figure. The correlations are such that increased rCBF in regions with positive salience leads to more positive brain scores and an increase in both accuracy and RT. Increased rCBF in regions with negative salience is associated with reductions in both behavioural measures. N = 9 in this figure due to missing behavioural data in one young participant.*

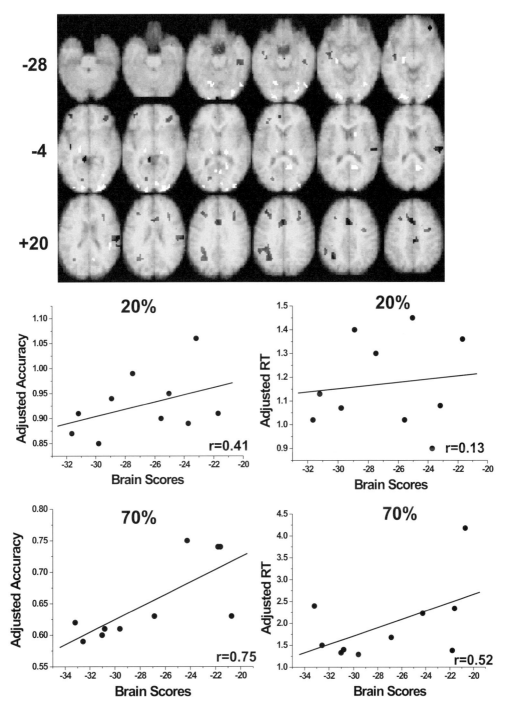

Fig. 4. *The first LV from the old subjects' behavioural analysis. Conventions for this figure are the same as for Fig. 2. Plots of brain scores vs. accuracy and response time for the 20% and 70% conditions are shown at the bottom of the figure. Increased rCBF in regions with positive salience leads to more positive brain scores and an increase in both accuracy and RT. Increased rCBF in regions with negative salience is associated with reductions in both behavioural measures across all degradation conditions.*

Table 5. *Regions where rCBF is Positively or Negatively Correlated with Accuracy and Reaction Time*

A. Positively Correlated

Region	Hem	BA	X	Y	Z	Task Effect
Young Adults						
Extrastriate						
GF	R	19	38	− 68	− 4	Face > Ctl, Dec
	R	37	52	− 42	− 20	Face > Ctl, Dec
GOm	L	19/37	− 54	− 62	− 4	Face > Ctl, Dec
Old Adults						
Extrastriate						
GF	L	18	− 22	− 92	− 12	Face > Ctl, Inc
	L	19	− 18	− 64	− 16	Face > Ctl
GOi	R	18	30	− 92	− 4	Face > Ctl
Thalamus	R		14	− 28	4	Face > Ctl
	L		− 16	− 24	4	Face > Ctl, O > Y
Hippocampus	L		− 22	− 26	− 8	O > Y
Cingulate (GC)	R	23/31	12	− 58	12	Ctl > Face

B. Negatively Correlated

Region	Hem	BA	X	Y	Z	Task Effect
Young Adults						
Premotor	L	6	− 54	− 4	12	Ctl > Face
Sensory	L	3	− 38	− 14	28	Ctl > Face
Temporal (GTs)	R	22	46	16	− 4	Ctl > Face
Parietal (LPi)	L	40	− 42	− 38	24	Ctl > Face
Old Adults						
Prefrontal (GFm)	L	9	− 38	32	32	Ctl > Face
Sensory	R	2	50	− 18	20	Ctl > Face
Insula	L		− 38	− 12	− 4	O > Y
Parietal (Gsm)	L	39	− 30	− 58	28	Y > O

Coordinates from regions seen in Figs. 3 and 4. Coordinates and Brodmann's areas from Talairach and Tournoux (1988). Abbreviations are the same as in Table 2. Task Effect refers to the contrast in the task analysis (or analyses) in which a similar brain region was found to be active: Face > Ctl = greater activity during nondegraded face matching vs. the control tasks; Ctl > Face = greater activity during the control tasks vs. nondegraded face matching; O > Y = greater increase during nondegraded face matching in the old adults; Y > O = greater increase during nondegraded face matching in the young adults; Dec = decreasing activity with increasing face degradation; Inc = increasing activity with increasing face degradation.

rCBF and a reduction in both accuracy and RT regardless of degradation level in the older group (Table 5B). Similar to the pattern seen in the young adults, two of these areas showing negative correlations with behaviour, the left prefrontal and right sensory regions, were more active during the control task. The other two areas showed a task by group interaction, the insula being more active in the old adults during nondegraded face matching, and the parietal region being more active in the young adults.

To summarise the brain-behaviour results, the correlations between rCBF and the two behavioural measures were in the same direction, reflecting the fact that accuracy and RT covaried directly within each face degradation condition. However, although both young and old adults showed correlations between increased activity in visual areas of the brain and increased accuracy and RT across all degradation levels, these regions were not the same in the two groups. In young adults activity in the fusiform gyrus was associated with increases in behavioural measures whereas in the old adults positive correlations were found between performance and activity in a system of regions composed of posterior occipital cortex, the pulvinar region of the thalamus, posterior cingulate and the hippocampal region. Negative correlations between rCBF and behavioural measures were generally found in perisylvian cortex and regions near the central sulcus in both groups.

DISCUSSION

The performance of young and old participants on these face matching tasks was notable in two respects. First, there was an age-related reduction in accuracy of face discrimination even in the nondegraded condition. This behavioural result differs somewhat from our previous work, in which we found equivalent performance in young and old adults on tasks of face matching (Grady et al., 1994). However, in that earlier study the face stimuli were taken from a standard test of face perception (Benton, 1990), in which the faces were photographed from different angles and under

varying lighting conditions, making matching of these faces more difficult for both young and older adults. This increase in task difficulty may have obscured any age-difference that might have been present. When using the current set of face stimuli, small but significant reductions in face matching accuracy in the older adults are observed, both in this experiment and in a previous one (Grady et al., 1995). Thus, when the face discrimination task is made easy, young adults perform almost at ceiling whereas older adults do not, although their performance is still quite good (90% or better).

The second interesting aspect of the behavioural data is that although the older adults were more susceptible to the effects of face degradation per se, the effect of *increasing* degradation was the same in both groups. Removing the influence of baseline face perception reduced the age difference in degraded performance but there was no significant interaction of age and amount of degradation on either accuracy or reaction time. This suggests that an age-related change in face processing per se accounted for most, but not all, of the reduction in accuracy seen during degraded face processing in these older adults, but the residual age-difference in degraded performance was not worsened by increasing the amount of stimulus degradation. This result is consistent with studies reporting equivalent changes in performance with stimulus degradation in young and old adults (Cremer & Zeef, 1987; Dollinger, 1995) or age × degradation interactions on some tasks but not others (Byrd & Moscovitch, 1984). In addition, these behavioural results suggest that age-related changes in more complex tasks, such as perception of degraded stimuli, can be greatly influenced by perceptual changes at more basic levels of function.

Brain Activity During Nondegraded Face Matching

Increased rCBF was found in both groups of subjects across widespread areas of ventral and dorsal extrastriate cortices when the nondegraded face-matching task was compared to the sensorimotor control task. Activation also was seen in premotor and parietal cortices, as well as in the thalamus. It is interesting that the areas with increased activity during nondegraded face matching compared to the control task appear to include both the ventral and dorsal visual processing streams. That is, they include the fusiform regions and ventral prefrontal areas thought to comprise the ventral object identification system (Ungerleider & Mishkin, 1982), as well as parietal cortex and premotor regions considered to be part of the dorsal localisation or visuomotor system (Goodale, 1996; Ungerleider & Mishkin, 1982). The dorsal system has not been previously delineated to this degree during face matching (Haxby et al., 1994). Both ventral and dorsal streams may be more involved in this experiment because the stimuli used were larger than those used in our previous face matching experiments. This might have resulted in more eye movements or a greater degree of visuomotor activity, thus involving the dorsal stream to a greater extent.

In both groups, there were regions in sensory, medial prefrontal, and temporal cortices that showed reduced activity during face matching compared to the control task. Reduced activity in these areas has been noted previously in face perception and memory tasks (Clark et al., 1996; Grady et al., 1998; Haxby et al., 1994), and has been interpreted as a suppression of unattended modalities in order to focus attention on the attended visual modality. In addition, sensory and temporal regions, including auditory cortex, showed a linear increase of activity with increasing face degradation. We reported a similar result in an experiment on memory for faces in which the retention interval varied linearly from 1 to 21 seconds (Grady et al., 1998). Such a finding suggests that deactivation of these regions during visual tasks is not constant, but varies as the demands of the task vary, whether it be a perceptual task or a memory task, and may indicate a lessening of cross-modality suppression with increasing task difficulty.

Some of the regions with differential activity during face matching compared to the control task showed greater activity in one group or the other. For example, young adults had greater activity during face matching in prestriate, ventral prefrontal, and parietal cortices. Greater activity in prestriate cortex in younger adults compared to older adults

has been found previously during face matching (Grady et al., 1994) and was interpreted as a reduction in low-level visual processing in the older individuals. We have also noted greater right ventral prefrontal activation in young adults compared to old adults in a face memory task (Grady et al., 1998), indicating that young adults may have a stronger input into this frontal region from ventral visual stream regions during face processing in general and perhaps in other kinds of visual tasks. Activity in the parietal areas could be related to eye movements or to the visuomotor operations involved in making the response as noted earlier (Goodale, 1996; Petit et al., 1996; Zihl & Hebel, 1997). On the other hand, young adults also had greater activity in a region of premotor cortex associated with sequencing of finger movements (Boecker et al., 1998), which may reflect differences in the motor programming of the manual response. In general, greater activity in the right hemisphere of young adults during face matching, compared to the older adults, is consistent with our previous finding of right hemisphere dominance in this task (Horwitz et al., 1992; McIntosh et al., 1994). This finding, coupled with that of greater left-hemisphere activation in older adults, may indicate a more bilateral involvement of the brain in nondegraded face matching with increasing age.

Old adults had greater activity during nondegraded face matching than young adults in a number of brain areas that were previously found to differentiate these age groups. The areas in the fusiform gyri that were more active in older adults are similar in location to regions that are more activated in older adults during short-term memory for faces (Grady et al., 1998) as well as other face matching tasks (Grady et al., 1994). Given the role of this region in face processing (Haxby et al., 1994; Kanwisher et al., 1997; Sergent et al., 1992), the additional activity here in older adults suggests that a greater demand is placed on this area during face processing in the elderly, perhaps in response to the reduction in prestriate activity. Left prefrontal cortex also was more active in the old adults in this experiment as well as in several previous ones involving both face perception (Grady et al., 1994) and memory (Grady et al., 1998), as well as verbal memory (Cabeza et al., 1997a; Madden et al., 1999). Prefrontal cortex in the left hemisphere has been implicated in visual encoding (Gulyas & Roland, 1995; Haxby et al., 1996), retrieval from semantic memory (Andreasen et al., 1995; Jennings, McIntosh, Kapur, Tulving, & Houle, 1997; Martin, Haxby, Lalonde, Wiggs, & Ungerleider, 1995), and visual working memory (Gold, Berman, Randolph, Goldberg, & Weinberger, 1996; Haxby, Ungerleider, Horwitz, Rapoport, & Grady, 1995). Older adults may thus rely more on associative strategies or those based on familiarity of the faces (Bartlett & Fulton, 1991), even when memory for the stimuli is not explicitly required, necessitating greater involvement of left prefrontal regions. The additional finding of greater activation of the hippocampal region in older adults supports this interpretation of strategy differences. In addition to the well-accepted role of this area in memory function (e.g. Squire, 1992), this region has been noted to be less active in older adults during both short-term memory for faces (Grady et al., 1998) and longer-term memory for faces (Grady et al., 1995). Increased activity in medial temporal regions in the elderly during face processing tasks not requiring memory may have an adverse impact on this region's ability to increment its activity level during memory processing as well as on our ability to detect such an increment.

Brain Activity During Degraded Face Matching

The multivariate analysis used in this study identified brain areas with changes in activity directly related to increasing face degradation that were similar to, but more extensive than, those reported previously for the young adults using a univariate analysis (Grady et al., 1996). Areas of increased activity in right prefrontal cortex and decreased activity in ventral extrastriate cortex were essentially identical in both analyses, with the added finding in the present report that this pattern characterised old as well as young adults. The main difference is that the multivariate approach was able to identify additional regions that showed a change in rCBF with increasing degradation. Although our previ-

ous analysis in young adults suggested that right prefrontal cortex was most directly related to increasing stimulus degradation, the current analysis identified additional right-hemisphere regions, including temporal and parietal cortices, as well as left prefrontal cortex. A recent experiment (Barch et al., 1997) that compared brain activity during working memory tasks (using letter stimuli) in which memory load and stimulus degradation were manipulated separately, also identified right prefrontal regions that had increased activity related to stimulus degradation, although these were ventral to the right prefrontal areas related to degradation in our experiment. These two findings taken together suggest that the right hemisphere, and specifically the right prefrontal cortex, is important for degraded viewing tasks. However, our results also indicate that a role for left prefrontal cortex cannot be excluded. Left prefrontal cortex is activated during visual encoding (Haxby et al., 1996; Owen, Milner, Petrides, & Evans, 1996), so that increased rCBF in this area is consistent with increasing demand on complex visual analysis. Alternatively, the left prefrontal region has been implicated during a number of difficult tasks, including increasing memory load (Braver et al., 1997; Grasby et al., 1994; Haxby et al., 1995), noncanonical object perception (Kosslyn et al., 1994), and learning of a motor sequence compared to overlearned performance (Jenkins, Brooks, Nixon, Frackowiak, & Passingham, 1994). This region may be involved in monitoring or organising performance on difficult tasks regardless of the exact nature of the task. Also of interest is the increased activity in cingulate and parietal regions with increasing face degradation. A number of years ago Bauer (1984) hypothesised that these two areas, in conjunction with limbic regions, were responsible for covert face recognition in a patient with an occipitotemporal lesion who was prosopagnosic. Bauer suggested that the dorsal visual stream interacted with regions involved in emotion and autonomic functions, effectively bypassing the damaged occipitotemporal area that normally would have been part of this loop, resulting in the autonomic arousal that was observed in response to familiar faces. In a similar fashion, parietal and anterior cingulate regions may participate in face recognition when activity in occipito-temporal regions is reduced temporarily, in this case via stimulus degradation.

Areas of decreased activity during degraded face matching are limited to ventral and dorsal extrastriate cortex, including the face-specific areas. This was true of the old adults as well as the young adults. This finding is consistent with the reduction in the number of stimuli easily recognisable as faces as degradation increases, and with the finding of reduced activity in face-selective neurons in monkeys during degraded face perception (Perrett et al., 1984; Rolls, Baylis, & Hasselmo, 1987; Rolls, Baylis, & Leonard, 1985). The lack of any age-related change in the pattern of degradation-related modulation of rCBF indicates that the basic response of the brain to face degradation does not change markedly with age. Indeed, our results suggest that differences in brain activity during baseline face matching far exceed any that might exist during degraded processing. However the way in which the brain's activity is related to behavioural output within the degradation conditions is markedly different in young and old adults.

Changes in rCBF Related to Behaviour

The correlations between brain activity and performance on the degradation tasks were in the same direction for both accuracy and RT, reflecting the speed/accuracy trade-off in performance that was found within the degradation conditions. In the young adults the extrastriate areas showing positive correlations with both accuracy and RT across all degradation conditions were similar to those found with a more traditional correlational analysis in these young subjects (Grady et al., 1996). An interesting finding is that there was considerable overlap between those areas with a task-related change in activity and those areas whose activity predicted behaviour. Most of the task-related changes were from the comparison of nondegraded face matching to the control task, despite the fact that the influence of this nondegraded task was removed from both the behaviour and the brain measures prior to the correlational analysis. This pattern of

results suggests that performance on the degraded tasks in young adults can be predicted to a large extent by activity in areas involved in nondegraded face processing. In general increased activity in areas more active during baseline face processing (e.g. fusiform gyrus) was associated with better accuracy on the degraded tasks, although at a cost of slowed response times. Conversely, increased activity in those areas *less* active during baseline face processing (e.g. perisylvian areas) was associated with poorer accuracy on the degraded tasks. This pattern indicates that those participants who were best able to both activate face-processing regions in extrastriate cortex and deactivate regions not required for face processing were most accurate at discriminating the degraded stimuli.

Older adults, like younger adults, showed considerable overlap between those areas with a task-related change in activity and those areas whose activity predicts behaviour. The older adults showed a set of brain areas where activity was associated with increased accuracy and RT across all conditions, as did the young group, but the specific brain areas were different. The extrastriate regions where activity was correlated with increased accuracy and RT were in more posterior regions of occipital cortex in the old adults, rather than the middle portion of the fusiform gyrus as seen in young adults. In addition, increased activation of the thalamus and hippocampus was associated with higher accuracy and slower response times in the elderly. The left thalamus and hippocampus are particularly interesting since these areas were also more active during baseline face processing in the old adults compared to the young adults. This conjunction of results, i.e. a differential task effect and a positive relation to behaviour, is evidence that increased levels of activity in the old group in these areas may represent a compensatory mechanism. This group of regions—extrastriate cortex, posterior thalamus, medial temporal, posterior cingulate—is involved in visual processing and is highly interconnected with other visual areas (Baizer, Desimone, & Ungerleider, 1993; Olson & Musil, 1992; Suzuki & Amaral, 1994; Ungerleider & Mishkin, 1982; Van Essen, Anderson, & Felleman, 1992), suggesting an as yet unspecified difference in how a face, and perhaps visual information in general, is processed in older adults.

CONCLUSIONS

This experiment shows that degraded face perception is less accurate in older adults compared to younger adults. This difference is accounted for largely, but not entirely, by a reduction in nondegraded face perception. The rCBF analyses show that the age groups differ significantly in the brain activity patterns that mediate nondegraded face processing, but they do not differ in the brain response to degradation of the stimuli. Rather, the way in which brain activity is translated into the behavioural output is different in the older adults. Performance of both younger and older adults during the degraded tasks can be predicted to some extent by activity in regions that also participate in nondegraded face perception, but the regions whose activity is related to performance are not the same in the two groups. Although these results need to be replicated or supported with additional converging evidence, they are nevertheless suggestive of considerable functional plasticity in the older adult brain during face perception. Both the behavioural and brain data from this experiment indicate that there may be considerable impact of visual perceptual factors on more cognitively demanding tasks. This influence may reflect a processing inefficiency, a type of "internal degradation," that decreases discriminability and affects regional activity in a distributed fashion throughout the brain.

REFERENCES

Andreasen, N.C., O'Leary, D.S., Cizadlo, T., Arndt, S., Rezai, K., Watkins, G.L., Boles Ponto, L.L., & Hichwa, R.D. (1995). Remembering the past: Two facets of episodic memory explored with positron emission tomography. *American Journal of Psychiatry, 152*, 1576–1585.

Baizer, J.S., Desimone, R., & Ungerleider, L.G. (1993). Comparison of subcortical connections of inferior temporal and posterior parietal cortex in monkeys. *Visual Neuroscience, 10*, 59–72.

Barch, D.M., Braver, T.S., Nystrom, L.E., Forman, S.D., Noll, D.C., & Cohen, J.D. (1997). Dissociating working memory from task difficulty in human prefronal cortex. *Neuropsychologia, 35*, 1373–1380.

Bartlett, J.C., & Fulton, A. (1991). Familiarity and recognition of faces in old age. *Memory and Cognition, 19*, 229–238.

Bartlett, J.C., & Leslie, J.E. (1986). Aging and memory for faces versus single views of faces. *Memory Cognition, 14*, 371–381.

Bartlett, J.C., Leslie, J.E., Tubbs, A., & Fulton, A. (1989). Aging and memory for pictures of faces. *Psychology and Aging, 4*, 276–283.

Bauer, R.M. (1984). Autonomic recognition of names and faces in prosopagnosia: A neuropsychological application of the guilty knowledge test. *Neuropsychologia, 22*, 457–469.

Benton, A. (1990). Facial recognition 1990. *Cortex, 26*, 491–499.

Boecker, H., Dagher, A., Ceballos-Baumann, A.O., Passingham, R.E., Samuel, M., Friston, K.J., Poline, J.-B., Dettmers, C., Conrad, B., & Brooks, D.J. (1998). Role of the human rostral supplementary motor area and the basal ganglia in motor sequence control: Investigations with $H_2^{15}O$ PET. *Journal of Neurophysiology, 79*, 1070–1080.

Braver, T.S., Cohen, J.D., Nystrom, L.E., Jonides, J., Smith, E.E., & Noll, D.C. (1997). A parametric study of prefrontal cortex involvement in human working memory. *NeuroImage, 5*, 49–62.

Burton, K.B., Owsley, C., & Sloane, M.E. (1993). Aging and spatial contrast sensitivity: Photopic vision. *Vision Research, 33*, 939–946.

Byrd, M., & Moscovitch, M. (1984). Lateralization of peripherally and centrally masked words in young and elderly people. *Journal of Gerontology, 39*, 699–703.

Cabeza, R., Grady, C.L., Nyberg, L., McIntosh, A.R., Tulving, E., Kapur, S., Jennings, J. M., Houle, S., & Craik, F.I.M. (1997a). Age-related differences in neural activity during memory encoding and retrieval: A positron emission tomography study. *Journal of Neuroscience, 17*, 391–400.

Cabeza, R., McIntosh, A.R., Tulving, E., Nyberg, L., & Grady, C.L. (1997b). Age-related differences in effective neural connectivity during encoding and recall. *NeuroReport, 8*, 3479–3483.

Carson, R.E., Berg, G.W., Finn, R.D., Patlak, C.S., Daube-Witherspoon, M.E., Stein, S. D., Simpson, N.R., Green, M.V., & Larson, S.M. (1987).

Tomographic measurement of LCBF with high-resolution PET and $H_2^{15}O$: Comparison of methods. *Journal of Cerebral Blood Flow and Metabolism, 7,* S578.

Clark, V.P., Keil, K., Maisog, J.M., Courtney, S., Ungerleider, L.G., & Haxby, J.V. (1996). Functional magnetic resonance imaging of human visual cortex during face matching: A comparison with positron emission tomography. *NeuroImage, 4,* 1–15.

Cremer, R., & Zeef, E.J. (1987). What kind of noise increases with age? *Journal of Gerontolology, 42,* 515–518.

Danziger, W.L., & Salthouse, T.A. (1978). Age and the perception of incomplete figures. *Experimental Aging Research, 4,* 67–80.

Dollinger, S.M.C. (1995). Effect of degraded viewing on visual asymmetry patterns in older adults. *Experimental Aging Research, 21,* 47–57.

Duara, R., Grady, C., Haxby, J., Ingvar, D., Sokoloff, L., Margolin, R.A., Manning, R.G., Cutler, N.R., & Rapoport, S.I. (1984). Human brain glucose utilization and cognitive function in relation to age. *Annals of Neurology, 16,* 702–713.

Edgington, E.S. (1980). *Randomization tests.* New York: Marcel Dekker.

Efron, B., & Tibshirani, R. (1986). Bootstrap methods for standard errors, confidence intervals and other measures of statistical accuracy. *Statistical Science, 1,* 54–77.

Frackowiak, R.S., & Friston, K.J. (1994). Functional neuroanatomy of the human brain: positron emission tomography—a new neuroanatomical technique. *Journal of Anatomy, 184,* 211–225.

Frazier, L., & Hoyer, W.J. (1992). Object recognition by component features: Are there age differences. *Experimental Aging Research, 18,* 9–14.

Gold, J.M., Berman, K.F., Randolph, C., Goldberg, T.E., & Weinberger, D.R. (1996). PET validation of a novel prefrontal task: Delayed response alternation. *Neuropsychology, 10,* 3–10.

Goodale, M.A. (1996). Visuomotor modules in the vertebrate brain. *Canadian Journal of Pharmacology, 74,* 390–400.

Grady, C.L., Horwitz, B., Pietrini, P., Mentis, M.J., Ungerleider, L.G., Rapoport, S.I., & Haxby, J.V. (1996). The effect of task difficulty on cerebral blood flow during perceptual matching of faces. *Human Brain Mapping, 4,* 227–239.

Grady, C.L., Maisog, J.M., Horwitz, B., Ungerleider, L.G., Mentis, M.J., Salerno, J.A., Pietrini, P., Wagner, E., & Haxby, J.V. (1994). Age-related changes in cortical blood flow activation during visual processing of faces and location. *Journal of Neuroscience, 14,* 1450–1462.

Grady, C.L., McIntosh, A.R., Bookstein, F., Horwitz, B., Rapoport, S.I., & Haxby, J.V. (1998). Age-related changes in regional cerebral blood flow during working memory for faces. *NeuroImage, 8,* 409–425.

Grady, C.L., McIntosh, A.R., Horwitz, B., Maisog, J.M., Ungerleider, L.G., Mentis, M.J., Pietrini, P., Schapiro, M.B., & Haxby, J.V. (1995). Age-related reductions in human recognition memory due to impaired encoding. *Science, 269,* 218–221.

Grasby, P.M., Frith, C.D., Friston, K.J., Simpson, J., Fletcher, P.C., Frackowiak, R.S.J., & Dolan, R.J. (1994). A graded task approach to the functional mapping of brain areas implicated in auditory-verbal memory. *Brain, 117,* 1271–1282.

Gulyas, B., & Roland, P.E. (1995). Cortical fields participating in spatial frequency and orientation discrimination: Functional anatomy by positron emission tomography. *Human Brain Mapping, 3,* 132–152.

Harmon, L.D. (1973). The recognition of faces. *Scientific American, 229*(5), 70–82.

Harmon, L.D., & Julesz, B. (1973). Masking in visual recognition: Effects of two-dimensional filtered noise. *Science, 180,* 1194–1197.

Haxby, J.V., Horwitz, B., Ungerleider, L.G., Maisog, J.M., Pietrini, P., & Grady, C.L. (1994). The functional organization of human extrastriate cortex: A PET-rCBF study of selective attention to faces and locations. *Journal of Neuroscience, 14,* 6336–6353.

Haxby, J.V., Ungerleider, L.G., Horwitz, B., Maisog, J.M., Rapoport, S.I., & Grady, C.L. (1996). Storage and retrieval of new memories for faces in the intact human brain. *Proceedings of the National Academy of Sciences USA, 93,* 922–927.

Haxby, J.V., Ungerleider, L.G., Horwitz, B., Rapoport, S.I., & Grady, C.L. (1995). Hemispheric differences in neural systems for face working memory: A PET-rCBF Study. *Human Brain Mapping, 3,* 68–82.

Hellige, J.B. (1976). Changes in same-different laterality patterns as a function of practice and stimulus quality. *Perception and Psychophysics, 20,* 267–273.

Holden, J.E., Gatley, S.J., Hichwa, R.D., Ip, W.R., Shaughnessy, W.J., Nickles, R.J., & Polycn, R.E. (1981). Cerebral blood flow using PET measurements of fluoromethane kinetics. *Journal of Nuclear Medicine, 22,* 1084–1088.

Horwitz, B., Grady, C.L., Haxby, J.V., Ungerleider, L.G., Schapiro, M.B., Mishkin, M., & Rapoport,

S.I. (1992). Functional associations among human posterior extrastriate brain regions during object and spatial vision. *Journal of Cognitive Neuroscience, 4,* 311–322.

Horwitz, B., McIntosh, A.R., Haxby, J.V., Furey, M., Salerno, J., Schapiro, M.B., Rapoport, S.I., & Grady, C.L. (1995). Network analysis of PET-mapped visual pathways in Alzheimer type dementia. *NeuroReport, 6,* 2287–2292.

Jenkins, I.H., Brooks, D.J., Nixon, P.D., Frackowiak, R.S.J., & Passingham, R.E. (1994). Motor sequence learning: A study with positron emission tomography. *Journal of Neuroscience, 14,* 3775–3790.

Jennings, J.M., McIntosh, A.R., Kapur, S., Tulving, E., & Houle, S. (1997). Cognitive subtractions may not add up: The interaction between semantic processing and response mode. *NeuroImage, 5,* 229–239.

Jonsson, J.E., & Hellige, J.B. (1986). Lateralized effects of blurring: a test of the visual spatial frequency model of cerebral hemisphere asymmetry. *Neuropsychologia, 24,* 351–362.

Kanwisher, N., McDermott, J., & Chun, M.M. (1997). The fusiform face area: a module in human extrastriate cortex specialized for face perception. *Journal of Neuroscience, 17,* 4302–4311.

Kosslyn, S.M., Alpert, N.M., Thompson, W.L., Chabris, C.F., Rauch, S.L., & Anderson, A.K. (1994). Identifying objects seen from different viewpoints. A PET investigation. *Brain, 117,* 1055–1071.

Madden, D.J., Turkington, T.G., Provenzale, J.M., Denny, L.L., Hawk, T.C., Gottlob, L.R., & Coleman, R.E. (1999). Adult age differences in the functional neuroanatomy of verbal recognition memory. *Human Brain Mapping, 7,* 115–135.

Martin, A., Haxby, J.V., Lalonde, F.M., Wiggs, C.L., & Ungerleider, L.G. (1995). Discrete cortical regions associated with knowledge of color and knowledge of action. *Science, 270,* 102–105.

McIntosh, A.R., Bookstein, F.L., Haxby, J.V., & Grady, C.L. (1996). Spatial pattern analysis of functional brain images using Partial Least Squares. *Neuroimage, 3,* 143–157.

McIntosh, A.R., Grady, C.L., Ungerleider, L.G., Haxby, J.V., Rapoport, S.I., & Horwitz, B. (1994). Network analysis of cortical visual pathways mapped with PET. *Journal of Neuroscience, 14,* 655–666.

Michimata, C., & Hellige, J. B. (1987). Effects of blurring and stimulus size on the lateralized processing of nonverbal stimuli. *Neuropsychologia, 25,* 397–407.

Olson, C.R., & Musil, S.Y. (1992). Sensory and oculomotor functions of single neurons in the posterior cingulate cortex of cats. *Cerebral Cortex, 2,* 485–502.

Owen, A.M., Milner, B., Petrides, M., & Evans, A.C. (1996). Memory for object features versus memory for object location: A positron-emission tomography study of encoding and retrieval processes. *Proceedings of the National Academy of Sciences USA, 93,* 9212–9217.

Owsley, C., Sekuler, R., & Boldt, C. (1981). Aging and low-contrast vision: Face perception. *Investigative Ophthalmology and Visual Science., 21,* 362–365.

Paus, T. (1996). Location and function of the human frontal eye-field: A selective review. *Neuropsychologia, 34,* 475–483.

Perrett, D.J., Smith, P.A.J., Potter, D.D., Mistlin, A.J., Head, A.S., Milner, A.D., & Jeeves, M.A. (1984). Neurones responsive to faces in the temporal cortex: studies of functional organization, sensitivity to identity and relation to perception. *Human Neurobiology, 3,* 197–208.

Petit, L., Orssaud, C., Tzourio, N., Crivello, F., Berthoz, A., & Mazoyer, B. (1996). Functional anatomy of a prelearned sequence of horizontal saccades in humans. *Journal of Neuroscience, 16,* 3714–3726.

Rolls, E.T., Baylis, G.C., & Hasselmo, M.E. (1987). The responses of neurons in the cortex in the superior temporal sulcus of the monkey to band-pass spatial frequency filtered faces. *Vision Research, 27,* 311–326.

Rolls, E.T., Baylis, G.C., & Leonard, C.M. (1985). Role of low and high spatial frequencies in the face-selective responses of neurons in the cortex in the superior temporal sulcus in the monkey. *Vision Research, 25,* 1021–1035.

Sampson, P.D., Streissguth, A.P., Barr, H.M., & Bookstein, F.L. (1989). Neurobehavioural effects of prenatal alchohol: Part II. Partial least squares analysis. *Neurotoxology and Teratology, 11,* 477–491.

Schreurs, B.G., McIntosh, A.R., Bahro, M., Herscovitch, P., Sunderland, T., & Molchan, S.E. (1997). Lateralization and behavioral correlation of changes in regional cerebral blood flow with classical conditioning of the human eyeblink response. *Journal of Neurophysiology, 77,* 2153–2163.

Sekuler, R., & Owsley, C. (1982). The spatial vision of older humans. In *Aging and human visual function* (pp. 185–202). New York: Alan R. Liss.

Sergent, J., Ohta, S., & MacDonald, B. (1992). Functional neuroanatomy of face and object processing. A positron emission tomography study. *Brain, 115,* 15–36.

Spear, P.D. (1993). Neural bases of visual deficits during aging. *Vision Research, 33,* 2589–2609.

Spear, P.D., Moore, R.J., Kim, C.B.Y., Xue, J.-T., & Tumosa, N. (1994). Effects of aging on the primate visual system: Spatial and temporal processing by lateral geniculate neurons in young adult and old rhesus monkeys. *Journal of Neurophysiology, 72,* 402–420.

Squire, L.R. (1992). Memory and the hippocampus: A synthesis from findings with rats, monkeys, and humans. *Psychological Review, 99,* 195–231.

Stuss, D.T., Picton, T.W., Cerri, A.M., Leech, E.E., & Stethem, L.L. (1992). Perceptual closure and object identification: Electrophysiological responses to incomplete pictures. *Brain and Cognition, 19,* 253–266.

Suzuki, W.A., & Amaral, D.G. (1994). Perirhinal and parahippocampal cortices of the macaque monkey: Cortical afferents. *Journal of Comparative Neurology, 350,* 497–533.

Talairach, J., & Tournoux, P. (1988). *Co–planar stereotaxic atlas of the human brain* (Mark Rayport, Trans.). New York: Thieme Medical Publishers, Inc.

Ungerleider, L.G., & Mishkin, M. (1982). Two cortical visual systems. In D.J. Ingle, M.A. Goodale, & R.J.W. Mansfield (Eds.), *Analysis of visual behavior* (pp. 549–586). Cambridge: MIT Press.

Van Essen, D.C., Anderson, C.H., & Felleman, D.J. (1992). Information processing in the primate visual system: An integrated systems perspective. *Science, 255,* 419–423.

Whitfield, K.E., & Elias, J.W. (1992). Age cohort differences in the ability to perform closure on degraded figures. *Experimental Aging Research, 18,* 67–73.

Zihl, J., & Hebel, N. (1997). Patterns of oculomotor scanning in patients with unilateral posterior parietal or frontal lobe damage. *Neuropsychologia, 35,* 893–906.

LOCALISED FACE PROCESSING BY THE HUMAN PREFRONTAL CORTEX: FACE-SELECTIVE INTRACEREBRAL POTENTIALS AND POST-LESION DEFICITS

K. Marinkovic

MGH-NMR Center, Harvard Medical School, Boston, MA, USA

P. Trebon

CHU-Pontchaillou-Neurology, Rennes, France

P. Chauvel

INSERM E9926, Marseilles, France

E. Halgren

MGH-NMR Center, Harvard Medical School, Boston, MA, USA and INSERM E9926, Marseilles, France

The patient described in the companion paper by Vignal, Chauvel, and Halgren (this issue) was studied with event related potentials (ERPs) recorded directly within the brain substance, as well as with neuropsychological tests before and after therapeutic cortectomy. Large ERPs were evoked in the prefrontal cortex to faces, as compared to sensory controls and words. The largest such ERPs were highly localised to the same right anterior inferior prefrontal site where direct electrical stimulation resulted in face hallucinations. Face-selective ERPs were also evoked in the right prefrontal sites that had shown projected activity during face hallucinations, and near the right anterior superior temporal sulcus. Selective responses began about 150msec after face onset. Words, but not faces or sensory controls, evoked large ERPs in distinct locations, mainly in the left hemisphere. A successful surgical therapy was performed by removing the cortex surrounding the right prefrontal site where face-selective responses were recorded and where face hallucinations were evoked by stimulation. This cortectomy resulted in a severe deficit in the recognition of emotional facial expressions, especially fear. No change was noted, however, in the recall of emotional words, or other tasks. The current results provide strong support for the early, specific, and sustained involvement of a multi-focal network in the right inferior fronto-temporal cortex in face-processing.

INTRODUCTION

In the companion paper by Vignal, Chauvel and Halgren, (this issue), a patient was described who had received implantation of electrodes in his left and right prefrontal, premotor, and anterior temporal cortices. Direct electrical stimulation of the right ventrolateral prefrontal cortex (VLPFC)

Requests for reprints should be addressed to K. Marinkovic, MGH-NMR Center, Bldg 149, 13th Street, Charlestown, MA 02129-2060, USA.

The study was performed at INSERM CJF 90-12, CHU Pontchaillou, Rennes, France.

Supported by INSERM, USPHS (NS18741), ONR and HFSPO (RG25/96). We thank I. Boissière and N. Hervé for experimental collaboration, and J.-P. Vignal and J.-M. Scarabin for clinical collaboration.

resulted in face-related hallucinations and illusions. This result was felt to support a contribution of right VLPFC to face processing, and is consistent with models wherein VLPFC activates representations in working or declarative memories (Goldman-Rakic, 1995b; Ungerleider, Courtney, & Haxby, 1998).

However, there are some difficulties in interpreting stimulation-evoked hallucinations and illusions. First, although the focality of the response is supported by the fact that face hallucinations were evoked only at one location among the many stimulated, the localisation of the critical area is confounded by the possible spread of the afterdischarge evoked by stimulation to distant sites that may not have been recorded. In addition, the fact that VLPFC stimulation can evoke face hallucinations provides little information regarding the nature of the contribution of the VLPFC to *normal* face processing.

In this paper, the same patient was studied with two additional techniques. One method involved recording of local field-potentials evoked by faces, in comparison to words and sensory controls. Such data can reveal the timing and location of cognitive activity with great precision. Unlike scalp EEG, the neural generators of EEG recorded with electrodes directly implanted in the brain substance (for identification of the seizure focus) can be localised with certainty if the potential shows large gradients over short distances in all directions. Unlike PET/fMRI, which have temporal resolutions greater than a second, intracranial EEG has temporal resolution equal to the sampling rate (about 5msec in this case). The other method entailed testing the same patient before and after the involved cortex was removed surgically. Such data can provide more direct evidence as to what the essential contribution of the area to normal behaviour may be.

Using these methods, the current study obtains results that reinforce the conclusions of the companion paper: A network of small regions in the right ventral prefrontal, temporal, and occipito-temporal cortices appears to be specifically involved in face processing.

EXPERIMENT 1: INTRACEREBRAL EVENT-RELATED POTENTIAL (ERP) RECORDINGS DURING COGNITIVE TASKS

Methods

Intracerebral recordings in response to faces, words, and control stimuli were obtained while monitoring for spontaneous seizures from the patient described in the companion paper (Vignal et al., this issue), in a session that took place prior to the clinical stimulations described therein. During a visual face/pattern task, the patient was asked to attentively observe images presented on a videomonitor (stimulus duration: 240msec, interstimulus interval: 1066msec). The images were superimposed on a grey background and they consisted of photographs of human faces and their sensory controls (the same faces after being distorted into nonrecognisable patterns by randomly moving the pixels but with similar surface texture, intensity, and general shape—see Fig. 1). In addition, the following images were presented in the same oval-shaped frame: colour and grey contours, entire frames filled with different colours (equated for intensity and brightness), and white frames. Since no reliable differences were noted in the current study between colour and grey meaningless contours, nor between colour and white blank frames, they were averaged together. During a lexical decision task, the patient was asked to press a button to real words (120 items, 3 or 4 letters long, average lexical frequency equal to 9493 according to the word count of Content, Mousty, & Radeau, 1990), mixed randomly among an equal number of pronounceable nonwords matched for length. Stimuli were presented for 300msec with 3600msec interstimulus interval (onset-to-onset).

Field potentials were recorded from 105 contacts (2mm in length, separated by 3.5mm centre-to-centre) on the following probes implanted in the right: G, O, P, A and left hemisphere: G', O' A' [see Fig. 1 in Vignal et al., this issue, for electrode localisation]. The recordings were referenced to the tip of the nose and digitised every 4msec (face/contour task) or 6msec (lexical decision task) at 12-bit

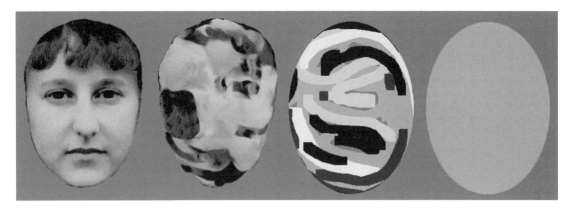

Fig. 1. *Examples of stimuli used.*

accuracy beginning 108msec before stimulus onset. The average ERPs were constructed from trials that were free of eye movements or epileptiform spikes.

Results

ERPs obtained during sensory-cognitive tasks from 19-right hemisphere and 19-left hemisphere sites are presented in Figs. 2 and 3, respectively. For each site, potentials evoked by faces (averaged waveform based on 47 trials) vs. nonfaces (57 trials) are shown superimposed in the first column; to contours (101 trials) vs. blank ovals (103 trials) in the centre column; and to words (112 trials) vs. nonwords (113 trials) in the right column. An oscillating potential was preferentially evoked by faces (thick line in the left column). The waveform had four phases of alternating polarity (positive-negative-positive-negative) with approximate latencies from stimulus onset to peak of 180, 240, 330, and 430msec. This waveform was widely distributed bilaterally within the anterior prefrontal area (contacts on probes G, O, P, G', and O'). The oscillating potential was also evoked by nonfaces, but with a much smaller amplitude (Figs. 2 and 3, left columns, thin lines), and by contours and blanks (Figs. 2 and 3, centre columns). Words and nonwords evoked potentials from these contacts differing in distribution, latency and waveform from those evoked by faces or sensory controls (Figs. 2 and 3, right columns).

A diffusely distributed potential is indicative of a diffusely distributed generator, or of a distant source. In contrast, steep *gradients* in the locally recorded potential imply a local neural generator. Such gradients in face-selective potentials were most prominent in G11, O5, and O9 (all in the right VLPFC), and A9 (in the right anterior temporal lobe). In G11, O5, and A9, the gradient appeared to be produced by the superposition of a sustained potential beginning before 200msec and lasting at least 500msec. In all cases, the sustained potential is absent in the immediately adjacent contacts medially and laterally. Since adjacent contacts are separated by only 1.5mm, this suggests local generation by a small area.

Statistical comparisons of the face vs. nonface average waveforms were performed across trials on the mean amplitudes within 200 to 600msec latency window. These average amplitudes were measured for the four contacts revealing face-selective ERPs (G11, O9, O5, and A9; left column of Fig. 2), as well as their immediately adjacent contacts that were paired during bipolar electrical stimulation reported in the companion paper. Univariate ANOVA revealed a significant interaction between the face/nonface factor and the amplitudes measured for the four pairs of channels, $[F(7,693) = 15.7, P < .0001]$. For each of the eight channels, pairwise comparisons between the face and nonface conditions were performed. Tukey post hoc procedure (Woodward, Bonett, & Brecht,

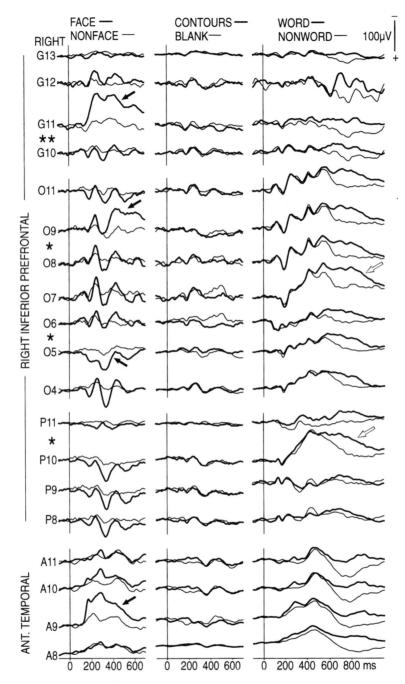

Fig. 2. *Potentials evoked in the right prefrontal and perirhinal cortices to faces. Large face-selective potentials (filled arrows) are evoked in the inferior frontal gyrus in the same contact (G11) where stimulation subsequently evoked hallucinations of faces (**), as well as the sites that showed projected activity during the face hallucinations (*: O5–6, O8–9, P10–11). A smaller triphasic face-selective response is noted diffusely in other prefrontal sites. A large face-selective response is also noted in a contact located just superior to the fundus of the inferior temporal sulcus (A9). In general, the focal responses are not seen in the immediately adjacent probes, separated by only 1.5mm. Details of electrode locations are shown in Fig. 1 of the companion paper (Vignal et al., this issue).*

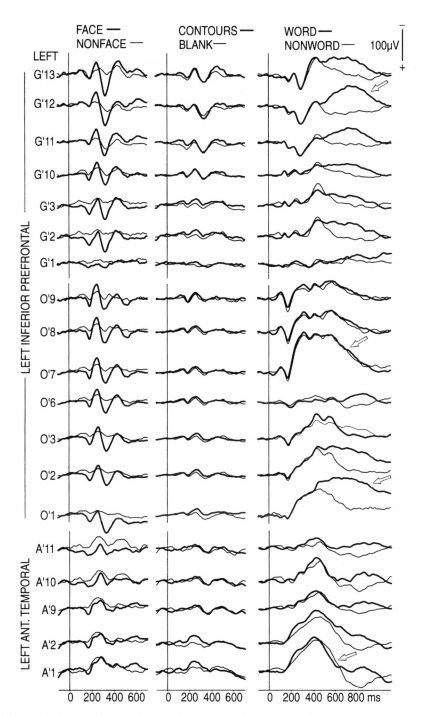

Fig. 3. *Potentials evoked in the left prefrontal and perirhinal cortices to words. Large word-selective potentials (open arrows) are recorded in several left inferior prefrontal sites (G'13, O'7, O'1), as well as the left amygdala (A'1, probably generated in periamygdaloid or perirhinal cortex). Comparison with Fig. 2 demonstrates a double-dissociation in the material-specificity of ERPs in the left and right ventral frontotemporal cortices, with large face-selective responses in the right hemisphere, and large word-selective responses in the left.*

1990) was utilised as a protection against inflated probability values and the corrected *P*-values are reported throughout. Large differences between the ERPs to faces vs. nonfaces that can be observed in Fig. 2, left column, (marked with filled arrows), turned out to be statistically significant for the four contacts [G11: $F(1,99) = 38.6$, $P < .001$; O9: $F(1,99) = 17.6, P < .05$; O5: $F(1,99) = 11.3, P < .05$; A9: $F(1,99) = 12.3$, $P < .05$]. These effects were highly focal as none of the differences observed at immediately adjacent contacts approached significance (*F* values ranging from 0.05 to 2.7).

A closer examination of latencies suggests that the anterior temporal response leads that in the VLPFC. Univariate ANOVAs were performed across trials for the average amplitudes measured at four 20msec latency windows spanning 120 to 200msec post stimulus for the contacts A9 and G11 and the simple comparisons protected with Tukey procedure. The response in A9 begins at about 124msec after stimulus onset, and its first peak appears at 168msec [face vs. nonface difference significant within 160–180msec latency window, $F(1,103) = 21.8, P < .01$, with a strong trend within 140–160msec, $F(1,103) = 8.4, P < .1$], with a second broader peak at 280msec. In contrast, the G11 response begins at about 152msec, with peaks at 244 and 268msec. The face vs. nonface difference does not attain reliable significance until the 180–200msec latency window, [$F(1,103) = 9.9$, $P < .05$]. In O9, the sustained potential began at about 300msec, peaked at 430msec, and lasted at least 400msec. These responses were completely absent to sensory controls and verbal stimuli.

Smaller oscillating potentials were observed to faces in P11 and G'1, as compared to adjacent sites. In both cases, smaller potentials were also seen in the same contacts to other stimuli (contours, blanks, words, and nonwords), suggesting a general decrease in amplitude due to biophysical factors, such as possibly being external to the cortex laterally (P11) or medially (G'1).

As has been detailed in the companion paper (Vignal et al., this issue), the patient reported seeing faces during direct electrical stimulation between contacts G11–12 in the right inferior frontal gyrus. These stimulations evoked a propagated spike/slow-wave discharge recorded between contacts O5–6, and propagated slow-waves between contacts O8–9 (shown in Figs. 2 and 3 of that paper). Thus, the clear face-specific focal ERP in the inferior prefrontal area was seen only in the contacts that were directly stimulated (electrode G), or where prominent propagated activity was evoked (electrode O).

The focal face-selective activity described earlier was seen only in the right hemisphere. In contrast, the large and focal potentials elicited by verbal stimuli were bilateral, but predominantly in the left hemisphere (Figs. 2 and 3, right columns). VLPFC sites with large amplitude and relatively steep voltage gradients to words and nonwords include O7 and P10 in the right, and G'12, O'7, and O'1 on the left. Large amplitude potentials to words without steep gradients were recorded in the left amygdala (A'1). None of these contacts showed any large or focal activity to faces or sensory controls. In the same contacts, face or contour visual stimuli evoked nonfocal distributed bimodal potential as described earlier. Overall, the meaningless contours evoked very small potentials bilaterally without indications of local generation.

In summary, focal face-selective activation was found in three locations in the right VLPFC, and in a site in the right anterior inferior temporal sulcus. The VLPFC locations corresponded to the precise locations where electrical stimulation either provoked hallucinations of faces, or where prominent propagated activity was recorded during the face hallucinations. A double-dissociation was demonstrated between these sites showing focal ERPs to faces, and the predominantly left fronto-temporal sites showing word-selective ERPs.

EXPERIMENT 2: BEHAVIOURAL TESTS BEFORE AND AFTER CORTECTOMY

Methods

As the final step in the surgical treatment of his seizures, the patient underwent a selective resection of the right prefrontal/orbital cortex. The cortectomy encompassed the right orbitofrontal and opercular area including the locations of electrodes O, P, and G, and extending to electrode F (see Fig. 1 in Vignal et al., this issue). Ventromedially, the cortectomy extended to (but did not include) the optic chiasm and branch A1 of the anterior cerebral artery, uncovering the corpus callosum at the medial end of the G electrode. As is often the case in frontal lobe epilepsy, no pathology was found in the surgical specimen. The patient remains seizure-free more than 4 years after the operation.

The patient was tested before and after the surgery with two equivalent versions of the following behavioural tests: Recognition of Facial Affect (Ekman & Friesen, 1976) and Recall of Emotional Words (adapted from Lieury, Boissiere, Jamet, & Marinkovic, 1997). The tests were administered 2½ months (Recognition of Facial Affect) or 2 days (Recall of Emotional Words) prior and 14 days after the selective cortectomy. In addition to these two testing occasions, the patient was retested with the Facial Affect task 3 years after surgery. The patient's performance on these behavioural tests is compared to the results of normal controls (N = 5, 3 females) that were matched in age, educational level and socioeconomic status. The patient was treated with comparable levels of antiepileptic medications on all three testing occasions.

Recognition of Facial Affect (Ekman & Friesen, 1976). On each of the two testing occasions (before and after surgery), and after familiarisation with the task and the list of emotions, the patient was presented with a randomised sequence of 55 photographic slides of 7 facial expressions (joy, sadness, fear, surprise, disgust, anger, and no emotion). The two versions of the test each contain from 7 to 10 pictures from each of the facial expression categories. After observing the picture for 2 seconds, the patient was prompted to give an answer by choosing the best fitting response among the 7 expressions.

Recall of Emotional Words. On each testing occasion, the patient was shown six lists of words, each consisting of nine items: three rated as emotionally positive (e.g. romance), three as negative (e.g. suicide), and three as neutral (e.g. scenario) in a coun-

terbalanced order. The words were presented on a computer screen for 240msec with 2700msec ISI. The patient was instructed to memorise the words in the list and was subsequently asked to recall as many words as possible after each list. The words were equated for their length and frequency based on the French language norms (Content et al., 1990). In addition, the emotional word categories were balanced for their valence as determined in a previously conducted study (Lieury et al., 1997) in which 239 independent judges rated their emotional characteristics.

General Neuropsychological Tests. A short neuropsychological battery was administered before and then 15 days after the surgery. This battery included naming (50 images of objects from Imagier Père Castor, France), verbal fluency (letters, furniture and animals, from the Batterie de Fluidité Verbale, 1989; Cardebat & Doyon, 1990), reading and writing from the Boston Diagnostic Aphasia Examination (Mazaux & Orgogozo, 1981), nonsemantic language comprehension (tested with the Token Test; DeRenzi, 1979), and arithmetic (from the Wechsler Adult Intelligence Scale: Wechsler, 1989). Verbal recent memory including immediate and delayed free recall of 12 words, as well as nonverbal recent memory, including immediate and delayed free recall of 12 abstract designs, were tested with the BEM 144: Batterie D'Efficience Mnésique (Signoret, 1991). The Test of Facial Recognition (Benton & Van Allen, 1968) was only administered 3 years after surgery.

Results

Recognition of Facial Affect. As can be observed in Fig. 4, the patient's performance before the surgery was somewhat impaired, but generally within the normal range (about 8% decrease in correct responses as compared to the controls, z-score = − 0.6). However, a much larger deficit in the patient's ability to recognise emotional expressions was seen 14 days after the frontal cortical resection (overall decrease of about 24%, z-score = − 1.75). Particularly striking was the patient's inability to recognize fear (0% correct), as all of the eight

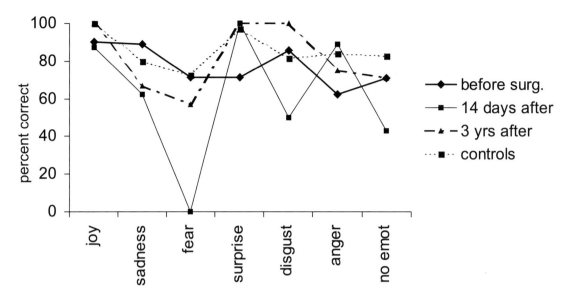

Fig. 4. *Behavioural recognition of emotional face expressions before and after therapeutic removal of right inferior prefrontal cortex. Performance is at near-normal levels before surgery to remove the epileptogenic focus. When retested 14 days later, the emotion of fear was not recognised on any of the eight presented faces with fearful expressions. Substantial recovery is apparent at testing 3 years after surgery.*

presented fear expressions were attributed to surprise. Recognition of disgust was at 50%, with 37.5% of the disgust expressions also mistaken for surprise. Three years later, there was a significant improvement in the patient's performance on this task (overall z-score = -0.35): disgust was recognised 100% correctly. However, the residual deficit in recognition of fear was still present: The expression of fear was correctly recognised 57% of the time, and was misattributed to surprise on 28.5% of the trials. One may note that in normal controls, the most common misattribution of fearful facial expressions is also as surprise (Ekman & Friesen, 1976). Recognition of the expression of sadness did not improve significantly 3 years after the surgery: 63% vs. 67% correct responses. The patient did not report being aware of any problems in emotional processing in general, nor in recognising emotional expressions in particular. Upon completion of the post-surgery testing session, the patient was queried about the apparent absence of the reported expressions of fear. Similar to other patients with frontal lesions (Marinkovic, Trebon, Halgren, & Chauvel, 1997), the patient commented that such expressions were shown "the last time, but not today."

Recall of Emotional Words. When compared to the normal controls, the patient's performance on this task was overall low before surgery (z-score = -1.07). However, it improved slightly after surgery (z-score = -0.6). This recall task was followed by a recognition task, wherein the 54 words used in the recall part were presented again, semirandomly mixed among 27 new (9 words in each emotional category), previously unseen words. The patient was instructed to press one of two keys for each repeated or new word with no emphasis on speed. The results of the recognition task are comparable to those from the recall portion. The patient's correct recognition rate increased by 8% and his error rate by 3% postoperatively. In addition, no significant psychomotor slowing was observed after the surgery as the reaction times increased only slightly, from 1346msec before to 1363msec after surgery. In summary, no change in recall or recognition memory for emotional words was observed after surgery.

General Neuropsychological Performance (Table 1). Naming, verbal fluency, reading, writing, and arithmetic, as well as verbal and nonverbal recent

Table 1. *Neuropsychological performance*

Tests:	Before Surgery	15 days after Surgery	6 months after Surgery
Naming (50 items)	98%	100%	100%
Fluency (animals, furniture) 60"	21	18	18
Fluency (letters b, s) 60"	26	24	23
Token test (max 156)	152	146	147
Reading: BDAE (max 10)	10	10	10
Writing: BDAE (max 12)	10	10	12
Arithmetic: WAIS (max 4)	3	4	4
Verbal Recent Memory: BEM144			
Immediate recall (max 12)	11	11.5	11
Delayed recall, 10'	11	11	12
Nonverbal recent memory: BEM144			
Immediate recall (max 12)	9	11	11
Delayed recall	11	11	12

memory, were normal before surgery, and unchanged when tested 15 days and 6 months after the surgery. The only possible exception to this pattern of normal and unchanged performance was a low-normal presurgical score on the Token Test, which deteriorated slightly after the surgery. Taken within the context of the other results, little significance can be ascribed to this finding. Importantly, performance on the Test of Facial Recognition was normal when tested 3 years after surgery (score on the long form of 43, normal range 41–54).

DISCUSSION

In this and the companion paper (Vignal et al., this issue), three lines of converging evidence are presented for an area related to faces in the right VLPFC of a single patient. Electrical stimulation of a single location resulted in hallucinations of faces. Large focal face-selective potentials were recorded from the same location and from two other VLPFC locations where the stimulation had resulted in projected activity. Surgical removal of this area and surrounding tissue led to a profound deficit in recognising certain emotional facial expressions, but no deficit in a variety of verbal tasks, including the recall and recognition of emotion-laden words. Although these observations

were made in a patient with epilepsy, there was no indication that any of these responses represented abnormal cortical organisation. Nonetheless, this possibility cannot be eliminated.

Multi-focal Activation to Faces

Two patterns of face-selective potentials were recorded within the prefrontal cortex in the current study, a nonfocal oscillation and a focal sustained ERP. Both patterns have been previously recorded in human frontal cortex, but sustained focal face-selective potentials were limited to the right premotor area (Halgren et al., 1994b). In addition, large sustained focal *word*-selective potentials were recorded in the left VLPFC in that study. Given that the responses in the current study were highly focal, it is likely that Halgren et al. failed to record large sustained focal face-selective potentials in the right VLPFC due to incomplete sampling. Furthermore, the location of most electrodes in that study were somewhat posterior to the VLPFC contacts showing focal face-selective responses in the current study. Finally, since bilateral prefrontal recordings with both words and faces were never obtained in the Halgren et al. study, it was not possible to demonstrate the within-patient double-dissociation between prefrontal areas with focal responses to faces *versus* those responding focally to words, as was done in the current study. The laterality and latencies of these prefrontal face-selective activations are consistent with those found in normal patients using whole-head magnetoencephalography (Marinkovic et al., 1999) and scalp EEG (Marinkovic & Halgren, 1999).

It should be noted that Halgren et al. (1994b) found a number of sites in the VLPFC that produced large focal sustained potentials to both faces *and* words, but not to simple visual or auditory stimuli (Baudena, Heit, Clarke, & Halgren, 1995). Halgren et al. used the same task for words and faces (delayed recognition), while the current study confounded task and material (the face task was "attentively observe" and the word task was lexical decision). Owen (1997) has criticised the activation evidence for material-specificity in the frontal lobe on just these grounds, asserting that when different materials were presented in different tasks, task rather than material differences could be the source of the different localisations. In the current study, no activation in either hemisphere was observed to the "attentively observe" instructions when contours or randomised faces were presented. Thus, the large responses to faces using the same instructions could not be due simply to the instructions, but some of the specificity could be related to the combination of the task and the stimulus.

In any case, combining the current results with the previous studies of Halgren et al. (1994b), large sustained focal face-selective potentials have been recorded in humans with depth electrodes in the ventrolateral, orbital, and premotor regions of right prefrontal cortex. These localisations are similar to those found for face-specific unit-responses in the macaque, possibly corresponding to ventrolateral (Ó Scalaidhe, Wilson, & Goldman-Rakic, 1997), orbital (Booth, Rolls, Critchley, Browning, & Hernadi, 1998; Ó Scalaidhe et al., 1997), and arcuate sulcal regions of prefrontal cortex (Ó Scalaidhe et al., 1997), respectively.

Although multiple areas contain locations with large focal face-selective responses, most locations within those areas are *not* focally responsive to faces. This suggests that face-selective processing is embodied in a distributed network of focal sites. Some indication of the size of these sites is suggested by the observation that typically no focal activity was recorded by contacts separated by 1.5mm medially or laterally from the active site. Spatial resolution in the anteroposterior or dorsoventral dimensions is limited by the electrode spacing of 15–20mm. In macaques, face-selective unit responses may show a similar pattern. Although such responses are highly localised to specific prefrontal regions, within any given region only a very small proportion of cells (1 to 5%) show face-selectivity (Booth et al., 1998; Ó Scalaidhe et al., 1997). These authors did not comment on whether face-responsive cells are clustered in the prefrontal sites. However, such clustering has been reported in the temporal lobe (Perrett, Hietanen, Oram, & Benson, 1992).

An alternative explanation for the multi-focal pattern of large face-selective responses would be that they are actually generated by all cortex, but fail to propagate due to their particular laminar distribution of sources and sinks (e.g., a tripolar rather than bipolar configuration). In this case, contacts would record the focal signal if and only if they lay in the cortical grey matter. We consider this explanation unlikely for several reasons. First, other contacts on the same electrodes showed large focal sustained responses to words but not to faces. Furthermore, neither a face nor word response was seen in some sites that according to anatomical criteria seemed to be in grey matter.

The most prominent prefrontal sites showing focal sustained face-selective responses were orbital site O5 and VLPFC site G11. The hallucinations evoked by stimulation of G10–11 also evoked spike-wave complexes in O5–6, suggesting that these sites are anatomically-connected parts of the same network. However, stimulation of O5–6 did not evoke face hallucinations, but rather resonating distortions of the physician's voice (Vignal et al., this issue). Vocal intonation is, of course, highly related to facial expression at many levels, suggesting the intriguing possibility that the network identified by these recordings may have a broader role than face-processing, for example the interpretation of communications from conspecifics.

Several studies have found face-selective prefrontal PET or fMRI activation, usually in the right hemisphere (for review see Ungerleider et al., 1998). However, the localisation of this activation across studies has not been highly consistent, nor clearly differentiated from other material. The multi-focal organisation of face-selective areas found in the current study can provide a partial explanation for these results. Given that the focal face-selective areas identified with intracerebral recordings and stimulation in the current papers are probably smaller than the spatial resolution of PET or fMRI, and that the focal face-selective areas are distributed across several regions and intermixed with word-selective areas, it is not surprising that PET/fMRI studies would sometimes fail to find significantly different distributions for different materials.

In sum, the current data from stimulation and recordings, together with earlier studies, suggests that specialisation for face-processing may be multi-focal, i.e. distributed across areas but highly localised within each area. Ojemann (1992) made a similar suggestion based on the pattern of disruption of function with stimulation of the exposed prefrontal cortical surface.

Fronto-temporal Interactions in Face Processing

In addition to the prefrontal activations, the current study found a large focal sustained face-selective potential in the most anterior part of the right middle temporal gyrus. Face-selective unit activity has been recorded in the apparently homologous area in monkeys, the lower bank of the superior temporal sulcus and subjacent cortex (Perrett et al., 1992). Furthermore, also in monkeys, these temporal areas project anatomically to the VLPFC locations where face-selective cells were recorded (Barbas, 1988; Ó Scalaidhe et al., 1997). In addition, the response properties of the face-selective cells in the VLPFC resemble those in the anteroventral temporal lobe (Ó Scalaidhe et al., 1997), as do the VLPFC and anteroventral temporal waveforms recorded in the current study. Finally, as noted later, VLPFC and anteroventral temporal lesions have similar effects on the judgement of facial emotional expressions. Thus, anatomical, physiological, and neuropsychological evidence suggests that these areas may participate in the same functional circuits.

Previous intracranial recordings have identified face-selective waveforms in the right fusiform gyrus (Halgren, Baudena, Heit, Clarke, & Marinkovic, 1994a). The probably homologous area in monkeys (part of TEO or TF: Halgren, Dale, Sereno, Tootell, Marinkovic, & Rosen, 1999), projects to the anterior temporal areas that in turn project to the VLPFC (Barbas, 1988). Like the face-specific response in the anterior temporal lobe reported here, those in the fusiform gyrus generally have a shorter latency to onset and to peak than those in the VLPFC. With intracerebral recordings, Klopp, Halgren, Marinkovic, Nenov, and Chauvel

(1999b) found a strong phasic face-selective increase in 40Hz coherence at latency of about 180–200msec between the fusiform gyrus and VLPFC. These responses show a consistent phase lag, with the VLPFC following the fusiform gyrus by about 15msec. These data suggest that the fusiform gyrus may participate in the same functional network with the face-selective anterior temporal and ventral prefrontal sites, and furthermore, at short latencies, the fusiform gyrus may lead the more anterior areas. The fusiform gyrus ERP continues for several hundred milliseconds, and thus is co-active with the prefrontal and anterior temporal sites. However, in the 300–700msec time window, the ventrolateral prefrontal cortex shows a wideband *increase* in power to faces, whereas the fusiform cortex shows a profound *decrease*, suggesting that the prefrontal sites may take a lead role during the later period of re-entrant processing (Klopp, Halgren, Marinkovic, & Nenov, 1999a). This interpretation is consistent with the ability of prefrontal stimulation to inject images of faces into awareness demonstrated in the companion paper (Vignal et al., this issue). In conclusion, the current study provides evidence that face processing involves multiple interacting highly focal locations in both temporal and prefrontal cortices.

Removing the region where focal face-selective responses were recorded produced a profound deficit in recognising the facial expression of fear and, to a lesser degree, impaired recognition of disgust. Recognition of other emotional face expressions appeared to be unchanged. The deficit in recognising fear, while unusually profound in this patient, is also seen in many patients with right prefrontal and/or temporal lesions (Adolphs, Damasio, Tranel, & Damasio, 1996; Marinkovic et al., 1997; Peper & Irle, 1997). A comparably profound deficit was found in a single patient with bilateral amygdala lesions (Adolphs et al., 1995), and amygdala stimulation commonly evokes fear in humans (Halgren, Walter, Cherlow, & Crandall, 1978). Intracerebral (Halgren & Marinkovic, 1995) and scalp ERPs (Marinkovic & Halgren, 1999) also have found evidence for differential responses to emotional facial expressions in both temporal and prefrontal areas. The fact that the patient in the current study recovered much of his ability to recognise fear when tested 3 years later is consistent with the contribution of multiple areas to this ability.

There appears to be no special requirement of the Recognition of Facial Affect test for working memory, response selection, semantic access, or other "executive functions." Furthermore, any requirement of the test for these faculties would appear to be equivalent across different emotional expressions. Thus, it is difficult to reconcile this result with theories that subsume all prefrontal functions under these rubrics. On the other hand, prefrontal lesions clearly produce deficits in many nonemotional tasks. For example, right prefrontal lesions may produce false recognition of unfamiliar faces (Rapcsak, Polster, Glisky, & Comer, 1996), as well as impaired recall (but not recognition) of famous faces (Shimamura, 1995). It thus appears that the prefrontal cortex may embody several distinct functions, even for face processing.

Implications for the Functional Organisation of Prefrontal Cortex

The current results strongly support the existence of material-specific processing in localised prefrontal areas, and thus are generally consistent with models of prefrontal function that posit such localisation, with processing of spatial material more dorsal, and that of object identity more ventral (for reviews see Goldman-Rakic, 1995a; Ungerleider et al., 1998). Recently, alternative models for prefrontal function have been proposed, in which the dorsal/ventral specialisation in prefrontal cortex is based on the nature of processing rather than the material that it is performed upon (Owen, 1997; Petrides, 1995). Ventral activation is thought to occur whenever working memory processes are required by the task, and more dorsal prefrontal cortex becomes involved when the task requires more complex executive processes, such as holding more information simultaneously in mind, needing simultaneously to process information and hold it in mind, and/or needing to decide amongst multiple response alternatives. Although the deficit in our patient did not appear to result from an impair-

ment in any of these functions, the distinct effects of stimulating different focal face-selective locations suggests that they may also have a functional specialisation based on processing requirements. The totality of our results are best accounted for in a model that posits multi-focal prefrontal and posterior areas specialised for both material and processing.

REFERENCES

Adolphs, R., Damasio, H., Tranel, D., & Damasio, A. R. (1996). Cortical systems for the recognition of emotion in facial expressions. *Journal of Neuroscience, 16(23)*, 7678–7687.

Adolphs, R., Tranel, D., Damasio, H., & Damasio, A. R. (1995). Fear and the human amygdala. *Journal of Neuroscience, 15(9)*, 5879-5891.

Barbas, H. (1988). Anatomic organization of basoventral and mediodorsal visual recipient prefrontal regions in the Rhesus monkey. *Journal of Comparative Neurology, 276*, 313–342.

Batterie de Fluidité Verbale. (1989). Paris: Les Editions du Centre de Psychologie Appliquée.

Baudena, P., Heit, G., Clarke, J.M., & Halgren, E. (1995). Intracerebral potentials to rare target and distractor auditory and visual stimuli: 3. Frontal cortex. *Electroencephalography and Clinical Neurophysiology, 94*, 251–264.

Benton, A.L., & Van Allen, M.W. (1968). Impairment in facial recognition in patients with cerebral disease. *Cortex, 4*, 344–358.

Booth, M.C.A., Rolls, E.T., Critchley, H.D., Browning, A.S., & Hernadi, I. (1998). Face-sensitive neurons in the primate orbitofrontal cortex. *Neuroscience Abstracts, 24*, 898.

Content, A., Mousty, P., & Radeau, M. (1990). Brulex: Une base de données lexicales informatisées pour le français écrit et parlé. *L'Année Psychologique, 90*, 551–566.

DeRenzi, E. (1979). A shortened version of the Token Test. In F. Boller & M. Dennis (Eds.), *Auditory comprehension: Clinical and experimental studies with the Token Test.* New York: Academic Press.

Ekman, P., & Friesen, W.V. (1976). *Pictures of facial affect.* Palo Alto, CA: Consulting Psychologists Press.

Goldman-Rakic, P.S. (1995a). Architecture of the prefrontal cortex and the central executive. *Annals of the New York Academy of Sciences, 769*, 71–83.

Goldman-Rakic, P.S. (1995b). Cellular basis of working memory. *Neuron, 14,* 477–485.

Halgren, E., Baudena, P., Heit, G., Clarke, J.M., & Marinkovic, K. (1994a). Spatio-temporal stages in face and word processing. 1. Depth-recorded potentials in the human occipital, temporal and parietal lobes. *Journal of Physiology (Paris), 88,* 1–50.

Halgren, E., Baudena, P., Heit, G., Clarke, J.M., Marinkovic, K., & Chauvel, P. (1994b). Spatio-temporal stages in face and word processing. 2. Depth-recorded potentials in the human frontal and Rolandic cortices. *Journal of Physiology (Paris), 88,* 51–80.

Halgren, E., & Marinkovic, K. (1995). Neurophysiological networks integrating human emotions. In M. Gazzaniga (Ed.), *The cognitive neurosciences* (pp. 1137–1151). Cambridge, MA: MIT Press.

Halgren, E., Dale, A.M., Sereno, M.I., Tootell, R.B.H., Marinkovic, K., & Rosen, B.R. (1999). Location of human face-selective cortex with respect to retinotopic area. *Human Brain Mapping, 7,* 29–37.

Halgren, E., Walter, R.D., Cherlow, D.G., & Crandall, P.H. (1978). Mental phenomena evoked by electrical stimulation of the human hippocampal formation and amygdala. *Brain, 101,* 83–117.

Klopp, J.C., Halgren, E., Marinkovic, K., & Nenov, V.I. (1999a). Face-selective event-related spectral changes in the human fusiform gyrus. *Clinical Neurophysiology, 110,* 677–683.

Klopp, J.C., Halgren, E., Marinkovic, K., Nenov, V.I., & Chauvel, P. (1999b). *Coherence evidence for early widespread cortical distribution of fusiform face-selective activity.* Manuscript submitted for publication.

Lieury, A., Boissiere, I., Jamet, E., & Marinkovic, K. (1997). Les mots grossiers et sexuels sont-ils mieux mémorisés que des mots neutres? *Le Langage et l'Homme, 32,* 17–37.

Marinkovic, K., & Halgren, E. (1999). Human brain potentials related to the emotional expression, repetition and gender of faces. *Psychobiology, 26,* 348–56.

Marinkovic, K., Halgren, E., Rabbel, C., Dhond, R. P., Paulson, K., Fischl, B., & Dale, A. (1999). Anatomically-constrained MEG activity to emotional expressions of faces. *NeuroImage, 9,* S363.

Marinkovic, K., Trebon, P., Halgren, E., & Chauvel, P. (1997). Effects of temporal and frontal cortectomies on emotional judgements of facial expressions and memory for emotional words. *Society for Neuroscience Abstracts, 23,* 1317.

Mazaux, J.M., & Orgogozo, J.M. (1981). *Boston Diagnostic Aphasia Examination: Echelle française.* Paris: Editions Scientifiques et Psychologiques, EAP.

Ojemann, G. (1992). Localization of language in frontal cortex. In P. Chauvel, A.V. Delgado-Escueta, E. Halgren, & J. Bancaud (Eds.), *Advances in neurology, Vol.57. Frontal lobe seizures and epilepsies* (pp. 361–368). New York: Raven Press.

Ó Scalaidhe, S., Wilson, F.A., & Goldman-Rakic, P.S. (1997). Areal segregation of face-processing neurons in prefrontal cortex. *Science, 278(5340),* 1135–1138.

Owen, A.M. (1997). The functional organization of working memory processes within human lateral frontal cortex: The contribution of functional neuroimaging. *European Journal of Neuroscience, 9,* 1329–1339.

Peper, M., & Irle, E. (1997). The decoding of emotional concepts in patients with focal cerebral lesions. *Brain and Cognition, 34(3),* 360–387.

Perrett, D.I., Hietanen, J.K., Oram, M.W., & Benson, P.J. (1992). Organization and functions of cells responsive to faces in the temporal cortex. *Philosophical Transactions of the Royal Society of London. Series B: Biological Sciences, 335,* 23–30.

Petrides, M. (1995). Functional organization of the human frontal cortex for mnemonic processing. Evidence from neuroimaging studies. *Annals of the New York Academy of Sciences, 769,* 85–96.

Rapcsak, S.Z., Polster, M.R., Glisky, M.L., & Comer, J.F. (1996). False recognition of unfamiliar faces following right hemisphere damage: Neuropsychological and anatomical observations. *Cortex, 32(4),* 593–611.

Shimamura, A.P. (1995). Memory and the prefrontal cortex. *Annals of the New York Academy of Sciences, 769,* 151–159.

Signoret, J.L. (1991). *BEM 144: Batterie D'Efficience Mnésique.* Paris: Collection Esprit & Cerveau, Elsevier.

Ungerleider, L.G., Courtney, S.M., & Haxby, J.V. (1998). A neural system for human visual working memory. *Proceedings of the National Academy Sciences USA, 95(3),* 883–890.

Vignal, J.P., Chauvel, P., & Halgren, E. (1999). Localised face processing by the human prefrontal cortex: Stimulation-evoked hallucinations of faces. *Cognitive Neuropsychology, 16,* 281–291.

Wechsler, D. (1989). *Wechsler Adult Intelligence Scale-Revised: Version française.* Paris: Editions du Centre de Psychologie Appliquée.

Woodward, J. A., Bonett, D.G., & Brecht, M.L. (1990). *Introduction to linear models and experimental design.* San Diego, CA: Harcourt Brace Jovanovich.

COGNITIVE NEUROPSYCHOLOGY, 2000, 17 (1/2/3), 201–219

SUPER FACE-INVERSION EFFECTS FOR ISOLATED INTERNAL OR EXTERNAL FEATURES, AND FOR FRACTURED FACES

Morris Moscovitch and David A. Moscovitch

University of Toronto at Mississauga and Rotman Research Institute, Baycrest Centre for Geriatric Care, Toronto, Canada

Two experiments were conducted to determine the contributions of the face and object systems to the recognition of upright and inverted faces. In Experiment 1, CK, a person with object agnosia and normal recognition of upright faces, and 12 controls attempted to identify faces when presented with upright or inverted versions of the whole face, or with only their internal or external features. CK recognised as many upright whole faces as controls and the performance of both dropped slightly in the upright, internal feature condition. CK's recognition, however, was impaired in the upright, external condition, and severely impaired in the inverted whole condition, whereas control performance was equivalent in the two, and only somewhat worse than in the upright whole condition. Recognition in the inverted internal and external condition was extremely poor for all participants, leading to a *super-inversion effect*. This super-inversion effect suggested that recognition depends on more than just piecemeal identification of individual features. Experiment 2 was conducted to determine whether relational information is needed even for the identification of inverted faces. Twelve controls were required to identify whole and fractured faces in the upright and inverted orientation. The fractured faces had all the parts in the canonical order (eyes above nose above mouth) but they were separated by gaps, thereby altering the spatial relation among them. Recognition of inverted fractured faces was much worse than recognition of upright fractured faces and inverted whole faces, producing yet another super-inversion effect. The deficit in the inverted fractured condition was equal to the combined drop in performance in the other two conditions, indicating that the effects of inversion and fracturing are additive. On the basis of these results, we proposed that the face system forms holistic representations of faces based on orientation-specific *global configurations* primarily of internal features. When this information is unavailable, as when viewing inverted or fractured faces, the object system is needed to integrate information about individual features, which themselves may be orientation-specific, with information about the *local or categorical relations* among them into an *object-system counterpart* of the face-system representation. The creation of the facial counterpart by the object system and the consequent identification by the face system involves an exchange of information between the two systems according to an interactive activation model.

Requests for reprints should be addressed to Dr. Morris Moscovitch, Rotman Research Institute, Baycrest Centre for Geriatric Care, 3560 Bathurst Street, Toronto, Ontario, Canada M6A 2E1 (Fax: 416-785-2862; Email: momos@credit.erin.utoronto.ca).

This research was supported by a grant from the Natural Sciences and Engineering Research Council of Canada to MM and a Savlov Summer Studentship at the Rotman Research Institute to DAM. We thank Marilyne Ziegler for technical assistance, Amy Siegenthaler for some of the materials, Heidi Roesler for help with data analyses and preparation of the manuscript, and Marlene Behrmann and two reviewers, Jim Tanaka and Anonymous, for their very helpful critique and comments.

201

INTRODUCTION

Yin (1969, 1970) was the first to report that inversion impairs recognition of faces much more than that of other objects. Since then, this inversion effect has become one of the primary criteria for distinguishing face-recognition from object-recognition, and has been the topic of investigation in its own right (e.g. Bartlett & Searcy, 1993; Searcy & Bartlett, 1996; Valentine, 1988). Thus, inversion has been used both as an assay for determining whether recognition of other stimuli resembles that of faces (e.g. Diamond & Carey, 1986; Farah, Tanaka, & Drain, 1995b), and as a tool for investigating what makes faces special (e.g. Farah et al., 1995b; Rhodes, Brake, & Atkinson, 1993; Searcy & Bartlett, 1996; Young, Hellawell, & Hay, 1987). Because inversion affects the perception of the spatial configuration among features more than identification of the features themselves (e.g. Rhodes, 1988; Rhodes et al., 1993; Searcy & Bartlett, 1996; Tanaka & Sengco, 1997), it has been proposed that face recognition is holistic or configurational. Object recognition, on the other hand, is part-based, relying as much or more on identification of individual features. What is often overlooked in these part-based accounts of face-recognition is that information about the spatial arrangements of parts is also critical, just as it is in object recognition. (Biederman, 1987; Suzuki, Peterson, Moscovitch, & Behrmann, 1997). The purpose of the present study is to gather more information about the relative contribution of internal and external features, and their orientation and spatial configuration, to the recognition of upright and inverted faces. In so doing, we hope to gain a better understanding of the processes and mechanisms that mediate recognition of upright and inverted faces.

The impetus for this study came from research conduced by Moscovitch, Winocur, and Behrmann (1997) on a unique patient, CK, who became dyslexic and visually agnosic for objects following a closed head injury but who retained a normal ability for recognising faces (for a full description of his case see also Behrmann, Moscovitch, & Winocur, 1994). CK afforded Moscovitch et al. the opportunity to investigate the operation of the face-recognition system in isolation from the contaminating influences of the object recognition system . They found that as long as a face was presented in its upright canonical orientation, CK's face recognition remained normal even when challenged by disguises, perceptual degradation of the face, its rotation in depth, or its transformation by ageing. Once the face was inverted, however, CK's recognition plummeted to a level far below normal. In investigating this phenomenon further, they discovered that this exaggerated inversion effect in CK was confined only to internal facial features—the unit formed by the configuration of the eyes, nose, and mouth. The remainder of the face comprised the external features. When the external features of a photograph were inverted as a unit (see Fig. 1), leaving the internal features upright, CK's recognition was normal.

There have been a few other studies on the relative importance of internal and external features to the recognition of upright faces. Despite some inconsistencies, the results of these studies can be summarised as follows: Recognition of unfamiliar faces depends more on external features whereas recognition of famous or familiar faces depends at least as much, if not more, on internal features (Ellis, Shepherd, & Davies, 1979; Haig, 1986; Nachson, Moscovitch, & Umilta, 1995; Ross & Turkewitz, 1982; Young, Hay, McWeeny, Flude, & Ellis, 1985).This is especially true if the tasks require participants to identify faces rather than merely match them with one another (Searcy & Bartlett, 1996). The same pattern of results is obtained in patients with unilateral lesions to the right or left hemisphere, though overall performance is poorer in the former group (de Haan & Hay, 1986). The findings regarding the identification of famous people accord with our own conclusions based on CK's performance. To our knowledge, there are no previous studies on the contribution of internal or external features to the recognition of inverted faces.

Based on the literature and their own observations of CK, Moscovitch et al. concluded that the face recognition system, which is intact in CK, is activated primarily by a configuration of internal features that must appear in the upright orientation. External features contribute less to recognition of famous people. Because CK's object-recognition system was damaged and because normal people could recognise whole inverted faces much better than CK could, Moscovitch et al. speculated, as others had, that inverted face recognition depends on the part-based object-recognition system alone, or more likely working in combination with the holistic face-recognition system (e.g. Farah et al., 1995b; Farah, Wilson, Drain, & Tanaka, 1998; Tanaka & Farah, 1993). We do not, however, have direct evidence of the contribution of internal and external features to the two systems, and therefore lack a full appreciation of their role in the recognition of upright or inverted faces.

We also do not know whether the features, when presented alone, contribute differently to the recognition of inverted faces, nor do we have sufficient evidence to determine whether internal or external features are processed preferentially by the face- or object-recognition system. The purpose of Experiment 1, therefore, was to gather more information pertaining to these issues. The results of Experiment 1 led us to re-examine the role that spatial relations among individual features and their orientation play in the recognition of upright and inverted faces. In so doing, we hoped to gain a better understanding of the operation of the face and object recognition systems and how they interact.

EXPERIMENT 1

CK provides us with a unique opportunity to address these issues. Based on our finding that CK's recognition of famous people was disrupted only when internal, but not external, features were inverted, we concluded that upright, internal features are processed preferentially by the face-recognition system. In addition, we speculated that external features are processed more effectively by the object recognition system but had no direct evidence to support this hypothesis. In the present experiment, we tested these hypotheses by asking CK and control participants to recognise faces of famous people based only on either their internal or

external features when presented upright or inverted. Our predictions were as follows: Because CK's face-recognition system is intact, but his object-recognition system is damaged, we predicted that (1) *CK should be as good as controls at recognising famous people from their upright internal features alone, but impaired at recognising people based only on their upright external features.* As a further test of the hypothesis that upright internal and external features are processed preferentially by the face- and object-recognition system, respectively, we examined how controls and CK performed when these features were inverted. On the assumption that it is the holistic face-recognition system that is most affected by inversion, we predicted that (2) *Controls would be affected as much as CK by inversion of internal features.* Indeed, controls should perform as poorly in this condition as CK if identification on the basis of only internal features depends almost exclusively on the processing of orientation-specific, configurational information by the face-recognition system, and if it is particularly this information that is lost with inversion. At the very least, the difference between CK and controls that we observed in recognising whole inverted faces should be greatly diminished when they are required to recognise faces from inverted internal features alone.

Last, to determine whether the object system relies primarily on external features in the recognition of inverted faces, or on the combination of internal and external features, we tested controls and CK's ability to identify faces based on inverted, external features alone or on the whole face. *(3) We expected CK to perform poorly with all inverted stimuli. Controls, however, may perform much better in some conditions than others, depending on which system mediates recognition of internal or external features.* If their recognition of inverted faces is much better in the external feature condition than in the internal feature condition, it would indicate that the object recognition system uses primarily external feature information in the identification of whole inverted faces. If, however, face-recognition is as poor with inverted external features as with internal ones, it would imply that recognition of whole, inverted faces results from a process that depends on the integration or interaction of internal with external features, a process that requires the participation of both the object and face recognition systems, rather than the object recognition system alone.

Method

Participants

CK, born in 1961, is a right-handed male with an MA degree. He sustained a closed head injury in 1988 when he was hit by a car while he was jogging. Initially in a coma, CK made a substantial recovery. When tested in 1991, he had a verbal IQ of 96 and performance IQ of 76, which, considering his severe object agnosia, probably underestimates his intelligence. His memory, language, reasoning, and recognition of upright faces is normal. In addition to his agnosia and dyslexia, CK has residual blindness in his upper left field and mild left-sided weakness in his limbs, which, despite his anticonvulsant medication (Tegretol), sometimes show clonus. Except for a hint of bilateral thinning in the occipitotemporal region, no damage was revealed on MRI or CT scans (for further information see Behrmann et al., 1994; Moscovitch et al., 1997). We tested him in the present experiment in September, 1997, at which point he had completed a manager-training programme and was working for a large organisation. He is married and has children.

Twelve people, three of them male, with an average age of 27 and 17 years of education, served as controls.

Stimuli

Stimuli consisted of 4 sets, each with 23 pictures of famous people taken from magazines. About 10 pictures in each set were coloured and were presented separately from the others. For each picture, we had a full-face version and internal and external feature versions. The internal features were derived by cutting the face just above the eyes, extending the cut perpendicularly from the outer edge of the eyes down to the mouth, and then angling the cut inward on either sides so that the two cuts met in the middle, just underneath the mouth (see Fig. 1).

Thus, the internal feature version consisted of the configuration formed by the eyes, nose, and mouth. What remained of the face comprised the external feature version (see Fig.1).

Procedure

All participants were presented with each of the four sets of pictures in counterbalanced order. One of these orders was presented to CK. Set A consisted of inverted whole faces, Set B of upright internal features, and Set C of inverted internal features. Because we did not have enough pictures, inverted and upright external features formed the single Set D. The pictures comprising each set were also rotated among the participants to control for stimulus effects. Thus, the pictures comprising, say, Set A for one participant formed another set, say, Set B for another participant.

The stimuli were mounted on 3" x 5" index cards and shown one at a time to participants, who were tested individually while sitting at a table with the pictures placed in front of them. For Set D, the external inverted version was shown first, followed by the same pictures rotated to the upright orientation. After each set was completed, the corresponding whole upright face of each picture was shown.

Participants were given 5 seconds to identify each picture. A response was scored correct if the name or some clearly identifying information was supplied.

Results

We first scored the results in terms of total correct in the whole upright condition. For the remainder of the conditions, however, the score was the proportion correct conditionalised on having identified the corresponding whole upright face correctly.

We took CK's performance to be deficient if it fell two or more SDs below the mean of controls. The results, presented in Table 1, show that CK performs as well as controls in identifying faces in the upright whole and upright internal condition and much more poorly than controls in identifying faces in the inverted whole and upright external condition. Both CK and controls performed very

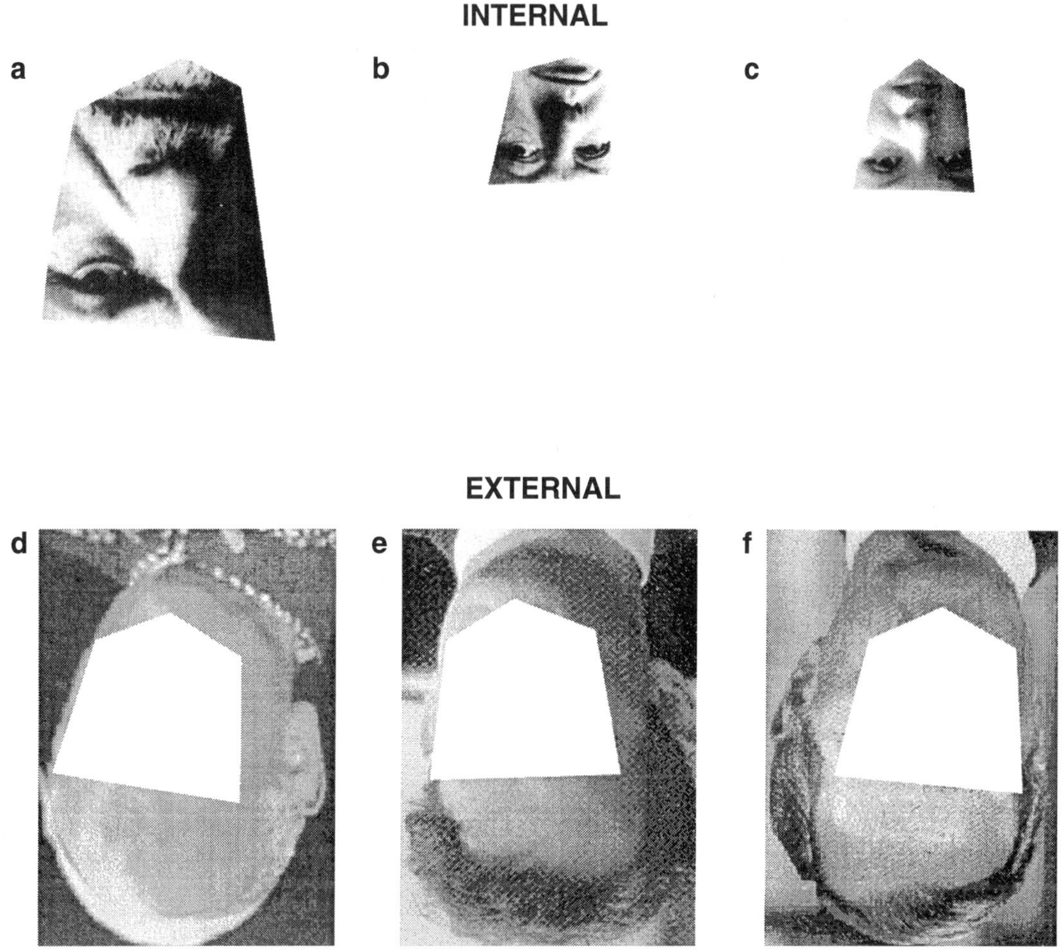

INTERNAL

EXTERNAL

Fig. 1 (A). *Examples of different internal and external features of faces that are inverted. The reader first should try to identify the inverted faces, then turn them upright, and then turn to Fig. 1(B).*

Table 1. *The Average Number of Correctly Recognised Faces in Each Whole Upright Condition and the Percentage (SD) of them Recognised in Each of the Other Conditions (Max = 23)*

	Whole Upright			Whole Inverted		Internal Upright		Internal Inverted		External Upright		External Inverted	
	No.	(SD)	%	%	(SD)	%	(SD)	%	(SD)	%	(SD)	%	(SD)
Controls (N = 12)	19.9	(2.95)	86.5	72.5	(15.2)	75.2	(17.1)	21.9	(13.3)	63.8	(10.1)	22.0	(9.7)
CK	21.8		94.7	22.7		86.4		4.5		33.3		9.5	

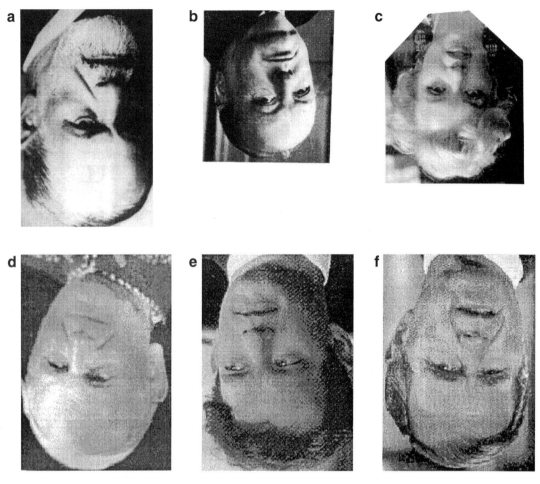

Fig. 1 (B). *The same six faces shown in Fig. 1(A) are here presented whole, but inverted. The reader should try to identify them inverted and then turn them upright. The faces are identified in the Note at the end of the paper.*

poorly in identifying faces in the inverted internal and external conditions.

Planned comparisons between the various conditions in controls showed that identification in the upright, internal condition was better than in the upright, external condition [$t(11) = 2.44$, $P < .03$]. Identification in the whole inverted condition was no different from that in the internal and external conditions when they were presented upright ($P < .2$) but much better than when they were presented inverted [$t(11) = 9.97$ and 9.92, respectively, $P < .001$]. Identification of whole inverted faces was even significantly better than the combined scores in the inverted internal and external conditions

[$t(11) = 5.03$, $P < .001$]. Performance in the latter two inverted conditions did not differ significantly from each other, nor did performance in the whole upright condition differ across the four sets.

Discussion

There were a number of interesting findings in our study. In the upright condition, we found, as predicted, that CK recognised faces normally from only their internal features but he was impaired at recognising faces from only their external features. Controls, by comparison, were only slightly worse at recognising faces from external than from internal features. With respect to inversion, we replicated our previous finding (Moscovitch et al., 1997) that CK was much worse than controls at recognising whole inverted faces. Also as predicted, we found a super-inversion effect in controls in the inverted internal feature conditions, in which they performed almost as poorly as CK, differing from him by less than 2 SDs. Nor were CK and controls any better at recognising faces based only on inverted external features. Each of these findings will be discussed in turn.

Our finding that CK could recognise faces normally when given only their upright internal features is consistent with our hypothesis that such stimuli preferentially engage the face-recognition system, which is intact in CK. When considered along with the finding that inversion of whole faces or just their internal features leads to severely impaired performance in CK, the result suggests that the face-recognition system relies primarily on information about the spatial configuration of internal features since it is this information that is lost with inversion. According to many investigators, (Rhodes, 1988; Rhodes et al., 1993; Searcy & Bartlett, 1996; Tanaka & Sengco, 1997), what is most crucial is not information about first-order relational features, which specify the invariant spatial relations of the parts across all exemplars (e.g. eyes above nose above mouth) of a class, but rather information about second-order relational features, which code for variations in spatial arrangement of features from individual to individual (e.g. the distance between the eyes and from the eyes to the nose) (Diamond & Carey, 1986). First-order relational features are sufficient to distinguish the class of faces from all other objects, a skill retained with inversion, whereas second-order relational features are needed to discriminate one face from another, a skill that suffers with inversion.

Because upright external features are impoverished with respect to such higher-order configurational information, CK, as predicted, was poor at recognising faces based only on their external features. This result suggests that in normal people, recognition based on external features also depends on the participation of the object-recognition sys-

tem, which is damaged in CK. Note, however, that his performance in the upright external feature condition, though impaired, was better than his performance on inverted whole faces both in absolute terms, and relative to that of controls. We return to this point later in the Discussion.

The conclusion that upright internal features engage the face-recognition system preferentially is supported by our finding that even controls were very poor at recognising faces from internal features once they were inverted. This result calls into question the prevailing view that recognition of whole inverted faces depends on the piecemeal identification of the individual internal features themselves, a process presumably mediated by the part-based object system. If this were the case, controls should have performed almost as well in the inverted internal feature condition as in the inverted whole face condition, which emphatically they did not.

The possibility remains that the part-based object-recognition system relies primarily on individual external features to support recognition of inverted whole faces in neurologically intact people. The evidence, however, does not support this hypothesis either. Controls performed as poorly in the inverted external feature condition as in the inverted internal condition and, in both conditions, almost as poorly as CK.

Perhaps recognition of inverted faces depends simply on the sum of information from inverted internal and external feature conditions, as would be predicted by a strong version of a model that states that inverted face-recognition depends on the piecemeal, part-based processing of individual features. There are too few correct responses to determine whether a simple additive model might account for CK's performance, though it is consistent with what we know of the operation of his object-recognition system. He seems able to identify individual features but not to integrate them with each other into a unified whole (Moscovitch et al., 1997, Experiments 15 & 17). An additive, part-based model, however, certainly falls well short of accounting for the performance of the controls. Their average combined score in the internal and external condition is 40% as compared to 75% for whole faces. For controls, internal and external features interact to yield performance that is better than the combined total from the two units.

The results indicate that recognition of inverted faces depends on more than the piecemeal identification of individual features. Information may be needed about the spatial arrangement of individual internal and external features, and their orientation. The latter suggestion raises the possibility that the representation of external and internal features is orientation-specific so that even at the level of individual features, identification is orientation-dependent. Until recently, this idea has not been given sufficient consideration because it is often assumed that recognition of individual parts is viewpoint-invariant (Biederman, 1987; Biederman & Gerhardstein, 1993). Recent evidence, however, shows that recognition of nonaccidental views of objects, especially of exemplars within a single category, and even of single geons, is influenced by rotation in depth and in the picture plane (Hamm & McMullen, 1998; Tarr, Hayward, Gauthier, & Williams, 1994; Hayward & Tarr, 1997; Suzuki et al., 1997; Suzuki, Peterson, Behrmann, & Moscovitch, 1999).

CK's performance in the upright, external feature condition lends support to both possibilities. His recognition of faces in this condition, though impaired, is better, both in absolute terms and relative to controls, than in any of the inverted conditions when compared to the whole, upright condition. This result suggests that some limited, but useful, configurational information is available even from external features, such as the relation of the forehead to the hair or chin, or all three in relation to the contour of the face. In addition, it may be the case that representation of even individual features, either by the face system or the object system, is orientation-specific. As a result, when a face is inverted, not only is some configurational information lost, but so is information about the individual features themselves. To test the hypotheses that some relational information is needed for recognition even of inverted faces, and that representation of individual features are themselves orientation-specific, we conducted a second experiment.

EXPERIMENT 2

To test CK's and controls' ability to recognise faces on the basis of individual features alone, Moscovitch et al. (1997, Experiment 15) constructed fractured faces that retained all the individual features in their general first-order relation (hair and forehead on top followed by eyes, nose, mouth, and chin) but altered the second-order relation of each of these components to each other (see Fig. 2). We reasoned that if inversion leads to a loss of configurational information, (second-order features relations) then fracturing faces in this way should have an effect similar to inversion. Recognition of fractured faces, as of inverted ones, should now be based primarily on the part-based object system rather than the holistic, configuration-based face system. The results confirmed our predictions. Controls were almost as impaired at recognising fractured faces as inverted ones, and CK far more so than controls.

The question we now ask is whether inverting fractured faces makes recognition even more deficient than inversion or fracturing alone. If recognition of intact, inverted faces depends only on the piecemeal identification of individual features, then performance should be no worse when fractured faces are inverted. If it is, it suggests that the intact, but not fractured, inverted face retains some relational information that is used to aid recognition. By the same reasoning, if recognition in the inverted, fractured condition is worse than in the upright, fractured condition, then it suggests that the representation of even individual features is orientation specific.

Method

Participants

Twelve people, five of them male, participated in the first version of the experiment. Their average age was 29 and they had an average of 18 years of education. Another six people, half of whom were male, participated in the second version. Their average age was 30 and their average years of education was 18.

Fig. 2(A). *Four fractured faces are presented in an inverted orientation. The reader should attempt to identify the inverted faces, then turn them upright, and then go to Fig. 2(B).*

Fig. 2(B). *The same faces as in Fig. 2(A) are presented whole but inverted. The faces are identified in the Note at the end of the paper.*

Stimuli

The stimuli were 40 pictures of fractured faces of famous people and their corresponding whole faces. The fractured faces were created by cutting photos into five or six parts and spreading them apart. The individual features eyes, nose, and mouth were preserved, as was their general relation to one another, with eyes above the nose, which in turn was above the mouth. Only the spatial relation among the features was altered (see Fig. 2). Each stimulus was mounted on an 8" x 11" sheet of paper and encased in plastic.

Procedure

In the first version of the experiment, half the participants viewed the entire set of 40 fractured faces initially in the inverted orientation, then in the upright orientation, followed by the corresponding intact faces in the upright orientation. The other half of the participants first viewed the intact face in the inverted orientation followed by the same intact faces in the upright orientation.

In the second version of the experiment, all the subjects viewed the faces in all conditions. For half the participants, the first 20 faces in the set were fractured and viewed first in the inverted orientation and then upright. The next 20 faces in the set were intact and viewed in the inverted orientation. All faces were then viewed in the intact, upright condition. For the other half of the subjects, the faces were interchanged, with the first 20 intact and inverted, and the second 20 fractured.

Participants were tested individually and the stimuli were presented one at a time on a table in front of them. Participants had 10 seconds to identify a face. A response was scored as correct if the name or some clearly identifying information was supplied.

Results

As in the previous experiment, the total correct in the whole upright condition is reported. For the other conditions, the score is the proportion correct of those faces identified correctly in the whole upright condition.

Table 2 shows that the average total correct in the whole upright condition of Version 1, 34.8, is very close to the score of 34 reported for CK, and of 33.1 reported for controls in Moscovitch et al., Experiment 15, where the same faces were used. Planned comparisons showed that participants in both Version 1 and 2 of the present experiment were significantly worse at identifying inverted fractured faces than either inverted, intact faces [Version 1: $t(10) = 2.72$, $P = .02$; Version 2: $t(5) = 3.02$, $P = .03$] or upright, fractured faces [Version 1: $t(5) = 11.23$, $P < 001$; Version 2: $t(5) = 3.77$, $P < .02$]. Their drop in performance from the whole upright condition to the inverted fractured condition (49% and 48% in Versions 1 and 2, respectively) did not differ significantly from the combined drop in performance in the fractured, upright and intact, inverted conditions (46% in both versions). Performance in the upright fractured condition was better than in the inverted whole condition in Version 1 [$t(10) = 2.64$, $P = .025$] but no different in Version 2 [$t(5) = .06$]. There were no significant differences between groups in Version 1, and between Sets in version 2, in the whole upright condition.

Discussion

The results show clearly that recognition of faces that are both fractured and inverted is much worse than recognition of inverted intact faces or of fractured faces alone. These findings support both our conjectures: (1) that the representation of individual facial features is orientation-specific, which accounts for the superior recognition of upright over inverted fractured faces; and (2) that some sort of relational information is used to support recognition even of inverted faces, which accounts for the superior recognition during inversion of intact over fractured faces. These conclusions indicate that the contrast between configurational processing of upright faces by the face-recognition system and the piecemeal, part-based processing of inverted faces by the object-recognition system is too stark in most current formulations and needs revision. We address this issue in our General Discussion

Table 2. *The Number (SD) of Correctly Recognised Faces in the Whole Upright Condition and the Percentage (SD) of Them Recognised in Each of the Other Conditions*

Version 1	Whole Upright[b]		Fractured Inverted		Fractured Upright		Whole Inverted	
	No.	(SD)	%	(SD)	%	(SD)	%	(SD)
Controls (N =6)	32.7	(6.1)	50.8	(12.3)	84.0	(7.0)		
Controls (N =6)	37.0	(2.8)					69.5	(11.5)
CK[a]	34				38			

Version 2	Fractured Set			Inverted Set	
	Whole Upright No.	Fractured Inverted %	Fractured Upright %	Whole Upright[c] No.	Whole Inverted %
Controls (N =6)	14.8	52	77	14.2	77

[a] From Moscovitch et al. (1997), Experiment 15
[b] Max = 40
[c] Max = 20

and consider its implication for the interpretation of our findings and for theories of face recognition.

GENERAL DISCUSSION

Our initial observation that CK's face-recognition was much more impaired by inversion of internal than external features provided the impetus for studying their relative contribution to recognition of upright and inverted faces. Our hope was that the knowledge gained from this investigation would clarify the roles that face and object systems play in face recognition.

Because CK can recognise faces normally despite being severely impaired at recognising objects, we assumed that only his object-recognition system is damaged. His performance on tests of face-recognition, therefore, could be used to gauge the operation of the face recognition system in relative isolation. By comparing his performance with that of neurologically intact controls, we then could determine the additional contribution that the object system made to face recognition.

We began with the working hypothesis, held by many investigators, that the face-recognition system processes information about holistic or config-

urational properties of the face that arise from the spatial relation that individual face parts or features, particularly the eyes, nose, and mouth, have with one another. The object-recognition system, on the other hand, is part-based, in that it processes information in a piecemeal fashion about individual parts or features of the face. As will become apparent, this hypothesis initially carried the weight of accumulating evidence well before it began to groan under its burden and needed some additional support.

Recognition of Faces from Upright Internal and External Features

Consistent with the working hypothesis, we found that CK could recognise faces normally when presented only with the configuration of upright, internal features but that he performed more poorly than normal when presented only with upright, external features. Presumably part-based, rather than configurational, properties dominate the unit of external features. In line with this interpretation, the superiority of controls in the upright, external condition indicated that optimal performance depends also on input from the object system, which is part-based.

Recognition of Faces from Inverted Internal and External Features

Because inversion selectively alters configurational, as opposed to part-based, information (though the eyes and nose are the same, their spatial relationship changes), CK's recognition of inverted faces was severely impaired whether it was based on the whole face or only on internal or external features. This was expected. Lacking an intact object system, CK was forced to rely entirely on his face-recognition system, which could not cope on its own with the altered configurational information. Controls fared no better than CK in the inverted, internal feature condition, thus lending additional support to our conjecture that recognition based only on internal features depends primarily on configurational information processed by the face system. As predicted, having an intact, part-based object system was of little help to controls in this case. In contrast, controls showed only a mild decline when the entire face was inverted, indicating that recognition of entire inverted faces benefits from the contribution of the object system and accords with the view that recognition of inverted faces is part-based. By a process of elimination, this finding suggested to us that recognition of entire inverted faces relies heavily on information derived from external features or their interaction with internal features.

The working hypothesis that had fared so well until now, however, began to falter when evidence was added from the controls' performance in the inverted, external feature condition. If recognition of faces based only on upright, external features is primarily part-based and requires the object system, then controls' performance should not have suffered much when external features were inverted. Recognition, however, was as poor in this condition as in the inverted internal condition, and was almost as poor in controls as in CK. Even when the controls' scores from both conditions were combined, the total was far below that in the whole, inverted condition. This super-inversion effect in the internal and external feature condition indicates that our working hypothesis, at best, is incomplete. The results from our studies of recognition of inverted fractured faces reinforced this opinion.

Recognition of Upright and Inverted Fractured Faces

When configurational properties of a face are altered by fracturing but the features themselves are left intact, recognition should rely primarily on part-based information. As expected, Moscovitch et al. (1997) found that controls were only mildly impaired on this task compared to CK, who performed many standard deviations below normal. If recognition of fractured faces is indeed primarily part-based, then inverting them should not have produced a much greater decline in controls' performance. Their performance should have resembled their recognition of inverted, intact faces. Contrary to the predictions of our working hypothesis, recognition of inverted, fractured faces fell well below the level for inverted intact faces and upright fractured faces.

What Activates the Face and Object Recognition Systems and How Do they Interact?

At this point, the weight of accumulating evidence may be too much for the holistic/part-based hypothesis to bear on its own. We can either replace it with another hypothesis or help it by adding some supports. We prefer the second alternative.

The Object System

Our proposal is to retain the basic premise of our working hypothesis: The face-recognition system operates primarily on holistic properties of the face whereas the object system operates primarily on its component parts or features. Two other assumptions about the object system are needed to sustain this model: (1) the representation of individual features is orientation-specific and normalisation processes are needed to deal with inverted faces (Harman & Moscovitch, 1996); (2) the integration or synthesis of parts into a whole by the object system depends on its having access to information about how the parts are related to each other. Though relational, this information need not be configurational in the sense that it forms a gestalt. Instead it may provide information about categorical relations (on top of, to the side of) about the piecemeal alignment and grouping of parts with one another, both within the internal and external units and between one unit and the other. Both assumptions are embodied in most conventional part-based accounts of object recognition (Biederman, 1987). The first assumption helps account for the superior performance with fractured faces and with external features when they are upright as compared to when they are inverted. The second assumption helps explain why controls perform so much better when inverted faces are intact as compared to when they are fractured.

Both of these added assumptions are needed to explain why controls perform better with entire inverted faces than with inverted internal or external features, and much better than the combined score on each of them, as might be expected if recognition was dependent only on the total number of features. This evidence forces us to reconsider exactly how the part-based object system contributes to face recognition.

One prevailing assumption is that faces are recognised on the basis of individual features when reliance on the object system is great. The evidence, however, suggests strongly that even under these conditions recognition depends on more than identification of single features. For example, our observation of CK indicates that despite his damaged object system he can identify individual features of a face as well as controls (see Moscovitch et al., 1997, Experiment 17). In fact, on those rare occasions that he can identify inverted or fractured faces, he may do so by relying primarily on information about individual features. This accounts for the nearly additive effects we observed in CK in our study. More importantly, the greatest deficit CK has in object recognition is not in identifying parts, but in appreciating their relation to one another and integrating them into a unified whole (Behrmann et al., 1994; Suzuki et al., 1999). It is for this reason that his *object agnosia* is of the *integrative* type.

These observations suggest that the object recognition system is part-based not only (or even primarily) because it is needed to identify individual parts but rather because it uses part-based, rather than holistic, configurational information to normalise the input and integrate individual features into a unified whole. It is the integrative operation of the part-based object system that is crucial for face-recognition when holistic, configurational information is degraded or unavailable, as it is when faces are inverted or fractured. Our study indicates that for integration to occur, information is needed not only about individual features but also about the spatial relations among individual features. As we stated earlier, this information is not configurational in the sense that it supports gestalt or holistic properties. Rather it may be either categorical in that it specifies the coordinate (left–right, up–down) relations among parts, or it may be piecemeal or local in that it indicates how individual features are aligned with each other, much in the way that local relational information is needed for alignment or grouping of pieces in a jigsaw puzzle. This analogy also makes it easy to appreciate the importance of orientation-specific information about individual features.

We can now understand why controls' recognition under inversion is much better for the entire face than for either the internal or external features alone or in total. Because integration is at the heart of the part-based system, interaction among features is to be expected. The integrative process depends on having information about individual features, their orientation, and their relation to one another to form a reasonably unified representation of the face, what Moscovitch et al. termed a *facial facsimile* but which is more properly termed a *counterpart* to the face representation. This counterpart is needed for recognition by the face system and the face system itself may contribute to its creation (see the following section on face system/object system interaction). In the inverted internal and external feature condition, the unavailability of adequate feature information and some higher-order categorical or local, relational information deprives the integrative process of what it needs to form a facial counterpart. On the other hand, when whole faces are inverted, integration is reasonably good because information about local relations needed to align or group features with one another is preserved. Similarly, for fractured faces, integration is good in the upright condition because information about identifiable features can be used to relate them to one another and patch over the gaps left by the fracture. Lacking a part-based system, CK is deficient in both these conditions. However, when fractured faces are inverted, the individual features are more difficult to identify because orientation-specific information needed for good identification is lost and the relational information needed to make up for the feature loss is absent. Integration fails and controls' performance drops dramatically.

There is one more point to note. The information lost by inversion and by fracturing is not identical. Each type of information contributes independently, and in an additive manner, to recognition. This is suggested by our finding that when the drop in performance by controls in the inverted whole and upright fractured conditions is added together it equals the drop in performance in the inverted, fractured condition. Our results indicate, therefore, that the contribution of information about local relations and about features to the integrative processes of the object system is probably additive.

It is conceivable that the additive, super-inversion effect observed for fractured faces in normal people does not result from specific challenges to the face and object system, but rather reflects the nonspecific effects of signal degradation, which tax the perceptual resources beyond their limits. Adding white noise to an inverted face would have the same effect as fracturing it. Although plausible, there are a number of reasons for rejecting this interpretation. Fracturing had a far more debilitating effect on CK's recognition of upright faces than did other kinds of signal degradation such as superimposing one face on another, adding disguises (Moscovitch et al., 1997), or deleting the external features. In contrast, in normal people, the latter manipulation had an effect equivalent to fracturing when the face was upright but a much greater effect when the face was inverted (see Tables 1 and 2). An interpretation in terms of nonspecific signal degradation cannot account for the differences between fracturing and other types of degradation, or explain why effects are additive in one case but more than additive in the other.

The Face System

Given our results, we believe that what distinguishes the face system from the object system is that the face system relies on orientation-specific, holistic, or *global* configurational properties to form a representation of the face rather than on *categorial* or *local* relations needed for the piecemeal integration of individual features. This proposal may be construed to favour gestalt or template models of face recognition (Farah et al., 1998) over models that rely more on relational properties (Carey & Diamond, 1994; Diamond & Carey, 1986; Rhodes, 1988; Rhodes et al., 1993) since in the latter models relations are calculated or defined with respect to individual features. We do not think, however, that the two types of models need to be placed in opposition to one another. As we argued elsewhere (Moscovitch et al., 1997), they complement each other.

According to the gestalt models (Farah et al., 1998, p. 495) "faces are represented holistically without explicitly representing … the local features." This undercomposed representation is essentially a template. According to this model, faces are distinguished from one another on the basis of overall (holistic) similarity (Valentine, 1991). Individual features such as eyes, nose, and mouth either have no privileged status or, if they do, it is only for them to serve as anchor points for bringing the observed face and the stored template into register (Yuille, 1991).

This view seems to us to be too extreme. To represent a face even as a template, some information is needed about the relation among the components that form the template, as the relational models posit. Also, there is evidence from CK that the face system codes information about individual parts. Given the face of a famous person but without eyes, or mouth, or nose, CK can identify the particular feature when it is presented in isolation as well as, or better than, controls (Moscovitch et al., 1997, Experiment 17). Farah et al. (1998) concede that templates contain information about configurations and about individual features, and that this information may even be extracted from templates when needed, as in the experiment we described. They maintain, however, that these features and configurations are not psychologically explicit or real, as whole faces are, in the same sense that in speech, phonemes or their features lack the psychological reality accorded to syllables and words (Bever, 1969; Carey & Diamond, 1994). For Farah et al. (1998), the dispute centres on which type of representation, relational or holistic, has computational precedence and psychological reality or saliency. Though we favour the compromise, complementary position, our data do not allow us to adjudicate among the models on the grounds proposed by Farah et al.

Interaction Between the Face and Object Systems: A Hypothesis

Whichever model is correct, it still needs to explain why upright, fractured faces and inverted faces are recognised as well as they are by controls. To appeal to the contribution of the object system is only part of the solution unless one believes that the object system alone is sufficient to support recognition under those conditions. There is little evidence to sustain that belief. Face recognition of prosopagnosic patients whose object recognition system is relatively well-preserved falls far below controls' recognition of inverted faces, though simultaneous or sequential matching of inverted faces after a very short delay can be preserved (de Gelder & Rouw, this issue; Farah et al., 1995). One is led to conclude that in controls the object system interacts with the face system to achieve good recognition of fractured and of inverted faces.

We suggested that the object system builds a facial counterpart by integrating information about facial features and the local relations among them (see earlier and Moscovitch et al., 1997). Information about this counterpart is then transferred to the face system, where it can be used to activate the appropriate representations needed for identification of the particular face. At this moment we can only speculate about the type of information that is transferred. Considering that the face system itself has access to information about individual parts and the configuration they form, it seems reasonable to suppose that it is information about parts and relations in the counterpart that is transferred. The information can then be used by the face system to activate candidate holistic representations of different faces. These representations can be used, in turn, to support the integration process of the object system. By the continued interaction between the face and object system, identification comes to be based on the most active of the candidate representations. In other words, an interactive activation model accounts for recognition of upright and inverted faces, with the interaction occurring not just between the stimulus and the internal, holistic facial representations, but also between them and representations formed by the object system.

The neuropsychological and neuroimaging evidence is consistent with our proposal. In object agnosia, damage to the object system leads to poor recognition of upright fractured faces and inverted faces even though the face system is intact; and when the face system is damaged, as in prosopagnosia, recognition even of upright, intact faces cannot be sustained by the preserved object system. Functional neuroimaging and electrophysiological studies confirm that there are face-sensitive areas in inferior temporal cortex, typically in the right hemisphere, that form a face-recognition system consisting of three components: (1) a region, probably in the occipital-temporal sulcus, which is sensitive to facial features, especially the eyes (Bentin, Allison, Puce, Perez, & McCarthy, 1996); (2) a region in the lateral fusiform gyrus that responds preferentially to whole upright faces, whether they are of humans or of animals, whether they are real or only cartoons, and whether they are familiar or unfamiliar (Allison, McCarthy, Nobre, Puce, & Belger, 1994; Haxby et al., 1994; Kanwisher, McDermott, & Chun, 1997; McCarthy, Puce, Gore, & Allison, 1997; Tong, Nakayama, Moscovitch, Weinrib, & Kanwisher, this issue), and which also responds, but less vigorously, to individual features; and (3) a region at the border of the fusifrom and parahippocampal gyrus that is sensitive to familiarity and facial identity (Sergent, MacDonald, & Zuck, 1994; Sergent, Ohta, & MacDonald, 1992). Areas more sensitive to objects are adjacent to the face areas but situated more medially and bilaterally (Allison et al., 1994; Kanwisher, Chun, McDermott, & Ledden, 1996a;

Kanwisher, Woods, Iacoboni, & Mazziotta, 1996b; Kohler, Kapur, Moscovitch, Winocur, & Houle, 1995; Malach et al., 1995; McCarthy et al., 1997; Sergent et al., 1992).

What is most relevant with regard to our proposal is that, as predicted, inverted faces activate the object system more than upright faces do (Haxby et al., 1999). If recognition of inverted faces also depends on the interaction of the object system with the face system, we also would expect inverted faces to activate the face system. In accord with our proposal, inverted faces activate the first two components of the system almost as vigorously as their upright counterparts do (Kanwisher, Tong, & Nakayama, 1998; Tong et al., this issue) but with a slightly greater delay (Aguirre, Singh, & D'Esposito, 1998, cited in D'Esposito, Zarahan, & Aguirre, 1999; Bentin et al., 1996; Jeffreys, 1989, 1993), as would be expected if the face system depended on the object system for the initial information about inverted faces.

CONCLUSION

The experiments we reported indicate that the face-recognition system is more sensitive to the configuration of upright internal than external facial features. A super inversion effect is obtained when isolated internal or external features or fractured faces are inverted. Recognition of faces from upright external features, and recognition of inverted and fractured faces, results from the interaction of the face and object system. Whereas the face system forms holistic representations of faces based on global configurations primarily of internal features, the object system integrates information about individual internal and external features and the local and categorial relations among them to form a normalised counterpart to the face-system representation. We proposed that the formation of a proper object-system counterpart and the selection of the appropriate holistic, face system representation depends on the exchange of information between the object and face system in accordance with an interactive activation model. The evidence from neuropsychological, neurophysiological, and

functional neuroimaging studies of face recognition is consistent with our proposal.

Note. The faces in Fig. 1 belong to (a) Sigmund Freud, (b) Winston Churchill, (c) Marilyn Monroe, (d) Pope John II, (e) Tom Hanks, (f) George Bush. The faces in Fig. 2 belong to (a) Michael Jackson, (b) President Bill Clinton, (c) Prince Charles, (d) Barbra Streisand.

REFERENCES

Aguirre, G.K., Singh, R., & D'Esposito, M. (1998). Timing and intensity of fusiform face area (FFA) responses to upright and inverted faces. *Society for Neuroscience Abstracts*, No. 355.8

Allison, T., McCarthy, G., Nobre, A., Puce, A., & Belger, A. (1994). Human extrastriate visual cortex and the perception of faces, words, numbers, and colors. *Cerebral Cortex, 5,* 544–554.

Bartlett, J.C., & Searcy, J. (1993). Inversion and configuration of faces. *Cognitive Psychology, 25,* 281–316.

Behrmann, M., Moscovitch, M., & Winocur, G. (1994). Intact visual imagery and impaired visual perception in a patient with visual agnosia. *Journal of Experimental Psychology: Human Perception and Performance, 30,* 1068–1087.

Bentin, S., Allison, T., Puce, A., Perez, A., & McCarthy, G. (1996). Electrophysiological studies of face perception in humans. *Journal of Cognitive Neuroscience, 8,* 551–565.

Biederman, I. (1987). Recognition-by-components: A theory of human image understanding. *Psychological Review, 94,* 115–147.

Biederman, I., & Gerhardstein, P.C. (1993). Recognising depth rotated objects: Evidence and conditions for three-dimensional viewpoint in variance. *Journal of Experimental Psychology: Human Perception and Performance, 19,* 1162–1182.

Carey, S., & Diamond, R. (1994). Are faces perceived as configurations more by adults than by children? *Visual Cognition , 1 ,* 253–274.

de Gelder, B., & Rouw, R. (this issue). Structural encoding precludes recognition of face parts in prosopagnosia. *Cognitive Neuropsychology, 17,* 89–102.

de Haan, E. H. F., & Hay, D.C. (1986). The matching of famous and unknown faces given either the internal or the external features: A study on patients with unilateral brain lesions. In H.E. Ellis, M.A. Jeeves, F. Newcombe, & A.W. Young (Eds.), *Aspects of face processing* (pp. 302–309). Dordrecht The Netherlands: Martinus Niijhoff.

D'Esposito, M., Zarahan, E., & Aguirre, G.K. (1999). Event-related functional MRI: Implications for cognitive psychology. *Psychological Bulletin, 125,* 155–164.

Diamond, R., & Carey, S. (1986). Why faces are and are not special: An effect of expertise. *Journal of Experimental Psychology: General, 115,* 107–117.

Ellis, H.D., Shepherd, J.W., & Davies, G.M. (1979). Identification of familiar and unfamiliar faces from internal and external features: Source implications for theories of face recognition. *Perception, 8,* 431–439.

Farah, M.J., Levinson, K.L., & Klein, K.L. (1995a). Face perception and within-category discrimination in prosopagnosia. *Neuropsychologia, 33,* 661–667

Farah, M.J., Tanaka, J.W., & Drain, H.M. (1995b). What causes the face inversion effect? *Journal of Experimental Psychology: Human Perception and Performance, 21,* 628–634.

Farah, M.J., Wilson, K.D., Drain, H.M., & Tanaka, J.R. (1995c). The inverted face inversion effect in prosopagnosia: Evidence for mandatory, face specific perceptual mechanisms. *Vision Research, 35,* 2089–2093

Farah, M.J., Wilson, K.D., Drain, H.M., & Tanaka, J.R. (1998). What is "special" about face perception? *Psychological Review, 105,* 482 – 498.

Haig, N.D. (1986). Exploring recognition with interchanged facial features. *Perception, 15,* 235 –247.

Hamm, J.P., & McMullen, P.A. (1998). Effects of orientation on the identification of rotated objects depends on the level of identity. *Journal of Experimental Psychology: Human Perception and Performance, 24,* 413–426.

Harman, K., & Moscovitch, M. (1996). *The inversion effect for faces and objects: Part-based/holistic encoding and the effects of format congruence.* Paper presented at the Annual Meeting of the Canadian Society for Brain Behavior and Cognitive Science. Montreal, Quebec, Canada.

Haxby, J.V., Horwitz, B., Ungerleider, L.G., Maisog, J.M., Pietrini, P., & Grady, C.L. (1994). The functional organisation of human extrastriate cortex: A PET-rCBF study of selective attention to faces and locations. *Journal of Neuroscience, 14,* 6336–6353.

Haxby, J.V., Ungerleider, L.G., Clark, V.P., Schouten, J.L., Hoffman, E.A., & Martin, A. (1999). The effect of face inversion on activity in human neural systems for face and object perception. *Neuron, 22,* 189–199.

Hayward, W.G., & Tarr, M.J. (1997). Testing conditions for viewpoint invariance in object recognition. *Journal of Experimental Psychology: Human Perception and Performance, 23,* 1511–1521.

Jeffreys, D.A. (1989). A face-responsive potential recorded from the human scalp. *Experimental Brain Research, 78,* 193–202.

Jeffreys, D.A. (1993). The influence of stimulus orientation on the vertex positive scalp potential evoked by faces. *Experimental Brain Research, 96,* 163–172.

Kanwisher, N., Chun, M.M., McDermott, J., & Ledden, P.J. (1996a). Functional imaging of human visual recognition. *Cognitive Brain Research, 5,* 55–67.

Kanwisher, N., McDermott, J., & Chun, M.M. (1997). The fusiform face area: A module in human extrastriate cortex specialised for face perception. *Journal of Neuroscience, 17,* 4302 –4311.

Kanwisher, N., Tong, F., & Nakayama, K. (1998). The effect of face inversion on the human fusiform face area. *Cognition, 68,* B1–B11.

Kanwisher, N., Woods, R.P., Iacoboni, M., & Mazziota, J.C. (1996b). A locus in human extrastriate cortex for visual shape analysis. *Journal of Cognitive Neuroscience, 9,* 133–142.

Köhler, S., Kapur, S., Moscovitch, M., Winocur, G., & Houle, S. (1995). Dissociations of spatial and object vision: A PET study in humans. *NeuroReport, 6,* 1865–1868.

Malach, R., Reppas, J.B., Benson, R.R., Kwong, K.K., Jiang, H., Kennedy, W.A., Ledden, P.J., Brady, T.J., Rosen, B.R., & Tootell, R.B. H. (1995). Object-related activity revealed by functional magnetic resonance imaging in human occipital cortex. *Proceedings of the National Academy of Sciences, USA, 92,* 8135–8139.

McCarthy, G., Puce, A., Gore, J.C., & Allison, T. (1997). Face-specific processing in the human fusiform gyrus. *Journal of Cognitive Neuroscience, 9,* 604–609.

Moscovitch, M., Winocur, G., & Behrmann, M. (1997). What is special about face recognition? Nineteen experiments on a person with visual object agnosia, and dyslexia but normal face recognition. *Journal of Cognitive Neuroscience, 9,* 555–604.

Nachson, I., Moscovitch, M., & Umiltà, C. (1995). The contribution of external and internal features to the matching of unfamiliar faces. *Psychological Research, 58,* 31–37.

Rhodes, G. (1988). Looking at faces: First-order and second-order features as determinants of facial appearance. *Perception, 17,* 43–63.

Rhodes, G., Brake, S., & Atkinson, A.P. (1993). What's lost in inverted faces? *Cognition, 47,* 25–57.

Ross, P., & Turkewitz, G. (1982). Changes in hemispheric advantage in processing facial information with increasing stimulus familiarisation. *Cortex, 18,* 489–499.

Savin, H.B., & Bever, T.G. (1970). The non-perceptual reality of the phoneme. *Journal of Verbal Learning and Verbal Behavior, 9,* 295–302.

Searcy, J.J., & Bartlett, J.C. (1996). Inversion and processing of component and spatial relational information in faces. *Journal of Experimental Psychology: Human Perception and Performance, 22,* 904–915.

Segui, J. (1984). The syllable: A basic perceptual unit in speech processing. In H. Bouma & D.G. Bouwhuis (Eds.) *Attention and performance X: Control of language processes.* Hove, UK: Lawrence Erlbaum Associates Ltd.

Sergent, J., MacDonald, B., & Zuck, E. (1994). Structural and functional organisation of knowledge about faces and proper names: A positron emission tomography study. In C. Umiltà & Moscovitch (Eds.), *Attention and performance XV: Conscious and nonconscious information processing* (pp. 203–228). Cambridge, MA: MIT Press/Bradford.

Sergent, J., Ohta, S., & MacDonald, B. (1992). Neuroanatomy of face and object processing. *Brain, 115,* 15–36.

Suzuki, S., Peterson, M.A., Behrmann, M., & Moscovitch, M. (1999). Identification of one-part and two-part volumetric objects: Selective deficits in encoding spatial arrangements of parts in visual agnosia. Manuscript submitted for publication.

Suzuki, S., Peterson, M.A., Moscovitch, M., & Behrmann, M. (1997). *Viewpoint specificity in the identification of single objects is evident in control partici-* pants and very exaggerated in visual object agnosia. Paper presented at the Annual Meeting of the Society for Cognitive Neuroscience, Boston, March 1997.

Tanaka, J.W., & Farah, M.J. (1993). Parts and wholes in face recognition. *Quarterly Journal of Experimental Psychology, 46A,* 225–245.

Tanaka, J.W., & Sengco, J.A. (1997). Parts and their configuration in face recognition. *Memory and Cognition, 25,* 583–592.

Tarr, M.J., Hayward, W.G., Gauthier, I., & Williams, P. (1994). *Geon recognition is viewpoint dependent.* Paper presented at the 35th Annual Meeting of the Psychonomic Society, St. Louis, MO.

Tong, F., Nakayama, K., Moscovitch, M., Weinrib, O., & Kanwisher, N. (this issue). Response properties of the human fusiform face area. *Cognitive Neuropsychology.*

Valentine, T. (1988). Upside-down faces: A review of the effects of inversion upon face recognition. *British Journal of Psychology, 79,* 471–491.

Valentine, T. (1991). A unified account of the effects of distinctiveness, inversion, and race in face recognition. *The Quarterly Journal of Experimental Psychology, 43A,* 161–204.

Yin, R.K. (1969). Looking at upside-down faces. *Journal of Experimental Psychology, 81,* 141–145.

Yin, R.K. (1970). Face Recognition by brain-injured patients: A dissociable ability? *Neuropsychologia, 8,* 395–402.

Young, A.W., Hay, D.C., McWeeeney, K.H., Flude, B.M., & Ellis, A.W. (1985). Matching familiar and unfamiliar faces on internal and external features. *Perception, 14,* 737–746.

Young, A.W., Hellawell, D., & Hay, D.C. (1987). Configurational information in face perception. *Perception, 16,* 747–759.

Yuille, A.L. (1991). Deformable templates for face recognition. Journal of Cognitive Neuroscience, 3, 59–70.

COGNITIVE NEUROPSYCHOLOGY, 2000, 17 (1/2/3), 221–239

ERPs Evoked by Viewing Facial Movements

Aina Puce, Angela Smith, and Truett Allison

VA Medical Center, West Haven and Yale University School of Medicine, New Haven, USA

Human neuroimaging and event-related potential (ERP) studies suggest that ventral and lateral temporo-occipital cortex is sensitive to static faces and face parts. Recent fMRI data also show activation by facial movements. In this study we recorded from 22 posterior scalp locations in 20 normal right-handed males to assess ERPs evoked by viewing: (1) moving eyes and mouths in the context of a face; (2) moving and static eyes with and without facial context.

N170 and P350 peak amplitude and latency data were analysed. N170 is an ERP previously shown to be preferentially responsive to face and eye stimuli, and P350 immediately follows N170. Major results were: (1) N170 was significantly larger over the bilateral temporal scalp to viewing opening mouths relative to closing mouths, and to eye aversion relative to eyes gazing at the observer; (2) at a focal region over the right inferior temporal scalp, N170 was significantly earlier to mouth opening relative to closing, and to eye aversion relative to eyes gazing at the observer; (3) the focal ERP effect of eye aversion occurred independent of facial context; (4) these differences cannot be attributable to movement per se, as they did not occur in a control condition in which checks moved in comparable areas of the visual field; (5) isolated static eyes produced N170s that were not significantly different from N170s to static full faces over the right inferior temporal scalp, unlike in the left hemisphere where face N170s were significantly larger than eye N170s; (6) unlike N170, P350 exhibited nonspecific changes as a function of stimulus movement.

These results suggest that: (1) bilateral temporal cortex forms part of a system sensitive to biological motion, of which facial movements form an important subset; (2) there may be a specialised system for facial gesture analysis that provides input for neuronal circuitry dealing with social attention and the actions of others.

INTRODUCTION

The human face is an important source of information. Viewing a familiar face can trigger the retrieval of a wealth of stored information concerning that person (Bruce & Young, 1986). A person's emotional state (Ekman, 1982) and attentional focus (Baron-Cohen, 1995; Baron-Cohen, Wheelwright, & Jolliffe, 1997) can easily be determined for both familiar and unfamiliar faces. Speakers in noisy environments are better understood when listeners read the speakers' lips (Campbell, Landis, & Regard, 1986). Monitoring facial expressions during social interactions allows us to infer the intentions of others. All of these analyses of facial gesture can proceed independently of facial familiarity.

When subjects view static faces, functional magnetic resonance imaging (fMRI) studies consis-

---

Requests for reprints should be addressed to Aina Puce, PhD, Brain Sciences Institute, Swinburne University of Technology, P.O. Box 218, Hawthorn Victoria 3122, Australia (Fax: +61 3 9214 5525; Email: puce@bsi.swin.edu.au).

This work was supported by the Department of Veterans Affairs and by NIMH grant MH-05286.

221

tently show activation of ventral and, to a lesser extent, lateral temporo-occipital cortex (Puce, Allison, Asgari, Gore, & McCarthy, 1996; Puce, Allison, Gore, & McCarthy, 1995; Puce, Allison, Spencer, Spencer, & McCarthy, 1997). Event-related potential (ERP) recordings made directly from the cortical surface reveal face-specific N200s from these same cortical regions (Allison et al., 1994a; Allison, McCarthy, Nobre, Puce, & Belger, 1994c; Allison, Puce, Spencer, & McCarthy, 1999; Puce et al., 1997). A critical locus for face perception appears to be located in the right posterior fusiform gyrus (Kanwisher, McDermott, & Chun, 1997; McCarthy, Puce, Gore, & Allison, 1997).

Recent fMRI studies suggest that moving faces preferentially activate lateral temporal cortex relative to ventral temporo-occipital cortex (Puce, Allison, Bentin, Gore, & McCarthy, 1998a). Indeed, evidence from human neuropsychological and neuroimaging studies suggests that there may be independent pathways for the processing of facial identity and for processing facial gesture and expression (Campbell et al., 1986; Humphreys, Donnelly, & Riddoch, 1993; Sergent, Ohta, Mac-Donald, & Zuck, 1994). Activation of the human bilateral temporal cortex occurs in response to changes in gaze direction (Puce et al., 1998a) and to linguistic (Calvert et al., 1997) and nonlinguistic mouth movements (Puce et al., 1998a). A left-hemisphere MEG study elicited neuronal responses with peak latencies around 200msec from the lateral temporal cortex in response to subjects discriminating mouthed phonemes (Sams et al., 1991). However, lateral temporal cortex is also active when subjects view static faces (Puce et al., 1995, 1996, 1997), so the functional significance of this region as yet remains undetermined. Given the response to both static and mobile faces, this region of cortex may find the *parts* of the face more salient than the whole if it is active in the processing of facial gestures. Although behavioural data from normal human subjects indicate that better judgements of gesture and expression are made when the face is mobile, this information can also be extracted from static faces (Bassili, 1978; Humphreys et al., 1993). Single-unit studies in monkeys viewing static faces indicate that some

neurones in the superior temporal sulcus (STS) are sensitive to head and eye direction (Hasselmo, Rolls, Baylis, & Nalwa, 1989; Perrett et al., 1985; Perrett, Hietanen, Oram, & Benson, 1992). The integration of visual form and motion is also thought to take place in regions of the primate STS (Oram & Perrett, 1996). Hence, it is thought that the cortex of the STS forms part of a system that deals with social attention in monkeys (Perrett et al., 1990).

Intracranial ERP recordings from ventral face-specific regions indicate that static face parts also evoke N200s, although their latency is longer than the N200 to full faces (Allison et al., 1994b; McCarthy, Puce, Belger, & Allison, 1999). Scalp ERP studies to static full faces and face parts also show this latency difference (Bentin, Allison, Puce, Perez, & McCarthy, 1996). Interestingly, the scalp N170 to isolated eyes is larger than to full faces at the temporal scalp, leading Bentin and colleagues (1996) to postulate the existence of a temporo-occipital "eye detector" in addition to a face-specific processor. Intracranial ERP recordings suggest that there may be separate regions of ventral temporo-occipital cortex that respond preferentially to static faces or face parts (Allison et al., 1999; McCarthy et al., 1999). A region of cortex *lateral* to ventral face-specific cortex that is preferentially sensitive to static isolated face parts (McCarthy et al., 1999) could be one source for the larger scalp N170 seen to isolated eyes by Bentin and colleagues (1996).

In this study, we sought to examine the behaviour of the "eye detector". We reasoned that it should be responsive to moving eyes with and without facial context, as well as to static isolated eyes. We also sought to examine neuronal responses to different types of mouth movements. In the fMRI study (Puce et al., 1998a), eye aversion and return were presented within a stimulus block (and similarly for mouth opening and closing), thus preventing assessment of the separate activation produced by these types of facial movement. Here we examined N170 and P350 ERPs evoked separately by eye aversion, eye return, mouth opening, and mouth closing. ERPs evoked by static and moving isolated eyes, and by nonbiological movement, were also investigated. A preliminary report of these results has appeared (Puce, Smith, & Allison, 1998b).

METHODS

Subjects

Twenty neurologically normal male subjects with an average age of 28.6 years (range 21–63 years) participated in this study. All subjects were strongly right-handed on the Edinburgh Handedness Inventory (mean: 85.8; SD: 10.2) (Oldfield, 1970). The ERP protocol was approved by the Human Studies Committee at VAMC, West Haven.

Experiments

Two experiments were run in which a colour stimulus was present on the screen at all times. A female face was used for Experiment 1, whereas a male face was used in Experiment 2. For both experiments stimuli were presented on a computer monitor and subtended a visual angle of 10.7° horizontally and vertically. Within each experiment the average luminance and contrast were equivalent across stimulus types. Subjects were instructed to attend to the stimuli at all times and to maintain fixation at a point at the centre of the eyes, or to an identical point in space for the control stimuli. No subject response was required.

In Experiment 1, ERPs evoked by viewing moving eyes (EYES) and mouths (MOUTH) were recorded. Six facial movements occurred on a continuously present face. There were four eye movements, which consisted of the eyes suddenly looking away from the viewer randomly to either the viewer's right or left [AWAY(R), AWAY(L)] and then back at the viewer (BACK). There were two mouth movements: mouth opening (OPEN) or mouth closure (CLOSED). The eye and mouth movements occurred randomly at 500msec intervals as shown schematically in Fig. 1, with the only constraint being that a baseline face condition (i.e. EYES BACK and MOUTH CLOSED) had to occur prior to any eye or mouth movement. This constraint was imposed so that other combinations

of facial movements could not occur (e.g. mouth opening while the eyes looked away). The face was presented on a background of black, gray and white concentric rings, which remained static during the experiment. These stimuli were a subset of those previously used in an fMRI study (Puce et al., 1998a).

In Experiment 2, ERPs evoked by viewing eye movements within and without the context of a full face were investigated, as were differences between ERPs evoked by static and moving stimuli. Three stimulus types consisting of a full face (FACE), eyes alone (EYES) or a checkerboard control (CHECK) were used. The display changed every 1500msec (Fig. 2). For example, the FACE replaced the previous stimulus on the screen (FACE ONSET). During FACE ONSET, the eyes in the stimulus face looked directly at the viewer. After 1500msec, the eyes looked away either to the left or the right (FACE AWAY). After 1500msec, the eyes then returned to look at the viewer (FACE BACK). The stimulus remained on the screen for another 1500msec. This three-part sequence with events spaced at 1500msec intervals occurred for each stimulus type. The direction of eye movement was randomized and there were an equal number of eye movements to the left and the right for the FACE and EYES stimulus types. The control stimulus (CHECK) was composed of a checkerboard the same overall size as the eye region in EYES. Isolated checks were alternated in spatially similar regions as the moving eyes, resulting in corresponding CHECK AWAY and CHECK BACK conditions. Hence there were a total of 9 stimulus conditions (Fig. 2).

ERP Recordings

Recording electrodes from the following 22 modified 10–20 system scalp sites (American EEG Society, 1990) were used: Cz, Pz, C3, P3, T7, TP7, P7, PO7, O1, TP9, P9, PO9, C4, P4, T8, TP8, P8, PO8, O2, TP10, P10, PO10. Horizontal and vertical EOG (EOGh and EOGv) recording electrodes were placed on the outer canthus of the eye and below the centre of the eye, respectively. For both EEG and EOG recordings electrodes on the

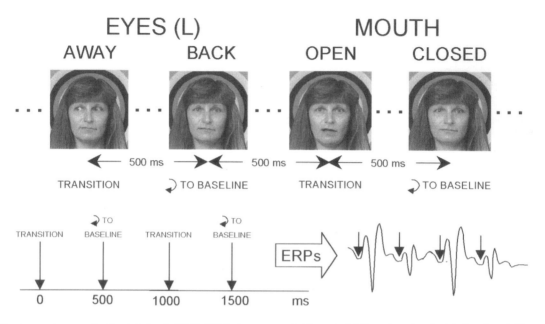

Fig. 1. *Experiment 1 stimuli and timing. In EYES AWAY, the eyes averted either to the left (L, as shown) or the right (not shown). The eyes then returned to look directly at the viewer (EYES BACK) in a baseline condition. In MOUTH OPEN, the mouth opened and remained open. The mouth was then subsequently closed (MOUTH CLOSED) in a baseline condition. These movements evoked ERPs every 500msec (bottom panel).*

forehead and chin served as ground and reference, respectively. Continuous EEG and EOG recordings were made during both experiments using a filter bandpass of 0.1 to 100Hz and a gain of 20,000. All electrode impedences were below 5kΩ.

ERP Analysis

Single-subject averaged ERPs, as well as grand averaged ERPs across subjects, were generated for both experiments and all stimulus conditions. Trials with EOG artefacts were detected and not included in the averages. N170 amplitudes and latencies were determined for each subject, experiment, and stimulus condition. This ERP component has previously been shown to be sensitive to faces and face parts (Bentin et al., 1996). A broad, positive ERP (P350) followed the N170. P350 usually had multiple peaks over its time course. Therefore area under the curve measurements were obtained over the latency range 200–500msec post-stimulus (P350 area).

Statistical Analysis

Experiment 1

Three-way repeated-measures analyses of variance (ANOVAs) were performed for each homologous electrode pair with Side (Left, Right), FacePart (Eyes Right, Eyes Left, Mouth) and Movement Type (Away/Open, Back/Closed) as factors. N170 amplitude, N170 latency, and P350 area were the dependent variables. Additional posthoc comparisons were performed as required.

Experiment 2

Differences between *moving* stimuli were assessed using three-way ANOVAs with repeated measures at homologous electrode pairs with Side (Left, Right), Stimulus Type (Face, Eyes, Check) and Movement Type (Away, Back) as factors. N170 amplitude, latency, and P350 area were the dependent variables in this and the comparisons described later. Similarly, a comparison between the *static* stimuli was made using a two-way

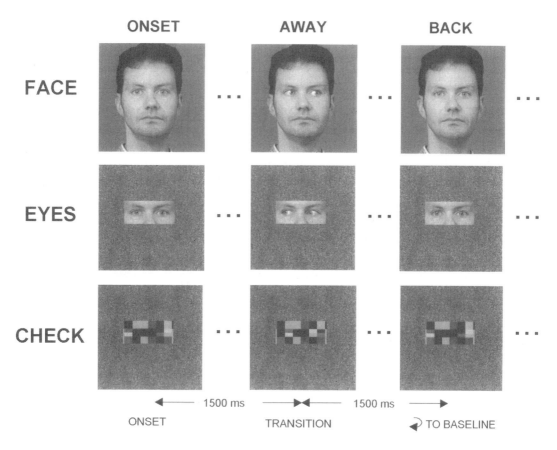

ONSET   AWAY   BACK

FACE

EYES

CHECK

ONSET   TRANSITION   TO BASELINE

1500 ms   1500 ms

Fig. 2. *Experiment 2 stimuli and timing. A stimulus was presented every 1500msec and consisted of a three-part sequence with ONSET, AWAY, and BACK conditions. There were three stimulus types: a full face (FACE), eyes alone (EYES), or a CHECKerboard control. In AWAY, the eyes averted (FACE AWAY, EYES AWAY) and then 1500msec later returned to look directly at the viewer (FACE BACK, EYES BACK). In the CHECK condition, checks were alternated at 1500msec intervals in positions spatially similar to the eyes.*

repeated measures ANOVA with Side (Left, Right) and Stimulus Type (Face, Eyes, Check) as factors. Finally, a comparison between moving and static stimulus conditions was made using only stimulus conditions in which eyes looked directly at the viewer. A three-way repeated-measures ANOVA was performed with Side (Left, Right), Stimulus Type (Face, Eyes, Check) and State (Static, Moving) as factors. Additional post-hoc comparisons were performed as required. For all analyses results with a significance level of $P < .01$ will be reported.

RESULTS

Experiment 1

Grand averaged waveforms from the 20 subjects are shown for all facial movement conditions in Fig. 3. The top set of ERPs depicts the EYES AWAY or MOUTH OPEN conditions, whereas the bottom set of ERPs depicts the EYES BACK or MOUTH CLOSED conditions. For all conditions triphasic ERPs (P100, N170, P350, e.g. electrode P7) were elicited. This triphasic waveform was not seen at the EOG electrodes (Fig. 3), and is thus not sec-ondary to eye movements associated with stimulus presentation. N170 had maximal amplitudes over the temporal scalp of both hemispheres. P350 was largest at centroparietal sites. P100 was generally insensitive to stimulus conditions and will not be discussed further.

Consistently larger N170s were observed in EYES AWAY relative to EYES BACK, and MOUTH OPEN relative to MOUTH CLOSED in both hemispheres (Compare the top and bottom set of ERP waveforms of Fig. 3). These differences were particularly evident at the temporal scalp and were confirmed with a three-way ANOVA with a significant main effect of Movement Type at these sites (Table 1). Post-hoc comparisons showed sig-nificant differences both for the two mouth (OPEN vs. CLOSED) and the eye (AWAY vs. BACK) conditions at the temporal scalp (Table 2). No main effects of either Side or FacePart were observed.

In general, N170 latency was fairly invariant across the facial movement conditions. The only significant main effect was observed at electrode pair P9/P10 for Movement Type (Table 1). Posthoc tests indicated that a significantly *earlier* N170 was elicited at P10 to eye aversion in either direction relative to eyes returning to look at the observer [EYES AWAY(R) vs. BACK: $F(1,19)$ = 14.32; EYES AWAY(L) vs. BACK: $F(1,19)$ =

14.58]. Also, significantly earlier N170 latencies were seen to mouth opening relative to mouth clo-sure [$F(1,19)$ = 18.84]. No significant differences were seen at P9.

P350 area was generally larger for eye aversion relative to eyes gazing back at the observer (Fig. 3). This observation was confirmed statistically. P350 area showed a significant main effect for Movement Type in the three-way ANOVA (Table 1) at ante-rior temporal and dorsal (Central and parietal) elec-trodes. Post-hoc testing indicated that conditions with eyes were responsible for these effects at right temporal and bilateral central/parietal sites (Table 3). A significant interaction effect at PO7/PO8 for Side × FacePart [$F(2,38)$ = 5.58] was produced by a larger P350 area in the right hemisphere for eyes returning to look at the observer from the right [$F(1,19)$ = 10.33].

EXPERIMENT 2

ERPs to Moving Stimuli

The ERPs evoked in Experiment 2 were similar to those of Experiment 1 and consisted of triphasic waveforms (P100, N170, P350) that were maximal over the temporal scalp. Figure 4 displays ERPs elicited to the moving stimuli. At each electrode three separate sets of ERP waveforms are shown for each stimulus type (FACE, EYES, and CHECK) with superimposition of the AWAY and BACK

Table 1. *Experiment 1: Results of a Three-way ANOVA for Side × FacePart × Movement Type*

Electrode Pair	N170 Amplitude		N170 Latency		P350 Area	
	$F(1,19)$	P	$F(1,19)$	P	$F(1,19)$	P
T7/T8					9.91	.005
TP7/TP8	28.92	.0001			10.23	.005
P7/P8	43.49	.0001				
PO7/PO8	47.31	.0001				
O1/O2	26.94	.0001				
TP9/TP10	34.45	.0001				
P9/P10	39.59	.0001	12.00	.003		
PO9/PO10	29.75	.0001				
C3/C4					13.64	.002
P3/P4					10.74	.004

Results show Significant ($P < .01$) main effects for Movement Type on N170 amplitude, N170 latency, and P350 area. There were no significant main effects for Side or FacePart. Electrode pairs consist of homologous regions in each hemisphere.

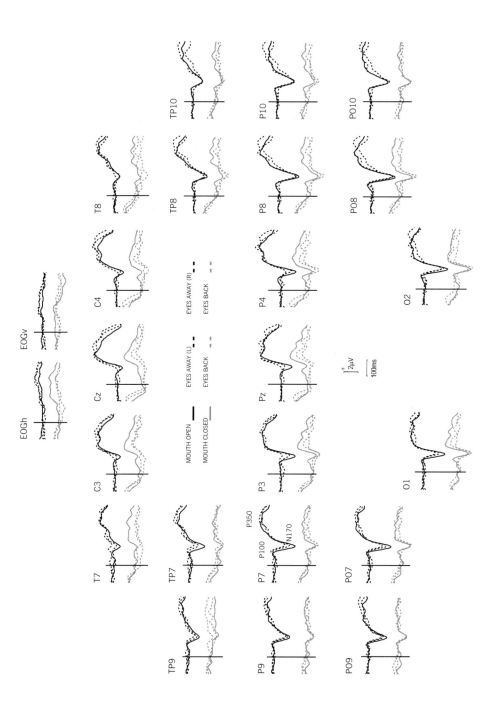

Fig. 3. Experiment 1. Grand averaged ERP waveforms for the EYES AWAY (LEFT, RIGHT) and BACK and MOUTH OPEN and CLOSED conditions from 20 subjects; the ERP lay-out mimics the approximate spatial position of the 22 scalp recording locations and EOG channels. Two sets of ERPs are shown at each electrode site. The top set of ERPs shows activity in a 500msec epoch during EYES AWAY(L), EYES AWAY(R) or MOUTH OPEN conditions; the bottom set for the EYES BACK (R or L) and MOUTH CLOSED conditions. A triphasic positive–negative–positive ERP consisting of P100, N170, and P350 was elicited for all facial movements (see labeled peaks at electrode T7). A 100msec pre-stimulus baseline is included in each trace. Time of stimulus delivery is indicated by the vertical line.

Table 2. *Experiment 1: Results of Significant (P < .01) Posthoc Comparisons (from Main Effects of Table 1) for N170 Amplitude as a Function of Movement Type*

Electrode Pair	Left Hemisphere			Right Hemisphere		
	FacePart	F(1,19)	P	FacePart	F(1,19)	P
TP7/TP8	MOUTH	14.11	.001	EYES L	15.56	.0009
P7/P8	MOUTH	28.38	.0001	MOUTH	12.80	.002
	EYES R	10.32	.005	EYES L	14.06	.001
	EYES L	8.28	.001			
PO7/PO8	MOUTH	17.19	.0005	MOUTH	17.44	.0005
	EYES L	9.30	.007	EYES L	15.80	.0008
O1/O2	MOUTH	23.04	.0001	MOUTH	19.76	.0003
				EYES L	9.23	.007
TP9/TP10	MOUTH	15.69	.0008	EYES L	23.67	.0001
P9/P10	MOUTH	14.79	.001	MOUTH	10.09	.005
	EYES R	21.20	.0002	EYES R	16.76	.0006
	EYES L	14.09	.001	EYES L	21.71	.0002
PO9/PO10	MOUTH	13.51	.002	MOUTH	13.94	.001
	EYES R	8.82	.008	EYES R	12.55	.002
	EYES L	9.93	.005	EYES L	13.99	.001

MOUTH = significantly larger N170 for MOUTH OPEN vs. CLOSED; EYES R = significantly larger N170 for EYES AWAY(R) vs. BACK; EYES L = significantly larger N170 for EYES AWAY(L) vs. BACK.

conditions. At electrodes O1 and O2 comparable N170 amplitudes were seen for the AWAY and BACK conditions of all stimulus types, implying that luminance and contrast in the AWAY and BACK conditions were comparable. At all electrodes, robust N170s were elicited to the CHECK control. N170 amplitudes were comparable for the AWAY and BACK conditions for the control (Fig. 4, third set of ERPs). N170 amplitude was larger for the AWAY condition and smaller for the BACK condition for FACES and EYES at electrode P10 (Fig. 4, inset) and at surrounding sites. Statistical analysis confirmed the N170 amplitude differences: A significant main effect of Movement Type was seen at electrode pair P9/P10 [$F(1,19)$ = 10.59]. Posthoc testing showed that the differences

Table 3. *Experiment 1: Results of Significant (P < .01) Posthoc Comparisons (from Main ffects of Table 1) for P350 Area as a Function of Movement Type*

Electrode Pair	Left Hemisphere			Right Hemisphere		
	FacePart	F(1,19)	P	FacePart	F(1,19)	P
T7/T8				EYES R	45.79	.0001
				EYES L	11.28	.003
TP7/TP8				EYES R	42.45	.0001
C3/C4	EYES L	14.78	.001	EYES R	33.10	.0001
				EYES L	26.43	.0001
P3/P4	EYES R	15.14	.001	EYES R	24.37	.0001
				EYES L	12.01	.003

MOUTH = significantly larger N170 for MOUTH OPEN vs. CLOSED;
EYES R = significantly larger N170 for EYES AWAY(R) vs. BACK;
EYES L = significantly larger N170 for EYES AWAY(L) vs. BACK.

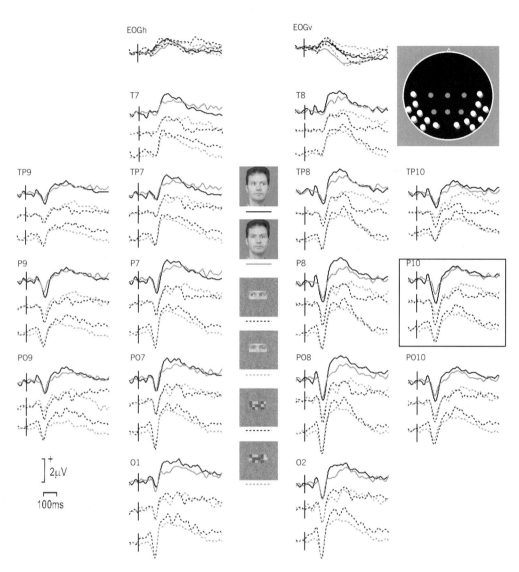

Fig. 4. *Experiment 2. Grand averaged ERP waveforms for electrodes overlying the temporal scalp and EOG channels for the six moving stimulus conditions. The selected electrodes are highlighted as white circles in a schematic electrode map at top right. ERPs from the temporal scalp electrodes are shown as three sets of ERP waveforms at each electrode site. The top, middle, and bottom sets of waveforms show ERPs to the FACE, EYES, and CHECK conditions, respectively. ERPs plotted in black denote AWAY conditions, whereas ERPs in gray denote BACK conditions. Time of stimulus delivery is indicated by the vertical line. Electrode P10 (enclosed by a black box) shows differences between AWAY and BACK conditions for FACE and EYES stimulus types.*

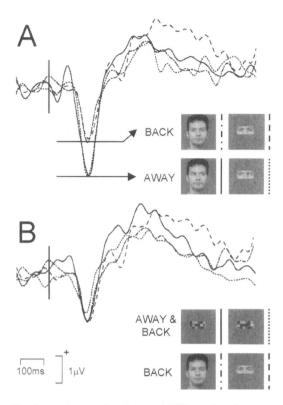

Fig. 5. *Experiment 2: Grand averaged ERP waveforms for electrode P10 for moving stimulus conditions. A. Comparison of AWAY and BACK conditions for the FACE and EYES stimulus types. B. Comparison of the CHECK conditions (AWAY and BACK) with the BACK conditions for the FACE and EYES stimulus types. Time of stimulus delivery is indicated by the vertical line.*

were significant at P10 only. Stimuli with eyes generated significantly larger N170 amplitudes for AWAY relative to BACK at P10 [FACE $F(1,19)$ = 12.87; EYES $F(1,19)$ = 9.70]. The ERPs at P10 have been superimposed in Fig. 5A to highlight the N170 amplitude differences between the AWAY and BACK conditions for stimuli containing eyes. Figure 5B depicts N170s of comparable amplitude for the control stimuli and the BACK conditions for stimuli containing eyes.

Significant main effects of Side for N170 amplitude were observed at electrode pairs PO7/PO8 and O1/O2. Post-hoc tests revealed that these effects were due to larger N170 amplitudes in the right hemisphere. At O2 relative to O1, signifi-

cantly larger N170s occurred for FACE [AWAY $F(1,19)$ = 10.54; BACK $F(1,19)$ = 8.80]. These effects were nonspecific at PO7/PO8: all stimulus types for the BACK condition, including CHECK, produced significantly larger N170s in the right hemisphere [FACE $F(1,19)$ = 9.61; EYES $F(1,19)$ = 16.30; CHECK $F(1,19)$ = 9.44]. No significant interaction effects were noted for N170 amplitude.

For N170 latency, the three-way ANOVA revealed a significant main effect for Stimulus Type at electrode pairs P7/P8 [$F(2,38)$ = 13.61] and PO7/PO8 [$F(2,38)$ = 8.47]. Posthoc tests indicated that these differences were due to slower N170 latencies to stimuli containing eyes for the BACK conditions [P7: FACE vs. CHECK $F(1,19)$ = 16.49; P8: EYES vs. CHECK $F(1,19)$ = 9.46; PO9: FACE vs. CHECK $F(1,19)$ = 10.21; EYES vs. CHECK $F(1,19)$ = 9.08; PO10: EYES vs. CHECK $F(1,19)$ = 9.54]. This effect can be seen in Fig. 4 at these electrodes and their neighbours. At PO9 there was also a significant difference between the AWAY conditions for the FACE and CHECK stimuli [$F(1,19)$ = 13.31], produced by a longer N170 latency for FACE relative to CHECK (Fig. 4). A significant main effect of Side was observed at electrode pair P9/P10 only. This was attributable to the EYES BACK condition: Significantly longer N170 latencies were seen at electrode P10 relative to P9 (Table 5). No significant interaction effects were noted for N170 latency.

P350 area showed significant main effects for Stimulus Type at electrode pairs C3/C4 and P3/P4. Posthoc testing indicated that these effects occurred because of a significantly larger P350 area for the CHECK stimulus [AWAY condition, P3: FACE vs. CHECK $F(1,19)$ = 9.18; P4: FACE vs. CHECK = 10.29, EYES vs. CHECK = 15.92; C3: FACE vs. CHECK = 8.44, EYES vs. CHECK = 8.67; C4: EYES vs. CHECK = 12.97, BACK condition, C4: EYES vs. CHK = 10.87].

ERPs to Static Stimuli

N170s to the three ONSET conditions showed the greatest differences at the temporal scalp of both hemispheres (Fig. 6), with CHECK producing small N170s relative to FACE and EYES. Statisti-

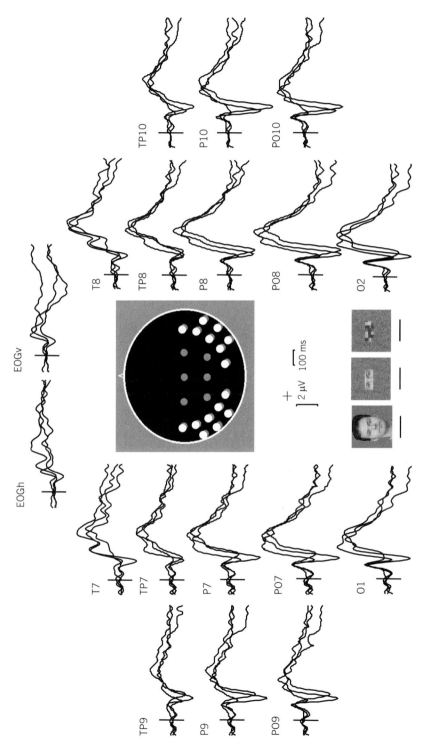

Fig. 6. Experiment 2. Grand averaged ERP waveforms for electrodes overlying the temporal scalp for the three static (ONSET) stimulus conditions. The selected electrodes are highlighted as white circles in a schematic electrode map. Time of stimulus ONSET is indicated by the vertical line.

cal analysis confirmed this observation. A significant main effect of Stimulus Type for N170 amplitude occurred at the temporal scalp (Table 4). Posthoc testing indicated that these differences were mainly due to a small CHECK N170 (Table 5), relative to FACE or EYES. A significant Side × Stimulus Type interaction effect at electrode pair TP9/TP10 [$F(2,38) = 6.66$] was also attributable to a smaller CHECK N170 relative to EYES at TP10.

Faces elicited bilaterally symmetrical N170s, whereas isolated eyes produced asymmetrical N170s which were largest at the right temporal scalp (e.g. electrode P10). By contrast, in the left hemisphere N170 to EYES was smaller than that to FACE (e.g. electrode P9). This finding was confirmed statistically at electrodes P7 and PO7: N170 amplitude to FACE was significantly larger than that to EYES (Tables 4 and 5). In the right hemisphere, N170 amplitude was not significantly different between FACE and EYES, despite the apparent amplitude difference in Fig. 6. Within each hemisphere, the largest N170s to EYES occurred in the most inferior row of temporal electrodes.

In both hemispheres N170 latency to isolated eyes was longer than that to FACE (e.g. Fig. 6, P9 and P10). Statistical analysis showed a main effect for Stimulus Type on N170 latency at P9/P10 and

PO7/PO8 (Table 4). Posthoc testing indicated that EYES produced significantly later N170s relative to CHECK at P9, whereas at P10 EYES were significantly later to either FACE or CHECK (Table 5). The main effect of Side at PO7/PO8 (Table 4) was due to a significantly later N170 at PO8 to EYES relative to CHECK (Table 5).

No significant main effects or interaction effects were noted for P350 area between the ONSET conditions.

Comparison of Static vs. Moving Stimuli

In this comparison the presented stimulus was structurally identical (ONSET, BACK), but the stimulus was either static or moving. Specifically, conditions in which the eyes looked directly at the viewer were compared. Hence, in this three-way ANOVA for Side (Left, Right) × State (Static, Moving) × Stimulus Type [Face, Eyes, Check), the main effect of interest was State. Significant main effects of State occurred at electrodes C3/C4 and at P9/P10 (Table 6). At the central electrodes, the CHECK control produced significantly larger N170s to the static stimuli bilaterally [C3: $F(1,19) = 9.02$, C4 $F(1,19) = 9.76$]. These differences were not seen in the stimulus conditions containing eyes. In contrast, at the temporal electrodes the static stimuli produced the largest N170s for all conditions with eyes in the right hemisphere [FACE:

Table 4. *Experiment 2: Static Stimulus Conditions*

	N170 Amplitude				N170 Latency			
	Stimulus	Type	Side		Stimulus	Type	Side	
Electrode Pair	*F(2,38)*	*P*	*F(1,19)*	*P*	*F(2,38)*	*P*	*F(1,19)*	*P*
T7/T8								
TP7/TP8								
P7/P8	6.94	.003						
PO7/PO8	11.18	.0002			9.44	.0005		
O1/O2								
TP9/TP10								
P9/P10	14.38	.0001	15.03	.001	15.61	.0001	15.03	.001
PO9/PO10	14.32	.0001						
C3/C4								
P3/P4								

Results of a two-way ANOVA for Side (L, R) × Stimulus Type [Face, Eyes, Check) showing significant ($P < .01$) main effects for N170 amplitude and latency.

Table 5. *Experiment 2: Static Stimulus Conditions*

| | N170 Amplitude | | | | | | N170 Latency | | | | | | |
| | Left Electrode | | | Right Electrode | | | Left Electrode | | | Right Electrode | | |
Electrode Pair	Type	F(2,38)	P	Type	F(1,19)	P	Type	F(2,38)	P	Type	F(2,38)	P
P7/P8	Face	10.01	.0005	Face	10.46	.004						
PO7/PO8	Face	24.31	.0001	Face	13.40	.002				Eyes	13.13	.002
	*****	8.79	.008	Eyes	15.96	.0008				*****	16.84	.0006
P9/P10	Face	19.31	.0003	Face	14.19	.001	Eyes	8.48	.009	Eyes	11.71	.003
				Eyes	28.50	.0001				*****	63.67	.0001
PO9/PO10	Face	19.94	.0003	Face	13.16	.002						
	Eyes	15.40	.0009	Eyes	22.10	.0002						

Results of significant ($P < .01$) posthoc comparisons (from main effects of Table 4) for Stimulus Type on N170 amplitude and N170 latency. Face = significantly larger N170 for FACE vs. CHECK; Eyes = significantly larger N170 amplitude for EYES vs. CHECK, or significantly longer N170 latency for EYES vs. CHECK; ***** = significantly smaller N170 for EYES vs. FACE, or significantly later N170 for EYES vs. FACE.

$F(1,19) = 12.87$, EYES $F(1,19) = 9.70$]. This effect was not seen to the CHECK control. Significant main effects of Side and Stimulus Type (Table 6) were also observed and were mainly caused by larger N170s in the right hemisphere to the static stimuli in the EYES condition, as described in the preceding section.

No significant main effect for State was observed for N170 latency. Significant main effects for Stimulus Type occurred at electrode pairs P7/ P8, PO7/PO8, and P9/P10 and were attributable to longer latencies in the static EYES condition. Similarly, a main effect of Side at P9/P10 was due to longer N170 latency at P10 for static EYES. These differences were described in the preceding section.

A large P350 potential was generated to the static version of all three stimulus types (see Figs. 4 and 6). Significant main effects of State occurred at electrodes C3/C4 and PO9/PO10. In the temporal

Table 6. *Experiment 2: Static and Moving Stimulus Conditions*

| | Side | | Stimulus Type | | State | |
Electrode Pair	F(1,19)	P	F(2,38)	P	F(1,19)	P
T7/T8						
TP7/TP8						
P7/P8			5.38	.009		
PO7/PO8	14.54	.001	8.71	.0008		
O1/O2	12.03	.003				
TP9/TP10						
P9/P10	10.97	.004	11.83	.0001	9.97	.0005
PO9/PO10			11.17	.0002		
C3/C4					9.07	.007
P3/P4						

Results of a three-way ANOVA for Side (L, R) × Stimulus Type [Face, Eyes, Check] × State (Static, Moving) showing significant ($P < .01$) main effects for N170 amplitude.

lobe, a larger P350 occurred to FACE and EYES relative to CHECK [PO10: FACE $F(1,19) = 8.86$, EYES = 21.07; PO9: EYES = 9.02]. At the central electrodes, EYES and CHECK produced larger P350s relative to FACE [C4: EYES = 12.97, CHECK = 10.87; C3: EYES = 8.67].

Summary of Results of Experiments 1 and 2

For Experiment 1, eye aversion and mouth opening produced larger N170s relative to eyes gazing at the observer and mouth closure at the temporal scalp bilaterally. N170 latency was later to eyes looking at the observer and mouth closure relative to eye aversion and mouth opening at a focal region on the right temporal scalp (P10). There was no hemispheric differentiation in N170 amplitude or latency as a function of eye or mouth movements. P350 area tended to be responsive to the eye stimulus, with larger P350 areas being seen in response to eye aversion at right anterior temporal and bilateral centroparietal sites.

Despite the difference in ISIs between Experiments 1 and 2, eye aversion produced significantly larger N170 amplitudes relative to eyes gazing at the observer. The effects in Experiment 2 were much more focal (electrode P10) relative to Experiment 1. Experiment 2 demonstrated that this effect occurred independently of facial context. In addition, N170 latency was significantly longer in the right (P10) hemisphere for stimuli with eyes in the BACK condition. This effect also occurred independently of facial context. As in Experiment 1, longer N170 latencies occurred in the BACK condition for stimuli containing eyes. The N170 changes seen to movements of the eyes cannot not be accounted for by stimulus onset or movement in the visual field per se, as there were no significant amplitude or latency differences between the CHECK AWAY and CHECK BACK conditions. Additionally, in both experiments N170 amplitude or latency at occipital electrodes did not vary as a function of facial movement.

The static stimuli of Experiment 2 generated larger N170s to the faces and eyes relative to the control in the right hemisphere, and larger N170s to faces in the left hemisphere. Isolated eyes produced longer N170 latencies relative to faces in the right hemisphere and relative to the control in both hemispheres. A comparison between static and moving stimuli indicated that overall the static stimuli produced larger N170s. At the right temporal scalp, static stimuli with eyes produced significantly larger N170s, whereas at the central electrodes the static checks produced the largest difference relative to their moving counterparts.

DISCUSSION

There were three major findings of this study. First, significantly larger N170s were seen over the bilateral temporal scalp when subjects viewed averting eyes and opening mouths relative to eyes gazing at the observer and mouths closing (Experiment 1). It is possible that N170 size was related to the perceived salience of the stimulus. At debriefing, subjects noted that they often had the urge to look in the direction of the averting eyes and also thought that the face was going to speak when the mouth opened. The full face was always present and facial movements occurred relatively rapidly in this experiment. (By contrast, subjects did not report this for Experiment 2, where a slower ISI was used and nonphysiological check stimuli and physiologically unlikely stimuli such as isolated eyes were included.) The bilateral temporal N170s could be a neuronal response to "biological motion". We did not explicitly study other types of biological motion, so it is not yet clear whether this is a response that is specific to facial movements. Facial movements (Calvert et al., 1997; Puce et al., 1998a) and movements of the hands and body (Bonda, Petrides, Ostry, & Evans, 1996; Grafton, Arbib, Fadiga, & Rizzolatti, 1996; Rizzolatti et al., 1996) are known to activate similar regions of temporal cortex. Given that intracranial recordings demonstrate ERPs to static faces (Allison et al., 1994a; Allison et al., 1999) and static hands (McCarthy et al., 1999) in temporal cortex, it is likely that neuronal responses would occur to moving hands as well as moving face parts.

Second, additional differentiation between facial movements occurred at a focal region of the right inferior temporal scalp. Significantly earlier N170s occurred to mouth opening and eye aversion relative to mouth closure and eyes looking back at the observer (Experiment 1). Third, the inferior temporal region responded with larger N170s to averted eyes either in isolation or within the context of a full face (Experiment 2). These focal changes suggest that some specialisation may exist within the biological motion system. In addition, the same region elicited the largest N170s to static isolated eyes (Experiment 2; see also Bentin et al., 1996). Bentin et al. postulated an "eye detector" acting in addition to a face processor. Our data suggest that regions of inferior temporal cortex may be functioning as a "facial gesture detector", rather than an "eye detector" per se.

The preferential response to moving mouths and static and moving eyes by a "facial gesture detector" is not surprising for several reasons. First, moving mouths are often associated with speech (e.g. Campbell et al., 1986). Second, nonverbal gestures conveyed by a moving mouth (e.g. smiles or sneers) send important affective messages (Ekman, 1982). Third, direction of gaze is an important indicator of another individual's focus of attention (Kleinke, 1986) and this information can be conveyed whether the face is static or mobile (Humphreys et al., 1993). Preliminary ERP data recorded from the scalp (Allison, Lieberman, & McCarthy, 1996) and from fusiform and inferior temporal gyri (McCarthy et al., 1999) using static faces demonstrate nonsignificantly larger ERPs to eye aversion to the left or up relative to eyes looking directly at the observer. These subtler effects of eye aversion using static faces indicate that the human physiological response, like the behavioural response (Humphreys et al., 1993) is driven more by a mobile rather than a static face.

In normal subjects, electrode P8 overlies the middle temporal gyrus and the posterior aspect of the STS (Homan, Herman, & Purdy, 1987). By extrapolation, P10 is likely to overlie the inferior temporal gyrus and ITS. Electrode pairs P7/P8 and P9/P10 showed the largest N170s to both static and moving faces, and it is possible that these electrodes

record ERPs generated both in the middle and inferior temporal gyri. Intracranial ERP recordings indicate that different regions of temporo-occipital cortex are preferentially tuned to static full faces and isolated face parts (Allison et al., 1994b; Allison et al., 1999; McCarthy et al., 1999). Face-specific cortex in the fusiform gyrus responds maximally to faces, but also responds to isolated face parts. Isolated eyes produce the largest ERP of all the face parts. A separate region of face-specific cortex is located in or near the middle temporal gyrus. This *lateral* face-specific region has similar response properties to ventral face-specific cortex. Finally, there is a region of cortex in or near the inferior temporal gyrus that exhibits a preferential sensitivity to face parts, especially eyes. This face-parts-sensitive cortex is located between the ventral and lateral face-specific regions. Thus neuronal activity sampled by scalp electrodes at P7/P8 or P9/P10 may be a combination of activity from the lateral face-specific cortex and the ventrolateral region preferentially responsive to face parts. It is unlikely that these scalp electrodes (Bentin et al., 1996) would sample activity from ventral face-specific cortex.

There are some differences in our ERP data to static stimuli (Experiment 2) and those of Bentin et al. (1996) that we believe are attributable mainly to differences in stimulus delivery. Bentin and colleagues demonstrated: (1) left-hemisphere (P7) N170s to faces and eyes that were not significantly different; (2) larger right-hemisphere (P8) N170s to eyes than to full faces. (They did not record from electrodes P9 and P10.) Our data showed: (1) smaller N170s to isolated eyes relative to full faces in the left hemisphere; (2) right-hemisphere N170s to faces and eyes that were not significantly different. This effect was maximal at P10; however, a similar trend was seen at P8. Stimulus delivery in the Bentin et al. study consisted of stimulus onset and offset from a blank screen, whereas in our study stimulus "onset" and "offset" consisted of the replacement of stimuli in a continuously present display. More importantly, eye onset could occur by replacing either a preceding checkerboard or a face (Fig. 2). In instances where the preceding stimulus was a checkerboard, the N170 could be a summed potential of responses from lateral face-specific cortex and ventrolateral face-parts-sensitive cortex. In instances where the preceding stimulus was a face, the face disappeared from the screen, but the eye region persisted. In this situation, lateral face-specific cortex could be inactive and only the ventrolateral region sensitive to face parts would generate a response. The net effect would be an eye onset N170 amplitude in our data that may have been reduced relative to that of Bentin et al. (1996).

A moving mouth has a strong association with speech, so that a left-hemisphere locus sensitive to mouth movements might be expected. A lip-reading deficit in a patient with a left temporal-occipital lesion has been demonstrated with no associated impairment in processing gaze direction or facial identity (Campbell et al., 1986). However, a clear left hemisphere effect is not seen when normal subjects are studied. (1) Although hemifield presentation of speaking faces elicited a left-hemisphere advantage in reaction time for phonemic matching judgements, judgement accuracy was not affected by hemifield of presentation (Campbell, de Gelder, & De Haan, 1996). (2) In the two fMRI studies to date examining activation patterns to moving mouths, both linguistic (Calvert et al., 1997) and nonlinguistic (Puce et al., 1998a) stimuli generated bilateral activation of lateral temporal cortex. (3) In our ERP study, larger N170s to mouth opening relative to closing were seen bilaterally, and earlier N170s to mouth opening occurred in the right hemisphere at P10. Taken together, the data suggest that both hemispheres possess the capability to process information from mouth movements.

A predominant right-hemisphere focus of neuronal activity for eyes might be expected as: (1) Campbell et al. (1986) studied a patient with a right-hemisphere temporal-occipital lesion and demonstrated a deficit in detection of gaze direction with no associated difficulties in lip-reading; (2) preliminary data in commisurotomy patients (Friesen & Kingstone, 1998) demonstrated a right hemisphere advantage for gaze discrimination in upright faces. The data are less clearly lateralised, however, when normal subjects are studied. The data of Bentin et al. (1996) indicate that although the right temporal scalp generates significantly larger N170s for static isolated eyes relative to full faces, similar, albeit nonsignificant, differences are observed in the left hemisphere. Although our N170 latencies to eye aversion were earlier at the right temporal scalp, larger N170s elicited to eye aversion relative to eye return occurred at the bilateral temporal scalp. Our fMRI study also found bilateral temporal activation in response to viewing eye movements. Although the activation appeared to be more extensive in the right hemisphere, the difference in activation across hemispheres was not significant. Taken together, the data suggest that both hemispheres are responsive to eye movements.

Although it is difficult to compare single-unit recordings in monkeys and ERP recordings in humans, studies in monkeys show parallels with human ERP studies. In monkeys a region of the STS (STPa) is responsive to static faces with different head and eye directions (Harries & Perrett, 1991; Hasselmo et al., 1989; Perrett et al., 1985, 1990, 1992). Different neurons were maximally sensitive to averted eyes or eyes looking directly at the observer. The preferred eye direction of a particular neuron usually matched its preferred head direction. Neurons sensitive to gaze direction were also tested with isolated eyes. In these instances, the magnitude of the response to eyes alone was equivalent to the response to eyes presented in the whole face (Perrett et al., 1985). The sensitivity of the monkey STPa to gaze direction has been verified in a lesion study. Bilateral removal of the banks and floor of the STS severely impaired performance on a task in which a face with averted gaze had to be selected (Campbell, Heywood, Cowey, Regard, & Landis, 1990). What is not currently known is whether neurons in the monkey STPa respond selectively to mouth movement.

Anatomical projections to STPa from the inferotemporal and posterior parietal regions have been demonstrated in monkeys (Baizer, Ungerleider, & Desimone, 1991), hence STPa is thought to be a region in which the integration of visual form and motion takes place (Oram & Perrett, 1996). Perrett and colleagues (1990) believe that STPa may form part of a neural system involved in analysis of social attention. This neural system may also include the amygdala and orbitofrontal cortex and is devoted not only to the analysis of social attention, but to social bonding and facial gesture as well (Brothers & Ring, 1993; Kling & Steklis, 1976; Perrett et al., 1990, 1992). The existence of such a system has also been postulated in humans (Baron-Cohen, 1995; Brothers, 1997). This study, fMRI studies of viewing facial movement (Puce et al., 1998a) and facial expression (Whalen et al., 1998), and behavioural data comparing normal subjects and individuals with autism and Asperger's syndrome (Baron-Cohen, 1995; Baron-Cohen et al., 1997) provide evidence for such a system in humans. Regions of human temporal cortex may receive input from the ventral and dorsal visual streams and may be the human homologue of monkey STPa. The N170s recorded in this study may in part reflect activity in the posterior portion of this system.

REFERENCES

Allison, T., Ginter, H., McCarthy, G., Nobre, A., Puce, A., Luby, M., & Spencer, D.D. (1994a). Face recognition in human extrastriate cortex. *Journal of Neurophysiology, 71,* 821–825.

Allison, T., Lieberman, D., & McCarthy, G. (1996). Here's not looking at you kid: An electrophysiological study of a region of human extrastriate cortex sensitive to head and eye aversion. *Society of Neuroscience Abstracts, 22,* 400.

Allison, T., McCarthy, G., Belger, A., Puce, A., Luby, M., Spencer, D.D., & Bentin, S. (1994b). What is a face?: Electrophysiological responsiveness of human extrastriate visual cortex to human faces, face components, and animal faces. *Society of Neuroscience Abstracts, 20,* 316.

Allison, T., McCarthy, G., Nobre, A., Puce, A., & Belger, A. (1994c). Human extrastriate visual cortex and the perception of faces, words, numbers, and colors. *Cerebral Cortex, 5,* 544–554.

Allison, T., Puce, A., Spencer, D.D., McCarthy, G. (1999). Electrophysiological studies of human face perception. I. Potentials generated in occipito-temporal cortex by face and non–face stimuli. *Cerebral Cortex, 9,* 415–430.

American Electroencephalographic Society. (1990). *Guidelines. Standard electrode position nomenclature.* Bloomfield, CT: Author.

Baizer, J.S., Ungerleider, L.G., & Desimone, R. (1991). Organisation of visual inputs to the inferior temporal and parietal cortex in macaques. *Journal of Neuroscience, 11,* 168–190.

Baron-Cohen, S. (1995). *Mindblindness. An essay on autism and theory of mind.* Cambridge, MA: MIT Press.

Baron-Cohen, S., Wheelwright, S., & Jolliffe, T. (1997). Is there a "language of the eyes"? Evidence from normal adults, and adults with Autism or Asperger syndrome. *Visual Cognition, 4,* 311–331.

Bassili, J.N. (1978). Facial motion in the perception of faces and of emotional expression. *Journal of Experimental Psychology: Human Perception and Performance, 4,* 373–379.

Bentin, S., Allison, T., Puce, A., Perez, A., & McCarthy, G. (1996). Electrophysiological studies of face perception in humans. *Journal of Cognitive Neuroscience, 8,* 551–565.

Bonda, E., Petrides, M., Ostry, D., & Evans, A. (1996). Specific involvement of human parietal systems and the amygdala in the perception of biological motion. *Journal of Neuroscience, 16,* 3737–3744.

Brothers, L. (1997). *Friday's footprint. How society shapes the human mind.* New York: Oxford University Press.

Brothers, L., & Ring, B. (1993). Mesial temporal neurons in the macaque monkey with responses selective for aspects of social stimuli. *Behavioral Brain Research, 57,* 53–61.

Bruce, V., & Young, A. (1986). Understanding face recognition. *British Journal of Psychology, 77,* 305–327.

Calvert, G.A., Bullmore, E.T., Brammer, M.J., Campbell, R., Williams, S.C.R., McGuire, P.K., Woodruff, P.W.R., Iversen, S.D., & David, A.S. (1997). Activation of auditory cortex during silent lipreading. *Science 276,* 593–596.

Campbell, R., de Gelder, B., & De Haan, E. (1996). The lateralization of lip-reading: A second look. *Neuropsychologia, 34,* 1235–1240.

Campbell, R., Heywood, C.A., Cowey, A., Regard, M., & Landis, T. (1990). Sensitivity to eye gaze in prosopagnosic patients and monkeys with superior temporal sulcus ablation. *Neuropsychologia, 28,* 1123–1142.

Campbell, R., Landis, T., & Regard, M. (1986). Face recognition and lip-reading: A neurological dissociation. *Brain, 109,* 509–521.

Ekman, P. (Ed.) (1982). *Emotion in the human face.* (2nd ed.). Cambridge: Cambridge University Press.

Friesen, C.K., & Kingstone, A. (1998). Reflexive social attention in a split–brain patient. *Cognitive Neuroscience Society Abstracts, 5,* 138, San Francisco.

Grafton, S.T., Arbib, M.A., Fadiga, L., & Rizzolatti, G. (1996). Localization of grasp representations in humans by positron emission tomography. 2. Observation compared with imagination. *Experimental Brain Research, 112,* 103–111.

Harries, M.H., & Perrett, D.I. (1991). Visual processing of faces in temporal cortex: physiological evidence for a modular organization and possible anatomical correlates. *Journal of Cognitive Neuroscience, 3,* 9–24.

Hasselmo, M.E., Rolls, E.T., Baylis, G.C., & Nalwa, V. (1989). Object-centered encoding by face-selective neurons in the cortex in the superior temporal sulcus of the monkey. *Experimental Brain Research, 75,* 417–429.

Homan, R.W., Herman, J., & Purdy, P. (1987). Cerebral location of international 10–20 system electrode placements. *Electroencephalography and Clinical Neurophysiology, 66,* 376–382.

Humphreys, G.W., Donnelly, N., & Riddoch, M.J. (1993). Expression is computed separately from facial identity, and it is computed separately for moving and static faces: Neuropsychological evidence. *Neuropsychologia, 31,* 173–181.

Kanwisher, N., McDermott, J., & Chun, M.M. (1997). The fusiform face area: A module in human extrastriate cortex specialized for face perception. *Journal of Neuroscience, 17,* 4302–4311.

Kleinke, C.L. (1986). Gaze and eye contact: A research review. *Psychological Bulletin, 100,* 78–100.

Kling, A., & Steklis, H.D. (1976). A neural substrate for affiliative behaviour in nonhuman primates. *Brain Behaviour and Evolution, 13,* 216–238

McCarthy, G., Puce, A., Belger, A., & Allison, T. (1999). Electrophysiological studies of human face perception. II. Response properties of face–specific potentials recorded from occipitotemporal cortex. *Cerebral Cortex, 9,* 431–444.

McCarthy, G., Puce, A., Gore, J.C., & Allison, T. (1997). Face-specific processing in the human fusiform gyrus. *Journal of Cognitive Neuroscience, 9,* 604–609.

Oldfield, R.C. (1970). The assessment and analysis of handedness: The Edinburgh Inventory. *Neuropsychologia, 9,* 97–113.

Oram, M.W., & Perrett, D.I. (1996). Integration of form and motion in the anterior superior temporal polysensory area (STPa) of the Macaque monkey. *Journal of Neurophysiology, 76,* 109–129.

Perrett, D.I., Harries, M.H., Mistlin, A.J., Hietanen, J.K., Benson, P.J., Bevan, R., Thomas, S., Oram, M.W., Ortega, J., & Brierly, K. (1990). Social signals analyzed at the cell level: someone is looking at me, something touched me, something moved! *International Journal of Comparative Psychology, 4,* 25–54.

Perrett, D.I., Hietanen, J.K., Oram, M.W., & Benson, P.J. (1992). Organization and functions of cells responsive to faces in the temporal cortex. *Philosophical Transactions of the Royal Society of London, B, 335,* 23–30.

Perrett, D.I., Smith, P.A.J., Potter, D.D., Mistlin, A.J., Head, A.S., Milner, A.D., & Jeeves, M.A. (1985). Visual cells in the temporal cortex sensitive to face view and gaze direction. *Proceedings of the Royal Society of London, B, 223,* 293–317.

Puce, A., Allison, T., Asgari, M., Gore, J.C., & McCarthy, G. (1996). Differential sensitivity of human visual cortex to faces, letterstrings, and textures: A functional MRI study. *Journal of Neuroscience, 16,* 5205–5215.

Puce, A., Allison, T., Bentin, S., Gore, J.C., McCarthy, G. (1998a). Temporal cortex activation in humans viewing eye and mouth movements. *Journal of Neuroscience, 18,* 2188–2199.

Puce, A., Allison, T., Gore, J.C., & McCarthy, G. (1995). A functional MRI study of face perception in extrastriate cortex. *Journal of Neurophysiology, 74,* 1192–1199.

Puce, A., Allison, T., Spencer, S.S., Spencer, D.D., & McCarthy, G. (1997). A comparison of cortical activation evoked by faces measured by intracranial field potentials and functional MRI: Two case studies. *Human Brain Mapping, 5,* 298–305.

Puce, A., Smith, A., & Allison, T. (1998b). Dealing with a poker face?: ERPs elicited to changes in gaze direction and mouth movement. *Neuroimage, 7*(4), S347.

Rizzolatti, G., Fadiga, L., Matelli, M., Bettinardi, V., Paulesu, E., Perani, D., & Fazio, F. (1996). Localization of grasp representations in humans by PET: 1. Observation versus execution. *Experimental Brain Research, 111,* 246–252.

Sams, M., Aulanko, R., Hamalainen, M., Hari, R., Lounasmaa, O.V., Lu, S.-T., & Simola, J. (1991). Seeing speech: Visual information from lip-movements modifies activity in the human auditory cortex. *Neuroscience Letters, 127,* 141–145.

Sergent, J., Ohta, S., MacDonald, B., & Zuck, E. (1994). Segregated processing of facial identity and emotion in the human brain: A PET study. *Visual Cognition, 1*, 349–369.

Whalen, P.J., Rauch, S.L., Etcoff, N.L., McInerney, S.C., Lee, M.B., & Jenike, M.A. (1998). Masked presentations of emotional facial expressions modulate amygdala activity without explicit knowledge. *Journal of Neuroscience, 18*, 411–418.

COGNITIVE NEUROPSYCHOLOGY, 2000, 17 (1/2/3), 241–255

PROSOPAMNESIA: A SELECTIVE IMPAIRMENT IN FACE LEARNING

Lynette J. Tippett
University of Auckland, New Zealand

Laurie A. Miller
University of Western Ontario, London, Ontario, Canada

Martha J. Farah
University of Pennsylvania, Philadelphia, USA

The structures required for new learning, and those required for the representation of what has been learned, are believed to be distinct. This counterintuitive division of labour when considered alongside the localised nature of knowledge representation for at least some stimulus domains, implies that circumscribed new learning impairments should occasionally be found as a result of disconnection between learning mechanisms and domain-specific representations. We describe the most narrowly circumscribed new learning deficit so far reported, consisting of a selective new learning impairment for faces, which we term "prosopamnesia." Logically, a diagnosis of prosopamnesia requires preserved face perception, preserved memory for material other than faces (including visual material), and preserved recognition of faces known premorbidly. We describe a patient who meets these criteria, thus supporting the division of labour between neural systems for learning and neural systems for knowledge representation, as well as providing further support for segregated face representation in cortex.

The hippocampal complex is necessary for the acquisition and consolidation of new memories (e.g. Squire, 1992). However, the neural substrate of consolidated, or long-term, memories themselves is believed to be neocortical, presumably the same regions of neocortex responsible for analysing the remembered stimuli in the first place (e.g. Hodges, 1995). One consequence of this hypothesised division of labour among the neural systems underlying memory is that it should be possible to find new learning impairments limited to specific stimulus domains represented in localised regions of cortex, without concomitant remote memory impairment. Such an impairment would result from functionally disconnecting the local cortical region from the hippocampus. Do such cases exist?

Asymmetries of verbal and nonverbal memory impairment following unilateral temporal lobectomy might appear to represent one instance of this phenomenon (e.g. Majdan, Sziklas, & Jones-Gotman, 1996; Milner, 1973). However, in these cases the hippocampus and related structures have themselves generally been damaged, and remote memory for verbal and nonverbal materials

Requests for reprints should be addressed to L.J. Tippett, Department of Psychology, University of Auckland, Private Bag 92019, Auckland, New Zealand (Email: l.tippett@auckland.ac.nz).

This research was supported by ONR grant N00014-93-10621, NIH grants R01 MH48274, R01 NS34030, R01 AG14082, and K02 AG00756. We thank Janice Howell for conducting the clinical neuropsychological testing of CT, and Morris Moscovitch, Marlene Behrmann, and an anonymous reviewer for helpful comments on an earlier draft of this article. We also thank Morris Moscovitch for lending us photographs of famous Canadians. Finally, we thank CT for his generous cooperation with this project.

L.A. Miller is now at the Royal Prince Alfred Hospital, Sydney, Australia.

has not been evaluated. These findings are therefore best interpreted in terms of some degree of hemispheric specialisation of the two hippocampal complexes. More relevant are the cases of Ross (1980a, b), with modality-specific new learning impairments in the visual and tactile modalities. Ross related their behavioural impairments to neuropathological mechanisms of disconnection between the modality-specific cortices and the medial temporal region. Most recently Hanley, Pearson, and Young (1990) reported a detailed case study of a patient with preserved learning ability for verbal materials, including nonword letter strings, and an impairment in the ability to learn visual material. The patient's anterograde amnesia was manifest in tests of recognition for both unfamiliar faces and objects.

In the present article we report an even more circumscribed new learning impairment, which appears to be the most selective material-specific anterograde amnesia yet described. The subject initially came to our attention because he was diagnosed as prosopagnosic on the basis of his inability to learn unfamiliar faces on the Warrington Recognition Memory Task (1984) as well as his inability to recognise hospital personnel and some members of his family. This diagnosis, however, was contradicted by his relatively good performance at recognising photographs of other family members, and at least some famous faces. Closer item-by-item scrutiny of his test results suggested that he was impaired specifically in the learning of faces and in the recognition of faces encountered since his brain injury. His ability to learn other kinds of visual information, as well as his learning of nonvisual information, appeared to be preserved. We therefore hypothesised that he was not prosopagnosic, but rather "prosopamnesic."

Our investigation is organised into three parts, corresponding to the three defining criteria for prosopamnesia. First, a prosopamnesic should perform normally on tasks that involve face processing without a memory component. Second, a prosopamnesic should perform poorly on any task that involves forming new memories of faces, but should be able to form new memories of other kinds of stimuli, including other types of visual stimuli.

Third, a prosopamnesic should be unable to recognise faces of people encountered subsequent to the brain injury, but recognition of faces known prior to the injury should be preserved.

SUBJECT DESCRIPTION

CT is a caucasian Canadian man, who was 35 years old at the time of testing. Left-handed as a child, he was forced to use his right hand for writing. CT left high school early, despite good grades, then returned several years later (after his head injury) and completed a diploma in public and business administration, followed by year and a half of college study towards a degree in accounting.

In 1982, at the age of 22, CT fractured his skull in a motorcycle accident and 3 months later began to experience complex partial and secondary generalised seizures, which were not well controlled by medication. In 1988 he underwent a right temporal lobectomy. For 3 months after the operation he was seizure free, but subsequently the seizures resumed, albeit with reduced frequency. An MRI in 1992 showed the right temporal lobectomy and increased signal on T2 weighted images in the left superior medial temporal region thought to represent an enlarged perivascular space. His EEG shows prominent left temporal frontal background abnormalities and independent bitemporal spikes. In sum, surgical, MRI, and EEG evidence suggests right and probably bilateral temporal damage, with possible left frontal dysfunction.

CT continues to have complex partial seizures (1–3/day) and has not held a job since 1992. His hobbies include listening to rock music and playing trivia games, at which he excels to such a great degree that a local radio station allows him only one attempt per week at answering their daily trivia question. He has seen few movies and his TV watching is limited to a few favourite programs. From 1979 to 1990 he lived in a small and isolated community in the Northwest Territories accessible only by air, which further limited his exposure to news of current events and entertainment through movies, magazines, and newspapers.

Neuropsychological Assessment

CT's most recent neuropsychological assessment was carried out in 1993, about 1 year before the testing reported here, and the results were consistent with earlier assessments conducted both before and after his right temporal lobectomy. CT's IQ on the WAIS-R (Wechsler Adult Intelligence Scale-Revised) fell in the Average to High Average range, with a Full Scale IQ of 110, and Verbal and Performance scores of 111 and 108, respectively.

CT was tested on the ability to learn and remember different types of material, including lists of words, stories, and geometric figures. As shown in Table 1, his performance was within normal limits with all materials excluding faces, even when the material to be remembered consisted of visual patterns. On the Wechsler Memory Scale, CT achieved a Superior Memory Quotient (135). Memory for verbal materials was good, as evidenced by immediate and delayed recall on the Rey Auditory Verbal Learning test, and the WMS Logical Memory subtest (see Table 1).

More relevant to the classification of this patient as prosopamnesic is his good performance on standard tests of memory for visual materials. He performed within normal limits and above average on the WMS Visual Reproduction subtest, both on immediate recall and after a 45-minute delay. His reproduction of the Rey Complex Figure following a 45-minute delay was also normal. Two versions of the Benton Visual Retention Test were administered to him; on the multiple choice version his performance was high average, and on the drawing version his performance was average.

Face Memory

Despite his good performance on a variety of memory tests, including memory for visual information, CT complained of memory difficulty, in particular difficulty recognising faces. He claimed that even with his wife, whom he met in 1985, he was forced to rely on details such as her hair, way of walking, or clothes. He reported that his brother-in-law walked by him in the hospital and he failed to recognise him. He tended to use cues such as con-

Table 1. *CT's Performance on Standardised Tests of Memory*

Test	CT's Score	Norms for Age-matched Control Subjects Mean (SD)
Rey Auditory Verbal Learning		
5th Learning Trial	14/15	11.4(2.6)
Delayed Recall	13/15	10.4(2.3)
Rey Complex Figure		
Copy	32/36	33.2 (6.1)
Delayed Recall	16.5/36	19.5(6.7)
WMS Visual Reproduction		
Immediate Recall	12.5/14	10.1 (2.6)
Delayed Recall	13/14	9.3(2.7)
Benton Visual Retention Test		
Recognition	14/15	14 = high average
Reproduction with delay	7/10	7 = average
Warrington Recognition Memory Test		
Words	48/50	75th percentile
Faces	26/50	5th percentile
Denman Neuropsychological Memory Test[a]		
Word Pair Learning	16	10 (3)
Word Pair Delayed Recall	14	10 (3)
Face Memory	6	10 (3)

[a]Age-scaled scores.

text and hair style and colour to make astute guesses at identification. CT's wife verified these reports, and said that he often fails to recognise people when they are met out of context. For example, he once walked by his wife in a shopping mall when he did not expect to see her there. We noted that he was unable to recognise the faces of familiar people in the hospital, even the psychometrist with whom he had spent 10 hours in the space of a 10-day period.

In order to explore his face recognition ability further, two additional investigations were undertaken. First, he was shown an updated version of the Famous Faces test of Albert and colleagues (Albert, Butters, & Levin, 1979), consisting of 60 faces of public figures from six decades, including the 1980s. CT identified only 9 of these faces, although, he was familiar with 37 of them when he was told their name. The 9 successfully identified faces were named rapidly, and when asked if he was guessing, CT insisted he was very confident of his answer. All 9 of these faces were well known prior to 1982.

For a second test of CT's face recognition ability, his wife supplied us with a set of personal snapshots of CT's family and friends, containing a total of 39 faces. An additional 20 faces from family photographs of strangers were added to the set. Backgrounds and clothing were largely masked out, although some bits of clothing inevitably remained visible. CT was asked to identify each familiar face and to tell us which faces were unfamiliar. CT correctly classified all 20 of the unfamiliar faces (100% correct). Of the 19 faces known to CT prior to 1982, he correctly identified them all (100% correct). Of the 20 faces first encountered after 1982, CT correctly identified 11 (55% correct). Some of these correct identifications were based on nonfacial cues, such as his wife's jacket. Even his daughter was not reliably recognised.

PART ONE: PERCEPTION AND IMMEDIATE VISUAL MEMORY FOR FACES

Problems perceiving faces have been noted in most, if not all, well-documented cases of prosopagnosia (see Farah, 1990). The question of whether face perception is ever intact in prosopagnosia and the possible role of face perception in distinguishing prosopagnosia and prosopamnesia will be taken up in the General Discussion. For present purposes, we need only observe that a functional disconnection between cortical face recognition areas and new learning areas should not affect the perception of faces, nor immediate visual memory for faces, as these abilities do not require learning. To test this part of the prosopamnesia hypothesis, we administered the Benton and Van Allen face matching task, which is a stringent test of face perception with no demands on learning, and a sequential same/different face matching task with upright and inverted faces, which tests immediate visual memory for faces as well as revealing the presence or absence of the normal "face inversion effect."

Methods

Test of Facial Recognition (Benton & Van Allen, 1968)

Materials. The test booklet developed by Benton and Van Allen (1968) was used, and CT was tested on the short form of the test (27 possible correct matches; Levin, Hamsher, & Benton, 1975). Each trial includes a single front-view black-and-white photograph of a face, and a choice set of six other photographs of faces, some of which depict the same person and some of which depict different (but same sex, age, and race) people. The subject's task is to locate all occurrences of the same person in the choice set. In one section the perspective and lighting are held constant between the face to be matched and the choice set; in the other two sections either the viewing angle or the lighting is changed.

Procedure. The subject is presented with one trial at a time, with the single face to be matched and the choice set simultaneously present, and is asked to find the matching face or faces in the choice set. Because the faces are unfamiliar and always visible throughout the trial, face learning and memory should not affect performance.

Sequential Face Matching, Upright and Inverted (Farah, Wilson, Drain, & Tanaka, 1995b)

Materials. Fifteen different shaded drawings of faces were generated using the Mac-a-Mug program, and were paired with themselves (same trials) or with another from the same set (different trials). Half of these occurrences of each face, in both same and different trials, were presented upright, and half were presented inverted. Both faces in a given trial were presented in the same orientation. There was a total of 300 trials.

Procedure. Faces were presented on a Macintosh Classic computer. The first face on each trial was presented for 750msec, followed by a 1.5sec blank interstimulus interval, followed by a 75msec presentation of the second face. The subject's task is to decide whether the two faces are the same or different, and respond as quickly and accurately as possible by key press.

Results

CT scored 21/27 on the short form of the Test of Facial Recognition. Correlations between the short and long forms of the test range from .88 to .94, implying that little information is lost by substituting the short for the long form. CT's short form score converts to a score of 43 on the long form; any score above 39 is considered normal (Benton, Hamsher, Varney, & Spreen, 1983). Although the testing session was not timed, CT did not appear to work slowly or slavishly, as has sometimes been reported in cases of prosopagnosia or face perception impairment (e.g. Newcombe, 1979; Young, Newcombe, de Haan, Small, & Hay, 1993).

As shown in Fig. 1, CT obtained 137/150 or 91% correct matching sequential pairs of upright faces, and 117/150 or 78% correct when the faces were inverted. His response times in these conditions were 1581msec and 1641msec on average, respectively. From a previous study involving this task (Farah, et al., 1995b), we have data from eight college-age normal subjects who saw each face for 1.5sec (as opposed to the 750msec duration used with CT). They obtained on average 141/150 or 94% correct with upright and 123/150 or 82% correct with inverted faces. Their average response times were 1086msec and 1253msec, respectively. We initially tried to test CT with the same exposure durations as the normal subjects and found that he performed too close to 100% correct to permit evaluation of the inversion effect. Therefore, although the normal subjects' testing situation is not strictly comparable to CT's, it errs on the side of conservatism. We can safely conclude that CT is not worse at sequential face matching than the normal subjects we tested.

In addition to assessing CT's ability to match sequentially presented faces, this experiment allows us to determine whether he shows a normal "face inversion effect." In a variety of tasks, involving face perception as well as face recognition, normal subjects perform markedly better with upright faces than with inverted faces (see Valentine, 1988, for a review). Although other stimuli may also show inversion effects, the pronounced effects observed when faces are inverted are characteristic of normal face recognition, a conclusion that is supported by such findings as absent face inversion effect in young children whose face recognition ability is poor (Carey & Diamond, 1977), abnormal face inversion effect in prosopagnosia (Farah et al., 1995b), and face inversion effects in the response

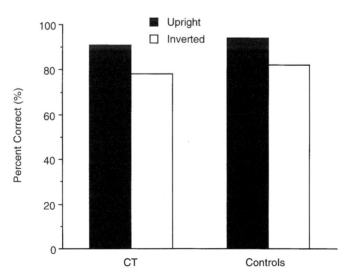

Fig. 1. *Accuracy of CT and normal control subjects in matching sequentially presented pairs of faces, upright and inverted.*

latencies of "face cells" in monkey temporal cortex (Perrett et al., 1988). CT shows an advantage for upright over inverted faces that is of normal magnitude in both accuracy and response time.

In sum, CT's performance on tasks involving the perception and matching of unfamiliar faces appears to be normal. He scores in the normal range on the Test of Facial Recognition, and can match sequentially presented faces at least as well as a group of normal college students. He also shows a normal advantage for matching upright faces relative to inverted faces.

PART TWO: LEARNING OF FACES AND NONFACE STIMULI

If CT is prosopamnesic, he should be impaired at learning new faces, but unimpaired at learning other types of material. The clinical tasks described earlier demonstrated good performance learning nonface material, even when the material was visual. CT performed within normal limits, and sometimes above average, on all standard tests of visual memory that were administered to him: the immediate and delayed recall versions of the WMS Visual Reproduction subtest, recall of the Rey Complex Figure, and both multiple choice and reproduction versions of the Benton Visual Retention Test.

In this section of the paper we report three additional studies aimed at assessing his learning of faces and contrasting his face learning ability with the learning of nonface materials within the same experiment. In the Denman Neuropsychological Memory Test (1984), learning of faces is contrasted with learning of auditory paired associate words. In the Recognition Memory Test of Warrington (1984), learning of faces is contrasted with learning of visually presented words. In a third task developed by us for use with a prosopagnosic (Farah, Klein, & Levinson, 1995a), learning of faces is contrasted with learning of eyeglass frames. The first task has the advantage of being a well-known clinical neuropsychology task that has been thoroughly normed. The second task has this same advantage,

and in addition includes visually presented words. The third task has the advantage of contrasting faces with another type of three-dimensional visual stimulus drawn from a large and visually homogeneous class, namely eyeglass frames.

Methods

Denman Neuropsychological Memory Test (Denman, 1984)

Materials. Verbal materials consist of 14 word pairs ranging from easy to difficult associations. Stimuli are presented in pairs at study, and a single stimulus from each pair is presented at test. Face stimuli consist of 48 black-and-white "yearbook style" photographs of male and female faces. Sixteen of these comprise the study set, with the remaining 32 serving as distractors.

Procedure. For the verbal materials, the 14 word pairs are read aloud to the subject and immediately following this the first word in each pair is read aloud and the subject must provide the associate. If the response is not correct, the subject is told the correct response. This procedure is repeated twice more, for a total of three administrations. After a 45–50-minute filled interval, a final test is administered. Scoring consists of summing the number of correct responses in the first three administrations, for a learning score, and summing the number of correct responses in the final adminstration, for a delayed recall score. For the faces, the 16 study faces are presented in an array and the subject is given 45 seconds to study them. After a 90-second filled interval, the full set of 48 faces are presented in an array and the subject must select the original 16. The score is the number correct.

Recognition Memory Task (Warrington, 1984)

Materials. The word stimuli consist of 50 study words and 50 distractors, all short (4–6 letters) commonplace words. For the study materials, words appear one at a time, printed in upper-case letters on white cards. For the test materials, a pair of words (one study word and one distractor) appear side by side, printed in upper-case letters on white cards. The position of the study and distractor words are varied. The face stimuli consist of 50 black-and-white photographs of men in the study set and 50 similar photographs in the distractor set. As with the words, the men were presented one at a time on white cards for study, and side-by-side for test.

Procedure. Subjects are asked to make "pleasant"/ "unpleasant" judgements about the 50 study words, and are instructed that their memory for the words will be tested. They are shown each of the study words, one at a timer, for approximately 3sec each. They are then tested immediately with a two-alternative forced choice. The same procedure is followed for the face stimuli.

Faces and Glasses Task (Farah, Klein, & Levinson, 1995)

Materials. The set of faces consists of 40 black-and-white professional portrait photographs of white male graduate students, selected to be clean shaven, without eyeglasses, and with unremarkable hairstyles and facial expressions. The set of eyeglass frames consists of 40 black-and-white photographs of eyeglass frames, photographed from the front, without visible logos or print. From each set of 40, 20 were selected for the study set. An attempt was made to divide "types" of faces or eyeglass frames between the study set and the remainder (e.g. blonde people or aviator frames did not occur predominantly in the study set or in the remainder).

Procedure. CT was shown the 40 study photographs with faces and glasses intermixed in a random order, one at a time. The complete set was viewed three times at a rate of 6 seconds per picture. He was then immediately shown the full set of 80 photographs, intermixed, and for each one responded whether he had seen it before.

Results

CT's scores on the verbal memory portions of the Denman were better than average according to norms for his age. His scaled score on learning was 16 (mean = 10, SD = 3) and his delayed recall score was 14 (mean = 10, SD = 3). In contrast, he performed worse than normal on the face memory task, with a scaled score of 6 (mean = 10, SD = 3).

CT recognised 48/50 of the words in the Recognition Memory Test, a nearly perfect performance which is at the 75th percentile of normal subjects. In contrast, his performance with faces was not different from chance, 26/50 correct. This falls well below the cutoff of 37/50 correct, the 5th percentile score for normal subjects.

In the faces and glasses task, CT achieved 23/40 correct with the faces and 25/40 correct with the eyeglass frames. Two small groups of normal subjects have been tested with this task, in both cases with just one study exposure of 3sec for each item. Ten college students achieved on average 35/40 and 27/40 correct with faces and glasses, respectively, and 10 individuals with advanced degrees and average age 43 years (range 33–48) achieved 34/40 and 28/40 correct with faces and glasses, respectively. Because the amount of study time was not equated between CT and the normal subjects, direct comparisons between his performance on faces or on glasses are not meaningful. In particular, we cannot determine whether his learning of eyeglass frames is within normal limits. However, because eyeglass frame performance was roughly equated, it is meaningful to compare the relative performance on faces and glasses between CT and the normal subjects. Whereas normal subjects generally performed better with faces, CT did not show this pattern. Combining the faces–glasses difference scores for CT and the control subjects, CT's score is an outlier among both the college students, $z = 2.37$, $P < .01$) and the older subjects ($z = 2.02$, $P < .05$). Figure 2 shows the performance of CT and of all of the control subjects combined.

In sum, CT is normal in his learning of both nonvisual material and a variety of visual materials, including novel visual patterns in the WMS visual reproduction, Rey Complex Figure, and Benton Visual Retention Test. Yet he is severely impaired in the learning of faces. His face learning is impaired even relative to his learning of exemplars from another visually homogeneous category of real objects, namely eyeglass frames.

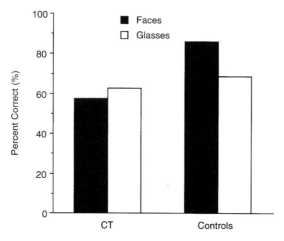

Fig. 2. *Accuracy of CT and normal control subjects in recognising faces and eyeglass frames.*

PART THREE: RECOGNITION OF FACES FIRST ENCOUNTERED BEFORE AND AFTER BRAIN INJURY

If CT has been unable to learn faces since his brain injury, then he should be unable to recognise faces of people who became famous in the 80s and 90s, after his brain injury, but should remain able to recognise people who became famous in earlier decades. To test this prediction, we collected pictures of celebrities (actors, musicians, sports figures, and politicians) who would be known to Canadians of CT's age and divided the pictures into two groups: those celebrities who became famous before 1982 and those who became famous after the early 1980s. We used these pictures in two tasks, a famous–nonfamous forced–choice task in which each famous face was paired with a nonfamous face, and an identification task.

Methods

Famous–Nonfamous Task
Materials. Faces of 23 people who became famous before 1982 and 17[1] people who became famous after 1982 were selected from magazines and books.

We attempted to select individuals that Canadian men of CT's age would probably know, and also attempted to avoid celebrities that CT might not have seen because of his narrow interests and his long isolation in the Northwest Territories. Only the most famous movie stars were used, because CT told us he rarely went to the movies, and only TV actors from shows that CT told us he watched regularly were used. The pre-1982 faces were: Alan Alda, Julie Andrews, Pierre Burton, Jimmy Carter, John Diefenbaker, Princess Diana, Ron Howard, Gordie Howe, John Lennon, Paul McCartney, Anne Murray, Richard Nixon, Lester B. Pearson, Elvis Presley, Paul Simon, Margaret Thatcher, Margaret Trudeau, Pierre Trudeau, Henry Winkler. The post-1982 faces were: George Bush, Bill Clinton, Hilary Clinton, Kim Campbell, Terry Fox, Wayne Gretzky, Tonya Harding, Michael Jackson, Madonna, Audrey McLaughlin, Brian Mulroney, Bob Ray, Brooke Shields, Boris Yeltsin, and three characters from the TV series Northern Exposure, Chris (John Corbett), Ed (Darren Burrows), and Joel (Rob Morrow). Each famous face was paired with a nonfamous face from magazines and books. The nonfamous faces were selected so that both photographs of a pair looked equally likely to be a famous face. All faces were duplicated

---

[1] Initially these counts were 22 and 18, respectively, because we had misclassified Princess Diana in the post-1982 group.

in black-and-white using a high-quality colour process photocopier.

Procedure. CT and 10 control subjects participated. Control subjects were matched with CT for nationality, sex, age (mean = 36 years, range = 31–43) and education (mean = 15 years, range = 11–18). Subjects were shown each pair of faces one at a time, and were asked to indicate which member of each pair was the famous face. Identification of the individual was not required. CT was administered this task twice, separated by a 3-hour filled interval. After both experiments involving this set of faces were completed, subjects' familiarity with the individuals was assessed by naming each one and asking subjects to provide information about the person's career or what they are known for.

Identification of Famous Faces
Materials. The same 40 famous faces used in the previous study were again used here.

Procedure. Each photograph was presented one at a time to subjects, who were required to name or identify each face. Only specific identifications were scored as correct. For example, "a TV actor" would not be sufficient, but "the Fonz" (a character played by the actor Henry Winkler) would be scored as correct.

Results

In the first administration of the Famous/Nonfamous task, CT was correct on 20/23, or 87% of the pre-1982 face pairs, but scored only 8/17 or 47% correct on the post-1982 face pairs. In the second administration, he obtained similar scores: 19/23, or 83% of the pre-1982 face pairs, and 9/17 or 53% correct on the post-1982 pairs. His performance on the two administrations, combined, is shown in Fig. 3. The difference in performance with pre- and post-1982 face pairs was significant by chi-squared test, comparing the frequency of consistently right item responses with wrong or split responses (11.83, $P < .001$). A comparison of responses on the two administrations of this task

added further support to the conclusion that CT recognised the pre-1982 faces with confidence but was guessing with the post-1982 face pairs: 18 of the 23 pairs that were correct on the first administration were also correct on the second, whereas CT's responses were consistently correct for only 4 of the post-1982 pairs.

As shown in Fig. 3, the control subjects were correct on average with 22.3/23 or 97% of the pre-1982 pairs (range 20–23) and 16/17 or 94% of the post-1982 pairs (range 13–17). Thus CT performed roughly normally—within the normal range on one administration, just below it on the other—with the pre-1982 face pairs, but was clearly abnormal with the post-1982 pairs.

Later questioning revealed that CT had relatively little familiarity with five of the individuals in the post-1982 group. This could artifactually decrease his performance with the post-1982 faces, as he cannot be expected to recognise the face of someone he knows little about. Therefore we recalculated his post 1982 performance with only the 12 faces of people with whom he was quite familiar. He was correct on 7/12 of these on the first administration, and 8/12 on the second, and only 4 of these were pairs on which he was correct both times. As before, control subjects performed well with all of the faces, obtaining 11.8/12 or 98% of the restricted set of post-1982 pairs (range 10–12). The average performance of CT and control subjects with the more conservatively selected subset of post-1982 faces is shown in Fig. 4. Despite the smaller stimulus set, the difference between his performance on the 12 high-familiarity items and his pre-1982 performance remained significant, (χ^2 = 6.82, $P < .01$).

Figure 5 shows that in the identification task, CT responded correctly for 13 /23 or 59% of pre-1982 faces and only 1/17 or 6% of post-1982 faces. This difference was significant: (χ^2 = 11.02, $P < .001$). CT remarked that he was guessing when he correctly identified the one post-1982 face. Figure 6 shows that when only the 12 post-1982 individuals with whom CT was definitely familiar were included, CT's performance was 1/12 or 8% correct, yielding, for the difference between pre- and post-1982, χ^2 = 7.63, $P < .01$.

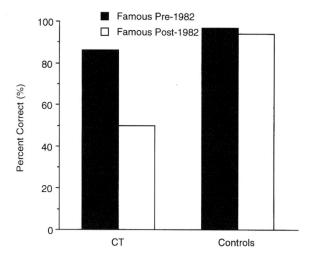

Fig. 3. *Accuracy of CT and normal control subjects in a forced-choice famous/nonfamous task, with faces that became famous before and after 1982.*

Normal subjects correctly identified an average of 20.8/23 or 90% of the pre-1982 faces (range 17–23) and 14.1/17 or 83% of the post-1982 faces (range 9–17), as shown in Fig. 5. When only the more conservatively selected set of 12 post-1982 faces was used, their accuracy was 11.3/12 or 94% (range 9–12), as shown in Fig. 6. For this set, normal subjects found the recent faces easier, whereas CT found them much harder. Although normal subjects performed better on the set of pre-1982 faces than on the full set of post-1982 faces, CT's difference was of a different magnitude: Considering the percentage point differences between pre- and post-1982 faces for CT and normal subjects as a distribution of 11 scores, CT was an outlier ($z = 2.46$, $P < .02$).

Unlike his performance in the Famous–Nonfamous task, CT's performance in this task was inferior to that of normal subjects, even with the pre-1982 faces. On reflection, this is not surprising

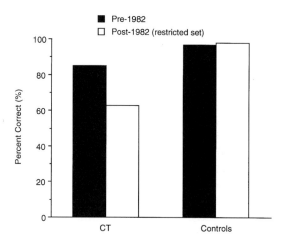

Fig. 4. *Accuracy of CT and normal control subjects in a forced-choice famous/nonfamous task, with faces that became famous before and after 1982, restricting the post-1982 faces to those of individuals about whom CT was knowledgeable.*

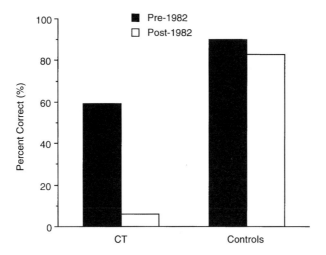

Fig. 5. *Accuracy of CT and normal control subjects in identifying faces that became famous before or after 1982.*

and does not necessarily imply a true retrograde face recognition impairment. Most of the faces in the pre-1982 set have continued to be seen occasionally in the 1980s and 1990s. Therefore, normal subjects have had the advantage of over a decade of relearning or refreshing their memories of these faces, whereas CT has not. An exception to this can be found in Lester B. Pearson, the former Prime Minister, whose name remains familiar to most Canadians but whose face is rarely seen. Consistent with

our conjecture about the importance of continued exposure to pre-1982 faces, only 3 of the 10 control subjects could identify Pearson. This factor may also contribute to CT's mediocre performance with the Famous Faces test, described in the Subject Description section.

If CT is a true prosopamnesic, he should also in principle show a retrograde gradient in face recognition. However, the role of continued exposure to faces, after their initial fame, would make it

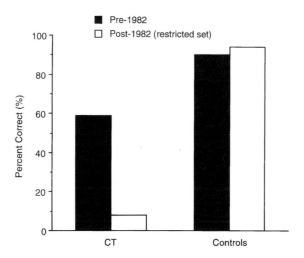

Fig. 6. *Accuracy of CT and normal control subjects in identifying faces that became famous before or after 1982, restricting the post–1982 faces to those of individuals about whom CT was knowledgeable.*

extremely difficult to test for a gradient in CT's retrograde face recognition. To be able to predict differential recognition performance for different pre-1982 faces, one would need to know, or control for, not only the year in which the face first became known, but also the amount of exposure in subsequent years. In addition, analyses that subdivide the pre-1982 faces would require a larger number of faces. It is therefore not feasible to test for a retrograde gradient in CT's memory for faces.

We have so far discussed the difference between CT's performance with faces of people who became famous before his brain injury and after in objective, numerical terms. This difference was also apparent in more qualitative ways. For example, when CT recognised the pre-1982 faces, he generally did so with an air of confidence, whereas he tended to hesitate and express puzzlement over the later faces. In one case in which he seemed to recognize a post-1982 face, Wayne Gretzky's, he confessed that this was a guess based on the appearance of a small visible portion of the shirt, which CT recognised as a hockey jersey. To test the role of this small bit of clothing in guiding CT's response, we took the photo out of the room without CT's notice and remounted it without any of the jersey showing. The photo was then added on to the end of the test. At this point, less than 15 minutes after the first viewing, CT neither recognised that he had seen the face before nor recognised it as Wayne Gretzky, saying instead that he thought the face might belong to a musician.

The contrast between CT's nonvisual knowledge of post-1982 celebrities and their faces was vividly illustrated in the case of Tonya Harding, the American figure skater associated with the attack on rival skater Nancy Kerrigan. CT spontaneously told us several Tonya Harding jokes in the first part of the day of testing, indicating that he was well aware of this skater and the news about her. Nevertheless, when CT encountered Tonya Harding's picture in the present testing, he was unable to identify her and consistently chose her foil in the Famous–Non-famous task.

An even more dramatic demonstration of the pre- and post-1982 difference in face recognition was demonstrated with a celebrity who is uniquely well suited to testing the prosopamnesia hypothesis. This individual has maintained his fame throughout the past several decades, but his face has changed dramatically. In the course of testing, CT was shown three pictures of the singer Michael Jackson. One of these was included in the Famous Faces test used as part of his original clinical assessment, and dated from the mid-1980s. At this time, the singer's facial appearance was very similar to his appearance in 1982, and on different occasions CT identified, by name, both the Famous Faces photograph as well as a 1982 photograph of Jackson, which appeared on one of his music album covers. Jackson's trademark tendril was edited out of the album photo in order to prevent the face from being recognised on the basis of this feature. A third photograph of Jackson was included in the set of post-1982 faces described in Part 3. This photograph dated from the 1994 scandal involving Jackson's allegedly improper relationship with a young boy. Jackson's face was seen frequently in the news media at this time, with a radically changed appearance owing to cosmetic surgery. CT consistently failed to identify, or recognise as famous, the post-surgical face of Michael Jackson.

GENERAL DISCUSSION

CT's pattern of performance across a number of clinical and experimental tasks of face perception, face memory, and memory for other types of stimuli indicates a selective impairment of new face learning, or prosopamnesia. He is normal in two rather demanding tests of face perception, and shows a normal face inversion effect. His ability to learn a variety of different materials is normal, and his learning of visual stimuli specifically is normal on some tests and at least reliably better than his face learning on others. Nevertheless, his ability to learn faces is exceptionally poor. Convergent evidence for his impairment in face learning comes from a famous faces task in which he performed relatively well on faces that had become famous before his brain injury, but was severely impaired on faces that had become famous since his brain injury.

The existence of prosopamnesia has relevance for at least three issues in neuropsychology. First, as mentioned at the outset, it provides a new type of evidence for a division of labour between the initial memory encoding of information and the storage of the information itself. This somewhat counterintuitive division of labour was initially suggested by two general neuropsychological observations: the observation that premorbid memories (particularly remote memories) can be preserved in amnesia, and the observation that when domain-specific knowledge is lost, as in prosopagnosia, it cannot be relearned despite the preserved ability to learn other types of information. Together, amnesia and prosopagnosia can be interpreted as a double dissociation between two separate faculties for learning and for domain-specific knowledge. If this interpretation is correct, then we should expect eventually to observe a third syndrome, prosopamnesia, in which the learning mechanism and the store of domain-specific knowledge are functionally disconnected. Although CT's brain damage is too widespread to suggest any specific anatomical hypotheses concerning disconnection, his pattern of abilities and deficits conforms in detail to the predictions of a disconnection between a learning mechanism and a face area.

The present case also sheds some light on two issues related to face perception and recognition. The first concerns the relation between face perception and face recognition. It has sometimes been suggested that prosopagnosics have normal face perception, and that their deficit emerges only when they must respond to a face on the basis of memory, for example identifying a face or making a famous/nonfamous judgement (e.g. Damasio, Damasio, & Tranel, 1990). However, for cases of prosopagnosia in which face perception has been carefully evaluated, perception of even unfamiliar faces is generally found to be deficient (for reviews see Farah, 1990; Shuttleworth, Syring, & Allen, 1982). One reason for overlooking the perceptual impairment of prosopagnosia may be the reliance on final scores in untimed tests, without attention to the speed and manner of completing the test. For example, Newcombe (1979) reports a prosopagnosic who appeared to perform well on the

Benton face matching task, but who achieved his success by relying on subtle variations in the models' hairlines. When hairlines were masked out, the patient's performance was dramatically impaired. Young et al., (1993) have shown that the appearance of dissociations between face recognition and face perception in a group of brain-damaged subjects is nullified when the time needed for the perception task is taken into account.

To these cautions we would add another: The appearance of good face perception in prosopagnosia could result from the misclassification of a prosopamnesic as prosopagnosic. It is also possible that a subject could suffer from a combination of mild prosopagnosia and prosopamnesia. Without careful testing that separates pre- and post-morbidly familiar faces, such cases might appear to be prosopagnosic, and yet could perform well on tests of face perception.

The issue of whether perception and recognition of faces can be dissociated is relevant to the computational architecture underlying face recognition. If it is possible to destroy stored face memories without affecting face perception, this would imply that the two are separate, and more generally that recognition processing is distinct from perceptual processing in the brain. Such an arrangement is consistent with traditional symbol manipulation architectures for computation, in which a representation derived from the stimulus would be matched with a separate stored representation in memory, but not with more recent and neurally plausible network architectures for computation (see, e.g., Farah, 1997). In the latter, the processing of a face progresses along a continuum of representation from early representations, in which the information extracted from the perceptual input is relatively independent of previous experience with faces, to later representations, in which the information extracted from the perceptual input is relatively more dependent on experience. In the later stages of such a system, there are not separate tokens of the face representation, one perceptual (i.e. derived from the stimulus) and one mnemonic (i.e. stored in memory). Rather, memory knowledge is being used to transform a visual perceptual representation derived from the stimulus, and the representation is therefore both perceptual and mnemonic. In contrast to the symbol manipulation architectures, in the kind of continuum of neural network processing described here it would be impossible to destroy stored memory information about faces and not change the final perceptual representation. The existence of prosopamnesia raises the possibility that any apparent case of prosopagnosia possessing good face perception could actually be a case of prosopamnesia. This in turn would deprive symbol manipulation architectures of a key source of empirical support in the realm of face processing.

Prosopamnesia is also relevant to the widely discussed issue of whether face recognition is "special," that is, whether it depends on pattern recognition mechanisms distinct from the recognition of other types of object. Prosopagnosia was for many years taken to imply that faces are special in this sense, because these patients can be impaired at face recognition while being roughly normal at nonface object recognition. However, this interpretation is based on the assumption that differences in the difficulty of recognising face and nonface objects cannot account for the relatively greater impairment of face recognition. Recent studies have assessed prosopagnosic recognition of faces and various nonface stimuli chosen to be equivalent in difficulty to faces (or even harder for normal subjects), and have found that prosopagnosics continue to do worse with faces (Farah et al., 1995a,b; McNeil & Warrington, 1993). This provides one source of neuropsychological evidence that face recognition is special.

Prosopamnesia provides another independent source of neuropsychological evidence for the hypothesis that faces are special. It shows that face recognition can be selectively disconnected from learning mechanisms, as well as selectively destroyed. In the present case, we have also shown that differences in the difficulty of learning faces and nonface visual stimuli do not account for the selectivity of the impairment because learning performance was measured relative to that of normal subjects with the same tasks.

REFERENCES

Albert, M.S., Butters, N., & Levin, J. (1979). Temporal gradients in the retrograde amnesia of patients with alcoholic Korsakoff's disease, *Brain, 36,* 876–879.

Benton, A.L., Hamsher, K., Varney, N.R., & Spreen, O. (1983). *Contributions to neuropsychological assessment.* New York: Oxford University Press.

Benton, A.L., & Van Allen, M.W. (1968). Impairment in facial recognition in patients with cerebral disease. *Transactions of the American Neurological Association, 93,* 38–42.

Carey, S., & Diamond, R. (1977). From piecemeal to configurational representation of faces. *Science, 195,* 312–314.

Damasio, A.R., Damasio, H., & Tranel, D. (1990). Impairments of visual recognition as clues to the processes of memory. In G. Adelman, E. Gall, & M. Cowan (Eds.), *Signal and sense: Global order in perceptual maps.* New York: Wiley-Liss.

Denman, S.B. (1984). *Denman Neuropsychological Memory Scale.* Charleston, SC: The author.

Farah, M.J. (1990). *Visual agnosia: Disorders of object recognition and what they tell us about normal vision.* Cambridge, MA: MIT Press/Bradford Books.

Farah, M.J. (1997). Computational modeling in behavioral neurology and neuropsychology. In T.E. Feinberg & MJ. Farah (Eds.), *Behavioral Neurology and Neuropsychology.* New York: McGraw Hill.

Farah, M.J., Klein, K.L., & Levinson, K.L. (1995). Face perception and within-category discrimination in prosopagnosia. *Neuropsychologia, 33,* 661 674.

Farah, M.J., Wilson, K.D., Drain, H.M., & Tanaka, J.R. (1995b). The inverted inversion effect in prosopagnosia: Evidence for mandatory, face specific perceptual mechanisms. *Vision Research, 35,* 2089–2093.

Hanley, J.R., Pearson, N., & Young, A.W. (1990). Impaired memory for new visual forms. *Brain, 113,* 1131–1148.

Hodges, J.R. (1995). Retrograde amnesia. In A. Baddeley, B. Wilson, & F. Watts (Eds.), *Handbook of memory disorders.* Chichester, UK: Wiley.

Levin, H.S., Hamsher, K. de S., & Benton, A.L. (1975). A short form of the Test of Facial Recognition for clinical use. *Journal of Psychology, 91,* 223–228.

Majdan, A., Sziklas, V., & Jones-Gotman, M. (1996). Performance of healthy subjects and patients with resection from the anterior temporal lobe on matched tests of verbal and visuospatial learning.

Journal of Clinical and Experimental Neuropsychology, 18, 416–430.

McNeil, J.E., & Warrington, E.K. (1993). Prosopagnosia: A face-specific disorder. *Quarterly Journal of Experimental Psychology: Human Experimental Psychology, 46A,* 1–10.

Milner, B. (1973). Hemispheric specialisation: Scope and limits. In F.O. Schmitt & F.G. Worden (Eds.), *The neurosciences: Third study program* (pp. 75–89). Cambridge, MA: MIT Press.

Newcombe, F. (1979). The processing of visual information in prosopagnosia and acquired dyslexia: Functional versus physiological interpretation. In D.J. Oborne, M.M. Gruneberg, & J.R. Eiser (Eds.), *Research in psychology and medicine.* London: Academic Press.

Perrett, D.I., Mistlin, A.J., Chitty, A.J., Smith, P.A., Potter, D.D., Broennimann, R., & Harries, M. (1988). Specialised face processing and hemispheric asymmetry in man and monkey: Evidence from single unit and reaction time studies. *Behavioural Brain Research, 29,* 245–258.

Ross, E.D. (1980a). The anatomic basis of visual agnosia. *Neurology, 30,* 109–110.

Ross, E.D. (1980b). Sensory-specific and fractional disorders of recent memory in man. I. Isolated loss of visual recent memory. *Archives of Neurology, 37,* 193–200.

Shuttleworth, E.C., Syring, V., & Allen, N. (1982). Further observations on the nature of prosopagnosia. *Brain and Cognition, 1,* 307–322.

Squire, L. (1992). Memory and the hippocampus: A synthesis of findings from rats, monkeys and humans. *Psychological Review, 99,* 195–231.

Valentine, T. (1988). Upside-down faces: A review of the effect of inversion upon face recognition. *British Journal of Psychology, 79,* 471–491.

Warrington, E.K. (1984). *Recognition Memory Test Manual.* Windsor, UK: NFER-Nelson.

Young, A.W., Newcombe, F., de Haan, E.H., Small, M., & Hay, D.C. (1993). Face perception after brain injury. Selective impairments affecting identity and expression. *Brain, 116,* 941–959.

COGNITIVE NEUROPSYCHOLOGY, 2000, 17 (1/2/3), 257–279

RESPONSE PROPERTIES OF THE HUMAN FUSIFORM FACE AREA

Frank Tong

Harvard University, Cambridge and Massachusetts General Hospital Nuclear Magnetic Resonance Center, Charlestown, USA

Ken Nakayama

Harvard University, Cambridge, USA

Morris Moscovitch

University of Toronto, Canada

Oren Weinrib

Harvard University, Cambridge, USA

Nancy Kanwisher

Massachusetts Institute of Technology, Cambridge and Massachusetts General Hospital Nuclear Magnetic Resource Centre, Charlestown, USA

We used functional magnetic resonance imaging to study the response properties of the human fusiform face area (FFA: Kanwisher, McDermott, & Chun, 1997) to a variety of face-like stimuli in order to clarify the functional role of this region. FFA responses were found to be (1) equally strong for cat, cartoon and human faces despite very different image properties, (2) equally strong for entire human faces and faces with eyes occluded but weaker for eyes shown alone, (3) equal for front and profile views of human heads, but declining in strength as faces rotated away from view, and (4) weakest for nonface objects and houses. These results indicate that generalisation of the FFA response across very different face types cannot be explained in terms of a specific response to a salient facial feature such as the eyes or a more general response to heads. Instead, the FFA appears to be optimally tuned to the broad category of faces.

INTRODUCTION

Numerous sources of evidence suggest that primate brains have special-purpose neural machinery that is selectively involved in the perception of faces. Physiological measurements, especially single-unit recordings in macaques and event-related potentials in humans, provide some of the richest sources of evidence on the specificity of these systems.

However, these techniques do not allow us to quantify responses from specific regions of the human brain. The goal of the present effort was to provide a detailed characterisation of the response properties of a region of human extrastriate cortex called the fusiform face area (Kanwisher, McDermott, & Chun, 1997). We begin with a brief outline of the neurophysiological evidence for face-specific neural systems.

Requests for reprints should be addressed to Frank Tong, Department of Psychology, Harvard University, 33 Kirkland St, Cambridge, MA 02138, USA, (Email: frank@wjh.harvard.edu).

This work was supported by a Human Frontiers and NIMH grant 56073 to NK, and an NSERC postgraduate scholarship to FT. We thank Bruce Rosen and many people at the MGH- NMR Center at Charlestown, MA for technical assistance and Yuan-Sea Lee for research assistance.

257

Early evidence that there may be specialised neural regions for face perception came from cases of prosopagnosia, the selective loss of face recognition abilities in patients with focal brain damage (e.g. Bodamer, 1947; Meadows, 1974). However, the first neurophysiological evidence of such specialisation came from the discovery of face-selective cells in the temporal cortex of macaques (Gross, Roche-Miranda, & Bender, 1972). Since this pioneering work, many studies have demonstrated that "face cells" may be tuned to certain facial attributes such as the identity (Yamane, Kaji, & Kawano, 1988), expression (Hasselmo, Rolls, & Baylis, 1989), viewpoint (Perrett et al., 1991), or parts of a face (Perrett, Rolls, & Caan, 1982; Yamane et al., 1988).

Intracranial recordings from the human temporal lobes and hippocampus (carried out for presurgical planning purposes) have also revealed individual neurons that respond selectively to faces, particular facial expressions, or gender (Fried, Mac-Donald, & Wilson, 1997; Heit, Smith, & Halgren, 1988; Ojemann, Ojemann, & Lettich, 1992). Evoked potentials recorded from strip electrodes implanted on the surface of the human brain have revealed distinct regions in the fusiform and inferotemporal gyri that produce face-specific N200 responses to faces but not to cars, butterflies, or other control stimuli (Allison et al., 1994). Furthermore, electrical stimulation of these regions frequently produced a temporary inability to name famous faces, suggesting that these cortical regions are not only engaged by, but necessary for, face recognition.

Although intracranial recordings provide impressive evidence for anatomically restricted responses to faces, with this technique it is difficult to collect enough data to clearly establish the face-specificity of the responses. Further, one can never be sure that the organisation of epileptic or damaged brains resembles that of the normal population. Noninvasive scalp recordings from normal subjects using event-related potentials (ERP) or magnetoencephalography (MEG) can circumvent these problems, and indeed face-selective responses have been reported in several studies (Jeffreys, 1989, 1996; Sams, Hietanen, Hari, Ilmoniemi, & Lounasmaa, 1997).

ERP and MEG studies provide excellent temporal resolution but incomplete information about the anatomical source of the signal. By contrast, recently developed neuroimaging techniques provide a method of localising functional signals with high spatial precision and therefore provide a critical new perspective. A large number of studies have demonstrated activation of human ventral extrastriate cortex during viewing of faces (e.g. Haxby et al., 1994; Puce, Allison, Asgari, Gore, & McCarthy, 1996; Sergent, Ohta, & MacDonald, 1992). Although these earlier studies did not attempt to establish the selectivity of these responses, two recent functional magnetic resonance imaging (fMRI) studies have addressed this question. McCarthy, Puce, Gore, and Allison (1997) found that a discrete region in the right fusiform gyrus responded preferentially to faces as compared to flowers or common objects. These findings agreed with other anatomical evidence showing that lesions in prosopagnosic patients (Meadows, 1974) and intracranial face-specific responses (measured preoperatively) in epileptic patients (Allison et al., 1994) frequently involve the fusiform gyrus. Kanwisher et al. (1997) demonstrated that this region, called the fusiform face area (FFA), responded in a highly selective fashion to faces as compared to objects, houses, scrambled faces, or human hands, even when subjects performed a demanding matching task that required attention to both face and nonface stimuli.

Kanwisher et al.'s results suggest that the FFA response is unlikely to be explained in terms of differences in the low-level properties of the stimuli, a general response to anything animate or human, or a tendency for subjects to attend more to faces than nonfaces during passive viewing tasks. However, they tell us little about what aspects of a face are responsible for activating the FFA. For example, is the FFA specifically tuned to human faces or does it respond more broadly, such that any type of face or the mere presence of a head will fully activate it? Does FFA activity reflect a response to the configuration of the face alone, without detailed information about face parts, or conversely are facial features sufficient to activate the FFA without information about the configuration of the face? By studying the response of the FFA to a variety of face-like stimuli, we hoped to elucidate the functional role of this area and address whether the FFA is primarily involved in face perception or some other type of processing such as gaze perception (Heywood & Cowey, 1992) or head recognition (Sinha & Poggio, 1996).

To address these questions, the present experiments incorporated several critical design features. For each experiment, we first functionally localised each subject's FFA on independent localiser scans conducted in the same session (see General Methods, also Kanwisher et al., 1997). Examples of the localised FFA of two subjects are shown in near-axial and near-coronal slices in Plate 3 of the colour section situated between pages 160 and 161. Such individual localisation was crucial because the FFA can vary considerably in its anatomical location and spatial extent across subjects (Kanwisher et al., 1997). By specifying our region of interest in advance, we could objectively measure the magnitude of FFA responses on experimental scans without having to correct for multiple comparisons across all scanned voxels. In each experiment, some subjects viewed stimuli passively while others performed a "one-back" matching task, which obligated them to attend to all stimuli regardless of inherent interest. To the extent that similar data were obtained in the two tasks, we could infer that the results did not reflect confounding differences in the engagement of visual attention by different stimuli.

The most important methodological advance in this study involved extending beyond simple pairwise comparisons to provide a richer description of the response profile of the FFA across a range of visual stimuli. It is well known that visual neurons tuned to simple or complex stimuli do not show all-or-none responses, but instead show a graded distribution of responses that peak around the optimal stimulus. By including four different stimulus conditions within each experimental scan, we were able to quantify the magnitude of FFA

response to each stimulus class relative to others in the same scan. Each scan contained two reference conditions: (1) an optimal stimulus condition consisting of front-view human faces that are known to produce strong FFA responses, and (2) a nonoptimal stimulus condition consisting of either nonface objects or houses that produce weak FFA responses, typically less than half the magnitude found for faces. Each scan also contained two new stimulus conditions of interest which could then be compared to these optimal and nonoptimal reference conditions. Thus we could determine whether each new stimulus category produced a weak FFA response no greater than those found for objects or houses, an intermediate level response, or an optimal FFA response as strong as those found for front-view human faces.

GENERAL METHODS

Subjects

Eighteen healthy normal adults (eight women), ages 18–39, volunteered or participated for payment in one to three of the following fMRI experiments. All subjects had normal or corrected-to-normal vision and gave informed written consent to participate in the study. Data from four subjects were discarded because of artefacts caused by excess head motion (two men) or because the FFA was not successfully localised on independent scans (two men).

Stimuli

For all experiments, stimuli consisted of an equal number of grayscale images from each of four different stimulus categories.

Experimental Procedures

Each subject was run on (1) two or more functional localiser scans, and (2) two or more scans from a given experiment. Each fMRI scan lasted a total duration of 330 seconds and consisted of four blocks of four consecutive 16-second stimulus epochs (one epoch for each stimulus condition) with a 16-second fixation baseline period occurring before each block (e.g. Fig. 1B). Across the four blocks, each stimulus condition appeared once in each serial position within a block. Images from the relevant stimulus condition were serially presented in random sequence during each epoch for subject viewing. During fixation baseline periods, subjects maintained fixation on a central fixation point.

In Experiments 1 and 2, images were centrally presented at a rate of one image every 667msec (stimulus duration = 450msec, interstimulus interval = 217msec) with a small spatial offset (10% of the image width) that alternated between a top-right and bottom-left position. In Experiments 3 and 4, images were centrally presented with no spatial offset at a rate of one image every 800msec (stimulus duration = 400msec, interstimulus interval = 400msec).

Subjects either performed a passive viewing or a one-back matching task in each experiment. For the passive viewing task, subjects were simply instructed to attentively view the sequence of images. In the one-back task, subjects were instructed to press a button whenever they saw two identical pictures in a row. Typically, one or two repetitions occurred in each epoch.

MRI Scanning Procedures

Scanning was done on a 1.5 T scanner at the MGH-NMR Center in Charlestown, MA, using a bilateral quadrature surface coil which provided a high signal to noise ratio in posterior brain regions. Standard echoplanar imaging procedures were used (TR = 2sec, TE = 70msec, flip angle = 90°, 180° offset = 25msec, 165 images/slice). Twelve 6mm or 7mm thick near-coronal slices (parallel to brainstem) covered the entire occipital lobe as well as the posterior portion of the temporal lobes, including the FFA. A bite bar was used to minimise head motion. In all other respects, imaging procedures were identical to those reported by Kanwisher et al. (1997).

fMRI Data Analysis

For each experiment, each subject's FFA was identified on separate functional localiser scans. The FFA was defined as the set of all contiguous voxels in the fusiform gyrus that showed significant differences in activity ($P < .0001$ uncorrected, incorporating a 6-second delay to compensate for haemodynamic lag) on a Kolmogorov-Smirnov test comparing front-view human faces to either houses or familiar objects. Because the localiser data were used to independently define the FFA region of interest for experimental fMRI scans, no correction for multiple voxel-wise comparisons was made.

Each subject's predefined FFA was then used to extract the time course of the magnetic resonance (MR) signal intensity during the experimental fMRI scans (averaging over all voxels identified in the localiser scan). After assuming a 6-second delay in haemodynamic response, FFA responses were then measured in terms of the average percentage change in MR signal during each stimulus epoch compared to fixation as a baseline.

A repeated-measures analysis of variance was performed by pooling the mean FFA response for each subject and stimulus condition with task (i.e. passive or one-back) as a between-subject variable. Planned comparisons were performed between stimulus conditions based on theoretical questions of interest.

Behavioural Data Analysis

The percentage of correct responses on the one-back matching task was calculated for each subject, experimental scan, and stimulus condition in terms of the percentage of hits minus false alarms. Table 1 shows a summary of the mean performance across subjects for Experiments 1–4. Discrimination performance was usually excellent (above 90%) except for stimuli that were perceived as highly visually similar, such as the schematic faces in Experiment 1, the capped faces and eyes alone stimuli in Experiment 3, and the different head views in Experiment 4. Because our main purpose was to study the response properties of the FFA and because we never found an effect of task on FFA responses, the behavioural data were not analysed further.

Table 1. *Summary of Behavioural Performance on one-back Matching Task: Percentage of Hits - False Alarms*

		Stimulus Condition			
Experiment 1	n	Human faces	Cat faces	Schematic faces	Objects
Mean	4	92	90	72	95
SE		7.8	1.6	4.8	3.0
Experiment 2	n	Human faces	Upright cartoon faces	Inverted cartoon faces	Objects
Mean	5	94	95	94	98
SE		3.4	3.8	4.0	1.5
Experiment 3	n	Entire faces	Faces with no eyes	Eyes alone	Houses
Mean	5	78	76	54	79
SE		5.8	6.8	10.9	7.4
Experiment 4	n	Front	Profile	Cheek	Back
Mean	2	87	75	61	70
SE		3.5	16.7	13.9	4.5

EXPERIMENT 1: HUMAN FACES, CAT FACES, SCHEMATIC FACES, AND OBJECTS

This experiment tested whether the FFA responds selectively to human faces or whether it generalises to other faces such as cat or schematic faces. Examples of the stimuli are shown in Fig. 1A and Appendix A.

Although cat faces possess animate and expressive qualities and are readily perceived as faces, they differ greatly from human faces in terms of their low-level features. For example, cat faces have highly textured fur and are often distinguished based on the patterns of colours in the fur itself. Regarding facial features, cats do not have lips or prominent eyebrows, and their ears, noses and mouths do not resemble those of human faces. The overall shape and aspect ratio of cat faces also differ from human faces. Thus, cat faces allowed us to test whether the FFA is specifically tuned to human facial features or to more general aspects of a face.

The use of cat face stimuli also allowed us to test whether the FFA is involved in expert recognition rather than face perception per se. Some researchers have suggested that the FFA response to human faces may instead reflect an effect of acquired expertise at identifying exemplars within a particular category (e.g. Gauthier, Tarr, Anderson, Skudlarski, & Gore, 1997b). If such a view were correct, one would predict a much greater FFA response to human than cat faces given that people are far more experienced at recognising human faces. However, single-unit studies in monkeys have shown that most face cells generalise equally well across monkey and human faces (e.g. Perrett et al., 1982). It was therefore conceivable that the FFA might also generalise to the faces of other species.

Schematic faces allowed us to test whether a basic facial configuration would be sufficient to activate the FFA. Even newborn infants appear to differentiate between simple schematic faces and scrambled faces, as evidenced by their preference to track a moving schematic face across a greater distance (Goren, Sarty, & Wu, 1975; Johnson, Dziurawiec, Ellis, & Morton, 1991). These results suggest that humans may have an innate preference for simple face-like visual patterns. However, single-unit recordings in monkeys have revealed that face cells show either no response or a weak

A

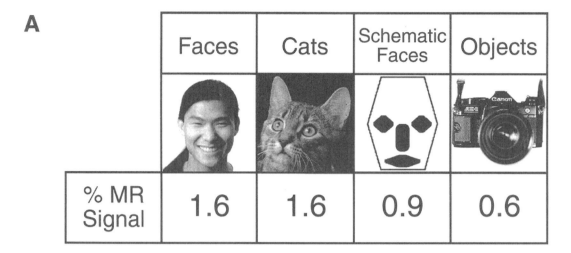

B

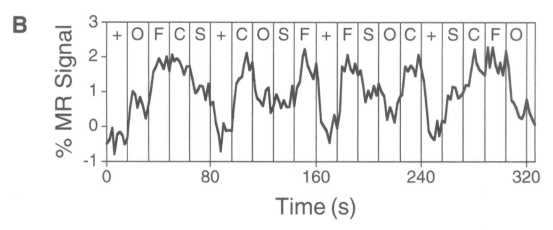

Fig. 1. *1A: Overall FFA response (expressed in percentage MR signal change from fixation baseline) to human faces, cat faces, schematic faces, and objects, averaged across eight subjects in Experiment 1. Example stimuli are shown. 1B: Time course showing mean FFA activity while subjects viewed sequences of human faces (F), cat faces (C), schematic faces (S), and objects (O). Note that FFA responses are delayed by approximately 6 seconds due to haemodynamic delay, and that responses are strongest for human and cat faces in each of the four blocks.*

response to simple line drawings of a monkey face (Perrett et al., 1982).

Unlike the schematic faces used in the above studies, our schematic faces were defined by the arrangement of nonfacial features consisting of simple geometric shapes. This allowed us to investigate the extent to which facial configuration alone, in absence of appropriate facial features, would activate the FFA. Front-view human faces and familiar (inanimate and animate) objects served as optimal and nonoptimal reference conditions respectively.

Method

Subjects

Eight subjects (five women) participated in Experiment 1; four performed the passive viewing task and four performed the one-back matching task.

Stimuli

The four stimulus conditions consisted of human faces, cat faces, schematic faces, and objects. In each condition, 35 different images were used. Figure 1A shows an example of each of these stimuli. Additional examples can be seen in Appendix A. Front-view human faces consisted of digitised college ID photos of undergraduate men and women. Cat faces were taken from a CD-ROM collection of cats and kittens (Corel professional photos). Schematic faces were created by using different rudimentary geometric shapes to compose the eyes, nose, mouth, and external contour of each face. Objects included both easily recognisable inanimate objects (e.g. camera, iron, tape cassette) and animate objects (e.g. cow, horse, caterpillar). All images were cropped and presented within a square window that subtended approximately $12° × 12°$ of visual angle.

Results and Discussion

Figure 1A shows the overall mean FFA response during each of the four stimulus conditions (expressed in percentage MR signal change from fixation baseline). The FFA responded most strongly to human faces and cat faces, much more weakly to schematic faces, and most weakly to objects. The consistency of these response differences can be seen in the average time course of FFA activity plotted in Fig. 1B. In each of the four blocks, the response to human and cat faces was always greater than the response to schematic faces or objects.

An ANOVA across subjects revealed a highly significant difference among stimulus conditions [$F(3,18) = 54.9$, $P < .00001$]. There was no significant effect of task [$F(1,6) < 1$] or interaction between task and stimulus [$F(3,18) < 1$]. (A summary of mean FFA responses during passive viewing versus one-back matching for all experiments can be found in Table 2.) Planned comparisons revealed significantly greater FFA activity for schematic faces than objects [$t(7) = 3.66$, $P < .01$] and for cat faces than schematic faces [$t(7) = 4.9$, $P < .002$]. However, no significant difference was

found between human and cat faces [$t(7) = 1.0$, $P = .35$].

The fact that the FFA responded as strongly to cat faces as human faces is quite striking, given that the FFA was localised on independent scans as the region in the fusiform gyrus that responded significantly more to *human* faces than to objects or houses. These results clearly indicate that the FFA can generalise to faces with very different low-level features, even those of another species. Given that our subjects were far more experienced at discriminating and identifying human faces than cat faces, it seems unlikely that the response of the FFA can be adequately explained in terms of visual expertise alone.

The much weaker response to schematic faces indicates that the presence of facial configuration alone, in absence of appropriate facial features, is not sufficient for fully activating the FFA. The weakness of this response does not seem attributable to the impoverished nature of the schematic faces given that simplistic two-tone Mooney faces have been shown to strongly activate the FFA (Kanwisher, Tong, & Nakayama, 1998), whereas complex objects do not. However, our results do suggest that facial configuration alone may lead to a partial or weak FFA response, as evidenced by the slightly greater response to schematic faces than familiar objects. The present results agree with the finding that face cells in monkeys generally show little or no response to simple schematic faces (Perrett et al., 1982).

EXPERIMENT 2: HUMAN FACES, UPRIGHT CARTOON FACES, INVERTED CARTOON FACES, AND OBJECTS

Experiment 2 tested whether the FFA would generalise to familiar upright and inverted cartoon faces that were loosely based on either animals (e.g. Mickey Mouse) or fictitious characters (e.g. Ernie and Bert; see Fig. 2A and Appendix B for examples of the stimuli). Unlike realistic faces, cartoon faces are drawn in a highly schematic and exaggerated fashion. The facial features of cartoon faces often

Table 2. *Summary of Mean FFA Response as a Function of Stimulus Condition and Task for All Experiments*

		Stimulus Condition			
Experiment 1	*n*	*Human faces*	*Cat faces*	*Schematic faces*	*Objects*
Passive	4	1.8	1.8	1.0	0.7
1-back	4	1.5	1.4	0.8	0.6
Experiment 2	*n*	*Human faces*	*Upright cartoon faces*	*Inverted cartoon faces*	*Objects*
Passive	4	1.7	1.8	1.4	0.7
1-back	5	1.8	1.7	1.4	0.8
Experiment 3	*n*	*Entire faces*	*Faces with no eyes*	*Eyes alone*	*Houses*
Passive	3	2.2	1.9	1.4	1.0
1-back	5	1.6	1.5	1.2	0.5
Experiment 4	*n*	*Front*	*Profile*	*Cheek*	*Back*
Passive	4	1.8	1.8	1.3	0.8
1-back	2	1.8	1.9	1.2	1.2

deviate from normal faces in colour, size, shape, and placement. Despite this fact, cartoons are readily perceived as animate faces, perhaps much more so than the schematic faces in Experiment 1.

There is some neuropsychological evidence suggesting that human faces and cartoon faces access a common face recognition system. Moscovitch, Winocur, and Behrmann (1997) reported an object agnosic patient, CK, who showed spared recognition for human faces as well as familiar cartoon faces. CK could identify both human and cartoon faces as well as normal controls, but was much more severely impaired than normals when the same faces were shown upside-down. Moscovitch et al. suggested that CK had an intact face recognition system that could only operate on upright faces, but an impaired object recognition system that would normally be used for identifying objects and also contribute to the identification of inverted faces. Consistent with this distinction between upright and inverted face processing, Farah, Wilson, Drain, and Tanaka (1995) reported a prosopagnosic patient who showed the opposite deficit of impaired recognition for upright faces but normal recognition for inverted faces.

This experiment used the same cartoon faces that were tested on patient CK to see if upright cartoon faces would activate the FFA as strongly as upright human faces. We also presented the cartoon faces upside-down to see if this would result in weaker FFA activity and, if so, whether FFA activity would drop to the level found for objects. Given the neuropsychological and cognitive evidence that face-specific processing is severely disrupted for inverted faces (Farah et al., 1995; Moscovitch et al., 1997; Tanaka & Farah, 1993; Tong & Nakayama, in press; Yin, 1971; Young, Hellawell, & Hay, 1987), one might expect that inverted faces should fail to access face-specific mechanisms. However, single-unit recordings in monkeys have revealed mixed results. Whereas most face cells in the lateral inferotemporal cortex respond more to upright than inverted faces (Tanaka, Saito, Fukada, & Moriya, 1991), cells in the superior temporal sulcus respond equally strongly to both types of faces (Perrett et al., 1982, 1985).

In previous fMRI studies of human observers, we have found that FFA responses are only slightly stronger for upright than inverted grayscale human faces, even though face discrimination performance is much poorer for the inverted faces (Kanwisher et al., 1998). By contrast, two-tone Mooney faces, which are difficult to perceive as faces at all after inversion, were found to yield a larger and more consistent FFA inversion effect.

Given that the subjects in the present experiment readily saw the inverted cartoons as faces, we predicted that the FFA inversion effect for cartoon faces would be rather small. In fact, even after inversion the cartoons often appeared easy to discriminate and identify because they contained highly distinctive features (e.g. the ears of Mickey Mouse or Bugs Bunny). We were therefore curious whether distinctive cartoon faces would still yield an FFA inversion effect.

Method

Subjects

Nine subjects (seven women) participated in Experiment 2; four performed the passive viewing task and five performed the one-back matching task.

Stimuli

Stimulus conditions consisted of upright cartoon faces (e.g. Mickey Mouse, Big Bird, Ernie, and Bert), inverted cartoon faces (i.e. the same cartoons shown upside-down), human faces (college ID photos), and objects. In each condition, 34 different images were used. All images were cropped and presented within a square window that subtended approximately 12° × 12° of visual angle. See Fig. 2A and Appendix B for examples.

Results and Discussion

FFA responses were strongest for upright human faces and upright cartoon faces, slightly weaker for inverted cartoon faces, and weakest for objects (see Fig. 2A). The consistency of these activation differences, including the cartoon inversion effect, could be seen in the average fMRI time course (see Fig. 2B) as well as in the individual subject data.

An ANOVA revealed a highly significant difference among stimulus conditions [$F(3,21) = 42.9$, $P < .00001$] but no significant effect of task

[$F(1,7) < 1$] or interaction between task and stimulus [$F(3,21) < 1$]. Planned comparisons revealed negligible differences in FFA response to upright cartoon faces and human faces [$t(8) = 0.56$, $P = .59$]. This indicates that the FFA response generalises equally well to upright cartoon faces as to human or cat faces (Experiment 1) despite their very different low-level image properties. These results are consistent with the preserved face recognition found in object agnosic patient CK, who could recognise both upright human and cartoon faces equally well (Moscovitch et al., 1997).

We found a small but significant decrease in FFA activity for inverted cartoon faces relative to upright cartoon faces [$t(8) = -6.74$, $P < .0001$] despite negligible differences in behavioural performance on the one-back matching task (inverted cartoons = 94% correct vs. upright cartoons = 95% correct). Compared to the small FFA inversion effect (upright cartoons − inverted cartoons = 1.7% − 1.4% = 0.3%), the FFA response to inverted cartoon faces was much greater than the response found for objects [1.4% vs. 0.7% respectively, $t(8) = 4.70$, $P < .002$], in fact almost twice in magnitude. The weak FFA inversion effect found here contrasts with the severe recognition deficit that CK showed for inverted cartoon faces (Moscovitch et al., 1997), but agrees well with the rather weak FFA inversion effects previously found for grayscale human faces (Kanwisher et al., 1998). Our results suggest that inverted faces can access face-specific mechanisms such as the FFA to a considerable extent, though not quite as effectively as upright faces.

EXPERIMENT 3: ENTIRE FACES, FACES WITHOUT EYES, EYES ALONE, AND HOUSES

Experiment 3 investigated the extent to which the FFA response could be attributed to the presence of the eyes. This was done by comparing the FFA response for entire human faces, faces with eyes occluded, eyes alone, and houses (see Fig. 3A and Appendix C for examples of the stimuli).

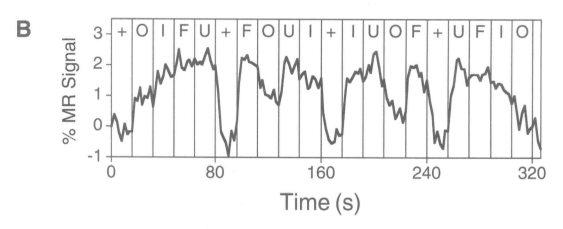

Fig. 2. *Example stimuli, overall FFA response (panel A) and time course of FFA activity (panel B) averaged across nine subjects in Experiment 2 during visual presentation of human faces (F), upright cartoon faces (U), inverted cartoon faces (I), and objects (O). Note that FFA responses are strongest for upright human and cartoon faces, somewhat weaker for inverted cartoon faces, and weakest for objects in all four blocks.*

One possible explanation of the generalised FFA response found across human, cat, and cartoon faces is that it reflects a more basic response to a salient facial feature such as the eyes. Perrett et al. (1985) found that for many "face cells" in superior temporal sulcus, selective responses for a particular face view (front or profile) could be better attributed to the gaze direction of the eyes. Furthermore, lesions of the superior temporal sulcus have been found to impair the discrimination of gaze direction but have little effect on face recognition perfor-

mance, suggesting that this region of monkey cortex may be specifically involved in gaze perception (Heywood & Cowey, 1992). ERP studies in humans have also revealed an N170 potential over the posterior temporal scalp that is greater for the eyes than for the nose, mouth, or entire face (Bentin, Allison, Puce, Perez, & McCarthy, 1996). Such an ERP may reflect an underlying gaze detection mechanism. However, such a mechanism has yet to be localised in the human brain. By using fMRI, we were able to test whether the FFA is selectively involved in gaze perception or involved in more global aspects of face perception.

Method

Subjects

Eight subjects (four women) participated in Experiment 3; three performed the passive viewing task and five performed the one-back matching task.

Stimuli

Front-view digital images of 38 men wearing a black ski hat were taken under controlled laboratory conditions. Stimuli consisted of 19 images of entire faces, a different set of 19 faces from which the eyes were digitally removed (and used for the eyes alone stimuli), 19 images of eyes alone, and 19 houses. All images were cropped and presented within a square window that subtended approximately 16° × 16° of visual angle, except for the eyes alone stimuli which subtended approximately 6° × 1.8°. See Fig. 3A and Appendix C for examples.

Results and Discussion

FFA responses were strongest for entire faces and faces without eyes, weaker for eyes alone, and weakest for houses (see Fig. 3A). The consistency of these activation differences can be seen in the average fMRI time course for each of the four blocks (see Fig. 3B).

An ANOVA revealed a highly significant difference among stimulus conditions [$F(3,18) = 28.5$, $P < .00001$], but no significant effect of task [$F(1,6) = 1.0$, $P = .30$] or interaction between task and stimulus [$F(3,18) < 1$]. Planned comparisons revealed a negligible difference in FFA response to entire faces and faces without eyes [$t(7) = 1.3$, $P = .23$], but a significantly greater response to faces without eyes than eyes alone [$t(7) = 3.30$, $P < .02$]. These results indicate that the eyes are neither necessary nor sufficient to fully activate the FFA. It further suggests that the FFA is not selectively involved in gaze detection (cf. Bentin et al., 1996; Heywood & Cowey, 1992), but instead is likely to be involved in global aspects of face perception. It

should also be noted that we found no other brain regions in our posterior slices that showed consistently greater responses to the presence of the eyes based on comparisons between eyes versus houses or entire faces versus faces without eyes.

The FFA response to eyes alone was much greater than the response to houses [$t(7) = 6.3$, $P < .0005$], even though the house stimuli were much larger and more visually complex. Apparently, a small isolated facial feature such as the eyes can still evoke a fairly large FFA response. However, when this feature was added to a face without eyes to form a complete face, no increase in FFA response was observed. This suggests that the FFA does not combine information from various facial features in a strictly linear fashion (see also Perrett et al., 1982, 1985).

EXPERIMENT 4: FRONT, PROFILE, CHEEK, AND BACK OF HEAD VIEWS

Experiment 4 investigated whether the FFA response is specific to faces or whether it reflects a more general response to a broader class of stimuli such as different views of heads. We tested four different head views: front view (0° rotation), profile view (90°), cheek view (135°), and back view (180°). Examples of the stimuli are shown in Fig. 4A and Appendix D.

A possible explanation of the generalised FFA response found across cat, cartoon, and human faces is that the FFA is more generally tuned to heads. For example, Sinha and Poggio (1996) have suggested that head recognition rather than face recognition is often used to identify individuals. By contrast, Perrett et al. (1991) have suggested that the reason why most "face cells" in the macaque superior temporal sulcus show specificity for various head views (including back of head and cheek views) is that these neurons are involved in coding the direction of another person's attention rather than facial identity.

We reasoned that if the FFA is generally tuned to heads, then one would predict equally elevated responses across all head views. However, if the

A

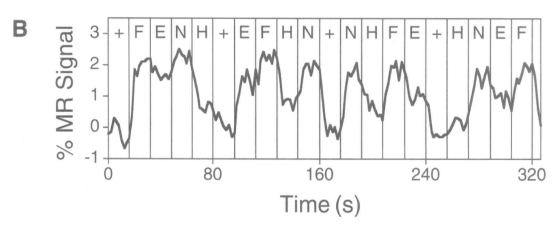

% MR Signal	Faces	No Eyes	Eyes	Houses
	1.8	1.7	1.3	0.6

B

Fig. 3. *Example stimuli, overall FFA response (panel A) and time course of FFA activity (panel B) averaged across eight subjects in Experiment 3 during visual presentation of entire human faces (F), faces with no eyes (N), eyes alone (E), and houses (H). Note that FFA responses are strongest for entire faces and faces with no eyes, weaker for eyes alone, and weakest for houses in all four blocks.*

FFA is more specifically tuned to faces, one would predict equally strong activity for front and profile views in which the internal features of the face remain visible, but declining activity thereafter as the face becomes progressively hidden from view.

Method

Subjects

Five subjects (two women) participated in Experiment 4. Three subjects performed only the passive viewing task, one subject performed only the one-back task, and one subject performed both tasks on different scans in the same session.

Stimuli

Images of 13 different men were taken from 4 different viewpoints which served as the 4 different stimulus conditions: front view (0° rotation), profile view (90°), cheek view (135°), and back view (180°). All images were cropped and presented within a square window that subtended approximately $12° \times 12°$ of visual angle. See Fig. 4A and Appendix D for examples of the stimuli.

Results and Discussion

The FFA responded most strongly to front and profile views, more weakly to cheek views and most weakly to back of head views (see Fig. 4A). The consistency of these activation differences can be seen in the average fMRI time course for each of the four blocks (see Fig. 4B).

An ANOVA revealed a highly significant difference among stimulus conditions [$F(3,12) = 12.9$, $P < .0005$], but no significant effect of task [$F(1,4) < 1$] or interaction between task and stimulus [$F(3,12) < 1$]. Planned comparisons revealed negligible FFA response differences between front and profile views [$t(5) = -0.08, P = .94$], but significantly greater activity for profile than cheek views [$t(5) = 4.01, P < .02$] and for cheek views than back of head views [$t(5) = 2.86, P < .05$]. Although an object control condition was not included in this experiment, the magnitude of FFA response to backs of heads appeared comparable to or only slightly greater than the response typically found for non-face objects.

FFA activity declined as the head rotated beyond profile view and the internal features of the face became progressively more occluded. This strongly suggests that the FFA responds specifically to faces and not more generally to heads. These results also rule out the possibility that the generalised FFA response found for cat and cartoon faces reflects a response to heads or animate forms in general. All subjects clearly recognised that they were viewing the back of human heads, and some subjects who were familiar with the persons shown even reported that they could identify people from the back of their heads. Despite the fact that such views were readily perceived as animate and were sometimes even recognised as belonging to a certain individual, the FFA failed to show much response to these views.

GENERAL DISCUSSION

The experiments reported here show that the FFA response generalises equally well across cat faces, cartoon faces, front-view human faces (with or without eyes), and profile-view human faces, even though the low-level visual features that compose these stimuli differ greatly. Such similar responses to very heterogeneous stimuli cannot be explained in terms of a more specific response to a salient facial feature such as the eyes or a more general response to heads or animate objects. Instead, our results strongly suggest that the FFA is optimally tuned to the broad stimulus category of faces.

Whereas cat, cartoon, and human faces evoked the strongest FFA responses, stimuli that conveyed only certain perceptual characteristics of a face (e.g. simple schematic faces, inverted cartoon faces, eyes alone, and cheek views of heads) evoked intermediate responses. By contrast, nonface stimuli such as objects, houses, and backs of heads consistently yielded the weakest responses. These results have a number of implications regarding the functional role of the FFA and the underlying processes that it may be performing. We address these issues below.

Is the FFA Selectively Involved in Gaze Perception?

There is some evidence that superior temporal sulcus lesions in monkeys may selectively impair the ability to perceive the direction of another's gaze without affecting face recognition performance (Heywood & Cowey, 1992). ERP recordings in humans have also revealed an N170 potential over the lateral occipital regions that is greater for the eyes than for the nose, mouth, or entire face (Bentin et al., 1996). These studies suggest that there may exist neural regions dedicated to the more specific task of gaze perception.

However, our results in Experiment 3 revealed no evidence of neural regions that respond selectively to gaze. Outside of the FFA, we failed to find preferential responses to the eyes. Note, however, that our brain slices extended from the occipital pole to the posterior temporal lobes; therefore it

A

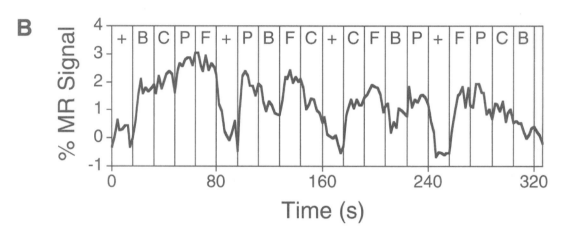

	Front	Profile	Cheek	Back
% MR Signal	1.8	1.8	1.3	0.9

B

Fig. 4. *Example stimuli, overall FFA response (panel A) and time course of FFA activity (panel B) averaged across six subjects in Experiment 4 during visual presentation of front (F), profile (P), cheek (C), and back (B) views of human heads. Note that FFA responses are strongest for front and profile views, weaker for cheek views, and weakest for back views in all four blocks.*

remains possible that one might find gaze-selective responses in more anterior regions.

Within the FFA itself, fMRI responses were equally strong for entire faces and faces without eyes, but significantly weaker for eyes shown alone. Thus, the eyes are neither necessary nor sufficient for evoking an optimal FFA response. This suggests that FFA is not *selectively* involved in gaze detection but instead is involved in more global aspects of face perception.

Does FFA Activity Reflect the Processing of Facial Features, Facial Configuration, or Both?

Although the processing of individual facial features contributes to face recognition, cognitive studies have generally emphasised the importance of configural or holistic processing for effective face recognition (Rhodes, Brennan, & Carey, 1987; Tanaka & Farah, 1993; Young et al., 1987). However, recent investigation of object agnosic patient CK, who appears to have a selectively spared face recognition system, suggests that both configural and featural information are encoded within a unitary system (Moscovitch et al., 1997). Our study likewise suggests that both global configuration and local facial features serve to activate the FFA.

In Experiment 1, we found that schematic faces defined by simple geometric shapes activated the FFA only slightly more than nonface objects. The weak response to schematic faces indicates that the presence of facial configuration alone, in the absence of appropriate facial features, is insufficient for evoking an optimal FFA response but can lead to a partial response.

In Experiment 2, subjects viewed upright and inverted cartoon faces that provided the same low-level feature information. However, FFA responses were significantly weaker for the inverted cartoon faces (see also Kanwisher et al., 1998), most probably because configural processing was disrupted for these faces. It is well known that face inversion severely disrupts configural or holistic processing, but generally has little effect on piecemeal processing of individual facial features (Tanaka & Farah, 1993; Tanaka & Sengco, 1997; Young et al., 1987).

These results suggest that neither configural information alone nor feature information alone is sufficient for evoking an optimal FFA response. Instead, optimal FFA activation appears to require both appropriate facial features and appropriate facial configuration. These response properties may reflect the fact that different FFA neurons are activated by different aspects of the face. Single-unit recordings in monkeys have revealed that face cells may be tuned to a particular facial feature (e.g. eyes, nose, mouth, chin), combination of features (e.g. mouth and chin) or the overall configuration of a face (Perrett et al., 1982; Yamane et al., 1988). If FFA neurons possess similar variations in tuning, one would predict that the FFA population would be most fully activated by a complete set of facial features presented in a proper configuration. By contrast, one would predict that fewer FFA neurons would respond to a face with inappropriate features (e.g. schematic faces), inappropriate con-

figuration (e.g. inverted faces), or to an isolated facial feature (e.g. eyes alone), as was found here.

Why Does the FFA Respond to Inverted Cartoon Faces?

Although we found a significant inversion effect for cartoon faces, the response to inverted cartoons remained almost twice as strong as the response to nonface objects. Perhaps one reason why inverted cartoon faces and inverted grayscale human faces (Kanwisher et al., 1998) evoke considerable FFA activity is that many facial features such as the eyes remain highly salient even after configural processing is disrupted by inversion. As Experiment 3 revealed, the eyes alone can evoke a fairly large FFA response.

Another possible explanation, which does not exclude the preceding one, is that the FFA is largely activated by successful acts of face *perception* rather than successful acts of face *recognition*. Inversion generally leads to rather small decreases in FFA activity, regardless of whether recognition performance is severely impaired, as in the case of grayscale human faces (Kanwisher et al., 1998), or unimpaired, as was found for cartoon faces. Even when these faces are inverted, they are still readily perceived as faces. By contrast, two-tone Mooney faces, which are difficult to perceive as faces once inverted, yield stronger FFA inversion effects (Kanwisher et al., 1998). This suggests that the FFA may be primarily activated by the perception of a face.

Supporting this view, Tong, Nakayama, Vaughan, and Kanwisher (1998) recently found that when subjects continuously viewed a bistable face/house display under conditions of binocular rivalry, the FFA showed a sharp increase in activity whenever subjects reported a perceptual switch from house to face. By contrast, the FFA showed a sharp decrease in activity during perceptual switches from face to house. FFA activity may therefore be tightly related to the phenomenal experience of seeing a face, even when it is the same face that is repeatedly perceived.

Might the FFA be Primarily Involved in Subordinate-level Categorisation or Expert Recognition?

Are there alternative accounts that might explain the apparent face-specificity of the FFA? Gauthier, Anderson, Tarr, Skudlarski, and Gore (1997a) have suggested that the FFA may reflect subordinate-level categorisation within a homogenous visual category rather than face-specific processing. However, such an account seems unlikely given that Kanwisher et al. (1997) previously showed that FFA responses were almost four times greater when subjects discriminated between individual faces than between individual hands. Here, we found that FFA responses were strongest for cat faces, upright cartoons, and human faces, intermediate for schematic faces, inverted cartoons, eyes alone, and cheek views, and weakest for houses and backs of heads, irrespective of whether subjects performed subordinate-level discriminations in the one-back matching task or a simple passive viewing task (see Table 2 for summary). These results suggest that the FFA response is quite automatic and far more dependent upon stimulus attributes than upon the difficulty of the visual discriminations involved (see Table 1) or the task at hand.

More recently, Gauthier et al. (1997b) have suggested that the FFA may instead reflect subordinate-level categorisation within a visual category for which one has acquired visual expertise. We think that such a modified account is also unlikely given the very strong FFA responses found here for cat faces. Although all of our subjects were far more experienced at recognising and individuating human faces than cat faces, the FFA showed equally strong activations to both face types. An expertise account would also have difficulty explaining why letters, which represent another highly overlearned visual category, activate different brain regions than faces (Puce et al., 1996). These findings suggest that the FFA response cannot be adequately explained in terms of the degree of visual expertise that one has for a particular category. Although some other modified subordinate-level classification account may still be viable, we

believe that the simplest account requiring the fewest ad hoc assumptions is that the FFA is primarily engaged in face perception.

Possible Roles of the FFA in the Detection, Perception, and Recognition of Faces

At present, there is little evidence to suggest that the FFA is involved in recognition memory for individual faces. Neuroimaging studies have shown that the FFA responds equally well to familiar versus novel faces, suggesting that the FFA might not be the site of memory storage for faces (Clark, Maisog, & Haxby, 1998; Haxby et al., 1996). These studies do not preclude the possibility that the FFA is involved in recognition memory for faces, but they do not support such involvement.

A plausible alternative is that the FFA plays a role in the *detection* of faces. By face detection, we mean the ability to discriminate between faces and nonfaces. The present study revealed that the FFA is optimally activated by cat, cartoon, and human faces but is weakly activated by nonface stimuli. This suggests that the FFA may not be specialised for recognising human faces but instead may serve a more basic function in detecting any type of face. In other studies, we have found that face inversion most severely impairs the FFA response when it impairs the subject's ability to detect the presence of a face (Kanwisher et al., 1998) and that the FFA automatically responds when the same face is repeatedly perceived in a bistable face/house display (Tong et al., 1998). These results suggest that the FFA response may reflect the conscious detection of a face.

Why might people develop a specialised mechanism for face detection? A face detection mechanism could signal the presence of humans or other animals in the immediate environment and thus serve as an alerting mechanism, providing important information for adaptive behaviour and survival. Face detection may also provide the necessary input for subsequent face recognition processes. For many computer vision algorithms, a face must first be located in a scene before face identification can proceed (e.g. *FaceIt*, 1998; Turk & Pentland, 1991) and, surprisingly, face detection in complex static scenes can sometimes prove as challenging as face identification itself (Leung, Burl, & Perona, 1995).

The FFA may also play a role in *face perception*, perhaps by representing the underlying shape or structure of a face. Inversion of grayscale human faces impairs both the FFA response (Kanwisher et al., 1998) and the perception of facial configuration (Tanaka & Sengco, 1997; Young et al., 1987), even though such inverted images are readily detected as faces. Thus, FFA activity may not only reflect face detection but may also reflect the perception of a face's shape and configuration.

One reason why face detection and face perception may rely on a common mechanism is computational efficiency. A common representational scheme such as a multidimensional "face space" (e.g. Rhodes et al., 1987; Valentine, 1991) could effectively serve both functions. Face detection would involve determining whether a particular item sufficiently resembles the central tendency of faces, whereas face perception would involve the complementary process of describing how a face deviates from this central tendency. Interestingly, when subjects must distinguish between intact and scrambled faces in a speeded-response task, faces that are highly atypical and recognisable are actually more difficult to classify as faces (Valentine, 1991). This suggests that face detection, like face perception, may involve coding a face in terms of its deviation from the central tendency of faces.

According to this framework, the FFA may play an important role in face detection and face perception, and may ultimately serve as a gateway to the higher-level areas where memories for individual faces are stored. FFA activity presumably reflects the activation of face-selective units that signal the presence of a face. These units may also provide a structural code for each face, perhaps by representing the local features and global configuration. Such structural information would provide the necessary input to higher-level recognition areas that match the incoming face input to stored face memories.

Concluding Remarks

We have shown that the FFA responds optimally to a variety of faces (humans, cats, and cartoons) and less strongly to stimuli that convey only certain perceptual characteristics of faces (e.g. schematic faces, inverted cartoons, eyes alone, cheek views of heads). The response profile of the FFA cannot be adequately explained in terms of low-level image properties given that upright and inverted faces with common image properties evoke different responses, and given that cat, cartoon, and human faces with very different image properties evoke comparable responses. Instead, the FFA response profile may be better understood in terms of higher-order representations for the general category of faces. One possibility is that activity in the FFA is tightly linked to the phenomenal experience of detecting or perceiving a face (Tong et al., 1998).

Regarding the functional role of the human fusiform face area, our results suggest that the FFA is not primarily involved in gaze perception, head detection, subordinate-level categorisation, or expert recognition. Instead, the FFA appears to be strongly involved in face detection and face perception, and may play a role in processing the local features and global configuration of faces.

REFERENCES

Allison, T., Ginter, H., McCarthy, G., Nobre, A.C., Puce, A., Luby, M., & Spencer, D.D. (1994). Face recognition in human extrastriate cortex. *Journal of Neurophysiology*, 71, 821–825.

Bentin, S., Allison, T., Puce, A., Perez, E., & McCarthy, G. (1996). Electrophysiological studies of face perceptions in humans. *Journal of Cognitive Neuroscience*, 8, 551–565.

Bodamer, J. (1947). Die Prosopagnosie. *Archiv für Psychiatrie und Nervenkrankheiten*, 179, 6–53.

Clark, V.P., Maisog, J.M., & Haxby, J.V. (1998). fMRI study of face perception and memory using random stimulus sequences. *Journal of Neurophysiology*, 79, 3257–3265.

FaceIt (1998). [Computer software.] Jersey City, NJ: Visionics Corporation.

Farah, M.J., Wilson, K.D., Drain, H.M., & Tanaka, J.R. (1995). The inverted face inversion effect in prosopagnosia: Evidence for mandatory, face-specific perceptual mechanisms. *Vision Research, 35,* 2089–2093.

Fried, I., MacDonald, K.A., & Wilson, C.L. (1997). Single neuron activity in human hippocampus and amygdala during recognition of faces and objects. *Neuron, 18,* 753–765.

Gauthier, I., Anderson, A.W., Tarr, M.J., Skudlarski, P., & Gore, J.C. (1997a). Levels of categorization in visual recognition studied using function magnetic resonance imaging. *Current Biology, 7,* 645–651.

Gauthier, I., Tarr, M.J., Anderson, A.W., Skudlarski, P., & Gore, J.C. (1997b). Expertise training with novel objects can recruit the fusiform face area. *Society for Neuroscience Abstracts, 23*(2), 2229.

Goren, C.C., Sarty, M., & Wu, P.Y.K. (1975). Visual following and pattern discrimination of face-like stimuli by newborn infants. *Pediatrics, 56,* 544–549.

Gross, C.G., Roche-Miranda, G.E., Bender, D.B. (1972). Visual properties of neurons in the infero-temporal cortex of the macaque. *Journal of Neurophysiology, 35,* 96–111.

Hasselmo, M.E., Rolls, E.T., & Baylis, G.C. (1989). The role of expression and identity in the face-selective responses of neurons in the temporal visual cortex of the monkey. *Behavioral Brain Research, 32,* 203–218.

Haxby, J.V., Horwitz, B., Ungerleider, L.G., Maisog, J.M., Pietrini, P., & Grady, C.L. (1994). The functional organization of human extrastriate cortex: A PET-rCBF study of selective attention to faces and locations. *Journal of Neuroscience, 14,* 6336–6353.

Haxby, J.V., Ungerleider, L.G., Horwitz, B., Maisog, J.M., Rapoport, S.I., & Grady, C.L. (1996). Face encoding and recognition in the human brain. *Proceedings of the National Academy of Sciences USA, 93,* 922–927.

Heit, G., Smith, M.E., & Halgren, E. (1988). Neural encoding of individual words and faces by the human hippocampus and amygdala. *Nature, 333,* 773–775.

Heywood, C.A., & Cowey, A. (1992). The role of the 'face-cell' area in the discrimination and recognition of faces by monkeys. *Philosophical Transactions of the Royal Society of London: Biological Sciences, 335*(1273), 31–37.

Jeffreys, D.A. (1989). A face-responsive potential recorded from the human scalp. *Experimental Brain Research, 78,* 193–202.

Jeffreys, D.A. (1996). Evoked potential studies of face and object processing. *Visual Cognition, 3,* 1–38.

Johnson, M.H., Dziurawiec, S., Ellis, H., & Morton. J. (1991). Newborns' preferential tracking of face-like stimuli and its subsequent decline. *Cognition, 40,* 1–19.

Kanwisher, N., McDermott, J., & Chun, M.M. (1997). The fusiform face area: A module in human extrastriate cortex specialized for face perception. *Journal of Neuroscience, 17*(11), 4302–4311.

Kanwisher, N., Tong, F., & Nakayama, K. (1998). The effect of face inversion on the human fusiform face area. *Cognition, 68,* B1–B11.

Leung, T.K., Burl, M.C., & Perona, P. (1995, June). *Finding faces in cluttered scenes using random graph matching.* International Conference on Computer Vision, Cambridge, MA.

McCarthy, G., Puce, A., Gore, J.C., & Allison, T. (1997). Face-specific processing in the human fusiform gyrus. *Journal of Cognitive Neuroscience, 9*(5), 604–609.

Meadows, J.C. (1974). The anatomical basis of prosopagnosia. *Journal of Neurology, Neurosurgery and Psychiatry, 37,* 489–501.

Moscovitch, M., Winocur, G., & Behrmann, M. (1997). What is special about face recognition? Nineteen experiments on a person with visual object agnosia and dyslexia but normal face recognition. *Journal of Cognitive Neuroscience, 9*(5), 555–604.

Ojemann J.G., Ojemann, G.A., Lettich, E. (1992). Neuronal activity related to faces and matching in human right nondominant temporal cortex. *Brain, 115,* 1–13.

Perrett, D.I., Oram, M.W., Harries, M.H., Bevan, R., Hietanen, J.K., Benson, P.J., & Thomas, S. (1991). Viewer-centred and object-centred coding of heads in the macaque temporal cortex. *Experimental Brain Research, 86,* 159–173.

Perrett, D.I., Rolls, E.T., & Caan, W. (1982). Visual neurones responsive to faces in the monkey temporal cortex. *Experimental Brain Research, 47,* 329–342.

Perrett, D.I., Smith, P.A.J., Potter, D.D., Mistlin, A.J., Head, A.S., Milner, A.D., & Jeeves, M.A. (1985). Visual cells in the temporal cortex sensitive to face view and gaze direction. *Proceedings of the Royal Society of London: B, 223,* 293–317.

Puce, A., Allison, T., Asgari, M., Gore, J.C., & McCarthy, G. (1996). Differential sensitivity of human visual cortex to faces, letterstrings, and textures: A functional magnetic resonance imaging study. *Journal of Neuroscience, 16,* 5205–5215.

Rhodes, G., Brennan, S., & Carey, S. (1987). Identification and ratings of caricatures: Implications for mental representations of faces. *Cognitive Psychology*, *19*(4), 473–497.

Sams, M., Hietanen, J.K., Hari, R., Ilmoniemi, R.J., Lounasmaa, O.V. (1997). Face-specific responses from the human inferior occipito-temporal cortex. *Neuroscience*, *77*, 49–55.

Sergent, J., Ohta, S., MacDonald, B. (1992) Functional neuroanatomy of face and object processing: a positron emission tomography study. *Brain*, *115*, 15–36.

Sinha, P., & Poggio, T. (1996). I think I know that face. *Nature*, *384*, 404.

Tanaka, J.W., & Farah, M.J. (1993). Parts and wholes in face recognition. *Quarterly Journal of Experimental Psychology*, *46A*(2), 225–245.

Tanaka, J.W., & Sengco, J.A. (1997). Features and their configuration in face recognition. *Memory and Cognition*, *25*(5), 583–592.

Tanaka, K., Saito, H.-A., Fukada, Y., & Moriya, M. (1991). Coding visual images of objects in the inferotemporal cortex of the macaque monkey. *Journal of Neurophysiology*, *66*, 170–189.

Tong, F., & Nakayama, K. (in press). Robust representations for faces: Evidence from visual search. *Journal of Experimental Psychology: Human Perception and Performance*.

Tong, F., Nakayama, K., Vaughan, J.T., & Kanwisher, N. (1998). Binocular rivalry and visual awareness in human extrastriate cortex. *Neuron*, *21*, 753–759.

Turk, M. & Pentland, A. (1991). Eigenfaces for recognition. *Journal of Cognitive Neuroscience*. *3*, 71–86.

Valentine, T. (1991). A unified account of the effects of distinctiveness, inversion, and race in face recognition. *Quarterly Journal of Experimental Psychology*, *43A*, 161–204.

Yamane, S., Kaji, S., & Kawano, K. (1988). What facial features activate face neurons in the inferotemporal cortex of the monkey. *Experimental Brain Research*, *73*, 209–214.

Yin, R.K. (1969). Looking at upside-down faces. *Journal of Experimental Psychology*, *81*, 141–145.

Young, A.W., Hellawell, D., & Hay, D.C. (1987). Configural information in face perception. *Perception*, *16*, 747–759.

APPENDIX A

Examples of stimuli in Experiment 1.

Faces Cats Schematic Faces Objects

APPENDIX B

Examples of stimuli in Experiment 2.

Faces · Upright Cartoons · Inverted Cartoons · Objects

APPENDIX C

Examples of stimuli in Experiment 3.

APPENDIX D

Examples of stimuli in Experiment 4.

Front Profile Cheek Back

COGNITIVE NEUROPSYCHOLOGY, 2000, 17 (1/2/3), 281–291

LOCALISED FACE PROCESSING BY THE HUMAN PREFRONTAL CORTEX: STIMULATION-EVOKED HALLUCINATIONS OF FACES

J.P. Vignal

University of Nancy, France

P. Chauvel

Faculté de Médecine, and INSERM E9926, Marseilles, France

E. Halgren

INSERM, Marseilles, France and MGH-NMR Center, Harvard Medical School, Charlestown, MA, USA

Left and right prefrontal, premotor, and anterior temporal sites were stereotaxically implanted in order to direct surgical therapy for epilepsy. Direct electrical stimulation of the right anterior inferior frontal gyrus resulted in face-related hallucinations and illusions. When the patient was viewing a blank background, stimulation induced the experience of a rapid succession of faces. When the patient was viewing a real face, stimulation induced a series of modifications to that face. Effective stimulations induced afterdischarges that remained localised to right ventrolateral prefrontal cortex (VLPFC). Stimulation of other frontal and anterior temporal sites, bilaterally, induced no face-related hallucinations or illusions. This result supports a contribution of right VLPFC to face processing, and is consistent with models wherein it activates representations in working or declarative memories.

INTRODUCTION

In one model of prefrontal function, stimuli in a specific category will activate a localised region within prefrontal cortex, as well as a corresponding site in posterior cortex. The posterior site is thought to generate a perceptual representation of the stimulus, whereas the prefrontal site is thought to maintain that representation in an active form permitting its utilisation in working memory (for reviews see Goldman-Rakic, 1995; Ungerleider, Courtney, & Haxby, 1998).

In the case of face stimuli, the most prominent posterior cortical region supporting specific processing was originally localised to the basal occipitotemporal junction using lesion studies of prosopagnosia (Damasio, Damasio, & Tranel, 1990; Meadows, 1974). More precise localisation to a small part of the fusiform gyrus has emerged from recent studies using positron emission tomography (PET: Haxby et al., 1994) and functional magnetic resonance imaging (fMRI: Clark et al., 1996; Courtney, Ungerleider, Keil, & Haxby, 1997; Halgren et al., 1999; Kanwisher, McDermott, & Chun, 1997; Puce, Allison, Gore, & McCarthy, 1995; see Kanwisher & Moscovitch, this issue, for a review). Magnetoencephalography (MEG: Halgren, Raij, Marinkovic, Jousmaki, & Hari, 1995; Sams, Hietanen, Hari, Ilmoniemi, & Lounasmaa, 1997) and intracranial electroenceph-

---

Requests for reprints should be addressed to E. Halgren, MGH-NMR Center, 149 13th street, Charlestown, MA 02129, USA.

This work was performed at INSERM CJF 90-12, CHU Pontchaillou, Rennes, France. Supported by INSERM, USPHS (NS18741), ONR, and HFSPO (RG25/96). We thank J.-M. Scarabin for implanting the probes.

alography (EEG) using subdural strips (Allison et al., 1994) or depth electrodes (stereo-encephalography, SEEG: Halgren, Baudena, Heit, Clarke, & Marinkovic, 1994a; Halgren et al., 1991) have confirmed this localisation and determined that a critical peak of activation occurs at 160–200msec after stimulus onset. Face-selective responses have also been seen in the region of the posterior superior temporal sulcus using fMRI (Puce, Allison, Bentin, Gore, & McCarthy, 1998) and SEEG (Halgren et al., 1994a), and may correspond to a location where face-selective unit-responses have been noted in monkeys (Perrett, Hietanen, Oram, & Benson, 1992).

The presence and location of a prefrontal area supporting face processing are much less well established. Using PET, Sergent, Shinsuke, and Macdonald (1992) found activation of orbitofrontal cortex (especially right) during the categorisation of familiar faces according to their professions. Haxby et al. (1994) found an area in the right VLPFC that was activated in a face matching task but not in a similar task matching locations. Also using PET, Courtney, Ungerleider, Keil, and Haxby (1996) found that the same area as well as a more dorsal area was activated in a working memory task where the identities of three faces needed to be kept in mind for comparison with a fourth, but not when the locations of the faces needed to be remembered. Using fMRI, Courtney et al. (1997) found that a right VLPFC area with sustained face-selective activation correlated with the period when the stimulus needed to be kept in mind. Recently, Kelley et al. (1998) found right dorsal prefrontal fMRI activation during the encoding of faces, with contralateral activation to words.

Electrophysiological evidence for a face-selective area in the prefrontal cortex has also been presented. In the macaque monkey, face-specific unit-firing has been reported in VLPFC (Booth, Rolls, Critchley, Browning, & Hernadi, 1998; Ó Scalaidhe, Wilson, & Goldman-Rakic, 1997; Pigarev, Rizzolatti, & Scandolara, 1979). In humans, using SEEG, Halgren et al. (1994b) and Klopp et al. (1999) showed that the VLPFC is strongly activated from 300 to 700msec after the presentation of faces in a declarative recognition memory task. Words also activated the same area, but simple visual and auditory stimuli in signal detection tasks did not. These data have been challenged, however, by an alternative view in which area specificity in the prefrontal cortex is due to differences in processing rather than in material (Owen, 1997). In this view, the apparent face-selectivity of the responses reviewed earlier may actually be due to confounding differences in the task context in which faces are presented.

The current study reports evidence from another technique, direct electrical stimulation of the human brain, for a role of the right VLPFC in face processing. Stimulation is thought to evoke experiential phenomena through a disruption of neural function near the stimulating electrode, together with an activation of neural processing in efferent structures (see Halgren & Chauvel, 1993, for discussion). For over a century, complex formed visual hallucinations during partial epileptic seizures have been associated with the medial temporal lobe (Bancaud, Brunet-Bourgin, Chauvel, & Halgren, 1994; Gloor, 1990; Gloor, Olivier, Quesney, Andermann, & Horowitz, 1982; Jackson & Colman, 1898; Jackson & Stewart, 1899; Penfield & Perot, 1963). Seizures involving the occipito-temporal junction may also evoke complex visual hallucinations, possibly via propagation to the medial temporal lobe (Blume, Whiting, & Girvin, 1991; Ludwig & Marsan, 1975; Salanova, Andermann, Olivier, Rasmussen, & Quesney, 1992; Williamson et al., 1992). These observations have been extended with electrical stimulation of (especially medial) temporal areas, where the precise location of the stimulating electrode is known. Such stimulations may produce vivid formed hallucinations (Bancaud et al., 1994; Gloor et al., 1982; Halgren, Walter, Cherlow, & Crandall, 1978; Penfield, & Perot 1963).

Schneider, Crosby, Bagchi, and Calhoun (1961) and Chauvel et al. (1995) reported complex visual hallucinations during partial seizures of probable frontal origin, but without describing the anatomical localisation of discharges during the hallucinations, nor the phenomenological details of the experiences. Thus, these experiences could have been due to spread of the discharge to the temporal lobe. Bancaud and Talairach (1992) briefly describe elementary hallucinations (grey or coloured veils, geometric figures) after dorsolateral frontal stimulation. We report an example of hallucinations and illusions of faces provoked by electrical stimulation of the right VLPFC of a patient suffering from seizures originating in that region. The inference that face-selective processing may occur in the human ventrolateral prefrontal cortex is supported by field-potential recordings and neuropsychological testing in the same patient, reported in the companion paper (Marinkovic, Trebon, Chauvel, & Halgren, this issue).

CASE REPORT

The patient is a 30-year-old married man of mixed handedness. He has 9 years of formal education and works as an upholsterer in a furniture factory. His intelligence, neurological examination, MRI, and interictal SPECT are all normal. Seizures began at age 14 and now usually occur at night. Seizures begin with an ascending sensation of warmth and a feeling of shame and guilt, followed by "gestural automatisms," tonic bilateral contraction of the facial muscles, blushing and pupillary dilation, and at the end of the seizure a vocalisation resembling the sound of an engine, and euphoria. Seizures last 20–30 seconds. Postictally, the behaviour and vigilance immediately return to normal. Tonic-clonic generalisation is rare.

In order to confirm the epileptogenic zone hypothesised from EEG recordings, depth probes were chronically implanted into multiple right and left prefrontal, anterior temporal, and premotor cortices (Fig. 1: see Bancaud, 1980; Chauvel, Vignal, Biraben, Badier, & Scarabin, 1996b; Talairach et al., 1967). These sites were stimulated in an attempt to provoke the patient's habitual seizure. Electrical stimulation used bipolar pulses with a duration of 1msec delivered for 5sec at a frequency of 50Hz.

Stimulation 1

(2mA between electrode contacts G11 and G12.)

During the stimulation, the patient was looking at the physician's white labcoat.

Patient: I see many faces that appear.
Doctor: The faces that appear, are they mine?
Patient: No, but a succession of portraits passing by.
Doctor: This succession of portraits, is it still going on?
Patient: No, it is over, I don't know, a bunch of people that it seems that I know, but which pass by one after the other, but it is possible to remember neither the first nor the second...
Doctor: People that you know?
Patient: Not necessarily, but someone who could live... with a hat, and one with glasses.
Doctor: It consists only of faces?
Patient: No, more or less the bust.
Doctor: There was one with a hat?
Patient: There was one with glasses, others with hats, at least one... it comes, but not only one block, one sees the image which comes... I looked at your shirt and I was seeing the entire group of successive images.
Doctor: These images were more on the right, or the left?
Patient: No, they were centred, like as if one was passing slides, one after the other, linked together.
Doctor: Were they in colour or black and white?
Patient: They were in colour, but not really well-defined colours.
Doctor: It was not familiar faces?
Patient: No, one might say of television celebrities, faces of people that one might encounter in everyday life, a face of a peasant, many, many faces ... it lasted 3 to 4 seconds.
Doctor: Of particular types of people?
Patient: Yes that's it, a peasant with his velvet hat and dark glasses.

The current provoked an afterdischarge that started 1.5sec after stimulus onset and lasted 8sec after the end of the stimulation in the right prefrontal cortex (Fig. 2). A frank afterdischarge of rhythmic spikes was limited to the immediate vicinity of the stimulated contacts. A slower rhythmic activity was also noted in other right

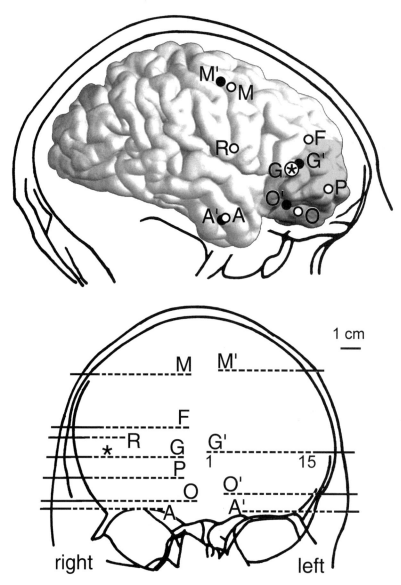

Fig. 1. *Probe locations. Actual probe locations relative to the skull are traced on lateral (above) and antero-posterior (below) teleradiographs, and superimposed on a standardised brain (above). Each probe has 5–15 electrode contacts, each being 2mm in length and separated by 1.5mm. Contacts are numbered starting with the deepest as 1. The electrode contacts (G11–12) where stimulation evoked hallucinations of faces are marked with an *. Probe locations with respect to the brain were determined by reference to the patient's MRI (Talairach & Tournoux, 1988). The internal contacts of probe G (1 and 2) were in the anterior cingulate gyrus (area 24), the external contacts (10 to 14) in the inferior frontal gyrus, and the intervening contacts (3 to 9) in the white matter. The stimulated contacts (G11–12) may have been in Brodman's area 45. However, given the variability in human prefrontal cytoarchitectonics, it may instead have been located in area 10, 46, or a transitional area (Rajkowska & Goldman-Rakic, 1995). The internal contacts of probe O (1 and 2) were in the middle frontal gyrus (area 11), and the more lateral contacts (5 through 12) in the inferior frontal gyrus (area 11 then area 47). Probe P was in the frontal pole (probably area 10). Probe A passed from the periamygdaloid cortex (contacts 1–2) through the amygdala (contacts 3–4) through the ventricle and temporal stem, then into the white matter of the middle temporal gyrus just superior to the fundus of the inferior temporal sulcus (contacts 9–10), and arriving at the cortical surface in contacts 13–14. Probes in the left hemisphere are marked with a prime, and are located in approximately homologous sites. The estimated extent of the therapeutic cortectomy is shown in darker grey.*

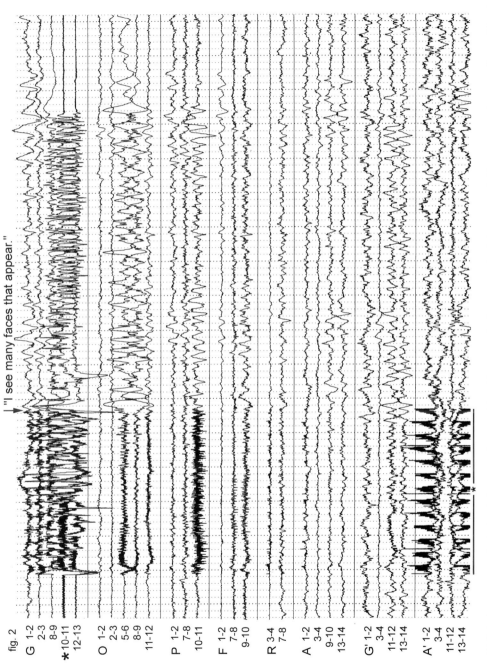

Fig. 2. *StereoEEG during prefrontal stimulation-induced hallucinations of faces. The artefact indicates when stimulation was applied between electrode contacts G11 and G12 in the right ventrolateral prefrontal cortex. An afterdischarge can be seen beginning during the stimulation period, with rhythmic spikes in the more lateral leads of G (G8–9, 10–11 and 12–13), and mainly slow waves in other right ventrolateral prefrontal contacts (O5–6, 8–9; P10–11). No significant change from baseline activity was noted in the right amygdala (A1–2, 3–4) or anterior middle temporal gyrus (A9–10, 13–14). Total epoch displayed 17.6sec.*

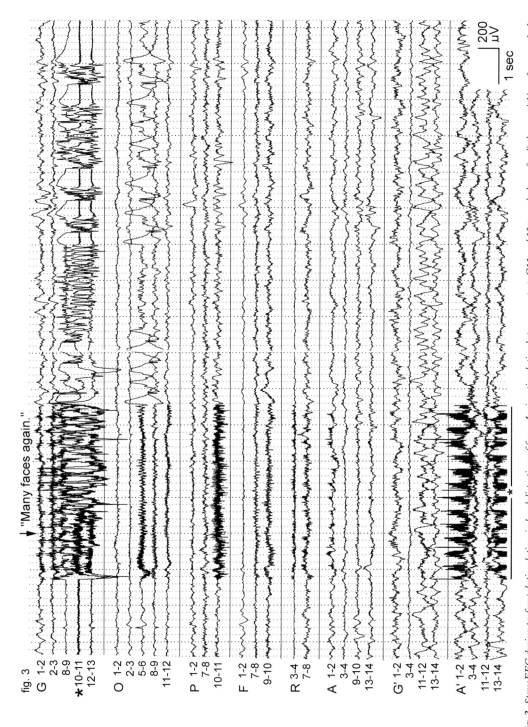

fig. 3

G 1-2
2-3
8-9
*10-11
12-13

O 1-2
2-3
5-6
8-9
11-12

P 1-2
7-8
10-11

F 1-2
7-8
9-10

R 3-4
7-8

A 1-2
3-4
9-10
13-14

G' 1-2
3-4
11-12
13-14

A' 1-2
3-4
11-12
13-14

↓ "Many faces again."

200 μV

1 sec

Fig. 3. StereoEEG during prefrontal stimulation-induced distortions of faces. Again, stimulation between contacts G11 and 12 provoked an afterdischarge within a few seconds that continued after the end of the stimulation. In this case, propagation was more limited in the right prefrontal cortex than that described above (G8–9 to G12–13, and only O5–6; no clear discharge in P). However, a rhythmic slow discharge occurred contralaterally (G'11–12, 13–14), presumably due to transcallosal propagation.

ventrolateral prefrontal contacts, of probe O (inferior to the stimulated site), with slow waves and occasional spikes in P (anterior and inferior to the stimulated site). No significant change from baseline activity was recorded by probe A in the right temporal lobe, passing from the amygdala to the anterior middle temporal gyrus. The patient commented on the content of his hallucinations immediately after the end of the stimulation.

Stimulation 2

(G11–12, 1.5mA, 10 min after stimulation 1.)

During the stimulation, the patient was looking at the doctor's face.

Patient: Many faces again.
Doctor: What are these faces?
Patient: They are you but transformed.
Doctor: Me transformed?
Patient: It's still happening to me.
Doctor: But transformed how?
Patient: It is difficult to explain.
Doctor: Is it over?
Patient: Yes. There I had the impression of warmth in the shoulders.
Doctor: What happened?
Patient: It is as if your face was transformed, one time without glasses, once with a hat, but always the same face.
Doctor: There was no modification of colours?
Patient: No.
Doctor: It was my head that changed, not my body?
Patient: No, it was as if you changed your face, that it was remodelled and that it became another face and so forth...

This stimulation (Fig. 3) provoked an afterdischarge that started 2sec after stimulus onset and lasted 9sec after the end of the stimulation with a more limited propagation in the right prefrontal cortex than that described earlier, but with a rhythmic slow discharge contralaterally. From second 2 of stimulation (i.e. at the moment of afterdischarge onset), the patient said "Many faces again." When he said "It's still happening to me," the after-

discharge ended. Contacts G11–12 were only stimulated on these two occasions.

Other Effective Stimulations:

Stimulation of the left amygdala (A'1–2) at 2mA evoked an impression of warmth in the head, and nausea, with a 30sec afterdischarge spreading to the left anterior cingulate gyrus (G'1–2). Stimulation of the right amygdala (A1–2) at 1.5mA evoked an impression of *déjà vécu* with an afterdischarge in the right amygdala and cingulate gyrus (G1–2). After stimulation of the right orbital cortex (O6–7, without afterdischarge: probable area 10) the patient reported that the tonality of voices was distorted, perhaps like an echo, with the impression of having already heard a similar distortion. Stimulation of the adjacent site (O5–6) 3 hours later again evoked a resonating distortion of the physician's voice, with a brief discharge in the external contacts of O and G. Stimulation of right SMA (M1–4) and bilateral dorsolateral area 6 (M5–7, M'5–10) gave motor responses typical of these areas: arrest, vocalisation, eye and head deviation (Chauvel, Rey, Buser, & Bancaud, 1996a).

Two typical seizures, similar in topography to the spontaneous ones, were provoked by stimulation of the right anterior cingulate gyrus (G1–2). Four spontaneous seizures were also found to begin in the right prefrontal cortex. Tailored surgery based upon these SEEG data (Bancaud, 1980; Chauvel et al., 1996b) eliminated all seizures (follow-up of over 4 years).

Ineffective Stimulations:

Contacts in most of the implanted electrodes were stimulated with the same parameters, with the sole exception of the current level, which changed as a function of the excitability of the stimulated structure. No subjective or objective phenomena were noted with stimulations of the following sites: with afterdischarge—F9–10, G'11–12, O'5–6, O'9–10; without afterdischarge—A11–12, F1–2, M7–8, M8–9, M10–11, O1–2, O10–11, P1–2, P8–9, A'10–11, G'1–2, M'1–2, M'2–3, M'3–4, M'4–5, M'5–6, O'1–2. No hallucinatory manifestations were provoked apart from those that were described earlier. In particular, note that F9–10, P8–9, and O10–11, where stimulation had no effect, were all within 2cm of G11–12, where stimulation evoked face hallucinations and illusions.

DISCUSSION

Stimulation of the right inferior frontal gyrus provoked hallucinations and illusions involving faces, accompanied by an afterdischarge localised to the right VLPFC. This afterdischarge and the hallucination began and terminated simultaneously. The afterdischarge did not involve the temporal lobe nor the cingulate gyrus, and stimulation of these areas did not evoke face-related hallucinations. The hallucinations consisted of portraits that appeared in rapid succession. The illusions consisted of a series of distortions of the physician's face, and in particular the removal or addition of an accessory (glasses or hat).

Similar phenomena have not been reported in previous studies of mental phenomena evoked by stimulation of the right VLPFC (Ojemann, 1992; Penfield & Jasper, 1954), nor in our own observations in about 10 such patients. The uniqueness of these data pose the question as to whether they are an idiosyncratic response resulting from abnormal epileptiform activation. Although this possibility cannot be absolutely excluded, it seems unlikely. First, these face-related hallucinations and illusions did not form part of the normal seizures of the patient. Second, no face-related phenomena were evoked by stimulation of the anterior cingulate gyrus, where the patient's typical seizure could be evoked. Third, presentation of faces failed to evoke any epileptiform activity in the critical contacts (Marinkovic et al., this issue).

Conversely, the failure in previous studies of VLPFC stimulation to observe face hallucinations could be explained if it occurs only when a relatively small location is stimulated. In the current study, face hallucinations were not seen after stimulation of any other electrode contacts, even including more dorsal, ventral, and anterior right VLPFC sites that were all within 2cm. Recordings from the

active site and its surroundings suggest that its mediolateral extent may be only a few millimetres (Marinkovic et al., this issue). In other studies stimulation was restricted to the cortical surface exposed during cortectomy, whereas the current results were obtained with stimulation of cortex buried in a sulcus. Other studies also tend to concentrate cortical stimulation to the left posterior prefrontal cortex in an attempt to identify eloquent cortex, whereas the face hallucinations in the current study were evoked from right anterior prefrontal cortex. Finally, many of the patients explored with intracranial electrodes have diffusely dysfunctional prefrontal cortex that may be generally unresponsive, whereas the patient in the current study had normal metabolism (as determined by SPECT) and background EEG in the right VLPFC. Thus, it seems likely that the failure of previous studies to observe face hallucinations may be due to insufficient sampling.

The phenomenological characteristics of the complex visual hallucinations reported here are clearly different from those that have been reported after temporal lobe stimulation. The complex hallucinations after temporal lobe stimulation occur within the context of the Dreamy State: an overall change in the quality of consciousness, often described by the patient as like a dream, or like a movie, with feelings of the doubling of consciousness (Bancaud et al., 1994; Halgren et al., 1978; Jackson & Colman, 1898; Jackson & Stewart, 1899; Penfield, & Perot 1963). Hallucinations evoked by temporal lobe stimulation are often associated with other experiential manifestations of medial temporal lobe activation, and in particular with a rising epigastric sensation or an emotion (Bancaud et al., 1994; Gloor, 1990; Halgren et al., 1978; Jackson & Colman, 1898; Jackson & Stewart, 1899). Frequently, a complex hallucination evoked by temporal lobe stimulation is described as a particular episode from the patient's life, and is accompanied by an intense feeling of familiarity (*déjà vu* or *déjà vécu*) or, conversely, an intense feeling of unfamiliarity (*jamais vu or jamais vécu*). In contrast, the face hallucinations after VLPFC stimulation reported here did not seem to be associated with any change in the quality in consciousness, nor were they accompanied by emotional phenomena. They were not described as related to the autobiographical memory of the patient, but rather as generic exemplars.

Another contrast between the hallucinations after VLPFC stimulation and those after temporal stimulation is that the former were of isolated faces, whereas the latter were of scenes. We examined the patients' verbatim experiential descriptions contained in Penfield and Perot (1963), Halgren et al. (1978), and Bancaud et al. (1994). In every instance where the patient could describe details of the experience, it was clear that an entire scene was experienced, not simply an isolated object or face. Furthermore, always prominent in the description was the location of the scene. In many instances, no person was present in the scene, and if so the entire person seemed to be viewed, not simply the face. Thus, phenomenologically, the effects of VLPFC stimulation seem to be directly upon the perceptual substrate of face processing, rather than upon the medial temporal substrate of autobiographical event memory.

It seems unlikely that the less elaborate hallucinations after frontal stimulation are due to characteristics of the electrographic response to the stimulation. In Halgren et al. (1978), afterdischarges were evoked in only 19 of the 44 medial temporal lobe stimulations that evoked memory- or dream-like complex hallucinations. It was noted that more bizarre hallucinations seemed to be associated with more extensive afterdischarges. The duration of the afterdischarges evoked by the two effective instances of stimulation in the current paper was 13–14sec, more than adequate to evoke the Dreamy State in responsive medial temporal lobe sites. Hence, the phenomenological differences between the Dreamy State and the hallucinations reported here appear to be due to the locus of the stimulation.

As reviewed earlier, numerous studies have identified a fusiform gyrus area that is highly and specifically activated by faces, and that according to lesion studies is essential for face processing. Anatomical, physiological, and neuropsychological data reviewed in the companion paper (Marinkovic et al., this issue) support an interaction between the fusiform and ventral prefrontal cortices during face processing, suggesting that the effects observed in this study are the result of activation of a pathway that is used for re-entrant or feedback processing of faces, from a secondary processing area in the frontal lobe to the primary processing area in the fusiform gyrus. The hypothesis of remote activation of the fusiform gyrus from VLPFC stimulation suggests a natural explanation for the experiential phenomena observed here. In the first stimulation, the patient was looking at the blank white labcoat of the neurologist and he reported a succession of typical faces. In the second stimulation, the patient was looking at the neurologist's face, and he initially reported a distortion of the neurologist's face that over time seemed to evolve again into a succession of faces, with different ancillary characteristics (hat, glasses, etc.). Under the hypothesis suggested earlier, in the first stimulation, activation from the frontal lobe would be projected to a quiescent fusiform g, selecting cell-assemblies representing particular faces, and resulting in simple face hallucinations. In the second stimulation, activation projected from the prefrontal site would distort ongoing activation (related to the actual sensory stimulus), rather than selecting a cell-assembly de novo. The implications of the current study for contrasting theories of prefrontal function are further examined in the companion study after presenting additional data (Marinkovic et al., this issue).

REFERENCES

Allison, T., Ginter, H., McCarthy, G., Nobre, A.C., Puce, A., Luby, M., & Spencer, D.D. (1994). Face recognition in human extrastriate cortex. *Journal of Neurophysiology, 71,* 821–825.

Bancaud, J. (1980). Surgery of epilepsy based on stereotaxic investigations. The plan of the SEEG investigation. *Acta Neurochirurgica, Supplementum (Wien), 30,* 25–34.

Bancaud, J., Brunet-Bourgin, F., Chauvel, P., & Halgren, E. (1994). Anatomical origin of déjà vu and vivid "memories" in human temporal lobe epilepsy. *Brain, 117,* 71–90.

Bancaud, J., & Talairach, J. (1992). Clinical semiology of frontal lobe seizures. In P. Chauvel, A. V.

Delgado-Escueta, E. Halgren, & J. Bancaud (Eds.), *Advances in Neurology, Vol. 57: Frontal Lobe Seizures and Epilepsies* (pp. 3–58). New York: Raven.

Blume, W.T., Whiting, S.E., & Girvin, J.P. (1991). Epilepsy surgery in the posterior cortex. *Annals of Neurology, 29,* 638–645.

Booth, M.C.A., Rolls, E.T., Critchley, H.D., Browning, A.S., & Hernadi, I. (1998). Face-sensitive neurons in the primate orbitofrontal cortex. *Neuroscience Abstracts, 24,* 898.

Chauvel, P., Kliemann, F., Vignal, J.P., Chodkiewicz, J.P., Talairach, J., & Bancaud, J. (1995). The clinical signs and symptoms of frontal lobe seizures. Phenomenology and classification. *Advances in Neurology, 66,* 115–125.

Chauvel, P.Y., Rey, M., Buser, P., & Bancaud, J. (1996a). What stimulation of the supplementary motor area in humans tells about its functional organisation. *Advances in Neurology, 70,* 199–209.

Chauvel, P., Vignal, J.P., Biraben, A., Badier, J.M., & Scarabin, J.M. (1996b). Stereo-electroncephalography. In G.S. Pawlik, (Ed.), *Multimethodological assessment of the localisation-related epilepsy* (pp. 135–63). Berlin: Springer Verlag.

Clark, V.P., Keil, K., Maisog, J.M., Courtney, S., Ungerleider, L.G., & Haxby, J.V. (1996). Functional magnetic resonance imaging of human visual cortex during face matching: a comparison with positron emission tomography. *NeuroImage, 4,* 1–15.

Courtney, S.M., Ungerleider, L.G., Keil, K., & Haxby, J.V. (1996). Object and spatial visual working memory activate separate neural systems in human cortex. *Cerebral Cortex, 6,* 39–49.

Courtney, S.M., Ungerleider, L.G., Keil, K., & Haxby, J.V. (1997). Transient and sustained activity in a distributed neural system for human working memory. *Nature, 386,* 608–11.

Damasio, A.R., Damasio, H., & Tranel, D. (1990). Face agnosia and the neural substrates of memory. *Annual Review of Neuroscience, 13,* 89–109.

Gloor, P. (1990). Experiential phenomena of temporal lobe epilepsy. *Brain, 113,* 1673–1694.

Gloor, P., Olivier, A., Quesney, L.F., Andermann, F., & Horowitz, S. (1982). The role of the limbic system in experiential phenomena of temporal lobe epilepsy. *Annals of Neurology, 12,* 129–144.

Goldman-Rakic, P.S. (1995). Cellular basis of working memory. *Neuron, 14,* 477–485.

Halgren, E., Baudena, P., Heit, G., Clarke, J.M., & Marinkovic, K. (1994a). Spatio-temporal stages in face and word processing. 1. Depth-recorded potentials in the human occipital, temporal and parietal lobes. *Journal of Physiology (Paris), 88,* 1–50.

Halgren, E., Baudena, P., Heit, G., Clarke, J.M., Marinkovic, K., & Chauvel, P. (1994b). Spatio-temporal stages in face and word processing. 2. Depth-recorded potentials in the human frontal and Rolandic cortices. *Journal of Physiology (Paris), 88,* 51–80.

Halgren, E., & Chauvel, P. (1993). Experiential phenomena evoked by human brain electrical stimulation. *Advances in Neurology, 63,* 123–140.

Halgren, E., Dale, A.M., Sereno, M.I., Tootell, R.B.H., Marinkovic, K., & Rosen, B.R. (1999). Location of human face-selective cortex with respect to retinotopic areas. *Human Brain Mapping, 7,* 29–37.

Halgren, E., Marinkovic, K., Baudena, P., Devaux, B., Broglin, D., Heit, G., & Chauvel, P. (1991). Human intracranial potentials evoked by faces. *Society for Neuroscience Abstracts, 17,* 656.

Halgren, E., Raij, T., Marinkovic, K., Jousmaki, V., & Hari, R. (1995). Magnetic fields evoked by faces in the human brain: I. Topography and equivalent dipole location. *Society for Neuroscience Abstract, 21,* 662.

Halgren, E., Walter, R.D., Cherlow, D.G., & Crandall, P.H. (1978). Mental phenomena evoked by electrical stimulation of the human hippocampal formation and amygdala. *Brain, 101,* 83–117.

Haxby, J.V., Horwitz, B., Ungerleider, L.G., Maisog, J.M., Pietrini, P., & Grady, C.L. (1994). The functional organisation of human extrastriate cortex: A PET-rCBF study of selective attention to faces and locations. *Journal of Neuroscience, 14,* 6336–6353.

Jackson, J.H., & Colman, W.S. (1898). Case of epilepsy with tasting movements and "dreamy state"—very small patch of softening in the uncinate gyrus. *Brain, 21,* 580–590.

Jackson, J.H., & Stewart, P. (1899). Epileptic attacks with warning sensations of smell and with intellectual aura (dreamy state) in a patient who had symptoms pointing to gross organic disease of the right temporo-sphenoidal lobe. *Brain, 22,* 534–549.

Kanwisher, N., McDermott, J., & Chun, M.M. (1997). The fusiform face area: a module in human extrastriate cortex specialised for face perception. *Journal of Neuroscience, 17,* 4302–4311.

Kanwisher, N., & Moscovitch, M. (this issue). The cognitive neuroscience of face processing: An introduction. *Cognitive Neuropsychology, 17,* 1-11.

Kelley, W.M., Miezin, F.M., McDermott, K.B., Buckner, R.L., Raichle, M.E., Cohen, N.J., Ollinger, J.M., Akbudak, E., Conturo, T.E., Snyder, A.Z., &

Petersen, S.E. (1998). Hemispheric specialisation in human dorsal frontal cortex and medial temporal lobe for verbal and nonverbal memory encoding. *Neuron, 20*, 927–936.

Klopp, J., Halgren, E., Marinkovic, K., & Nenov, V. (1999). Face-selective event-related spectral changes in the human fusiform gyrus. *Clinical Neurophysiology, 110*, 677–683.

Ludwig, B.I., & Marsan, C.A. (1975). Clinical ictal patterns in epileptic patients with occipital electro-encephalographic foci. *Neurology, 25*, 463–471.

Marinkovic, K., Trebon, P., Chauvel, P., & Halgren, E. (this issue). Localised face-processing by the human prefrontal cortex: Face-selective intracerebral potentials and post-lesion deficits. *Cognitive Neuropsychology, 17*, 187–199.

Meadows, J.C. (1974). The anatomical basis of prosopagnosia. *Journal of Neurology, Neurosurgery and Psychiatry, 37*, 489–501.

Ojemann, G. (1992). Localisation of language in frontal cortex. In P. Chauvel, A.V. Delgado-Escueta, E. Halgren, & J. Bancaud (Eds.), *Advances in neurology, Vol.57. Frontal lobe seizures and epilepsies* (pp. 361–368). New York: Raven.

Ó Scalaidhe, S., Wilson, F.A., & Goldman-Rakic, P.S. (1997). Areal segregation of face-processing neurons in prefrontal cortex. *Science, 278*, 1135–1138.

Owen, A.M. (1997). The functional organisation of working memory processes within human lateral frontal cortex: The contribution of functional neuroimaging. *European Journal of Neuroscience, 9*, 1329–1339.

Penfield, W., & Jasper, H. (1954). *Epilepsy and the functional anatomy of the human brain.* Boston, MA: Little Brown.

Penfield, W.P., & Perot, P. (1963). The brain's record of auditory and visual experience: A final summary and discussion. *Brain, 86*, 595–696.

Perrett, D.I., Hietanen, J.K., Oram, M.W., & Benson, P.J. (1992). Organisation and functions of cells responsive to faces in the temporal cortex. *Philosophical Transactions of the Royal Society of London.Series B: Biological Sciences, 335*, 23–30.

Pigarev, I.N., Rizzolatti, G., & Scandolara, C. (1979). Neurons responding to visual stimuli in the frontal lobe of macaque monkeys. *Neuroscience Letters, 12*, 207–212.

Puce, A., Allison, T., Bentin, S., Gore, J.C., & McCarthy, G. (1998). Temporal cortex activation in humans viewing eye and mouth movements. *Journal of Neuroscience, 18*, 2188–2199.

Puce, A., Allison, T., Gore, J.C., & McCarthy, G. (1995). Face-sensitive regions in human extrastriate cortex studied by functional MRI. *Journal of Neurophysiology, 74*, 1192–1199.

Rajkowska, G., & Goldman-Rakic, P.S. (1995). Cytoarchitectonic definition of prefrontal areas in the normal human cortex: II. Variability in locations of areas 9 and 46 and relationship to the Talairach coordinate system. *Cerebral Cortex, 5*, 323–337.

Salanova, V., Andermann, F., Olivier, A., Rasmussen, T., & Quesney, L.F. (1992). Occipital lobe epilepsy: electroclinical manifestations, electrocorticography, cortical stimulation and outcome in 42 patients treated between 1930 and 1991. Surgery of occipital lobe epilepsy. *Brain, 115*, 1655–1680.

Sams, M., Hietanen, J.K., Hari, R., Ilmoniemi, R.J., & Lounasmaa, O.V. (1997). Face-specific responses from the human inferior occipito-temporal cortex. *Neuroscience, 77*, 49–55.

Schneider, R.C., Crosby, E.C., Bagchi, B.K., & Calhoun, H.D. (1961). Temporal or occipital lobe hallucinations triggered from frontal lobe lesions. *Neurology, 11*, 172–179.

Sergent, J., Shinsuke, O., & Macdonald, B. (1992). Functional neuroanatomy of face and object processing: A positron emission tomography study. *Brain, 115*, 15–36.

Talairach, J., Szikla, G., Tournoux, P., Prossalentis, A., Bordas-Ferrer, M., Covello, L., Jaco, M., & Mempel, E. (1967). *Atlas d'anatomie stereotaxique du telencephale.* Paris: Masson et Cie.

Talairach, J., & Tournoux, P. (1988). *Co-planar stereotaxic atlas of the human brain.* New York: Thieme Medical Publishers.

Ungerleider, L.G., Courtney, S.M., & Haxby, J.V. (1998). A neural system for human visual working memory. *Proceedings of the National Academy Sciences USA, 95*, 883–890.

Williamson, P.D., Thadani, V.M., Darcey, T.M., Spencer, D.D., Spencer, S.S., & Mattson, R.H. (1992). Occipital lobe epilepsy: clinical characteristics, seizure spread patterns, and results of surgery. *Annals of Neurology, 31*, 3–13.

SUBJECT INDEX

Affective response, face processing 3, 55, 56, 60, 63, 65–70, 193

Age, face recognition effect 6, 165–86

Amnesia, new faces 2, 241–55

Amygdala 58, 61–64, 69, 127, 197, 287

Animal faces 3, 4, 92–94, 261–63

Apperceptive prosopagnosia 57, 63, 66

Associative prosopagnosia 57, 63, 66, 68, 69, 122

Attention, face-specific ERPs 103–16

Behavioural studies 2
   after epilepsy surgery 192–95
   age-related changes 167, 169, 173–79
   categorisation 137–38
   face learning 241–55
   facial expression recognition 73–87
   image orientation and size 31–32

Biographical knowledge 55, 64, 67

Biological information 3, 14, 234–35

Capgras syndrome 3, 55, 56, 63–64, 65, 68–70

Cartoon faces 263–65, 271

Categorisation see Discrimination systems

Cats, recognition 3, 261–63

Children, localised neural substrates 117–23

Cingulate gyrus 58, 61, 64, 181

Cognitive models, face processing 55, 64–68

Computer vision 7–8

Configural processing systems 4–5

expertise effect 158

fusiform face area 271

novel objects 126, 135

orientation effect 201, 202, 208, 211–13, 217

sensitivity 130, 135

structural encoding 91–92, 94, 97

Contextual effects 89, 91–92

Cortical microstimulation 2, 187–99, 281–91

Delusions, misidentification syndromes 3, 55, 56, 63–64, 65, 68–70

Detection of faces 7, 272–73

Discrimination systems
   age effects 166
   early development 117–23
   non-face objects 125, 137–38
   subordinate-level categorisation 3, 4, 7, 143–63, 272

Dogs, recognition 3, 4

Dorsal visual pathway 55, 56, 58, 59–61, 68–70, 180

Emotional expression, recognition 2, 7, 73–87, 187, 193–94, 197–98

Emotional memory, amygdala role 61–62

Emotional responses 7, 57, 59

Encoding processes
   face processing 125, 135–36, 253
   image size and orientation 29–31

motor-program 74
structural 6, 7, 35–54, 65–67, 89–102
Epilepsy 2, 59, 187–99, 281–91
Event-related potentials (ERPs)
　face identification and encoding 35–54
　face-specific 103–16
　facial movements 221–39
　localised face processing 187–99
　N1 6, 103, 114–15
　N170 2, 4, 7, 8, 35–54, 105, 221–39
　N400 45–50, 51–52
　P350 221–39
　VPP 104–05, 114, 115
Experience
　amygdala role 62
　configural processing 136, 158
　face processing role 8, 118, 125
　fusiform face area 138, 272
　object recognition 125, 136, 138
　orientation and size of image 29, 30
Eyes
　fusiform face area response 266–67, 270
　movement, ERP response 221–39
　see also Gaze

Face processing
　age-related changes 6, 165–86
　cognitive model 64–68
　configural systems 4, 5, 125
　detection of faces 7, 272–73
　discrimination systems 3, 4, 7, 117–23, 125,
　　137–38, 143–63, 166, 272
　encoding and identification 35–54, 125,
　　135–36, 253
　face-specific ERPs 2, 103–16, 187–99, 258
　face-specific mechanisms 2–4, 6, 8, 117–23,
　　127–34
　facial movement ERPs 2, 221–39
　functional organisation 2, 6–7, 73, 241
　fusiform face area 143–63, 257–79
　future research 6
　hallucinations 188, 192, 196, 281–91
　infants 117–19, 126
　inversion effect 4–5, 7, 36, 89–102, 201–19,
　　244–46, 263–65, 271
　learning new faces 2, 68, 241–55
　part-based systems 4–5, 9, 89–102, 203,
　　207–14
　perception 7, 36, 103, 222, 253–54, 272–73
　prefrontal cortex 2–3, 6, 165–66, 172,
　　180–81, 187–99, 281–91

recent research 1–11
single-route models 62–70
stimulus selectivity 8–9, 14, 36, 125–42,
　143–44, 254, 257
structural encoding 6, 7, 35–54, 65–67,
　89–102
subordinate-level categorisation 143, 156–59,
　272
two-route model 55–62, 65–70
Face recognition 4, 6
　attentional modulations 103–16
　cognitive 64–68
　covert 3, 55–71
　fusiform face area 272–73
　Möbius syndrome 77–79
　overt 56, 58, 63, 65, 68, 69
　and perception 253
　prosopagnosia 89–102
　structural encoding 35–54
Facial expression
　event-related potentials 221
　production/recognition 2, 7, 59, 73–87, 128
Facial paralysis 2, 73–87
Frontal cortex, face processing 2–3, 6
Functional magnetic resonance imaging (fMRI)
　face processing mechanisms 221–22
　facial movement 222
　fusiform face area 104, 128, 257–79
　monkeys 4, 7, 9, 137
　novel objects 4, 138, 139
　subordinate-level categorisation 143, 148–63
Fusiform face area (FFA) 3–4, 5, 6, 7, 8
　object discrimination 128, 137, 138
　plasticity 119
　response properties 104, 257–79
　subordinate-level categorisation 143–63

Gaze
　event-related potential study 221–39
　fusiform face area 266, 269–70
　neural mechanisms 2, 128–29
Greebles 4, 138, 158

Hallucinations, faces 188, 192, 196, 281–91
Heads
　fusiform face area response 267–69
　orientation importance 13, 30, 128
Hippocampal complex 241–42
Holistic processing system
　faces 4–5, 90, 99, 126, 130
　objects 92

orientation effect 99, 103–4, 201, 215–16, 217

Identification of faces 35–54, 74, 125, 135–36, 253
Infants, face processing 117–19, 126
Inferior frontal gyrus 74
Inferotemporal cortex
    experience effect 4
    face-specific cells 36, 104, 138–39, 143
    image size 30
    monkeys 125, 127, 129, 130, 131, 135
    role 9
    visual pathways 58–59, 61
Inversion of faces
    cartoon 263–65, 271
    face-processing mechanisms 4–5, 7, 36
    orientation and size 13–34
    prosopagnosia 89–102
    prosopamnesia 244–46
    structural encoding 36
    super inversion effect 201–19

Learning, new faces 241–55
Localised neural substrates 117–23, 187–99, 281

Machine face recognition 7–8
Magnetoencephalography (MEG) 258
Matching, face processing 165–86
Memory, new faces 241–55
Möbius syndrome 2, 73–87
Monkeys
    face-specific mechanisms 2, 6, 7, 104, 125–42, 197
    gaze sensitivity 236, 266
    image orientation and size 13–34
    novel object recognition 4
    visual pathways 58–59, 127
Motor-program code 74, 86
Mouth, movement, ERP response 221–39

Object recognition 4, 5, 8
    encoding systems 36, 136
    event-related potential study 103–16
    fusiform face area 269
    inversion effect 203–04, 207, 208, 212, 216–17
    localised neural substrates 117–23, 198
    monkeys 131–34, 136, 138
    novel objects 4, 138, 139
    orientation and size 13–34
    subordinate-level categorisation 143–63

view-independent representations 29
visual pathways 60
Orientation of image 4–5, 7, 13–34, 89–102, 201–19
    see also Inversion effect

Parietal lobe 6, 59
Part-based processing system 4, 5, 9, 89–102, 203, 207–14
Prefrontal cortex, face processing 2–3, 6, 165–66, 172, 180–81, 187–99, 281–91
Prosopagnosia
    covert face recognition 3, 55–71
    inversion effect 5, 126
    localised neural substrates 117–23
    structural encoding 36, 89–102
    subordinate-level categorisation 4, 157–58
Prosopamnesia 2, 241–55

Selective attention 103–16
Semantic information
    emotional words 193, 195
    face processing 3, 35, 36, 51–52, 55, 64, 67
    subordinate-level categorisation 143–63
Single-unit studies 8, 9, 13–34, 130, 137, 139
Size of image 13–15, 22–34
Skin conductance response (SCR) 56, 57–58, 61–68
Sound, emotional 81
Spatial location
    face processing 143, 159
    facial features arrangement 201–13
    objects 60–61
Stimulus selectivity, face processing 8–9, 14, 36, 125–42, 143–44, 254, 257
Structural encoding 6, 7, 35–54, 65–67, 89–102
Superior temporal sulcus (STS)
    face-specific cells 6, 7, 104, 125, 128–30, 236–37
    facial movement 2
    gaze perception 266
    image orientation and size 5, 13–34

Temporal cortex
    face recognition 63, 115, 125
    facial movements 236–37
    macaque monkeys 13–34

Ventral cortical stream 26, 29, 31
Ventral extrastriate cortex 9, 181, 258

Ventral occipitotemporal cortex 3, 59, 118
Ventral visual pathway 55, 56, 58, 60, 62–63,
   69–70, 157, 180
View-sensitive representations 29, 30, 61, 128,
   138, 208
Visual agnosia 36
Visual recognition systems
   age effects 166, 180

categorisation 146, 156, 158
early damage 118
single-route models 62–70
specificity 4, 36
two-route model 55–62
Visuospatial tasks 60–61
Vocal expression, recognition 79, 81